MONEY LIKE YOU MEAN IT

PERSONAL FINANCE TACTICS FOR THE REAL WORLD

ERICA ALINI

An imprint of
Srishti Publishers & Distributors

Srishti Publishers & Distributors
A unit of AJR Publishing LLP
212A, Peacock Lane
Shahpur Jat, New Delhi – 110 049

editorial@srishtipublishers.com

First published in India by Bold,
an imprint of Srishti Publishers & Distributors in 2023

Original English language edition published by
Dundurn Press Ltd. PO Box 19510 RPO Manulife,
Toronto Ontario M4W 3T9, Canada.

Arranged via Licensor's Agent: DropCap Inc.

10 9 8 7 6 5 4 3 2 1

The views expressed in this publication are those of the author alone and should not be taken as expert instruction or commands. While all attempts have been made to verify the information provided in this publication, neither the author nor the publisher assumes any responsibility for errors, omissions, or contrary interpretation of the subject matter herein.

Printed and bound in India

For Sale in India Only

To Chris, who makes everything possible, including writing a book during a pandemic. To my parents. And to my "patato" — Luca.

CONTENTS

INTRODUCTION

HOW TO MONEY LIKE YOU MEAN IT

PERHAPS YOU KNOW this scenario. You and your partner have good jobs and promising careers. You're so-called DINKs — dual income, no kids. You treat yourself to craft beer and — dare I say it — avocado toast, perhaps? But you've been diligently squirrelling away a hefty chunk of your paycheques for years, and now you have what feels like a significant pile of money. You're ready to buy a house but you just … can't.

Or maybe you did buy a house, but only because your parents swooped in with a generous contribution to your down payment. Grateful as you are for the help, you're also ashamed of needing it.

If you have kids at this stage in your life, you're probably juggling rent or a mortgage, stratospheric child-care fees that amount to a whole other rent or mortgage, and the after-effects of seeing your income drop to half or less for a year or more during parental leave. And you may also still be paying off your student loans.

Or perhaps you're hopping from shift to shift or from freelance contract to freelance contract. You're working evenings, weekends, and holidays. And yet you're barely stitching together a living.

We are millennials and the older Gen Zers. We work hard. We're doing all the right things (or at least some of them, anyway). And yet we do not have our financial ducks in a row. Purchasing a home with our own money, raising kids while also being able to pay for the occasional vacation, building up a retirement nest egg — these are mundane middle-class financial goals. But many of us are struggling mightily to reach them.

This book is about understanding why you're struggling and about getting the financial know-how you need to fight back.

Even if you make a good living and are happy with your housing situation, managing your money can feel like wading through a daunting, overgrown jungle. It's easier than ever to wander in the wrong direction, end up with far more debt than you can afford, or unwittingly put your money in the wrong investments. Because sure, you can download an app that will let you buy a stock with a few thumb strikes. But did anyone ever teach you the first thing about investing? And do you have an employer pension that will actually pay for your life when you're too old to work? Unlikely.

Get a job, work hard, spend less than you make, and retire at 65. That's advice for a world that has largely disappeared. To make it in today's economy, you need a whole new financial tool kit. And you need to know what you're up against. In this book, I draw on a decade of reporting on personal finance and economics to give you both the hands-on money basics you need to navigate day-to-day life and an understanding of the big forces that are shaping your financial reality.

I'm the personal finance reporter at Global News, and I'm an older millennial. This is the personal finance guide I wish I'd had when I ventured out into the world of financial grown-upedness as a wide-eyed Bambi, right into the financial crisis of 2007–2008.

Back then I was living and working in the United States, the epicentre of the quake that threatened to bring down the global financial system. I had a front-row seat to the devastation of the Great Recession and the economic dark age that followed the financial crisis and dragged on for years. In New York, coffee shops and libraries were packed with recent graduates spending all day — day after day — applying for jobs. Positions they qualified for, jobs they didn't qualify for, gigs for which they were way overqualified. Answering calls, waiting tables, moving furniture. Anything would do. *Anything.* But there were so very few jobs to be had.

Even in Canada, where the recession and its fallout were less intense, things felt quite bleak if you were just starting out. And yet the world did not cut millennials — back then more commonly called Gen Y — much slack. We couldn't find jobs because we were lazy, spoiled, or clueless. Or all of the above. Those of us who went back to living with our parents for a while were dubbed the boomerang generation, a spineless breed that just wanted to live rent-free and play video games in the basement. I even found myself writing one of the articles decrying the supposed spendthrift ways of my own kind. (The telltale headline was "Generation Spend." All I can say is I did not pitch the story.)

The disconnect between what was happening in the economy and the money advice I'd hear was painful. On my U.S. tax returns I had to identify myself as a "nonresident alien," which always sounded weird. But when I listened to or read about personal finance at the time, I truly felt like I had come from outer space. "You should have the equivalent of 100 percent of your salary saved up by age 30." *With what money?* I wondered. At the time my husband and I were switching jobs and moving cities and sometimes countries every one or two years, constantly chasing short-term contract positions. Whatever savings we had built up were almost wiped out by moving expenses with alarming regularity.

Personal finance has come a long way since then. There are now millennial financial planners giving advice that actually reflects the world we live in. And among older generations, the best financial experts are acutely aware of the challenges facing young people.

Of course, it's not like setting yourself up financially was ever a walk in the park. In 1990, when the last cohort of boomers was hitting the age of home ownership, housing affordability was, by some metrics, as bad as today. Many in our parents' generation finished school in the late 1980s, just before a vicious recession. And Gen Xers hit the labour market when middle-class wages were in a bigger funk than they are now.

And yet both generations found their footing. Generally speaking (of course, talking about generations means painting large, diverse groups of people in broad strokes), they did okay. A significant number of millennials, on the other hand, are still spinning their wheels. And more than a decade after I started out, things do not look better for the Gen Zers following in millennials' steps.

The pandemic, of course, has made things worse. While unfathomably high home prices were an issue mostly in and around Vancouver and Toronto before Covid-19, they have now become a national emergency. As hotels, restaurants, and stores shut down, and as companies in other sectors temporarily froze hiring or let go of young recruits, the job losses disproportionately hit low-income, racialized, and young workers. Six months after the onset of the health emergency, the bulk of the 1.3 million Canadians who'd been jobless for that long was under the age of 35.

The combined effect of the real estate craze and those labour-market convulsions has widened the divide between Canada's housing haves and have-nots. The young, lower-earning, and racialized Canadians who accounted for most of the job losses were also more likely to be renters. Homeowners, who usually have higher incomes and better jobs, sailed through largely unscathed. Stuck at home, many wealthier renters rushed to buy homes in smaller towns and lower-cost neighbourhoods. Many of those who couldn't — or didn't — are now wondering whether they'll ever get to be homeowners.

It has become impossible to talk about personal finance without also talking about how the economy is affecting the financial challenges we face. Everywhere you turn, making, keeping, and growing your money takes more initiative, more out-of-the-box thinking, and more stamina than it once did. The path to financial stability and security has turned into a wilderness where it's easy to get turned around and become lost.

This book will help you slash through the bush. Each section explores a major area of personal finance. We'll talk about debt and what research shows are some of the best mental hacks to make it psychologically easier to save and avoid borrowing too much. We'll also talk about many different species of debt and how they can threaten your financial well-being or be made to work for you. We will take a close-up look at credit scores. And then, of course, we'll speak about housing: from how to decide whether to rent or buy to the ins and outs of mortgages and the cost of home ownership (because all houses — even the newest ones — are inevitably money pits).

We will then move on to the question of how it is that one makes money. We'll compare paycheques and freelance pay, talk about how to ask for more (whether you're a new hire, an employee looking for a raise, or self-employed and negotiating with clients), and look at how to evaluate whether a side hustle is really worth the hassle. We'll talk about DIYing your way to retirement and investing (and, yes, we'll go over Bitcoin, NFTs, and all that).

We'll learn about insurance and how climate change is making home insurance more expensive. We'll talk about starting a family and paying for babies. And finally, we'll delve into the pesky but oh-so-crucial subject of whether and how to accept financial help from the Bank of Mom and Dad (a.k.a. BOMAD).

I want to be clear that this book is for the middle class. For low-income Canadians and those living in poverty, the rules of personal finance are often quite different. With the weekly personal finance newsletter I write for Global News, called *Money123,* I have tried to create a resource that also serves this woefully neglected group of Canadians, who really need quality money guidance catered specifically to their situation. Happily, more financial planners are taking on the task (and many of them contribute to *Money123*). This book, though, is for people with middling or even pretty good incomes.

I should also spare a word about "general" rules. Personal finance blogs and articles are full of them. You'll find a few of them here, too, so I should clarify what to make of them. The best course of action when it comes to your money often depends on a myriad of individual variables tied to your particular circumstance and individual preferences. So a general rule isn't a prescription. It's more a starting point. It provides a framework for thinking about a certain issue. But as you analyze your own situation and needs, you may find yourself straying quite far from the general rule — and that's perfectly okay.

You'll find a lot of practical information in here, but, as I mentioned, this book is also about the big picture. How did housing become so incredibly expensive? Why do so many of us have so much debt? Why does it feel like middle-class wages have been stuck for decades? These are big, simple, common-sense questions I hear all the time from readers and friends. This book has no simple answers, but you'll find a nuanced overview of a lot of the trends and developments that are complicating our financial lives — along with many concrete tactics to help you reach your money goals in spite of the challenges.

So stretch your arms, make yourself comfortable, and fill up your favourite mug. Here's how to money like you *mean* it.

CHAPTER 1

MIND OVER MONEY

WHY DO YOU HAVE DEBT?

Don't worry, I'm not looking for a confession. This isn't about making you feel like a weakling because you drank the proverbial $5 latte this morning instead of a homemade cup of joe. Nor am I under the illusion that sticking religiously to your French press and forsaking takeout guarantees you'll be able to pay off your credit card balance at the end of the month. I know this from experience. When it comes to food and drink, I have things down to a science. I buy my favourite brew in bulk on Amazon and plan meals a week at a time. And sure, this saves me money. But if the transmission of my 10-year-old car suddenly gave out tomorrow, I'd have to make some tough financial choices (and let's hope I didn't just jinx myself with that).

What I'm asking here is this: Do you know why you and I and most other people have so much debt?

It's not just because of the choices we've made or because of our individual circumstances. We live in a world that makes it extremely easy to borrow. I know you didn't crack open this book for a history lesson, but stick with me for a minute while we speed through the decades — understanding how we got here will help you put your own debt struggles in context. Once we've had a close look at the larger forces that shape why and how we borrow, I'll talk about some simple strategies you can use to fight back, kick your debt, and turbocharge your savings.

Canadians owe more than $2 trillion in household debt. That's roughly equal to the size of our entire economy. It means that the value of all the mortgages, credit card debt, and other loans we collectively carry is roughly the same as the value of all the goods and services we produce as a country. Measured as a percentage of gross domestic product (GDP), our pile of household debt is one of the biggest in the world. We have the dubious honour of being ahead of both the United States and the United Kingdom.

But living in the red is hardly a uniquely Canadian thing. When you look at how much debt Canadians carry compared to their after-tax income, we don't come close to leading the pack. The Swiss, Norwegians, and Australians — to name just three — have higher household debt levels.

People didn't always have this much debt. At the start of 1990, Canadians' debt was 87 percent of their collective after-tax income. By the end of 2019, it had skyrocketed to 181 percent. Another way to think about that: for every dollar of income we bring home on average, we owe $1.81. And while the relative size of our debt load shrunk immediately after the start of the pandemic, because many of us rushed to save up, it soon started climbing again.

So *why* did we start racking up so much debt? Did someone put something in the water? Did we develop a gene mutation that turned most of us into spend-more-than-you-make zombies?

I won't pretend to have the full answer. Heck, economists don't have all the answers, either. But it's pretty clear that how we got here has a lot to do with low interest rates, high prices, and easy access to credit.

• • •

Low Interest Rates

Interest rates were once much, much higher than they are now. Chances are, if you were born in the 1980s or 1990s, the idea of your parents borrowing money at a rate of 18 or 19 percent interest leaves you gobsmacked. I'm an older millennial — I have a husband, a kid, a house, and the aforementioned aging car — and mortgage rates have been in the low single digits for as long as I've been aware of what a mortgage is.

Why are rates so low now?

Interest rates started to decline in the 1990s — not just mortgage rates and not just in Canada. It had a lot to do with a number of countries figuring out a new and better way to keep inflation in check.

But let's rewind the clock a little further. By the late 1970s, high and unpredictable inflation had become a major pain in the neck for everyone. Constantly rising prices forced consumers and companies to waste a lot of time worrying about what they'd be able to afford in the future. Workers demanded higher wages to keep up with the cost of living, and businesses, in turn, had to raise prices so they could pay those higher wages. It wasn't pretty.

By 1981 Canada's annual rate of inflation was a mind-boggling 12 percent, and things weren't much better in many other rich countries. That's why central banks spent much of that decade cranking up interest rates to wrestle inflation back under control. When interest rates go up, it costs more to borrow and pays more to save. This creates an incentive for both people and businesses to squirrel away more of their money. Overall, everyone tends to spend less, which prompts companies to increase their prices more slowly, or even to lower them, bringing down the inflation rate.

But, in Canada at least, beating down inflation by jacking up interest rates turned out to be like a game of whack-a-mole. As soon as the Bank of Canada eased off interest rates, prices would spike again, and the cycle would repeat.

No one was enjoying that constant hammering, so in the early 1990s the Bank of Canada, along with central banks of other countries, came up with a better system. They started to actively aim for a desirable low level of inflation. In 1991 Canada declared it would start targeting inflation of 2 percent per year. This helped everyone know what to expect in terms of future inflation, and a few years later the bank finally reached its target. Canada's annual rate of inflation hasn't strayed too far from 2 percent ever since.

That has gone a long way toward solving the problem of high and volatile inflation, but it also helped create a new problem: persistently lower interest rates made it cheap to borrow money.

The financial crisis of 2007–2008 didn't help. Even though a lot of the crisis had to do with reckless lending and borrowing, interest rates dropped even lower as central banks scrambled to soften the impacts of the recession in various ways. When interest rates are low, people and companies save less and spend and borrow more, creating economic activity. The economy took a really long time to re-emerge from that swamp — I can attest to this first-hand, as a proud graduate of the class of 2008 — and interest rates got stuck in ultra-low gear.

More than a decade after that crisis, interest rates in Canada, the U.S., and other countries had just started to come up a bit when along came the Covid-19 pandemic. The global economy went into another funk, and down went interest rates again.

Central banks, to their credit, are well aware that low interest rates have made it easier for people to borrow too much. They're worried about it. The Bank of Canada has called our massive household debt one of the key vulnerabilities of the Canadian economy. But there isn't much central banks can do about it, says Christopher Ragan, a professor at McGill University and one of Canada's best-known monetary policy experts. Central banks "have dedicated their one policy instrument to their primary thing, which is keeping inflation low and stable," he says.

There is no magic wand the central banks can wave to keep inflation at the target while also making borrowing a little costlier for people — nor do they have a mandate to rein in household debt. The Bank of Canada has one job when it comes to monetary policy, and that is to manage inflation, which has proven tricky enough.

Central banks aren't the only force keeping interest rates low. Many economists think another reason borrowing is cheap is because right now the world's savers outweigh its borrowers. You may be wondering what the heck they're talking about, since so many people have a lot of debt and little savings. But population aging, for example, means that there are scores of people who've been saving up for retirement. Also, some rich countries like China and oil exporters in the Persian Gulf have been building giant reserves of savings. At the same time, technological change means that many companies can make oodles of money by selling things like digital advertising. They don't need to borrow to build factories and invest in heavy machinery like the industrial giants of yore. All in all, the result is too little demand to borrow money, which keeps interest rates low.

We've definitely seen a bit of inflation recently, starting about a year after the onset of the pandemic. A sustained and significant increase in consumer prices would send interest rates up and make it costlier to borrow. But as I write, economists and investors are divided as to how concerned we should be about those slightly higher inflation rates.

• • •

High Prices

Achieving low and stable inflation was central bankers' big feat of the past 25 years or so. The prices of most things have been rising gradually, which is a very good thing for companies and for consumers like you and me.

But the prices of *some* things have been growing much faster than both inflation and salaries. Take tuition, for example. In a 2018 report for RBC, economist Gerard Walsh figured that back in 1990, a student would have to work around 290 hours at a minimum-wage job to make enough money to pay for one year of tuition.[1] Today, you're looking at more than 500 hours — and that wouldn't even cover the cost of books or those pesky mandatory student fees.

But tuition costs are a sideshow compared to what happened in the housing market. From 2007 to 2017, the prices of single-family homes in Canada's cities grew 2.5 times faster than Canadians' incomes — and that was before the pandemic housing boom. In February 2021, a report by the National Bank of Canada noted that for a median-earning household squirrelling away 10 percent of their pre-tax income, it would take 60 months — five years — to save up for the minimum down payment on a house in a major urban centre.[2] "At a national level, there has never been a worse time to accumulate the minimum down payment," economists Kyle Dahms and Camille Baillargeon, the report authors, noted. And that includes the previous peak linked to the housing bubble of the late 1980s.

For a time this was a problem primarily for those living in or around Toronto and Vancouver. The situation there has long been completely ridiculous. In Vancouver, it takes a household with a median income an unfathomable 32 years to save up for a down payment on a house. To look at housing affordability a different way, that same household would have to spend around 78 percent of their income every month on mortgage payments for the average non-condo home. In Toronto, you're looking at more than 24 years to save for a down payment on a house, with mortgage payments taking up 60 percent of median incomes. To put that in perspective, the general rule of thumb is that people should spend no more than 30 percent of their pre-tax income on housing.

But buying an average house with an average family income is also getting tougher in Montreal and Ottawa, not to mention smaller cities like Hamilton, Ontario. The pandemic prompted scores of millennials to pull the trigger on purchasing their first home. And buyers of all ages ditched their urban digs in favour of bigger properties and backyards. This helped fuel a housing craze that swept across Canada, with some of the steepest price increases in smaller communities.

I'll have much more to say about housing — including for renters — in chapter 3, but here, let me highlight this: even in cities where homes remain relatively affordable, property values are significantly higher compared to incomes than they once were. What that means is, as borrowing costs shrank, our mortgages became that much bigger. Today, Canadians are carrying $1.7 trillion of mortgage debt, up 70 percent from just a decade ago.

• • •

Easy Access to Credit

Borrowing didn't just get cheaper — it also became easier. Since 1985, Canada's adult population has grown from 19 to 31 million people. The number of credit cards in circulation, meanwhile, has ballooned from 14 million to 76 million, and that's only counting Visa and Mastercard. And fully 30 percent of us are in the habit of having a carry-over balance.

Are we piling on credit card debt because it's cheap? No, we do it because it's easy. But let's be clear: this isn't just about swiping your card for a Carrie Bradshaw–style shoe-shopping spree. Or because you *need* alloy rims on your truck. I'm also talking about when your dog needs shots and now you're $150 short at the end of the month. Are you going to take out a loan? Borrow from your parents? Probably not. You quietly put that bill on your credit card, and just hope you'll be able to pay it off soon.

Credit cards are tricky because, with a typical annual interest rate of 20 percent, they can sink you into debt really quickly. But, for Canadians collectively, that's not where most of our liabilities come from. Credit cards account for just 5 percent of this country's pile of household debt. Mortgages, unsurprisingly, make up the lion's share, about 70 percent. But another big slice, almost 20 percent, comes from lines of credit.

With lines of credit, borrowing is both cheap *and* easy. The interest rate is generally higher than that for mortgages but much lower than that for credit cards. But, as with credit cards, you can get away with making just minimum payments every month. Lenders bill this as "flexibility," and it *is* a feature that can come in very handy in some cases. But it also enables you to keep taking on debt for a very long time.

Then there are auto loans. Another thing that makes borrowing easier is stretching out the time frame for repaying your loan. If you're allowed to take longer to extinguish your debt, you can make smaller payments. That's exactly what lenders did with auto loans. Canadians used to have up to five years to pay off their cars. Today, it's common to take eight years.

So here we are now. We have collectively gotten to the point where, today, we owe something like $1.75 to $1.80 for every dollar of after-tax income *on average* — many of us have way more debt than that. (And the average figure may have gone up since this book went to press.)

Of course, none of this means that racking up a ton of debt is inevitable. But I would argue that falling into a debt trap these days is a lot easier than it used to be. And whether you're trying to avoid getting into a vicious debt cycle or struggling to get out of one, you should know you are waging an unequal battle. On one side, there are big macroeconomic forces at work. There are also lenders, who are mainly interested in your ability to service your debt — not in your ability to pay it off comfortably and in a reasonable amount of time. On the other side, there's little old you, with your busy life and limited willpower.

The debt epidemic reminds me a lot of the obesity epidemic. We all know that we need to eat healthy food. But the problem isn't knowing; it's executing. We live surrounded by temptation: stacks of candy bars strategically placed at the checkout inviting that last-minute impulse buy, entire supermarket aisles devoted just to pop and chips, and constant ads about everything we should not be eating. Let me tell you, it was way easier to eat healthy when I was growing up in Italy. Yogurt didn't have the same number of calories as ice cream, and no one was putting sugar into bread. But now things are changing in Italy, too. Portion sizes are getting bigger — and so are waistlines.

This isn't to say that everything was better in the past. Far from it. But with debt, as with our diets, life has become a David-versus-Goliath clash for many of us. And, for the most part, we're getting some pretty useless directions about how to tackle that battle.

Much of the advice we hear about debt seems to rely on two main assumptions. One is that if you have debt, you must not understand the importance of spending less than you make. But survey after survey shows we are worried sick about our finances. Clearly, understanding is not the issue. Another is that if you've got too much debt, you must be irresponsible. This approach tries to appeal to your heart rather than your head. If you're deep in the red, you should be ashamed.

But a growing body of research shows that neither of these approaches is very helpful. This kind of finger wagging makes a pretty crappy weapon in the ongoing, daily fight against debt. When you're pitted against such mighty enemies, you need to fight smarter, not harder. The key is to know yourself and know your debt.

• • •

Know Yourself: Mental Hacks to Help You Fight Debt and Turbocharge Your Savings

As we've seen, there are big, powerful trends in today's economy that make it *so* easy to spend and borrow too much. By knowing yourself, you can use some simple mental tricks to nudge yourself in the opposite direction, making it a less heavy lift, psychologically, to pay down your debt and build your savings.

Below are four steps that will help you rewire yourself and stay on track. First, most of us need a vision for our financial goals. It's hard to get motivated if you don't have one. Second, you need to break up the big goals into smaller, more achievable, intermediate-term ones. Third, you need to figure out how much you can afford to spend and then set your savings, bill payments, and debt repayments on autopilot as much as you can.

STEP ONE: BUILD A VISION FOR YOUR FINANCIAL GOALS

There's another way in which money and food are similar: our New Year's resolutions. January pledges generally revolve around losing weight and paying off debt. That's when gym memberships spike and new diets take off. It's also when foot traffic tends to increase in the direction of financial advisers and debt counsellors. But by May, the gym pass sits unused in your wallet, and Friday evenings are once against spent scooping ice cream in front of the TV. Debt resolutions often meet a similar fate.

Why does this happen? Why does our motivation run out of steam before we've had a chance to build up our cardio?

I've been there. In my 20s, I rarely worked out. My glory days of winning school track-and-field events had quickly faded during my teens, when my height stopped being enough to allow me to outrun or outjump other girls. Without the thrill of the podium, I quickly lost interest, not just in track and field but in any kind of sport. The gym loomed in my head, now a massive chore. My first few jobs in journalism saw me putting in 11- or 12-hour days, often working on weekends, too. I didn't find that exercise helped me manage the stress — it was just another thing to do. My idea of unwinding had a lot more to do with curling up on the couch with a good book than sweating it up on the treadmill. Giving up on the gym in May would have been an achievement for me. I was usually done at week two.

Then one day I tried yoga. I never thought I'd be a yogi, to be honest. It all seemed too trendy and hipstery. But I was seven months' pregnant and had a work-from-home job. My back was killing me, and I was slowly losing my mind from spending too much time cooped up in the house alone. So I broke down and went to a prenatal yoga class around the corner from my house. By the end of it, I was so relaxed I fell asleep during savasana. You know when you wake yourself up with a snore? That was me. Within a couple of weeks, my back pain was gone, and I was hooked. I kept practising yoga twice a week without fail for more than three years, until the pandemic. Why? Because exercising had become something I actually looked forward to, rather than something I had to do, or else.

It's the same with paying off debt: you'll probably have an easier time following through if it becomes something you *want* to do, rather than something you *have* to do. One way to trigger that mind shift is to think about *why* you want to pay off your debt. What will life look like once your debt is back under control, or gone entirely? What will you be able to do once that $500 a month is no longer going toward credit card payments?

One goal that gets a lot of people going these days is the idea of an extra-early retirement. That's the big concept behind the FIRE movement — which stands for "financial independence, retire early." Most FIRE enthusiasts are willing to commit to extreme frugality in the name of reaching financial independence as early as their 30s. The point isn't necessarily to spend the rest of your life in retirement, but to be able to choose to work only because you want to. In other words, smash your debt and turbocharge your savings so you can escape the make-ends-meet hamster wheel and live the life you want.

I don't personally adhere to the FIRE philosophy. I'm lucky enough to already be doing what I really want to do, so I'm in no rush to quit my job. (Plus, if I were hoping to be able to put $1 million in the bank by 35 on a journalist's salary, good luck to me.) But I do think the FIRE movement has hit the nail on the head in terms of what it takes to set a really ambitious financial resolution and stick to it for the long term. In a world that makes it easier than ever to buy and borrow, you need to attach a powerful vision to your saving and debt-smashing goals.

The pressure to spend is real. Perhaps, before going to sleep, you've been flipping through pictures of your friend's beautiful kitchen reno on Instagram. In the morning, you walk up to your eight-year-old sedan, which happens to be parked right next to your neighbour's brand-new SUV. After work, everyone's going out for drinks at $13 a pop — or, I should say, a cocktail. Are you going to be the one who orders tap water?

To shut all that out, you're going to need something more powerful than a mental image of your shrinking credit card balance or your growing savings account. You need to envision what you're going to do with your money instead. You need to see yourself hiking up Machu Picchu on a trip that will leave only good memories because you paid for it with your savings. Or imagine your partner's face when you tell them you're finally debt-free. Or picture yourself at your kids' university graduations, knowing they won't be struggling with student loans because you saved for their education. When you can see your vision for the future, that's when you start saving because you want to. You're not resisting the temptation to spend anymore — you're choosing what you really want to use your money for.

STEP TWO: CHOP THOSE BIG GOALS INTO SMALLER ONES

Having a vision for your financial goals is powerful. But if your goal is a big one, like paying off tens of thousands of dollars of debt or saving for a down payment on a house, you'll probably need some help along the way to keep up your motivation. One thing you can do is break down your big goal into smaller, more manageable ones.

If you've ever run a race, you've probably noticed that no matter how tired and out of breath you're feeling, you find it in yourself to push a little harder when the finish line is in view. Researchers have found that the closer you feel to achieving a goal, the more oomph you'll get to reach it. For example, one study found that coffee shop customers who received a 12-stamp reward card with two bonus stamps already on it would earn their free coffee faster than those who were given a simple 10-stamp card.[3]

This also works well when trying to pay off debt or save up for a big purchase. It's easier to get there if you set a series of intermediate finish lines — you'll get a little jolt of adrenalin every time you cross one. There are countless stories of people who say this trick has helped them crush massive amounts of debt.

In a September 2018 interview with *Money*, Joshua Holt, a New York lawyer and personal finance blogger who graduated with more than $200,000 of debt, said he hung a paper chain from his staircase with each ring representing $1,000 of his debt. Every time he paid that much off his loans, he'd get a little satisfaction by ripping off one of the loops.

Lauren Torres (a.k.a. Kitty), one of the hilarious and sharp-tongued co-authors of the money blog *Bitches Get Riches*, came up with a colouring book–style aid to help herself stay motivated about paying off her $252,000 of mortgage debt. She drew a digital brick wall, with each brick representing $500 in principal. She coloured in the bricks as she gradually hacked away at her debt. She also tracked how far behind in completing her wall she would have been if she'd only made regular mortgage payments, which helped her keep going with the lump-sum payments. "Updating [the wall] is fun," she wrote, "because it feels like I'm racing against someone else's expectations of me — and I'm lapping them."[4]

Torres says she is now happily mortgage-free and still several birthdays away from turning 40. She'd be the first one to tell you that she and her partner were able to extinguish their debt quite quickly in large part because of their incomes. But the colouring wall helped along the way.

STEP THREE: STAY ON TRACK

Motivation is great, but you also need method. You need to know where your money is going and how much you can afford to set aside in savings.

Before I go any further, though, let's clear up what knowing where your money goes really means. Although many people say they don't know where their dollars disappear to, the truth is few adults sail through life unaware of how much money they make or how much they spend on things like rent and utilities. Most actually have a pretty good handle on their major financial inflows and outflows. Many of them even have a budget. And yet, somehow, they are often a few hundred dollars short at the end of the month.

As money goes, this can be a deadly problem. There's a common belief that it takes an extravagant lifestyle to end up with unmanageable debt. But according to debt counsellors and financial planners, many people start sinking into debt slowly. The credit card charges pile up little by little because you keep spending just a tad more than you bring in. It's like quicksand. At first you're in it up to your ankles, then up to your knees. Keeping up with just the minimum payment on your credit card becomes a struggle. Then one day your furnace gives out, your car breaks down, or you lose your job — one large, unexpected crisis and you're in over your head.

» THE TROUBLE WITH BUDGETING WITH SPREADSHEETS

So what can you do to avoid this treacherous debt quagmire? Some people will tell you that you need a better budget. Track every cent you spend, they say. Keep all receipts. Create a spreadsheet with every imaginable spending category.

This doesn't work for me, for two reasons. First of all, who has the time to do all that? Sure, after I've worked all day, wrestled some dinner into my five-year-old, played with Lego for an hour, tackled the laundry I didn't get to over the weekend, and finished up some more work after dinner ... yes, after all that I will gladly sit down and spend the last of my waking hours collecting receipts and entering numbers into a spreadsheet. I truly cannot think of a better use of my time.

But even if you did do all that, and even if, unlike me, you enjoy doing it, the second issue with this kind of budgeting is you cannot possibly predict things like a parking ticket, your kid going through two shoe sizes in six months, or having to fly across the country for a funeral. Research shows human beings are exceptionally bad at handling these sorts of extraordinary expenses. One study by researchers at Princeton University and New York

University, for example, found that, because we treat these costs as one-offs, we are more likely both to exclude them from our budget and to overspend on them.[5] Unexpected expenses are *always* coming up — and always will. I once tracked my surprise costs for six months and found they occurred almost as regularly as my weekly trips to the grocery store. You can't predict what the unpredictable spending will be, but you can be sure there will be some.

Detailed budgets can be very useful for simple, short-term goals. How much do you need to save for that vacation? You can budget for that. You're going to have line items like airfare, hotel, car rental, gas, food, and a bit of fun money. Chances are, your trip will play out more or less as planned. It's also easier to stick to a rigid budget if it's only for a short period of time. Coaxing your day-to-day spending into a sprawling spreadsheet, on the other hand, is hopeless. Life is too complicated and unpredictable.

» THE MONEY-BUCKET SYSTEM

Luckily, you can get around this issue by setting up different accounts for money that serves different purposes. You probably already have a chequing account that's the landing place for your paycheque, freelance income, government benefits, and any other money coming in. This is what you use to pay for everything. You may also have a savings account and an investment account for your retirement savings, to which you send monthly transfers (for more on how much to save for retirement, see chapter 5). You can think of each of those accounts as a money bucket.

To manage your cash flow effectively without a spreadsheet, you might need a few more buckets. For example, if you have important longer-term savings goals, like setting money aside for a down payment, it's useful to set up an account for those as well. You may also want to open another chequing account to which you send money for your monthly fixed expenses, like mortgage or rent, utilities, insurance, and other bills, as well as any non-mortgage debt repayments, like a car loan. It's also helpful to set up routine transfers to this account for predictable but infrequent bills such as property taxes. These money buckets help you take care of your predictable expenses.

Now, here's what my husband and I do for unpredictable expenses. First, we have a savings account for small emergencies and repairs. It's our money bucket for larger expenses we couldn't see coming and need to take care of right away. This is the bucket we tapped for the $500 insurance deductible after a huge tree branch smashed the front of our car and to repair the AC unit when it started spitting out ice in the middle of a blistering summer.

Then we have a pool of money for the mother of all emergencies: unemployment. The unemployment fund is cash you set aside for a run-of-the-mill layoff or, you know, in case a global pandemic wipes out not just your job, but your entire industry. It's the financial equivalent of the bunker stocked with months' worth of canned beans where you drag the family in case of an alien invasion — which, after a year like 2020 and the Pentagon UFO videos, doesn't seem all that far-fetched. The point of the unemployment fund is to keep you alive — again, financially speaking — until you can go back out and resume earning a living.

After the Covid-19 pandemic, I'm sure we all have a deeper appreciation for the importance of this cash cushion. In fact, it was pretty striking to watch Canadians' savings rate shoot up in the months after the lockdowns began. We went from stashing away something like 3 percent of our disposable income to nearly 30 percent in the early days of the pandemic. The huge spike on the savings rate chart looked like we were running for the hills, which probably isn't too far from what it felt like in real life.

But, short-term savings binges aside, how much should you keep in your doomsday fund? The classic rule of thumb is three to six months of living expenses. I think about it a little differently. I start with this question: How many months would it take me to land another job? Even in good years, finding a spot in a newsroom is a bit like a blood sport, and it might very well take me more than six months. On the other hand, I could probably bring home some money by freelancing while looking for a steady, full-time gig.

My target is to be able to stay financially afloat for eight or nine months. But that doesn't mean I have nine times my salary socked away in a savings account. If I were laid off from my current job, I'd get several months of severance pay, which greatly reduces my savings needs. I'd also be eligible for employment insurance, or EI, which is a huge help. But when I used to work as a full-time freelancer — self-employed, with no benefits or access to EI — I did have a cash pile that would have paid for close to six months of my life.

In short, how much you're likely to need in an unemployment emergency depends a lot on the job you do. If you don't have an employer-funded safety net and wouldn't be able to go on EI if you lost your job, it makes sense to aim higher. If you're thinking of changing jobs, it may also be a good idea to top up your doomsday money bucket before you do, in case the new gig doesn't pan out and you haven't been around long enough to earn much in severance pay. The silver lining if your income takes a dive is that you'll probably have to trim your spending. There's no ordering dinner in when you're sheltering in a bunker. And while that's a bummer in one way, it also lowers your savings target for covering several months of expenses. It's a good idea to run through your regular expenses to see which line items you could nix in lean times so you have a clear idea of what your essential expenses amount to.

Also on the plus side, our two emergency-related money buckets don't require constant funding. We save aggressively when they've been depleted, but once we've reached our targets, I generally pause the transfers and channel the money elsewhere until the next minor disaster strikes, and the cycle begins again.

Once you've set up your transfers for fixed expenses, whatever is left over needs to cover your monthly and annual variable expenses. I find it helpful to have savings accounts set up for regular but infrequent spending like clothing and car maintenance as well as short-term savings goals like vacations or home upgrades.

The flow chart on page 24 shows what the money-bucket system I just described looks like. I should note this set-up was heavily influenced by financial planner Shannon Lee Simmons's eye-opening book *Worry-Free Money: The Guilt-Free Approach to Managing Your Money and Your Life*, and I owe a hat tip to the financial planners at Spring Planning, whose excellent flow chart inspired my own.

Banks have limits on how many accounts you can open, so channelling your money through several money buckets may require relying on two

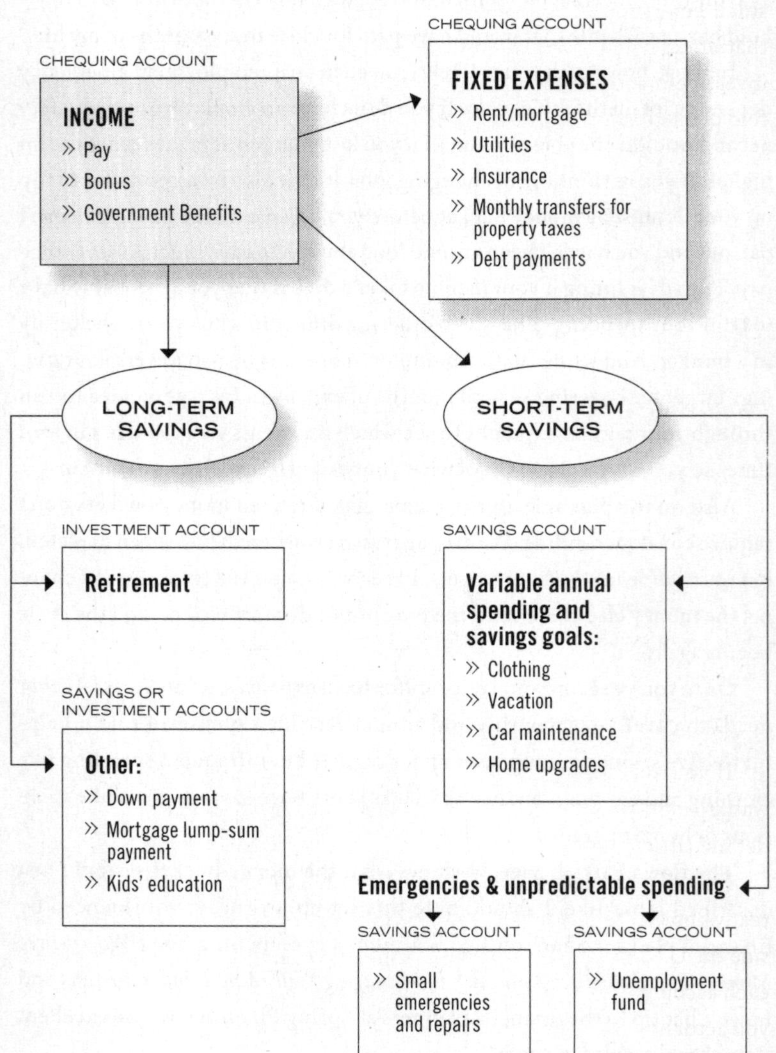
The Money-Bucket System
CHEQUING ACCOUNT
INCOME
» Pay
» Bonus
» Government Benefits
CHEQUING ACCOUNT
FIXED EXPENSES
» Rent/mortgage
» Utilities
» Insurance
» Monthly transfers for property taxes
» Debt payments
LONG-TERM SAVINGS
SHORT-TERM SAVINGS
INVESTMENT ACCOUNT
Retirement
SAVINGS OR INVESTMENT ACCOUNTS
Other:
» Down payment
» Mortgage lump-sum payment
» Kids' education
SAVINGS ACCOUNT
Variable annual spending and savings goals:
» Clothing
» Vacation
» Car maintenance
» Home upgrades
Emergencies & unpredictable spending
SAVINGS ACCOUNT
» Small emergencies and repairs
SAVINGS ACCOUNT
» Unemployment fund

or three financial institutions. I have my catch-all chequing account and small-emergencies fund at one bank and everything else at another bank that offers competitive interest rates on savings accounts. Then I have my investment accounts with a robo advisor and a discount brokerage (you'll find plenty on how to invest in chapter 6).

WHAT TO KNOW ABOUT BANK FEES

I don't pay fees on any of my bank accounts. The money-bucket system can get pricey if your bank is helping itself to a bit of what's in each of your many buckets every month. So I'll shout this from the rooftops: *You don't have to put up with fees to have a bank account.* The whole notion of paying for the privilege of accessing your own money is absurd. There are a number of online banks and other financial institutions that offer no-fee banking. I've been a happy customer of two of them for years. You can use sites that compare financial products, like Ratehub.ca and RATESDOTCA, to find non-fee chequing and savings accounts with the features you need, such as unlimited transactions and free e-transfers.

If you're building up your money-bucket system as a couple, you may want to make all or most of your buckets shared accounts. You'll find a more detailed discussion of how to money-bucket for two in chapter 7.

Finally, a note for those of you with U.S. citizenship. As you likely already know, if you have more than a minimum total amount in accounts outside the U.S., the U.S. government demands to know how much you have in each account every year — no matter what country you live in and whether you actually owe U.S. taxes. Having many accounts may further complicate the already complicated process of filing your annual U.S. paperwork.

If you don't want to set up a lot of separate accounts, you can try what will likely become the money-bucket system of the future: a budgeting app that allows you to set savings goals and create virtual money buckets. When you think about it, there's no need to have so many bank accounts if you can visually divide and track your money within one account. For example, the Scotiabank MomentumPLUS Savings Account allows you to save for multiple goals in one account and earn a tiered interest rate depending on how long you leave the money in there. Another example is KOHO, a Canadian app that comes with a reloadable prepaid Visa card. KOHO lets you set aside money for various savings goals and automatically deducts those transfers from your spending balance. With KOHO, the money in your account is held by Peoples Trust, which is a member of the Canada Deposit Insurance Corporation. These types of apps can help you reduce the number of accounts you need to set up, but read the fine print to make sure they're truly a good fit for you.

Now let's run an example with some actual numbers. Here's how a single person with an after-tax income of $4,700 a month might distribute the money among various buckets in a given month:

MONTHLY INCOME AFTER TAX	$4,700
FIXED EXPENSES AND SAVINGS	
Fixed expenses	$2,350
Retirement	$650
EMERGENCIES AND VARIABLE ANNUAL SPENDING	
Small-emergencies fund	$100
Unemployment fund	$200
Short-term savings	$400
LEFT OVER FOR REST OF MONTHLY SPENDING	$1,000

The above is just an example — it's not meant to be a model for how *you* should channel your money. Also note that while transfers to long-term savings and your fixed-expenses buckets should be, well, fixed, what goes into your other buckets is flexible. Settling on the right amounts for each of the buckets may take some trial and error, but if you can carve all of that from your monthly income, you'll be in good shape.

» THE DRAWBACKS OF SUBSCRIPTIONS

Before we move on to the next step, I should add a note about fixed expenses. Most of these are tied to things we all need: keeping a roof over our heads, the lights on, and our homes warm in winter. But if you take a close look at your spending patterns, you'll probably find a number of regular bills that don't quite fit the definition of necessary expenses. And I'm willing to bet a lot of them are subscriptions.

I'm not just talking about magazines, streaming services, and your gym membership — although those count, too, of course. Do you have a subscription to cloud storage? A meal delivery service? Did you sign up to have a curated box of clothes shipped to your door every month? More and more services are subscription-based these days. There are a whole host of software programs you can no longer buy outright but have to subscribe to instead. Amazon pushes subscriptions for everyday items from diapers to disposable razors. You can even subscribe to get ink refills for your printer.

In one sense, subscriptions can make it easier to budget, says Mariel Beasley, principal at Duke University's Common Cents Lab. That's because they smooth out your cash flow. Instead of, say, dropping $250 for clothes at the mall every six months, you spend $50 a month to have a company pick your outfits. Your spending becomes predictable, and you're avoiding the temptation to overspend in store, Beasley says.

But there are potential drawbacks, she warns. People often end up overspending even with subscriptions. Now you're spending $300 on clothing every six months instead of $250.

Also, it can be tricky to keep track of all your subscriptions. As much as the human brain struggles with unpredictable costs, it is also not great at tallying up lots of tiny expenses. Research suggests we tend to dramatically underestimate just how big a chunk of our budget goes to subscriptions. One U.S. survey, for example, found that respondents were, on average, spending almost three times as much as they thought they were.[6]

And the fact we have so many subscriptions means a chunk of our discretionary spending has now become a routine expense. Have your fixed costs been creeping up, by, say, $10 or $25 a month with subscriptions? Over time, this will leave less and less space for spur-of-the-moment expenses, which could make it harder — not easier — to spend within your limits.

Also, if you're thinking you'll just cancel the subscriptions you no longer want or need, think again. "We asked credit union and bank execs this question: 'How many of you have a subscription that you've been meaning to cancel, but just not today?'" Beasley recalls. It turned out everyone had one, she says. That's because there usually isn't much urgency to stop a subscription. You won't go broke if $10 comes out of your account for one more month.

And cancelling can be a real pain. You've probably forgotten the password you need to log into the account and click the "unsubscribe" button. Or maybe you're dreading having to pick up the phone to tell the customer agent you no longer want the service. Even when you do get around to making the phone call, the conversation often drags on. The agent, who's just doing their job, will likely have a script to run through. Are you really sure you want to cancel? How about a discount instead? What if we throw in this other freebie you never asked for? The process, Beasley says, is designed "to add friction in that system to make you decide, 'Maybe I'll think about it a little bit more,' which they know [means] they've got you for at least another three months."

This isn't to say you should forsake all subscriptions. Just choose carefully. When pondering whether to sign up for something, don't ask yourself whether you can afford, say, $10 a month. Ask yourself whether you're prepared to spend $120 a year. If not, then whatever you're thinking of subscribing to is not worth $10 a month, either.

Too many routine costs — small as they may be — will do you in. So keep a running tally of all your monthly dues. While tracking your entire spending through spreadsheets is usually a hopeless enterprise, this is one case in which a simple ongoing tabulation will do the trick.

STEP FOUR: SAVE YOURSELF THE MENTAL STRUGGLE

You're going to be in a fight against debt your whole adult life, whether you're paying it off or trying to stay out of it, so it's important to conserve your energy. Try to spare yourself the mental struggle as much as you can. Once you've set goals and figured out how much money you can realistically set aside each month, automate your bill and debt payments from your chequing account. You should also think about putting at least some of your savings on autopilot, with regular transfers to your savings and investment accounts. If you can't see the money in your everyday bank account, you won't spend it.

This is one of the key insights of behavioural economics: people who automate their savings tend to save more — sometimes a lot more. Behavioural economists are big on small changes that can help people make better financial choices. Automating payments and savings is one tiny change that can make a huge difference, research shows.

In one study by Nava Ashraf, Dean Karlan, and Wesley Yin, participants who set up automatic deposits to their savings accounts boosted their savings by 81 percentage points within a year compared to the control group.[7] It's easy to see why: automating transfers to your savings account requires just one good decision. You set things up and you're done, sheltered from temptation for the long term. The authors compare this to Odysseus, the king of ancient Greek mythology, who famously survived listening to the seductive but deadly call of the Sirens. Many a sailor had fallen for their mesmerizing song never to return, so Odysseus, who wanted to hear the music but was wise enough not to trust his own willpower, tied himself to the mast of his ship. As the *Odyssey* has it, he sailed through just fine. By setting your savings on autopilot, you'll be tying yourself to the mast of your own ship.

Making debt repayments by default also works well. To make things simple, you can set up your payments to go out the day after your payday. That way, the money that's meant to help you kick your debt makes just a fleeting appearance in your chequing account, and once the payment is made, you'll know exactly how much you have left until the next cheque lands.

My only word of caution about automating savings and debt payment is this: have a well-tested budget in place before you do it. Nothing saps motivation like being overzealous in setting up your default savings and then having to pluck the money back out of your savings account — or borrowing again because you didn't leave yourself enough to get to the end of the month. Automated payments are a thing of beauty, but it is possible to overdo them.

BONUS MOVE: PAY WITH CASH OR DEBIT FOR ALMOST EVERYTHING

If you have a simple budget in place and everything is going according to plan, using your credit card as your default payment method is perfectly fine. You just pay it off in full right after your paycheque comes in, and you're set. But if you're in the early stages of establishing a budget or find that, despite your best-laid plans, you keep busting your spending limits, switch to paying with cash or debit for everything you *want* to spend money on. This will make it easier on your brain to avoid overspending.

The issue with credit cards, as behavioural economist Dan Ariely often puts it, is that they delay "the pain of paying." Giving up money is unpleasant and, recent research has found, actually activates some of the same regions of the brain that are involved in processing pain.[8] Credit cards and any other buy-now, pay-later schemes separate the joy of buying from the pain of paying, which encourages consumption. That's why many non-profit debt counsellors advise people struggling with debt to pay with cash. The moment you pay, there's less money in your wallet, and it feels kind of crappy.

If you're not so keen on walking around with rolls of cash in your pocket or if you do most of your overspending online, use your debit card. The experience isn't quite as palpable as handing over your cash, but you'll still know in your mind that your bank account balance drops the instant you buy something.

Still, if you're like most people, banishing credit cards from your life probably isn't a good idea. Most of us need to have a credit score (we'll talk more about those in chapter 2), and that usually means having at least one active credit card. One way to get around the problem is to use credit only to pay for your fixed expenses, like your utility bills. Set up automatic payments and you'll start building a credit history without even needing to carry your credit card in your wallet.

A NOTE ABOUT MATH VERSUS PSYCHOLOGY

Psychology can trump math. Sometimes it makes more sense to choose what seems doable rather than what you know to be the best course of action mathematically — unless there's a smart way to reconcile the two.

One example of this is tax refunds. When you look at the numbers, getting a large tax refund isn't a great idea. When too much money is deducted from your paycheque throughout the year, it means the government is hanging on to money that should be sitting in your bank account instead. Technically, you could invest that extra money and earn a return on it. Instead, you've unwittingly made an interest-free loan to the tax collector.

Math suggests that the best course of action is to minimize the amount of money you'll get back during tax season. Canada Revenue Agency (CRA) has forms you can fill out to let your employer and the government know about changes that would affect your tax load, like whether you're financially supporting your spouse or are paying tuition fees.

It's good to know that you can get the government to scale back your payroll withholdings in some instances if you have the paperwork to back up your claims. That can come in very handy if you're so cash strapped that every little bit helps. But gunning for the smallest possible amount of tax throughout the year doesn't make sense for everyone. We often think about tax refunds as bonus money — a sudden gift that plops into our bank accounts in April or May. That, of course, doesn't make any sense. The money was ours all along. But you can harness the funny way your brain works to your advantage here. The beauty of a large tax refund is that it takes a single good decision to direct that money straight to your savings account or toward paying off debt. It's much easier to do that with, say, a $1,500 cheque from the government than by keeping track of an extra $125 that shows up on your monthly paycheque thanks to smaller payroll deductions. Still, there's a smart hack that may allow you to get the best of both worlds: you could set up automatic monthly transfers for that extra $125, although you may have to do some fine analysis of your pay stub to figure out exactly how your deductions have changed.

Another example of psychology versus math involves debt repayment. When you have a number of outstanding debts, there are two well-known strategies for attacking them: one is to prioritize paying off the loan with the highest interest rate, and the other is to start with your smallest debt and work your way up to the largest. The first strategy is the sensible one from a mathematical point of view. Because your highest-interest debt is the one that's growing the fastest, that's where you want to put your spare cash, while still keeping up with minimum payments on all your other debts. After that loan has been extinguished, you move on to the one with the second-highest interest rate, and so on. This approach minimizes the interest you're paying overall and allows you to get out of debt faster.

However, most financial advisers and debt counsellors I've spoken with swear by the "snowball method" of repaying debt popularized by personal finance guru Dave Ramsey, the bestselling author of *The Total Money Makeover*. The idea is that, while still keeping up with all your minimum payments, you pay off your smallest debt first, regardless of what interest rate it carries. That early win, goes the argument, creates the psychological momentum to move on to bigger and bigger debts. While it's not the most efficient way to get rid of debt, it's the most likely to keep people motivated, supporters say.

Some research, though, suggests that debt-snowballing doesn't always work well. In a series of experiments, Dan Ariely, Moty Amar, Shahar Ayal, Cynthia Cryder, and Scott Rick found that, while there was a noticeable inclination among participants to reduce the number of outstanding debt accounts, there was also a tendency to flounder after paying off some of the smaller loans.[9] Especially when smaller debts have lower interest rates and bigger debts are the costlier ones, the snowball method may "enable consumers to win the battle but lose the war against debt," the authors concluded. Given what I've heard from professionals on the front line of the debt crisis, I wonder whether the snowball method works best when you have the support of a financial coach to encourage you to move on to the larger debts.

That said, if you're trying to tackle multiple debts on your own, here, too, there may be a way to blend the best that math and psychology have to offer. The ultimate ninja move would be to consolidate all your debts into a single, lower-interest loan and then set yourself intermediate goals to pay it off, allowing yourself a little celebration every time you reach the next one. I have to warn you, though, that debt consolidation can be a death trap, depending on how you choose to do it. This leads me to my next point: you need to know not only yourself, but your debt, too, which we'll talk about in the next chapter.

• • •

Wrap-Up

If you've been beating yourself up about your daunting debt or puny savings, I hope this chapter has helped you realize how the availability of cheap and easy credit and the mind-bending cost of things like housing have likely contributed to your struggles. But this chapter isn't about ditching individual responsibility and blaming the system for all your financial woes. Instead, it's about letting go of shame and self-blame and using specific psychological techniques to make it easier to change your behaviour and get on the right track.

Before we move on to talking about different kinds of debt, here are some points to help you get started on getting rid of oppressive debt or start saving for what you really want:

» You need to know what you're saving or paying down debt for. Can you envision what your life will be like once you've reached your goals?

» You also need a plan for reaching your big financial goals — a plan made up of smaller, more manageable intermediate goals. You know what they say: a goal without a plan is just a wish. As much I try to stay away from cheesy tropes, this one's true.

» To keep your finances on track, you need more than goals. You need a simple and reliable system for managing the money coming into and going out of your bank accounts. You can start by drawing your own flow chart of the money-bucket system.

» Once you have a system, it helps to automate as much of it as you can. Setting up automatic transfers means choosing the autopilot option once you've punched in the coordinates of your financial goals. You can kick back, relax, and stop worrying about where you're going all the time.

CHAPTER 2

KNOW YOUR ENEMY: DEBT IS NOT CREATED EQUAL

DEBT IS NOT EVIL. There are some who preach a lifelong abstinence from it, but for most people, that is neither realistic nor practical.

Borrowing gives us the ability to use today money we think we're going to have in the future. Interest is the money we pay creditors in addition to the amount we've borrowed, as a reward for letting us access their money. We need interest because, without it, what incentive would those with surplus cash have to lend it? They're not only refraining from using the money themselves, they're also facing the risk that borrowers won't repay them. There has to be something in it for them. In return, borrowers get to do things like live in a house they can call their own for decades before they've fully paid for it. It's brilliant, when you think of it. Debt is one of humankind's great inventions.

But as useful as it is, debt isn't your friend. It's a frenemy at best. You allow debt into your life with the goal of eventually getting rid of it.

So if you're afraid of debt, I get it. Some of us just have a mental block for anything to do with money, so we, say, sign the loan papers without even attempting to read the fine print first. We simply want to get it over with fast.

For some of us, the ever-growing debt balance triggers that panicky feeling. Our defence mechanism is to hide our heads in the sand, throwing unopened past-due notices straight into the trash, because we simply can't face reality.

But here's the thing: you need to know your enemy to fight it effectively. Credit is available in all shapes and forms. You need to understand how different kinds of debt work in order to choose the ones that work best for you and to devise the best repayment strategy. This chapter gives you some tools to help you get the most out of different forms of debt without letting it get the better of you.

• • •

How to Wrestle Credit Card Debt to the Ground

Everyone knows that credit card debt is bad. But how bad exactly? And why?

The short answer is that it's bad because your carry-over balance grows like bread dough in the oven even if you stop actively adding to it. Your interest rate is pure yeast. The typical rewards credit card in Canada carries an interest rate of 19.99 percent, which is very high. See the box for an example of how quickly the interest charges can add up.

You can use two simple steps to attack credit card debt. Step one: stop using that innocent-looking piece of plastic. Take the card out of your wallet entirely. Until your credit card balance is back to zero, pay for everything with debit or cash instead. Step two: using an online tool like the FCAC's credit card payment calculator, figure out how much you can realistically afford to pay back every month and how long it will take you. If it's going to take several months, use one of the mental hacks we talked about in chapter 1: Set up intermediate goals and throw yourself a mini-party when you reach

HOW LONG DOES IT TAKE TO PAY OFF $1,000 IN CREDIT CARD DEBT MAKING ONLY MINIMUM PAYMENTS?

Let's say you put a single charge of $1,000 on a credit card to buy a dishwasher, and then stop using that card for a year. Your first monthly interest charge might be about $16.66, which is 19.99% of $1,000 divided by 12 (as in 12 months of the year). The monthly minimum payment is often 3 percent of the balance, or $30 in this case. If you pay just that, your balance will go down to $986.66. The next month, your interest charge will be 19.99% of $986.66 divided by 12, or $16.44. Your minimum payment is 3 percent of the same balance, or $29.60.

And on it goes.

After 12 months, you'll have racked up $186 in interest charges, which means you've already paid almost 20 percent more for your dishwasher — and you're not done yet. If you keep making only minimum payments, it will take you a mind-blowing 131 months — nearly 11 years — to pay off that debt. Your interest charges will reach $990, nearly doubling the cost of your washer.

But it doesn't take much to pay off that balance faster and at a much lower cost, even if you don't have $1,000 at hand to erase it all at once. According to the credit card payment calculator of the Financial Consumer Agency of Canada (FCAC), paying just $10 more than your minimum payment every month will cut down your repayment time by six years and three months. You'll also save almost $543 in interest.

The FCAC tool may not match exactly how your credit card calculates interest, as the formula tends to vary slightly from credit card company to credit card company. But the calculator will give you a pretty good idea of what you're up against (and, yes, the deck is stacked!). The point is, making only minimum payments on your credit card is a road to nowhere, but throwing just a little bit more at it can make a huge difference if you also stop the spending.

each of them. Buy yourself a cupcake, a pack of M&M's, a new set of strings for your guitar — whatever brings a little joy to your soul. The following day, head back to the front line rejuvenated and ready to conquer the next target.

In an ideal scenario you would pay off your credit card balance in full every month. Paycheque lands; credit card balance goes back to zero. Treating your credit card like a debit card that earns you reward points means having the best of both worlds.

To recap, here are some things to think about when it comes to credit card debt:

» If you have a carry-over balance, use the FCAC's credit card payment calculator to figure out just how much that's costing you in interest charges.

» If you're making just minimum payments, the credit card payment calculator, again, is your friend. You may find that paying just a few dollars more every month would significantly cut down your repayment timeline.

» If knocking out your credit card debt is going to take several months, set up intermediate targets for yourself and take time to celebrate when you reach each of them.

» If your credit card debt has gotten so out of hand you can't beat it on your own, you'll find a section at the end of this chapter on what you can do if you can't repay your debt in full.

• • •

Lines of Credit Are False Friends

Credit cards get a bad rap, but don't be fooled — a line of credit (LOC) can be just as dangerous.

LOCs work somewhat like credit cards: You can borrow only what you need, up to your credit limit. You pay interest only on the amount you borrow, and as you pay back your balance, you free up room to borrow again. You can usually access funds by using a card at the ATM, writing cheques, and transferring money with online banking. Also like credit cards, LOCs allow you to make minimum payments rather than holding you to a schedule with fixed repayments. But LOCs typically have relatively low interest rates, easily less than half those of credit cards. So far so good, but there's more.

There are two main kinds of LOCs: unsecured, which do not require collateral, and secured, which are backed by collateral such as your house, your car, or your investment portfolio. With unsecured LOCs, the maximum credit limit you can hope for is usually in the tens of thousands of dollars. With secured LOCs, credit limits can easily reach the hundreds of thousands of dollars, depending on the value of your collateral, because the lender can take possession of your collateral if you don't pay back what you owe. Having collateral usually allows you to access higher credit limits, lower interest rates, and more flexible repayment terms. Secured LOCs also often allow you to make interest-only payments.

A personal LOC is an example of an unsecured LOC. Home-equity lines of credit, or HELOCs, are the best-known type of secured LOC. Student LOCs, which you can use to pay for anything from tuition to living expenses while in school, are a rather bizarre species of unsecured LOC. Although they aren't linked to collateral, you may be allowed to make interest-only payments while you're a student and for a period of time after graduation. And if you're a graduate or professional student, you may be able to get a student LOC with a credit limit well into the six figures.

Because of their lower interest rates, you might think LOCs are credit cards' more benign cousins. You'd be wrong. If credit cards can be a slippery slope toward persistent debt, LOCs are, for many people, waterslides leading straight into the debt pit. The real problem is their higher borrowing limits. You can borrow *a lot* of money through an LOC. Combined with relatively low interest rates and low minimum payments, that makes it incredibly easy to keep borrowing, kicking the can down the road. HELOCs can be especially dangerous in this regard, as I explain in the box.

Scott Terrio, manager of consumer insolvency at Hoyes, Michalos and Associates, an Ontario-based debt insolvency firm, says his clients typically have debt from both credit cards and LOCs. And the really big balances tend to be on the latter. "Inevitably they have a couple of credit cards, a couple lines of credit. And the lines of credit are always twice as much or significantly more," Terrio says. But because of the lower interest, he says, "people think that carrying a larger balance isn't so bad."

There are other drawbacks. For one, LOCs usually come with variable interest rates that can go up or down with the general level of interest rates in the economy. The bank can increase your interest rate at its discretion, something that 85 percent of HELOC holders do not realize, according to a recent FCAC survey.[1] Lenders can also lower your credit limit or ask that you repay your balance at any time, although they have to give you advance notice of any changes to your credit agreement.

Terrio could talk all day about the frivolous pursuits he's seen being financed through LOCs, from exotic pets to someone buying a horse for their kid who'd taken up horseback riding. Never tap an LOC to pay for things like vacations or Christmas gifts.

Also, be cautious about using LOCs to consolidate debt. Terrio is no fan of debt consolidation in general. He says he's seen enough people who've gone the route of using one big loan to pay off a bunch of smaller loans, only to end up having to file for insolvency further down the line.

A SPECIAL WARNING ABOUT HELOCS

HELOCs, Scott Terrio warns, can be especially dangerous debt traps. That's because your ability to borrow is often tied to your home equity — the portion of your house you truly own. Home equity, in other words, is what's left when you take your current home value and subtract from it what you still owe on your mortgage and any other debts backed by the property. With a HELOC you can borrow up to 65 percent of your home value.

Here's what you really need to watch out for with HELOCs: Paying down your mortgage is only one way in which your home equity increases. It also increases when the value of your home goes up. For years, soaring home prices have forced home buyers to take on monster mortgages. But for those who already owned a home, rising values have created more room to borrow via HELOCs. The average Canadian with a HELOC has a credit limit of $180,000 and owes a whopping $67,000.[2]

It's like having a credit card that lets you borrow hundreds of thousands of dollars at relatively low interest rates and with a potentially ever-rising credit limit. "It's pretty tempting to use that," Terrio says. And the ability to make interest-only payments makes it even easier to let the debt pile on, he adds.

The idea behind consolidating your debt is you have only one payment to keep track of, and you may be able to get a lower interest rate. I've heard different opinions on debt consolidation over the years, but nearly every debt counsellor or financial adviser I've spoken with is very wary of using LOCs for that purpose. The low interest rate and flexible payment terms make it exceedingly easy not just to put off paying down the debt, but also to keep adding to it.

If you're thinking about debt consolidation, you may want to consider a term or personal loan instead. They usually have higher interest rates and can require significantly bigger payments, but they can be worth it. With a firm end date and mandatory installments, they make it way easier to stick to the schedule and pay off your debt in a reasonable amount of time.

Now, I'm not trying to put you off LOCs altogether. I just want to make sure you don't trip up like many others before you. So how do you make an LOC work for you?

Many people treat LOCs, and especially HELOCs, as credit they can access in an emergency. Having an untouched LOC you can tap for cash in a rare, desperate moment isn't a bad idea. But as many independent financial advisers will tell you, an LOC isn't a substitute for having a rainy-day fund. Your first go-to for anything like a job loss or an enormous bill from the vet should be your own cash reserve. "No HELOC is ever going to be a better emergency fund than cash," Terrio says.

Still, an LOC is nice to have as a second-tier emergency fund because nothing prevents your furnace from going on strike the same day you receive your pink slip. Anything can happen. Tapping an LOC once you've exhausted your emergency fund is never ideal, but it can buy you some time while you find a way to get back on your feet. But once you're there, you should come up with a plan to pay off the debt.

Another way to bend LOCs to your will is to use their flexibility to your advantage without falling for the temptation to overspend. Take home renovations, for example. It's not by chance HELOCs are a popular method for financing things like kitchen overhauls, bathroom facelifts, and third-floor additions. As anyone who's ever lived through the process of remaking their own house knows, renovations are full of surprises. Some things go way over budget, so you have to cut out others you can no longer afford. The contractors are running late, so you have to keep renting the Airbnb. The ability to borrow what you need at low rates comes in handy when your costs are so variable.

The trick, though, is to save and budget for that reno ahead of time. Have a pile of cash to throw at your outstanding balance as soon as you've verified the house is still standing, moved back in, and unpacked your boxes. And have a plan for paying off the rest of it in regular monthly installments, as if it were a loan with a deadline and strict repayment schedule.

If you have or are considering taking out an LOC, here are some things to think about:

» If you owe money on an LOC, what's the maximum monthly payment you could afford without stretching yourself too thin? And how long would it take you to extinguish your balance at that pace?

» If you're thinking of using an LOC for a renovation, have you sketched out a tentative schedule for repaying what you're about to borrow?

» If you've been keeping your LOC for emergencies, do you also have a cash cushion you could tap first? If not, how much would you need to borrow on your LOC if you were unemployed for six months? And how long would it take you to repay that money once you've found a new job?

• • •

Student Loans Aren't as Scary as You Think

While LOCs are more treacherous debt creatures than many would have you believe, student loans don't really live up to their scary reputation. I'm talking about government loans provided by the federal, provincial, and territorial governments. Private student loans are another matter, as I discuss later.

To be clear, I'm not dismissing what a huge financial drag student loans are. But here in Canada at least, it's not the features of the loans themselves that make them dangerous. It's when they hit you. This is debt that you typically have to confront in the most financially fragile phase of your adult life, when you're just beginning on the job market. The lowest-earning years of your career are also the ones in which you face the largest student loan balance.

Still, it's important to emphasize that student loans, in and of themselves, aren't as formidable a type of debt as they're often cracked up to be. The web is full of blogs, articles, and social media threads about how you should crush your student debt as fast as you can, eliminate that scourge from your life as soon as possible. But a lot of this advice is about U.S. student loans, which are an entirely different and far more fearful beast. Thankfully, up here north of the 49th parallel, student debt is generally a more manageable enemy — and not only because going to school costs a lot less than in the U.S.

There are more than a few reasons not to be so scared of student loans. First, they're cheap — and the Covid-19 pandemic made them even cheaper. Some provincial and territorial student loans are interest-free (although sometimes that comes with conditions). For Canada Student Loans that have a variable interest rate, the federal government usually charges a rate equal to Canada's prime rate. For those with fixed rates, it's prime plus two percentage points. The Bank of Canada's prime rate is an average of the big banks' prime rates, which are their benchmarks for setting interest rates for variable-rate loans. The point is, at the start of 2020, the prime rate being used stood at a low 3.95 percent, but during the pandemic it dropped even lower, to 2.45 percent. Rates are similar — and sometimes lower — for provinces and territories that charge their own interest (keep in mind that Canada Student Loans aren't available in Nunavut, the Northwest Territories, or Quebec, which run their own student aid programs). Even better, during the health emergency the federal government first temporarily froze principal and interest payments and then, once payments were required again, suspended the accumulation of interest on various types of federal loans. Many provincial and territorial governments also introduced their own Covid-19 financial relief measures for students.

Also, a neat feature of borrowing from the government is that you often get a six-month grace period after finishing school during which you don't have to make payments. And as of November 2019, interest does not accumulate on federal loans during the non-repayment period, although that's not necessarily the case with money coming from the provinces.

Second, student loans are flexible. Another bonus of many government loans is that you can tweak your repayment terms. With federal loans, for example, you can change the date on which your payments are due, as well as increase or decrease the payments and how long it will take to pay back the loan. Adjusting the due date means you can set your student loan payment to come out of your account, for example, right after you get paid. Dialing up your payment amount means you can pay off your loan faster and save on the total interest you'll pay. Shrinking your payments, on the other hand, means it will take you longer to get rid of the debt and you'll end up paying more interest over the life of the loan, but could come in handy if you're going through a rough patch financially.

Third, student loans are forgiving — the government is a pretty understanding lender. With the Repayment Assistance Plan (RAP), if you can't keep up with your loans, you can get your payments capped at 20 percent of your income, or temporarily waived. If your income is under $25,000 a year, you won't have to make any payments at all. And after enough years, if you're still struggling, the government will start to pay for both the interest and the principal exceeding your payments. After 15 years, any leftover debt is forgiven. One thing to keep in mind, though: you need to reapply for the assistance plan every six months. If your loan doesn't qualify for RAP, there are also provincial and territorial payment assistance or payment deferral plans.

Finally, government student loans have tax perks. If your loan was obtained under the Canada Student Loans Act, the Canada Student Financial Assistance Act, the Apprentice Loans Act, or a similar provincial or territorial law, you can claim the interest on your tax return and receive a tax break.

WHEN STUDENT LOANS BECOME DANGEROUS

Even though only a small portion of Canadians default on their student debt, two situations can turn student loans from relatively tame creatures into deadly fiends.

The first is not graduating. Taking on student debt makes sense when you're investing in your education, which will boost your earning potential. But when you don't finish school, you've basically taken on the cost of higher education without enjoying the returns typically associated with it. Research shows that Canadians are more likely to default on their student loans if they've dropped out of school.[3]

The second is getting stuck in a low-paying job right after graduation. This is a much more common problem, especially for certain majors. Earning a living in the first few years after school often means stitching together a number of unpaid or barely paid internships and low-wage gigs. And, depending on your industry, you may be first in line to be let go if there are layoffs.

Sure, the government stands ready to help, by giving you the ability to lower your own payments and to apply for repayment assistance, but you have to know to reach out for that lifeline. It doesn't happen automatically.

Also, be careful about using expensive debt to make ends meet during a cash crunch when you could easily take advantage of your student loan repayment options instead. If you're keeping up with your standard student loan payments but racking up a credit card bill, you're opening the gates to a much more insidious debt creature.

All of the above make Canada's government student loans a pretty sweet deal as far as debt goes. So tread carefully when weighing the option of taking on a private student loan or a student LOC instead of a government loan. They may have lower interest rates, but the repayment terms likely won't be as generous, and you'll give up the tax credit. Even adding your student loans to a debt-consolidation arrangement means your creditor is no longer the government but a private lender, who may not be as lenient.

Still, like all debt, government student loans must be handled with care. As described in the box, there are situations when student loans can become financially threatening. And let's face it: between soaring housing prices and staggering daycare fees, the start-up costs of adult life have gone up sharply for many of us. Student loans add to that. Even if you have a pretty high income early on, student loans can feel like a massive chain holding you down while you're revving up your engine, trying to take off. I'm thinking of young doctors, for example, who easily graduate with more than $100,000 in debt.

Here are some points to think about with respect to government student loans:

» Is your credit card debt slowly creeping higher while you dutifully keep up with your student loan payments? Consider stretching out your repayment period, which will result in lower payments. Or check out whether you're eligible for repayment assistance.

» If you're thinking of consolidating your government student loans into a student LOC, have you considered that you would no longer be able to take advantage of the student loan interest tax credit or apply for repayment assistance?

» If you're about to become a parent (congratulations!) and still have student loans, can you realistically accelerate your payments and eliminate your student debt before you're changing nappies and likely facing a reduced income while on parental leave?

• • •

Watch Out for Longer Car Loans

If you have a good credit score, car loans aren't an aggressive species of debt. I often hear from people in my parents' boomer generation that the advice from their own parents was to save up and buy a car or truck with cash. But there's nothing wrong or financially unsound with taking out a loan of three to five years to buy a vehicle. The old-fashioned car loan is something any qualified borrower can pay off relatively quickly so they can enjoy years — possibly a decade or more — of car-payment-free driving.

But a more dangerous breed has emerged in the last decade or so: auto loans longer than five or six years. "For the longest time, five years was it" when it came to borrowing to buy a vehicle, recalls George Iny of the Automobile Protection Association, a consumer advocacy group. Then five years became six, then seven or even eight years, he says.

For a given principal amount and interest rate, the obvious drawback of a longer loan term is you'll end up paying more interest. What's attractive is the low payments; the longer you have to repay the loan, the smaller the installments. And with today's ultra-low interest rates, chances are you won't pay that much interest anyway. In theory, a longer loan with a low rate is a great deal, Iny says. Whatever money you're saving in car payments, you can use to pay off expensive debt like your credit card balance. Or you can use the funds to top up your investments for retirement.

But that assumes you'd buy the same "rinky-dink" car you would have bought with a shorter auto loan, Iny says. That's what would happen if we were perfectly rational personal finance robots with hearts and minds of steel.

In practice, what happens to many of us flesh-and-bone borrowers is quite different. In all likelihood, you start out with a car payment in mind. You know what you can afford to pay every month. When you get to the dealership floor, the salesperson may show you that you can actually buy a more expensive car than you thought. That's the magic of longer loans: same payment, better ride. So why not? You sign the papers and happily drive off the lot with a spiffy new car and, let's say, a longer-than-you'd-planned seven-year loan.

For a few years, all is well. But around year four your once-new vehicle starts to feel a little dated. Your smartphone technology has moved on, and your car hasn't kept up. It's no big deal, but you start checking out new models, just for kicks. That's when you learn you could actually upgrade your car for *the same monthly payment* — or perhaps even a slightly lower payment! So again, why not? Once more you drive off the lot happy. Except this time you have an eight-year loan that covers not just the price of your latest purchase but the leftover balance of your old loan.

Now, wait a second, you might say. Waaaait a second! Didn't I just trade in my older car? Yes, but that wasn't quite enough.

This is where negative equity comes in. Equity is negative when what you bought is worth less than what you still owe on it. In real estate it's called being underwater. If you remember the headlines from 2008 and 2009, after the U.S. housing bubble burst, you probably know it's bad news even if you're not entirely sure why. Let me explain. Home prices generally go up. But if housing values take a sharp downturn, someone who made a very small down payment and took out a big mortgage may end up with their home being worth less than what they still owe. Being underwater can be a real headache because it means if you sold your home, you'd lose money. In the U.S., this forced many Americans to sit tight in areas of high unemployment instead of moving to where the jobs were.

When it comes to vehicles, though, having negative equity is very common. That's because cars and trucks lose value over time. New vehicles generally shed one-third of their value in the first year, says Brian Murphy, who was vice-president of research and analytics at Canadian Black Book when he spoke to me for this book. Thankfully the pace of depreciation slows down considerably after that. But unless you make a big down payment, negative equity is inevitable in the first few years of a long auto loan. The good news is that, since the pace of depreciation slows down, eventually you reach positive equity, meaning your loan balance falls below the value of your vehicle.

However, the longer your loan term and the smaller your payments, the longer it will take you to get there. Now, if you switch to a new vehicle before you've reached positive equity, you'll be left with a balance on your old auto loan that wasn't covered by the trade-in. That money will be added to your new car loan. You can check out the box for a detailed example of how this works. By making a few early trade-ins and taking out longer and longer auto loans, you can dig yourself into quite the debt hole.

BY THE NUMBERS: AN EIGHT-YEAR VERSUS A FIVE-YEAR AUTO LOAN

Let's look at an example with some numbers. Say you bought a compact SUV for $38,000 with zero down and a 1.9 percent interest rate. With a five-year loan, it would take you about two years to get to positive equity, as shown in the first chart on page 52.

NEGATIVE EQUITY WITH A 5-YEAR AUTO LOAN

	BALANCE	MARKET VALUE	AMOUNT OF EQUITY
MONTH 12	$33,108	$26,300	-$6,808
MONTH 24	$25,065	$24,250	-$815
MONTH 36	$16,868	$21,500	$4,632
MONTH 48	$8,514	$18,950	$10,436
MONTH 60	$0	$16,800	$16,800

With an eight-year loan, on the other hand, it would take you nearly five years — five years! — to get there, according to numbers provided by Murphy, as shown in the second chart.

NEGATIVE EQUITY WITH AN 8-YEAR AUTO LOAN

	BALANCE	MARKET VALUE	AMOUNT OF EQUITY
MONTH 12	$36,209	$26,300	-$9,909
MONTH 24	$31,326	$24,250	-$7,076
MONTH 36	$26,350	$21,500	-$4,850
MONTH 48	$21,278	$18,950	-$2,328
MONTH 60	$16,109	$16,800	$691
MONTH 72	$10,841	$14,450	$3,609
MONTH 84	$5,472	$12,500	$7,028
MONTH 96	$0	$10,650	$10,650

SOURCE: CANADIAN BLACK BOOK

If you had $4,000 left over from your previous car loan, your starting balance wouldn't be $38,000, but $42,000. You've basically added a "negative down payment," Murphy says. Now it will take you even longer to get to a position of positive equity.

How did we as a society get here, you ask? How are we allowing people to end up with auto loans that are so much bigger than their vehicles were worth brand new? According to both Iny and Murphy, it all started with the financial crisis. "Car sales tanked quite badly in 2008," Iny recalls. "Consumers were actually kind of kneecapped. They didn't have the liquidity to buy vehicles." So the industry came up with seven- and eight-year loans, which kept payments enticingly low, he says. Murphy puts the emphasis on how the crisis affected the leasing market. "The banks didn't want to lend money to companies that were doing leasing, because they often became incredibly risk averse," he says. But loan payments were dramatically higher than what people were used to paying when leasing, so the solution was longer-term loans, he adds.

The problem, though, is many borrowers with longer loans don't hang on to their vehicles for long enough, so they end up in the negative-equity spiral.

5-year vs. 8-year car loan

Vehicle price: $38,000 **Interest rate:** 1.9%

5-year loan

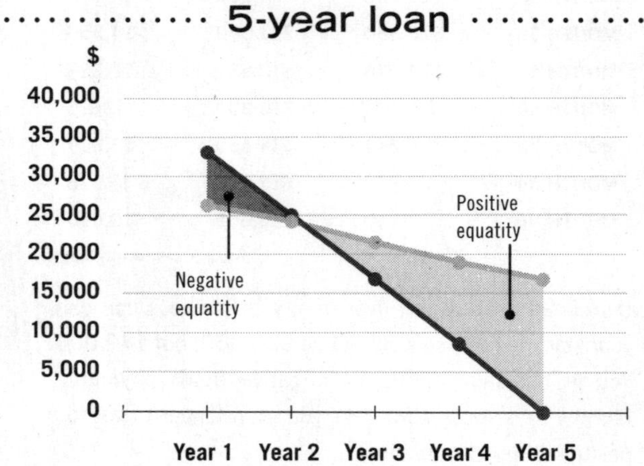

8-year loan

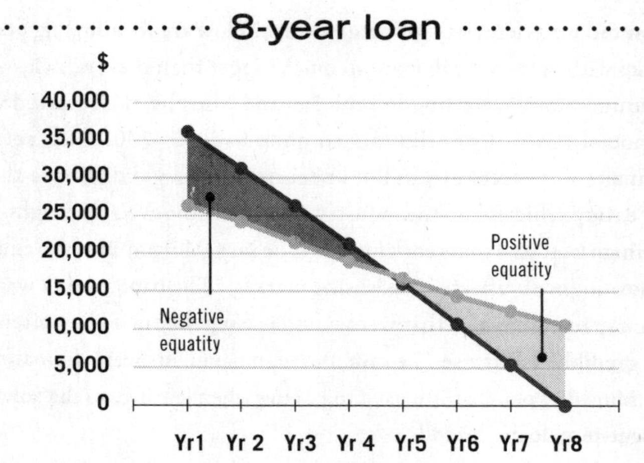

Source: Canadian Black Book

Now that leasing is popular again, it's probably the better option if you like to switch cars every few years, both Murphy and Iny say. You'll never be car-payment-free, but you'll sidestep the negative-equity problem.

If you're set on buying rather than leasing, there's something more you should know about negative equity. If your vehicle is stolen or declared a total loss due to a bad accident, there's a chance the market value of your car will be less than what you still owe on it. This means the insurance payout wouldn't fully cover your loan. If you're buying a new vehicle, you can protect yourself from this risk with optional insurance coverage that will pay out the original purchase price of the vehicle, says Matthew Turack, president of CAA Insurance Company. For example, if your car cost $40,000 but was worth $30,000 at the time it was stolen or totalled, your insurance payout would be $40,000 (instead of the $30,000 you'd get with standard coverage). Some of that money would go to cover your outstanding loan balance, and the rest would go back to you, Turack says.

This is called a waiver of depreciation or replacement cost coverage. You can choose it as an add-on to your insurance policy or, if you live in a province where auto insurance is provided by the government, buy it as part of optional insurance coverage offered by private insurers. With CAA Insurance, you can get depreciation waiver coverage for up to five years, Turack says. And if you're leasing, leasing companies commonly require you to have depreciation waiver coverage for at least a couple of years.

Another option is guaranteed asset protection insurance, commonly known as GAP insurance, sold by dealerships and financing companies. It can extend for up to eight years and is available on used vehicles as well. Keep in mind that, unlike replacement cost coverage, GAP insurance does not pay out the original purchase price — it simply covers the difference between what you still owe on your vehicle and the vehicle's actual cash value.

In general, the more you can put down when buying a car, the better, says Anne Marie Thomas, who was an insurance expert at InsuranceHotline.com when I spoke with her for this book. "Not only will that reduce your car payment, it also will reduce the potential of you finding yourself in a negative-equity position," Thomas says.

Also, the higher the interest rate on your auto loan — all else being equal — the longer it will take you to get to positive equity. That's because more of your payment goes toward interest and less goes toward reducing the principal balance. Also, the better your vehicle retains its value, the sooner you'll get rid of negative equity. Of course, cars and trucks that have a reputation for high resale value often come at a premium price, but it's worth it, Murphy says.

And one last thing: by buying a second-hand vehicle that's only three or four years old, you can skip the steepest part of the depreciation curve. That means a big discount on the purchase price and many years of slower depreciation ahead of you. "You can save yourself a lot of money," Murphy says.

You can also save a ton of money by not having a car, if you can avoid it. If you include depreciation, the cost of owning a car in Canada averages a shocking $9,000 a year, according to the CAA.[4] If you can get by with public transport, a bike, or the occasional rental car or car-share ride, why not put that money in your savings account rather than your gas tank?

Here are some points to consider if you're thinking of taking out a car loan:

» Just because you think you can afford the monthly car payment doesn't mean you can actually afford the car. Before you put your autograph on an auto loan, look at how much you'd be borrowing overall, how long it would take you to pay that off, and what you'd be shelling out in interest alone.

» If you'd still have a balance on your auto loan after trading in your car, you're not ready to trade up.

» If you really, *really* like to get a new car every few years, consider leasing instead of buying.

» If you're buying a vehicle with a loan longer than five years or with a high interest rate, consider buying a replacement cost endorsement on your existing policy or GAP insurance. Both of these options will avoid your having to foot the difference between your vehicle's cash value and what you might still owe on it if the vehicle is stolen or you get into an accident and your ride is declared a total loss.

» If you're researching your next car, take a look at websites like Canadian Black Book for an estimate of how well various models retain their value.

• • •

Don't Judge a Mortgage (Only) by the Interest Rate

Mortgages are arguably the most popular creature in the debt zoo. Not only do they have a reputation for being docile — with their decades-long repayment periods and low interest rates — but having one can also be a status symbol. I mean, can you even call yourself an adult if you're not a homeowner with a mortgage? Some people would say no. I strongly disagree, but we'll get to that in chapter 3.

For now, let me just point this out: a mortgage is an elephant of a loan, the biggest debt most of us will ever take on. And you should do your research before approaching this majestic tusker.

The obvious part of the prep work is comparing mortgage rates. When I started out as a financial reporter in 2010, I heard so many stories of people simply signing up for whatever their bank had to offer. Thankfully, by now many prospective home buyers seem to know better than that. According to a 2019 survey by the Canada Mortgage and Housing Corporation, 87 percent of home buyers were going online to compare mortgages, and most people contacted up to three lenders and two mortgage brokers for information or advice.[5]

Rate-comparison sites are a mandatory first step when you start your research. With a few clicks, you'll see rates from a variety of lenders and likely get a pretty good idea of what you qualify for. Usually, you can then inquire about a specific loan directly through the site. Even if you're hoping to eventually sign up with your bank or a mortgage broker, knowing what's out there will help you understand whether you're getting a good deal. Make sure to repeat your search on several of the major sites, as they don't all list the same lenders and offers, says Sean Cooper, a mortgage broker and the author of *Burn Your Mortgage: The Simple, Powerful Path to Financial Freedom for Canadians.*

A mortgage broker is an intermediary between borrowers and lenders and will do the comparing for you. And take note: it's usually the lender, not you, who foots the commission once the mortgage closes, although you'll probably have to pay a fee if you don't qualify for a conventional loan. Also, in a highly competitive market, brokers may be willing to give up part of their commission to negotiate a better rate for the client.

A good broker can help you choose the right mortgage term, decide between a fixed and a variable mortgage rate, and generally find the best deal based on your specific situation. They may also have access to lenders that only deal with brokers. And if you're self-employed, working on commission, or have a less-than-stellar credit score, turning to a broker is probably your best bet to secure a loan.

Still, one risk with brokers, who are paid based on commission, is that they may steer you toward just a handful of lenders. And since brokers get paid when you take out a mortgage, some of them might go to great lengths to get you a loan, when maybe you'd be better off waiting a little longer to save up for a larger down payment or to improve your credit score. As a starting point, Cooper says, make sure you understand how a broker is getting paid, and feel free to ask lots of questions.

A third possibility when it comes to mortgage-deal hunting is to haggle with your own bank. If you're really keen on getting a mortgage at the same institution that looks over your chequing account and retirement savings, you can ask them whether they'd be willing to match the best rates you've seen in your research. It may not work, but it could be worth a shot.

If you're dealing with one of the big banks, though, beware of steep penalties for breaking fixed-rate mortgages, Cooper warns. "I haven't really heard of a bank talk about the fact that their penalties are pretty high," he says. And few borrowers would know to ask the question, he adds.

That's why mortgage shopping should go beyond interest rates. Don't let that benign-elephant image fool you: many a borrower has been gored by pricey penalties. A large penalty for breaking your mortgage contract can cost you tens of thousands of dollars — easily far more than a lower interest rate would save you over the life of the loan. You may not think you're going to break your mortgage, but life happens. Historically, about one-third of borrowers end up breaking their mortgage early for one reason or another, according to mortgage broker David Larock of Integrated Mortgage Planners. Maybe you'll find a job in another city, get divorced, or become unemployed. Or perhaps you'll want to pay off your mortgage early or you'll be tempted to refinance at a lower rate. Whatever the reason you have for wanting to get out of your mortgage early, the lender will charge you a fee that compensates it for the interest payments it's going to lose out on.

That might sound fair enough, but not all penalties are created equal. If you have a variable mortgage rate, you'll generally pay three months' worth of interest. The real risk is with fixed-rate mortgages, where the penalty is usually the greater of three months' interest or something called the interest rate differential, or IRD. This is a calculation based on your remaining mortgage balance and the difference between your original rate and a comparison rate, which is effectively the rate at which your lender says it can relend what you're paying back early. A bigger mortgage balance and a larger gap between those rates will result in a higher penalty.

The size of IRD-based penalties can vary significantly based on which formula lenders use to calculate it, warns Larock. The comparison rate the big banks and some credit unions typically use for the IRD is what's called their posted rate, which is typically much higher than the discounted rate often used by lenders that focus solely on mortgages and by some online banks and some credit unions. An IRD penalty that is based on the posted rate instead of the discounted rate can cost you thousands of dollars more.

Let me show you an example of what this might look like based on numbers provided by Larock. Let's say you need to get out of your five-year fixed-rate mortgage contract early, and that it has an interest rate of 1.94 percent, a balance of $300,000, and two years remaining on the term. What kind of penalty will you have to pay for breaking your contract? With a penalty of three months' interest, you'd be able to break free for $1,455:

FORMULA:

Contract rate × Mortgage balance × (3 months remaining / 12) = 3-month penalty

....

EXAMPLE:

1.94% × $300,000 × (3 / 12) = $1,455

Now let's look at the IRD calculation. Some lenders that focus only on mortgages, along with some online banks and credit unions, use a straightforward IRD formula that goes like this:

FORMULA:

(Contract rate - Current rate that most closely matches your remaining term) × Mortgage balance × (Months remaining / 12) = Simple IRD

....

EXAMPLE:

(1.94% - 1.89%) × $300,000 × (24 / 12) = $300

The lender calculates the difference between your mortgage rate and the interest it can charge on a two-year loan (which in this example is 1.89 percent). It then multiplies that by your mortgage balance and the time remaining on your term (expressed as the number of months left to the end of the term divided by 12 months of the year). The simple IRD formula yields a penalty of just $300. But since the three-month penalty of $1,455 is higher, that's what you end up paying.

If you think that sounds like a lot of money, wait until you see what the math yields with a different IRD calculation. According to Larock, in one formula used by the big banks and some of the smaller banks and credit unions, the lender takes your contract rate and subtracts from it the difference between the posted rate that most closely matches your remaining term and the discount you received off the posted rate. In this case, let's say the five-year posted rate when you signed your mortgage was 4.79 percent (remember: your contract rate is 1.94 percent, meaning you received a discount of 2.85 percent on the posted rate) and the two-year posted rate is 3.19 percent. Behold what this formula produces:

FORMULA:

[Contract rate - (Posted rate that most closely matches your remaining term - Discount received on posted rate)] × Mortgage balance × (Months remaining/12) = IRD with posted rate

....

EXAMPLE:

[1.94% - (3.19% - 2.85%)] × $300,000 × (24 / 12) = 1.6% × $300,000 × 2 = $9,600

No, you did not read that wrong. You could get saddled with an eye-watering penalty of $9,600 if your lender uses the IRD calculation with posted rates.

All of the big banks and many credit unions charge far bigger penalties than what's required to make them whole, Larock warns. Such inflated penalties generate substantial profits for the lenders that use them, he adds. That's why it pays to do your research and sign up with what are called fair-penalty lenders, which charge reasonable fees that are only meant to compensate them when you break your contract. Lenders that focus only on mortgages usually have fair penalties, according to Cooper. Some large-volume credit unions and online banks also charge very reasonable penalties. If you search for *fair-penalty lenders* online, you should be able to find some good lists.

As you might be able to tell from the formulas on pages 58–59, the size of the penalty depends on current interest rates and on the number of months you have left in your mortgage. See the box on page 61 for more details on why the timing of your decision to break your mortgage matters.

Penalties aren't the only commonly overlooked trait of a mortgage. Another feature you should pay attention to is prepayment privileges. How quickly would you be able to pay down your mortgage without incurring penalties if you had extra cash lying around?

What's neat about making a lump-sum payment is that, unlike your regular payments, all of the money goes toward reducing your principal balance. Another way to shrink your mortgage faster is to increase your regular payments. Also, taking advantage of generous prepayment privileges can help you reduce your penalty, should you need to break your contract, because your balance is smaller.

But as Cooper says, prepayment privileges vary significantly from lender to lender. Is the cap on your lump-sum payments 10 percent or 20 percent of your mortgage balance? Will you be able to make lump-sum payments any time or just once a year? And can you double up your payments? All of this matters when evaluating a mortgage contract, Cooper says.

Another feature that can come in handy is portability. This allows you to bring your mortgage with you if you move to a new home and, if needed, to combine it with a new loan *sans* penalty. Another potential advantage of transferring your old mortgage: if rates have gone up since you bought your first home, you'll be able to secure a rate that's lower than what you would have gotten by signing up for an entirely new mortgage.

But portability clauses also vary, Cooper warns. For example, some lenders may give you 30 days to port your mortgage without penalty, and others 60 or even 90 days, he says. The difference can be crucial. Imagine, for example, that you're moving into a newly built home. The contractor assured

WHEN YOU BREAK YOUR MORTGAGE MATTERS

There's a little more you need to know about penalties (sorry!).

First, if you're trying to break free of a fixed-rate mortgage, it matters whether interest rates have been rising or falling. For example, the drop in interest rates triggered by the economic impact of Covid-19 increased the difference between pre-pandemic mortgage rates and the comparison rate, resulting in appallingly high penalties that slammed many Canadians who were forced to break their mortgages. High mortgage penalties also kept many others from being able to refinance at lower rates.

Another issue to keep in mind: IRD penalties can grow as you get closer to the end of your mortgage term. This may seem counterintuitive, because the further along you are in repaying your loan, the smaller your outstanding balance is. But the time remaining in your term also affects which comparison rate lenders use for the IRD calculation.

Lenders use the comparison rate that most closely matches how much time is left on your current term. In the example above, the comparison rate was for a two-year mortgage term. But what if you have 17 months left on your term? Then your lender would likely pick a comparison rate based on a one-year mortgage (12 months remaining). The problem here is the discount that banks apply on short-term mortgages is much smaller than what they grant on five-year terms. This can skew the IRD calculation and result in a bigger penalty.

you the new property would be available by a certain date but — lo and behold — they run late by a month and a half. If your portability option has a 30-day expiry date, you'll have to get a new mortgage and pay a (potentially horrific) penalty on your old one. A longer portability window also gives you more breathing room to close your buying and selling transactions when the dates don't line up closely, Cooper notes.

Remember, a mortgage will likely be the biggest debt of your life. Be sure to take your time doing the research, read the fine print, and never be afraid to ask questions. And keep the following points in mind:

» If you were to buy a winter coat, you'd probably check out a few models and maybe a few retailers, am I right? Your mortgage is likely the biggest loan you'll ever have, so you owe it to yourself to shop around, just like you would for a new parka.

» The mortgage with the lowest interest rate isn't necessarily the best mortgage. Check out other important features like the penalty you'd have to pay for breaking it, prepayment privileges, and whether you'd be able to transfer your mortgage to a new home.

» In particular, watch out for prepayment penalties, which could cost you tens of thousands of dollars. Fair-penalty lenders will charge you reasonable fees should you ever break your mortgage contract.

• • •

Micropayments: Tiny but Dangerous

Micropayments are a newer addition to the varied microcosm of debt, and they're spreading fast. As tiny as they may be, do not underestimate them. Confused about what the heck I'm saying? I'm talking about the new incarnation of the buy-now, pay-later (BNPL) system.

This isn't a new idea of course. If you've ever bought a mattress or a laundry machine, you've probably come across this scheme: Get the thing now and don't pay for six months interest-free! What we should do with that, of course, is figure out whether we can afford to pay off the bill in full within the fateful six months. If so, it's a sweet deal: pay for a big-ticket item in smaller installments at zero additional cost. But what our impressionable brain often does instead is think it's getting something for free right now; forget about the bill for six months; and then, when the bill comes due, curse itself for having to shell out a ton of money plus interest for something that no longer feels new.

Much like using a credit card, BNPL separates the pain of paying from the actual purchase, says Mariel Beasley of Duke University's Common Cents Lab. "There's something super powerful about 'free today.'" This age-old offer also takes advantage of our natural inclination to discount what's going to happen in the future, she says. As animals, we're hard-wired to worry about the present much more than about what's to come. The prospect of a big charge coming down the pike in six months is much less likely to deter us from a purchase than if we had to fork out the money right away.

Micropayments have taken all this to the next level. The grandchildren of the classic BNPL system are online services and apps that let you split small purchases into tiny installment payments. You may have started to notice these offers at checkout when you're buying something on the web. You can pay for that $150 pair of shoes in one go, or your can make three monthly payments of $50.

BNPL 2.0 has been around for a while in the U.S., but in Canada it really took off during the pandemic, with consumers largely limited to online shopping and many retailers pivoting to digital sales overnight.

Proponents of the new BNPL say it's way better than using a credit card. The payments come out of your account automatically, which means there's no danger of incurring extra interest charges as you would if you didn't pay off the full balance on your credit card. But when you have the option of paying in tiny installments, your brain tends to zero in on the smaller dollar amount of the monthly charge rather than the total cost, something behavioural economists call anchoring.

On the other hand, when you pay with plastic, you are still looking at the full cost of a purchase. Sure, you can put off *paying* it off in full, but the price tag on which you're basing your buying decision is the full amount. This forces you to think about whether whatever you've got your eye on is really worth the cost. "There is still at least a little bit of pain in thinking, 'Is this purchase worth $235, even though I won't have to pay it today?'" Beasley says. "Whereas these smaller fixed installments — these micropayments — essentially what they're doing is they're anchoring you on 'You can get this item for $47.'"

Micropayment can be a better option for something you were going to buy no matter what. But for anything else, they likely make it easier to overspend because they refocus your attention on the smaller installment payment rather than the bigger, overall number, Beasley says.

Be aware that BNPL apps may collect fees and interest. Also, in some cases you can set the payments to be charged to your credit card, which eliminates any advantage of using installments instead of paying with plastic. Finally, with some BNPL micropayment options, you may be signing up for a miniature loan, which could affect your credit score.

If you're thinking of taking advantage of micropayments, here are some things to consider:

» What should you do when you discover you can get a fabulous $235 pair of jeans for just $47 a month with five monthly installments? You should stop, breathe, and do the math. Can you really afford to drop $235 on jeans?

» Okay, so maybe you did treat yourself to those designer jeans — because you could afford them (and good for you; splurging when you know you can feels great). But now you're looking at new headphones. They cost $300, but you can pay $50 a month. Fifty bucks a month doesn't seem too bad, but remember, you're still paying off the jeans. If you add the headphones, you'll be out $97 a month. You get the point: micropayments are a slippery slope.

» Remember the issue with subscriptions I mentioned in chapter 1? Small installment payments are similar: they're easy to forget, but they add up fast.

• • •

How to Tame Your Credit Score

Your credit score, of course, isn't debt. But it is a gatekeeper to the debt universe. Getting to know this creature and how to handle it is essential.

You may already know that a credit score is a three-digit number in the range of 300 to 900 that helps lenders determine your creditworthiness. Scores from the mid-600s to low 700s are generally considered good, and the higher the score, the better. Credit scores affect your ability to get credit, how much you can borrow, through what means and at what cost. Pretty much everyone knows they're important.

But credit scores are also shrouded in mystery. There are all kinds of urban legends about how they really work and how you can boost your numbers.

Many people seem to treat credit scores as if they were a grade for their financial savvy. That's understandable. The word *creditworthiness* itself encourages this idea: the bigger your number, the higher your worthiness. No wonder some people take it personally when their credit score dips.

But that's not what credit scores are. They're the product of algorithms that classify your information based on data points from millions of other borrowers. It's a bit like what insurance companies do when they gauge the chances you will, say, get into a car accident. Credit scores predict the likelihood you'll repay what you've borrowed on time.

The most thorough explanation I've ever heard of how credit scores work comes from Julie Kuzmic, senior compliance officer for consumer advocacy at Equifax Canada. Let's pretend we're going to come up with our very own, brand-new credit-scoring algorithm, Kuzmic suggests. The first thing we want to do is go back a couple of years and collect the credit files of, say, 10 million borrowers. Let's say right now is January 2022; we might have to go back to January 2020. "You want to have a good cross-section of old credit files, new credit files, people who've missed a lot of payments, people who have a solid background, people who have declared bankruptcy.... You want the whole spectrum," Kuzmic says. And, of course, all the files are completely anonymized.

First we look at the files as they were in 2020. Then we look at the same credit files one to two years later. As of January 2022, some people will be humming along, others will have declared bankruptcy, and yet others will have climbed out of bankruptcy and resumed making payments on time — to cite a few of many possible scenarios. Statisticians will then look "for the elements of the credit file from that first sample that ended up being most predictive of what actually happened a year or two later," Kuzmic says.

That's how credit scores are intended to help level the playing field in terms of who gets to borrow money from the bank, she says. "If you think about what may have happened a hundred years ago or more if somebody was applying for a loan at a bank," Kuzmic says, "a big part of whether or not it was granted was probably related to whether the bank manager knew the family of the person who was applying."

Credit scores are far from being a perfect equalizer. In the U.S., for example, low-income households are far more likely to have neither a bank account nor a credit score due to their limited or non-existent credit histories. But lenders relying on your score, rather than on your connections, certainly seems a better approach.

In Canada there are two main credit bureaus: Equifax and TransUnion. Each of them compiles a credit report based on information lenders send them. Each of them uses their proprietary algorithms to arrive at credit scores based on your credit report. In addition, lenders often have their own formulas to score creditworthiness. That's why you don't have just one credit score. Your scores may be different based on who's calculating it and what information they're using.

Even your credit reports don't always match up, so it's a good idea to check periodically with both credit bureaus to make sure everything is accurate and up to date. You can mail or phone to request a hard copy of your credit report for free. TransUnion also allows consumers to order their credit reports online once a month without paying. In 2020, Quebec enacted legislation that requires both TransUnion and Equifax to allow residents of the province to access their credit reports and scores online at no charge. Since then, Equifax has also started offering free online access to credit reports and credit scores for everyone in Canada.

While credit-scoring models differ, there are generally five main factors that go into the calculation:

1. Payment history: This shows how well you've been keeping up with your payments and is usually the biggest deal. How many of your accounts are in good standing? Are there any late or missed payments? How late were you? How much did you owe? And how long ago did that happen? There are many other variables at play, but you get the gist. This generally accounts for around 35 percent of your score, according to Equifax.

---

2. Credit utilization: This measures how much you're borrowing on things like credit cards and LOCs compared to your credit limit. This is mostly concerned with revolving credit, which

frees up room to borrow, up to the available limit, as you repay. It's also a major factor, accounting for roughly 30 percent of your score, Equifax says. In general, a lower utilization rate is better, according to Kuzmic.

---

3. Credit history: This looks at the age of your credit files. How old is your mortgage? How long have you had your current credit card? A longer credit history is generally better. This accounts for around 15 percent of the score, Equifax says.

---

4. New credit: This weighs things like how many new accounts you have, when you last opened an account, and how many credit products you've recently applied for. If a lender asks to review your credit report as part of a credit application, this is known as a hard inquiry, and may affect your credit score. Some scoring formulas lump multiple hard inquiries about the same type of loan, such as a mortgage, into a single inquiry if they're made within a short period of time. That's because this often reflects consumers shopping around for the best deal on a financial product. Obtaining your own credit report or score is a soft inquiry, and has no effect on your scores. If your lender pulls your record to make a pre-approved credit offer, it also doesn't impact your score. This factor accounts for around 10 percent of your score.

---

5. Credit mix: This reflects the variety of the types of credit you have. Generally, a mix of installment credit, such as a mortgage or an auto loan, and revolving credit, such as a credit card, is preferable. Credit mix makes up roughly 10 percent of your score.

One thing jumps out from all this: you have to borrow to have a credit score. I once reported about a young Canadian with a fantastic job who had always paid his bills on time and saved up a large amount for a big down payment on a house. It turned out he did not remotely qualify for a mortgage and eventually had to ask his parents to put their names on the loan. Why? Because he didn't even have a credit card. He'd always used his debit card to force himself to pay in full and on time all the time. I could have described this guy like my five-year-old's book describes the origins of Captain America: "He was a kid working hard and doing the right thing." But lenders don't care much about Captain America unless he has a track record of taking on debt and repaying it. Rent and utility bills don't count (see the box below for an explanation). Without that track record, the bank doesn't have much to go on to assess whether he's a reliable borrower.

You do *not* start out with a perfect credit score of 900. I hear this is a common misconception. My guess is some people assume you have to make mistakes to lose points.

WHY YOUR RENT DOESN'T FACTOR INTO YOUR CREDIT SCORE

Why don't credit scores take into account things like rent and utilities? If you always pay your bills, aren't you also likely to pay off your credit card balance?

That would be my intuitive assumption, but credit scores aren't based on intuition. They run on huge amounts of data and statistical analysis about borrowing. They have started to include some bill-paying history, such as for cellphone bills. And the industry has been looking at ways of incorporating more data points like that. It's likely that rent will become a more common input in credit scores at some point.

For now, though, credit scores are mostly based on information directly related to the behaviour they are meant to rate: borrowing.

For a lender, a new borrower is like a novice driver is to an insurer. Are you a cautious driver or a speeder? Someone who always checks his blind spot or someone who spends Saturday night doing doughnuts in a parking lot? The more you drive, the better your insurance company gets to know you. And a long record of being a good driver helps push down your premium. Similarly, it takes time to build up your credit score from scratch. The longer you've been using credit and making your payments, the likelier you are to see your score improve.

Another important takeaway: beware of generalizations about the perfect utilization rate or credit mix to boost your score. Credit scores don't work like that, Kuzmic says.

To understand why, you have to look under the hood of credit-scoring algorithms, she says. "When the statisticians do all this work to start figuring out what elements of the credit file are most predictive of future behaviour, they actually take a step where they group together people who behave similarly based on statistical analysis," she says.

As a simplified example, some credit-score versions reflect three factors statisticians use to sort people into these different groups: how long people have been borrowing, how many credit accounts are on their file, and whether their record contains something like payments gone into collection or a bankruptcy. Different combinations of these three traits make for eight different groups.

Every borrower falls into one of those groups, Kuzmic says. And each group has its own algorithm, because the people in it tend to behave in a similar way. This means that "statistically there are some things that are true in [one] group that are not true in another group," she explains. For example, suppose someone with a shorter credit history and some payments in collection applies for new credit, which produces a hard hit on their credit report. For that kind of borrower, statistically, more credit tends to result in more missed payments. But if you take a borrower with a long credit history, a variety of credit lines, and an impeccable record of paying everything off in full and on time, when a hard hit appears on their credit report, it may not be a potential predictor of future missed payments.

The example above is "a gross simplification," Kuzmic says. But the bottom line is clear: the same action or credit event can affect two different borrowers in different ways.

Be wary of anyone peddling overly specific advice about credit scores. Is someone claiming to know, say, that two credit cards, a mortgage, and an auto loan is the debt combo preferred by credit-scoring algorithms? Is a lender promising to quickly fix a battered credit score with a new loan? Here's how you should respond: walk away.

Don't get me wrong. It's entirely possible that many people with two credit cards, a mortgage, and an auto loan have fantastic credit scores. But this doesn't mean having that combination will help *your* score. Similarly, a new loan can certainly help you build a credit history and improve your score, but it's no sure thing. If you're already borrowing through several channels and have a spotty record of repaying, lenders may see one more loan as added risk. If you ever comb through the fine print of a contract for a credit-repair loan, you'll probably find a line or two stating there's no guarantee the product will actually boost your score.

At the same time — hear me say it again — a perfect credit score is not the be-all, end-all. Your score may fluctuate at times, as explained in the box below. And even if your score is high, that doesn't mean all is well.

WHY DOES MY CREDIT SCORE GO UP AND DOWN?

Small fluctuations in your credit score are normal and nothing to worry about. Let's say you made a one-time large purchase with your credit card. You had the money to pay it all off, but you wanted to use your card for points. It's possible this would temporarily lower your score from great to very good. But the numbers should bounce back up after you pay off your balance and your credit utilization rate drops. Unless you happen to be applying for something like a new mortgage or auto loan right then, that small, temporary credit-score dip doesn't matter. There's no reason to avoid putting a big purchase on your credit card so you can rake in the points.

That said, check your credit reports every six months or so to make sure everything is in order. Credit reporting errors happen, and it's good to spot them and address them sooner rather than later.

Douglas Hoyes, a licensed insolvency trustee and co-founder of Hoyes, Michalos and Associates, says he's seen his fair share of people with good and even great credit scores who ended up having to file for insolvency. "It is possible to be in serious financial trouble and still have a good credit report because the credit score does not capture everything," he says. Credit scores, for example, don't know whether you owe a lot of money in taxes, Hoyes says. Nor do they pick up on debts from certain payday lenders that do not report to credit bureaus, he adds.

There are many other aspects of your financial situation that don't appear in a credit report. What's your income? How secure is your employment? Do you have an emergency fund? If you lost your job tomorrow, for how long would you be able to keep up with your bills? A credit-scoring algorithm doesn't factor in any of that. That's why your bank will ask for much more than your credit score when you apply for a mortgage, Kuzmic notes.

Credit scores are also backward-looking, Hoyes says. They're based on your credit history — and history isn't always a good indicator of what's going to happen next.

Also, some people can keep up appearances for some time. "You can borrow from your line of credit to make the payment on your [credit] card, and then you could do a cash advance on your [credit] card to make the payment on your line of credit," Kuzmic says. It's the age-old trick of robbing Peter to pay Paul — except you are both Peter and Paul. Your credit history may not show signs of trouble for a while. And the greater your ability to borrow, the longer you might be able to keep going. Eventually, though, you'll run out of room to borrow or out of cash to make even minimum payments.

Hoyes says clients who walk into his office with decent credit scores are typically the ones who decided to act before they reached the end of the road. A licensed insolvency trustee can help you eliminate all or some of your debt through a consumer proposal or bankruptcy.

I'm going to say this one last time for good measure: credit scores are important but not something to obsess about. It doesn't make sense, for example, to delay seeking professional help with your debt for fear of damaging your credit score. Sure, letting your creditors know you won't be able to repay everything will hit your score. But the damage won't last forever.

Finally, keep in mind that it takes some time to build up a great credit score. Thankfully, though, it doesn't have to be expensive. Whether you're building up your credit history from scratch or fixing a bruised score, a good place to start are secured credit cards, which are backed by a deposit. This means a credit card with a borrowing limit of, say, $500 requires the borrower to put down $500 in cash, which the lender can use toward any missed payments. If you keep making your payments in full and on time, you'll graduate to a regular credit card and can move up from there.

It may take you some time to save up for the secured card's initial deposit, but it often pays to be patient. You may be better off putting some money aside into a savings account every month to save for the deposit than pouring your cash into an expensive credit-repair loan. "You might pay $3,000 in fees and interest to have a $2,000 loan showing up on your credit report," Hoyes warns.

Here are some things to think about when it comes to your credit score:

» Credit scores rate you as a borrower. To have a credit score, you need to borrow money.

» There isn't just one credit score. If you have a credit history, then you probably have more than one score. Credit scores can vary depending on how they're calculated and the information used to formulate them. That's why it's important to make sure that information is accurate and up to date. Regularly check your credit report from both Equifax and TransUnion. You can check your credit report from both credit bureaus online for free.

» Do not trust overly specific advice about how to boost your credit score — it doesn't work like that.

» Building up your credit score takes time but doesn't have to be expensive. Think very carefully before taking out a pricey credit-repair loan and always, *always* take your time to read the fine print before you sign.

» Credit scores are only a partial picture of your financial situation. A high score doesn't necessarily mean all is well financially.

• • •

Wrap-Up and What to Do if You Can't Repay Your Debt

In chapter 1 we looked at why our brains have a tendency to fall for certain common financial traps and how to avoid that. In this chapter, we examined different types of debt and how they can be useful or turn into those financial booby traps. Now you can put two and two — or rather, chapter 1 and chapter 2 — together and devise some strategies to get the most out of various types of credit without debt getting the better of you. For example, it may make sense to choose to borrow via a personal loan instead of a personal LOC if the loan's fixed repayment schedule will help you stay on track; this may be worth it even if the loan has a slightly higher interest rate.

Knowing yourself also makes it easier to climb out of any debt hole you've already fallen into. Drawing up a repayment plan and setting intermediate goals, as you've heard me say a few times, helps your brain stay focused and motivated.

Still, not all debt battles can be won on your own. Maybe the debt is accumulating faster than you can pay it off. Perhaps you can't even keep up with minimum payments or you find yourself using one credit card to pay off another. If you can't repay everything you owe, be wary of the undergrowth of loosely regulated companies peddling all sorts of pricey consolidation loans and other debt-fixing snake oil. Instead, consider these three main options:

» A debt management plan (DMP): A credit counselling agency can help you consolidate your debts into one payment that's more manageable. Keep in mind that a DMP is an informal process. Your creditors have to voluntarily agree to it. A DMP will often reduce or eliminate the interest on your debt, but you'll still have to repay all of the principal. Also, your monthly payments through a DMP may include an administrative fee. Non-profit credit counselling agencies typically cap these fees and will either charge you based on your ability to pay or waive those costs entirely.

» A consumer proposal: As the name implies, this involves making a proposal to your creditors. Usually, you propose to pay back less than the principal. If creditors claiming a majority of your debt agree, it becomes legally binding for all of them. Note that a consumer proposal can only be administered by a licensed insolvency trustee, a federally regulated professional who helps people with debt. Part of the money you repay through a consumer proposal goes to the trustee, but because the fees are federally regulated, every trustee in Canada charges the same way.

- A bankruptcy: This is also a legally binding process that can only be administered by a licensed insolvency trustee. Usually you don't get to keep your assets in a bankruptcy, but there are some notable exceptions. Depending on where you live, you may be able to keep your car or the savings in your RRSP. There may also be options to keep your home. The fees involved can vary significantly based on your situation.

I know, I know, the thought of seeking help to tackle your debt can be scary. It's why people often put it off for a long time. But if your debt is more than you can realistically fight on your own, teaming up with a pro to defeat the fiend is nothing to be ashamed of. It is the wise and sensible thing to do.

And now that we've learned about the psychology of money and the diverse world of debt, let's move on to that epic enterprise known to many of us millennials and Gen Zers as finding an affordable place to live (or finding a way to afford a place to live).

CHAPTER 3

EVERYTHING STARTS WITH HOUSING

HOUSING IS WHERE it all starts. There aren't too many decisions that can set the course of the rest of your life, but how much you're going to spend to keep a roof over your head is one of them. Whether you have a mortgage or a landlord, shelter is very likely your largest monthly outlay. And if that fixed cost takes up too much of your income, you're going to have a hard time finding money for an emergency fund, retirement, vacations, or anything else worth saving for.

Balancing the cost of shelter with the cost of everything else has become the biggest financial challenge of our generation. A 2019 study by Generation Squeeze, a non-profit that advocates for young adults, offers some important historical perspective.[1] In the mid-1980s, the report shows, the average home price in Metro Vancouver was around $250,000 in 2018 dollars, five times the median salary of a Vancouverite between the ages of 25 and 34, which would be around $50,000 a year in 2018 dollars. Fast forward to 2018, and the average Vancouver home price had surpassed $1 million. Meanwhile, your typical local 25- to 34-year-old was still making around $50,000 a year.

And it keeps getting worse. During the pandemic, the soul-crushing cost of real estate went from being an issue largely restricted to Vancouver and Toronto to being a problem in much of Canada. Even before Covid-19, home prices were on the rise in places like Winnipeg, Hamilton, Ottawa, and Quebec City. But the pandemic accelerated that trend, triggering a home-buying stampede as Canadians — and especially millennials — grasped for bigger homes and backyards in lower-cost neighbourhoods, smaller cities, and the suburbs. And then, of course, once prices took off, real estate investors and everybody and their cousin with enough money in the bank piled into the real estate craze, pushing prices even further into the stratosphere.

My husband and I bought our home in Toronto in 2015 for what seemed back then — and, frankly, still seems — like an obscene amount of money. We have since dodged two cycles of absurd price increases that would have surely shut us out of the market had we waited to buy.

The housing market in so much of Canada has turned into a kind of sick birth-year lottery, with younger home buyers generally facing the toughest odds. We've come to the point where being able to step onto the property ladder often requires a significant financial push from family, usually in the form of a gift or loan from Mom and Dad (much, much more on that in chapter 9). If your parents don't have that kind of starter capital to share, you may feel like you'll never be able to buy a home.

If you're angry about what Canada's real estate market has become, you're right. The housing crisis needs fixing. It needs people advocating for solutions and vigorous debate about the best ways to move forward. But solving, or even marginally improving on, big problems doesn't happen overnight. And in the meantime, you need a place to live.

This chapter is about navigating the warped housing reality we have right now. We're going to look at how to tell whether you can really afford to buy a home. Even if you live in a place where home prices and rents still seem pretty reasonable, it's easy to buy too much house.

We're also going to take a cool-headed look at owning versus renting, because buying a house isn't a mandatory rite of passage into adulthood. If you're better off renting, you should rent. But we're not going to sugar-coat the realities of renting, either. Let's face it, the cost of housing isn't an issue only for home buyers. It's easy to say, "If you can't buy, rent." But while renting is often cheaper than buying, that doesn't necessarily make it affordable. In much of Canada, many renters spend half or more of their income to pay the landlord and utilities. Nor is it easy in many parts of Canada to find a place to rent. The rental vacancy rate in 2020 was just 3.2 percent across the country, and that was after the pandemic and travel restrictions spurred scores of landlords to make short-term rentals available to long-term tenants.

So how does one approach the question of housing? With clear eyes and full hearts, to paraphrase *Friday Night Lights*. (Who couldn't use a bit of Coach Taylor when contemplating home prices or long-term renting in much of Canada?)

But first, let's have a look at how housing became so ridiculously expensive. A deeper understanding of the housing market will help you make better housing decisions.

• • •

How Housing Became So Expensive

It's easy to sum up Canada's housing problem: home prices and — to a lesser but still significant extent — some rents have gone up much, much faster than incomes. In February 2021, BMO economist Sal Guatieri quipped in a note to clients, "Your house makes more than you do."[2] Across much of Canada and particularly in Ontario, he noted, home prices over the previous 12 months not only rose faster than incomes, but also rose by more than families would earn in an entire year. In Woodstock, Ontario, for example, the benchmark home price climbed by more than $118,000, or more than 30 percent, between January 2020 and January 2021. Meanwhile, the typical

Woodstock family had an annual income of around $87,000. "Draw your own conclusions," Guatieri wrote.

How did we get here? There is no single or simple explanation. In fact, there is no comprehensive or widely accepted narrative about what happened to the housing market. Here, I'm going to give you an overview of at least some of the major forces that helped make housing unaffordable for so many of us.

Let's start with the basics. The price of housing, like almost anything else, depends on supply and demand. In the simplest form, when a lot of people want to buy or rent a home but there aren't a lot of homes available to buy or rent, home sellers and landlords can charge more. Vice versa, when there are a lot of homes for sale or lease but not a lot of buyers or prospective tenants, prices generally go down. This dynamic sounds pretty simple, but when it comes to residential real estate, many factors can complicate the relationship between demand and supply. For example, low interest rates make it easier for more people to borrow money to buy a place, and to spend more on it, which generally helps push up prices. Low interest rates and rapidly rising home prices, in turn, can attract real estate investors. Cheap borrowing makes it easy for investors to finance real estate purchases, and rapid appreciation fuels their belief that they'll be able to resell what they bought for a higher price at some point in the future and pocket a nice gain.

As we saw in chapter 1, interest rates have been at historically low levels for a long time in much of the rich world. This also means there aren't a lot of low-risk options where investors can stash their money and earn decent returns. Some see buying houses and condos in coveted real estate markets as one way to do just that. This may help explain why so many big cities have become unaffordable for the people who live there. It's not just Vancouver and Toronto (and now increasingly Montreal and Ottawa). It's London (the one in the United Kingdom), Amsterdam, Sydney, and Melbourne, just to name a few. According to a 2018 report from the International Monetary Fund, housing prices in 44 major cities around the world had been moving in an increasingly synchronized way before the pandemic, and global investors may be partly why.[3]

Another factor that influences housing demand when prices start to accelerate is FOMO, the fear of missing out. Just like the stock market, the real estate market is "a very emotional creature," says Diana Petramala, senior economist at the Centre for Urban Research and Land Development at Ryerson University. When home prices are on the rise, real estate becomes "an asset that everybody wants to own," she says.

Overall, housing demand can change rather quickly. Supply, on the other hand, is typically slow to adjust. For example, it can take almost two years for builders to complete a high-rise building — and that's once they have their building permits, Petramala notes. And despite rising home prices, homeowners may be reluctant to sell if they don't want to move, can't afford to upsize, or think they're better off sitting still and waiting for property values to increase even more.

The mismatch between demand and supply can lead to housing market booms, when demand outstrips supply, and busts, when home-building, often delayed, ramps up and overshoots demand. That's what happened in Canada in the 1980s and 1990s, according to Petramala. At first the country faced a housing shortage as the baby boomers reached the home-buying age. This prompted more construction, but by the time many of the new units were completed, demand was no longer as strong, which helped lead to the 1990s housing bust.

As the chart shows on page 82, home prices stagnated for a decade or so. Then, around the early 2000s, they started climbing again. By 2006, the average price of a home was around the equivalent of $355,000 in today's dollars, compared to an inflation-adjusted average price of about $235,000 in 1996. At the same time interest rates were trending lower, and the federal government was loosening some mortgage regulations, making it considerably easier for home buyers to borrow. By the end of 2006, Canadians could get mortgage default insurance on 40-year mortgages and zero-down-payment mortgages.

That set the wheels of the housing market in motion, says John Pasalis, president and founder of Toronto real estate brokerage Realosophy Realty.

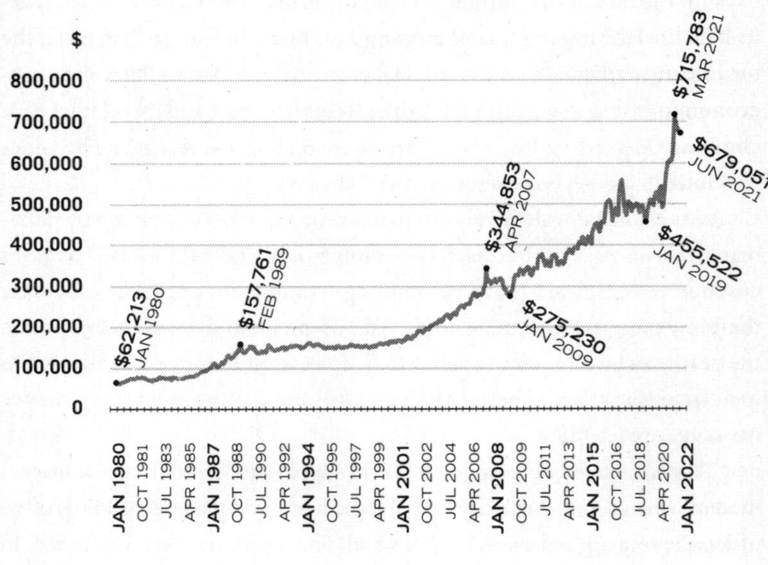

Source: Canadian Real Estate Association (CREA); unadjusted average residential home price

"And once the housing market starts accelerating like that, it's very hard to slow down."

After the U.S. housing market cratered and set off the global financial crisis in 2007, the Canadian federal government quickly backtracked on mortgage rules, reducing the maximum length of a mortgage (eventually, all the way down to 30 years) and requiring down payments of at least 5 percent, among other measures. But as we saw in chapter 1, the massive recession that swept the world after the financial crisis also prompted central banks, including Canada's, to push interest rates to new lows.

In Canada the Great Recession was relatively mild — certainly compared to the devastation it wrought in the U.S. — and in the housing market it registered only as a short-lived blip. In general, home prices fell in 2008, but by 2009 they were already bouncing back. Interest rates inched back up in the following years, but in 2015 the Bank of Canada lowered its benchmark rate once again, as low oil prices sent Canada's energy sector into a tailspin. And while oil-rich provinces struggled with a painful economic downturn, real estate prices in Vancouver and Toronto kept on climbing.

Until 2016 low interest rates were a main factor lighting a fire under Canada's hottest housing markets, Petramala says. Fanning the flames were real estate investors attracted by the prospect of big profits thanks to low-cost borrowing and fast-rising prices. In 2016, Metro Vancouver had more than 65,000 homes either lying empty or occupied for only a short period of the year, more than double the number of empty homes in 2001, according to an analysis by Simon Fraser University's Andy Yan.[4] In Toronto, investors accounted for as much as one in five sales of existing homes in certain neighbourhoods, according to data compiled by Pasalis. Canada's lax anti-money-laundering regime made it exceedingly easy for drug money and other illicit capital to flow to — or, rather, flood — the real estate market, as my Global News colleague Sam Cooper has extensively reported.[5] Amid the frenzy, home prices in Vancouver jumped by an astonishing 40 percent, and in Toronto by a similarly eye-popping 31 percent between the end of 2014 and the end of 2016.

Eventually, the public outcry over runaway property values and rents, along with worries about foreign and domestic speculation, prompted the government to crack down. In August of 2016, the B.C. government rolled out a 15-percent tax on foreign home buyers in Vancouver. Shortly after, in 2017, Vancouver adopted an empty-homes tax, a measure meant to incentivize investors to make those empty properties available for long-term rental. Ontario then followed suit with its own non-resident speculation tax for Toronto and a number of other areas. Since then, British Columbia has also enacted a speculation and vacancy tax, and Prince Edward Island has been under pressure to tighten restrictions on land purchases by non-residents. As I write, Toronto has announced plans for its own vacancy tax, and the federal government said in its 2021 federal budget that it would roll out a tax on vacant or underused residential property held by foreign homeowners.

Whether you love or hate these types of measures, there's little question that both the Vancouver and Toronto markets cooled off for a while after they were implemented. Around the same time, another cold shower came from a set of new mortgage rules. Between 2016 and 2018, the federal government started mandating that mortgage applicants undergo a mortgage stress test, proving that they would be able to keep up with payments even if interest rates were substantially above their actual mortgage rate. The process often means home buyers can't borrow as much as they otherwise would have, forcing them to settle for a less-expensive home. The government tightened those stress-test rules in June 2021 in an effort to cool the pandemic housing boom.

But as Toronto and, to a greater extent, Vancouver took a bit of a breather, other housing markets were starting to heat up. Ottawa, for example, was experiencing "exceptionally high" demand, a Royal LePage report noted in late 2017.[6] And prices were climbing fast in Montreal as well.

By the end of 2019 the housing market had come roaring back in much of the country. "An ongoing shortage of homes available for purchase across most of Ontario, Quebec and the Maritime provinces means sellers there hold the upper hand," the Canadian Real Estate Association wrote in its December 2019 sales report.[7] By January and February of 2020, real estate agents were getting ready for a record spring market.

Then the pandemic hit. But, it turned out, even the economic downturn linked to Covid-19 couldn't lower the market's temperature for very long. Much like the Great Recession, the economic downturn triggered by the health emergency caused only a short-term hiccup in sales activity. By the summer of 2020, the market was as hot as ever. But unlike the real estate craze of 2016–2017, which was concentrated mostly around Vancouver and Toronto, this time the sharpest price gains happened in places like Woodstock, Ontario; Kamloops, British Columbia; and Yarmouth, Nova Scotia. Home buyers in search of more space and lower prices swarmed to the suburbs, the country, and lower-cost cities in central, eastern, and western Canada, driving record price increases of 30 percent and more in a number of smaller markets.

How did Canada's housing market manage to defy even a global pandemic? The answer has less to do with interest rates (which dropped, once again, to rock-bottom levels amid the economic crisis) than with demographics, according to Petramala. Sure, it didn't hurt that lenders were offering unfathomably low fixed mortgage rates of 1.5 percent, or even less. But the pandemic housing boom started as, first and foremost, a millennial land grab.

The demographic pressure had been building up for years. For example, take the Greater Golden Horseshoe, which, for the uninitiated, is the chunk of southern Ontario that stretches, roughly, from Toronto to the Niagara region along the western shore of Lake Ontario. Between 2016 and 2021, the area added an astounding 60,000 new households (meaning families, groups of roommates, or people living alone) on average every year, compared to an average of 47,000 new households a year in the previous decade, Petramala says. The supply of new homes, however, remained steady at an average of roughly 47,000 new homes per year.

Where did all these new people come from and why the heck didn't we start building more homes you ask? Good questions. The growth in the number of households is the result of many trends. For one, it reflects millennials reaching the home-buying age. As of the 2016 census, there were more than 800,000 millennials living at home who'd be looking to move out on their own in the following 10 years, Petramala says.

Now add to that immigration. Between 2016 and 2019, Canada admitted a massive 310,000 new permanent residents a year on average, nearly 20 percent more than the yearly average of the previous four years. And in 2019 alone, Canada welcomed around 800,000 new temporary foreign workers and international students. Of all the new arrivals, around 40 percent of permanent and temporary residents and half of international students tended to go to Ontario. By age, the largest cohort of new immigrants consisted of 25- to 39-year-olds, a.k.a. millennials. And with federal programs fast-tracking immigration to the tech sector, it wasn't just more young workers, but also more high-earners, who concentrated in and around Toronto and other big cities, Petramala says.

Then, rather than freezing the housing market, the pandemic lit a fire under the demographic powder keg. "You have a whole lot of millennials who may have been living at home longer than they would have liked, but saving more," Petramala says. The pandemic restrictions likely prompted scores of wannabe home buyers who'd been squirrelling away for a down payment to finally pull the trigger. At the same time, the rise of remote work encouraged people to move to places where they could get more square footage for their buck. And while the pandemic ravaged the labour market, the job losses largely spared higher-income workers, who are more likely to become home buyers. In early 2021 Royal LePage published a survey suggesting that a quarter of Canadians between the ages of 25 and 35 had bought a home during the pandemic.[8]

Later on, as prices kept rising, real estate investors piled in once again, adding to the demand for homes and the pressure on property valuations. Ever since the housing market started bouncing back from its brief plunge in the spring of 2020, I kept asking real estate agents across the country whether the buyers they were helping were investors or people who wanted homes to live in. Through the summer and fall of 2020, the answer, over and over, was that there wasn't much sign of investors. Toward the end of that year, though, I started getting more and more reports that investors — those based in Canada, at least — were back. According to data gathered by the Bank of Canada, by February 2021 investors accounted for one out of five home purchases in Canada, a share that was lower than a previous peak in 2018 but showed a clear upward trend compared to the period immediately before the pandemic.[9] In June 2021, Toronto-based Core Development Group made headlines with a plan to buy $1 billion worth of single-family homes and turn them into rentals, a strategy that stoked fears about investors crowding out young home buyers.

Still, even before Covid-19, Canada's housing supply was failing to keep up with millennial demand. A 2018 study from the Canada Mortgage and

Housing Corporation found that home-building in Vancouver and Toronto was especially slow to respond to increases in demand, compared to other big cities like Edmonton, Montreal, and Calgary.[10] The problem isn't just the quantity of homes, but also the type of housing we've been building. If you live in a big city and are hoping to start a family, you're probably well acquainted with this dilemma: much of what's on offer are detached homes that are ridiculously outside your budget or tiny condos that are really glorified broom closets. Although many cities are starting to address the problem (or at least starting to talk about it), for buyers looking for in-between options, there isn't much.

Pasalis, the Toronto real estate broker, calls this "a massive policy screw-up." Since the 1970s, he says, governments at the federal, provincial, and municipal levels have failed to promote the construction of purpose-built rentals, leaving it to condominiums to fulfill housing needs in high-density areas instead. "The idea was mom-and-pop investors will buy up condos and that's going to fill our rental supply," he says. Indeed, around 30 percent of condos in Canada's major cities are rented, according to Canada Mortgage and Housing Corporation data.[11] But there's only so much that moms and pops can afford to buy, which has created an incentive for developers to build uber-small units of 500 square feet or less (for reference, 400 square feet is the size of a two-car garage). Meanwhile, zoning laws have often kept low-rise buildings out of low-density residential areas, which have remained dominated by detached homes.

The problem isn't just that there are very few mid-sized housing units, Petramala says. It's also that "the market is not actually delivering housing for middle-income households."

In pre-pandemic times, another squeeze on housing supplies in big cities came from short-term rentals. A 2019 study by McGill University researchers, for example, estimates Airbnb alone had effectively removed 31,000 homes from Canada's long-term rental market, with 46 percent of those housing units located in Montreal, Toronto, and Vancouver.[12] Responding to the report in a *Globe and Mail* article, Airbnb noted the researchers had no way of knowing whether landlords would have made those homes available to long-term renters if they hadn't been able to use them for short-term rental.[13] Still, at least as far as Toronto goes, several estimates have shown that if all short-term rental units would come onto the long-term rental market, that alone would bring demand in line with supply and perhaps even lead to a bit of excess supply, Petramala says.

Indeed, Covid-19 has offered a glimpse of this. As travel ground to a halt and Quebec and Ontario imposed temporary restrictions on home-sharing, short-term-rental listings collapsed in cities like Montreal, Toronto, and Vancouver, with many of the units flooding the long-term-rental market instead. Take Toronto, for instance. Over the first three months of 2020 — after the city followed Vancouver and Quebec's examples with stricter rules on home-sharing in late 2019, and largely before the pandemic started — Toronto had already seen an almost 30 percent annual increase in listings of apartments that likely used to be short-term rentals. Between April and June, once the health emergency was in full swing, the number of short-term rentals converted into long-term rentals soared by more than 50 percent, to 1,877 units, compared to the same period in 2019, and was equal to 12 percent of all condo rental listings during that three-month period at the start of the pandemic, according to real estate research group Urbanation.[14,15]

Over the second half of 2020, asking rents across Canada declined by a spectacular 8.5 percent on average, according to an analysis by rental listings site Rentals.ca.[16] Of course, there are many reasons for the drop, from the pandemic exodus from downtown cores to the dearth of new immigrant and international student arrivals, among others. But there's little question that more landlords giving up on short-term renting, at least for a while, helped.

As I write, it's unclear whether those extra units will remain available to long-term renters when the world goes fully back to normal, but here's a safe prediction for the post-pandemic world: even as more millennials start to have children and reach for more space, most boomers aren't likely to scooch over for another 20 years. Many of them have no intention of downsizing any time soon. They're healthy and wealthy and perfectly capable of going up and down the stairs or tending to the garden, thank you very much. And while that's perfectly legitimate and understandable, it creates yet another housing headache. In Ontario, for example, there are an estimated 5 million empty bedrooms — equivalent to 25 years' worth of construction — owned mostly by empty nesters aged 65 and up. But as demand for bigger homes increases from millennial families, "you have two major demographics coming head to head in the housing market," Petramala says.

As for Gen Z, most of them are still a long way off from even thinking about buying a home, but if immigration trends resume to what they were before the pandemic, that generation will become as big as millennials, according to Petramala. Here's hoping Canada will be well on its way to tackling its festering housing problem by then.

Coming back to the present, though, if you're thinking about buying your first home — or about whether you should buy in the first place — here's what you should know.

• • •

Can You Afford to Buy a Home?

For millennials, and likely in a few years for Gen Z, this is the million-dollar question. In fact, if you live in or around Toronto and Vancouver, finding anything big enough for a family for an even million looks like a steal.

Thankfully, in most of the rest of Canada, the average home price remains far below seven figures. But with the pandemic housing craze bringing staggering price increases to cities, towns, and neighbourhoods that had, until 2020, remained relatively affordable, being able to buy the home you want where you want may no longer be a given, even if you live nowhere close to the country's most expensive real estate markets.

But before we get to that, I need to ask a quick preliminary question: How long do you see yourself living in the place you're thinking of buying? If your answer is five years at most, you may want to stick with renting. Buying and selling a home is incredibly expensive. If you don't plan to stay long, you'll be paying real estate agent commissions, lawyer fees, and land transfer taxes (except in Alberta and Saskatchewan) twice in the span of a few years. These are massive costs that could easily wipe out any gains you might see from an increase in the value of your home (and that's assuming housing prices go up). Also keep in mind that the issue of staying in your home longer than five years isn't just about being ready to settle down or whether your job or life in general may soon take you elsewhere. It's also about planning ahead. If you want to buy, aim for something that will still fit your needs many years down the line. If you're planning to have a family, ideally you want to avoid outgrowing your home in a few years.

Now that we've cleared that up, let's move on to the big dilemma: How much house, or condo, can you afford? The first step is to recognize that there are two components to home affordability. There's the question of how much you'll need to save up front and the issue of whether you'll be able to comfortably carry the costs of home ownership.

UPFRONT COSTS

Upfront costs and carrying costs, of course, are linked. The more money you can come up with to start, the smaller the amount you need to borrow from the bank and the lower your mortgage payments, which are a big chunk of your costs as a homeowner. This probably sounds obvious, but managing both sides of the home ownership equation may be trickier than you think.

For one, if your down payment is less than 20 percent of the value of the home you're buying, you'll be saddled with the extra cost of mortgage default insurance. This, as you may guess from the name, protects your lender in case you end up defaulting on your mortgage. The coverage is mandatory; if you put down less than 20 percent, you have to have it. Mortgage default insurance is calculated as a percentage of your mortgage loan and works out to thousands of dollars. In Canada you can buy a home with as little as 5 percent down, but the less you save up front, the more you'll have to pay in mortgage default insurance.

THE HOME BUYERS' PLAN

If you're a first-time home buyer, the Home Buyers' Plan (HBP for those in the know) allows you to take up to $35,000 out of your RRSP tax-free to buy or build a home. If you're buying a place with your partner or spouse, you can join forces for a combined maximum withdrawal of $70,000.

But before you decide to raid your RRSP for a down payment, keep in mind the following:

1. You'll need to repay that money. The HBP is a loan to yourself, and the government will keep you honest. You'll have 15 years to put back the money you took out, which is a pretty generous schedule. But if you miss any payments, you could end up paying taxes on that money, just like with any regular RRSP withdrawals (more on that in chapter 5).
2. You'll need to get the paperwork right. Not only do you have to keep up with repayment, you have to designate the fund as HBP payments rather than regular RRSP contributions.
3. If you default on your HBP repayments, you'll permanently lose some of your RRSP contribution room. Data from Statistics Canada suggests at least some of those who default on their HBP repayments do so simply because they don't know they should label their RRSP contributions.

If all this is making your head spin, you might want to save for a down payment in a tax-free savings account (TFSA), which comes with far fewer strings attached. And if all this is gibberish to you right now, head over to chapters 5 and 6, where I talk about RRSPs and TFSAs.

For example, as of February 2021, if you bought a $400,000 house with just $20,000 (5 percent) down, the value of your mortgage would be $380,000. You'd be charged 4 percent of that value, or a whopping $15,200, for mortgage default insurance. That's an added $15,200 the bank will tack on to your mortgage payments and on which you'll be paying interest (unless you pay it upfront, which few people do). By comparison, with $40,000 (10 percent) down, your insurance premium shrinks to 3.1 percent of a $360,000 mortgage, or $11,160. You can use the Canada Mortgage and Housing Corporation's mortgage calculator to estimate your mortgage insurance costs (Sagen and Canada Guaranty also provide mortgage insurance).

In an ideal world, we'd all put 20 percent down. In the real world, though, not all of us can. Saving until you've got 20 percent can feel like a hopeless game of catch-up if home prices keep running away from you as they have for years in Vancouver and Toronto.

Still, this doesn't mean you should settle for 5 percent down. Not only will you pay a lot in mortgage insurance, you may end up with negative equity if home prices fall. This is the problem we discussed in chapter 2 of owing more on something than that something is worth. It's a common issue when buying a car, but, as I mentioned, it can also happen when you buy a home if you put very little down. In a situation where what you owe the bank is considerably more than your place is worth, you'd be practically stuck in your home without possibility of selling unless you were able to come up with the cash to cover the difference. I know what you're thinking: *Home prices will never fall!* But sometimes they do, and that tends to happen during recessions. The nightmare scenario is losing your job and then being unable to move somewhere you could find employment because you can't offload your home — something scores of U.S. homeowners experienced first-hand during the subprime mortgage crisis. See the boxes on the Home Buyers' Plan on page 91 and the First-Time Home Buyer Incentive on pages 93–94 for two ways you can consider for coming up with a larger down payment.

Also, note that the minimum down payment required varies based on the value of the home. With 5 percent down, you can only buy a place valued at $500,000 or less. For anything above $500,000 and up to $999,999, you'll need 5 percent on the first $500,000 and 10 percent down on the rest. And if you have your heart set on anything worth $1 million or more, you'll need to come up with 20 percent down.

THE FIRST-TIME HOME BUYER INCENTIVE

The First-Time Home Buyer Incentive (FTHBI) is an interest-free loan from the federal government that is meant to help you buy a home if you are — as the name says — a first-time home buyer. In fact, though, it may be more intuitive to think of it as buying a home *with* the government, with Ottawa pitching in some of the down payment but also hanging on to a portion of the value of the property.

As of September 2021, here's how it works: The FTHBI provides 5 or 10 percent of the purchase price of the home to top up your own down payment money. The larger down payment means you can take out a smaller mortgage with lower payments, including for mortgage insurance. The incentive comes in the form of a second mortgage on the home. The nice thing is you don't have to make any payments toward this second mortgage. The not-so-nice part is you'll have to pay 5 or 10 percent of the value of the home back to the government after 25 years or when you sell the property, whichever comes first.

If your home appreciates quickly, you may end up repaying more than you saved through the lower mortgage payments. On the other hand, if the value of your home declines, you'll have to repay less than the original down payment top-up you received, and the government eats the loss.

Also, in most of Canada the incentive is available only to buyers with a household income of up to $120,000 who are taking out a mortgage worth no more than four times their income. In Toronto, Vancouver, and Victoria, the income cap is $150,000 and the borrowing limit is 4.5 times that income. And the FTHBI is available only for mortgages greater than 80 percent of the home value. If you're planning to put down 20 percent or more, this isn't for you.

The down payment isn't the only immediate cash outlay you'll face as a home buyer. There are also closing costs and what I call settle-in expenses. The closing costs usually include things like the land transfer tax or fee, legal fees, and title insurance, at a minimum. They can easily amount to between 1.5 and 4 percent of the purchase price, according to financial-product comparison site Ratehub.ca.[17] I often hear from financial planners that many home buyers are caught off guard by these administrative and legal costs.

And then there are the settle-in expenses. This is the cost of moving into your home and making it livable. I'm not talking about redoing the kitchen, installing built-in cabinets, or giving your bathroom a facelift. All of that can wait until you've rebuilt your savings. I'm talking about any immediate repairs or upgrades you might need, like redoing an ancient roof, replacing lead pipes, or buying a new couch because your old one won't fit through the door. These expenses can vary significantly based on where you're moving to and from. For example, older homes are more likely to have issues, and if you're going from a condo to a house, you'll probably have to buy some furniture ASAP. But they will easily add at least a few thousand dollars to your upfront costs even in the most optimistic scenario. It's a good idea to reserve a small cash cushion for these costs or scale back your down payment if you foresee big expenses you'll need to take care of right away.

If you really want to buy a home but can't afford these costs, you might think about joining forces with a friend or family member. See the box on page 95 for some things to consider.

BUYING A HOME WITH FRIENDS OR FAMILY

If you can't buy a home on your own, one possible solution is to team up with friends or family. As they say, there is strength in numbers. Pooling your financial resources with close friends or family can bring home ownership within reach.

Some people enjoy co-owning a home because of the opportunity for communal living — whether it's building memories in a multi-generational home or sharing your morning coffee with some of your best friends. But co-ownership doesn't necessarily mean sharing the kitchen and the toothbrush holder. One possibility, for example, is to buy a bigger house that you can carve into two or more independent units.

Still, getting co-ownership right requires a lot of careful planning. You'll need to come up with a long and detailed list of house rules, think about how you'll split up costs for maintenance and repairs, and devise a system for making decisions about issues you can't foresee (which are guaranteed to come up). It makes sense to put all of this in writing to minimize the potential for future conflict.

But before you even buy a property, you'll have to choose between two types of ownership structure: joint tenancy or tenancy in common. You can skip to chapter 9 for a more detailed discussion of that.

CARRYING COSTS

When you're renting, you pay your landlord every month, and that's pretty much it. Sure, maybe you have to foot some of the utility bills, take out renter's insurance (if you haven't already, you should), and pay for phone and internet. But rent is by far your biggest housing cost. The mortgage payment is not the homeowner's equivalent of rent. There are a ton of other fixed and variable costs you'll have to carry if you buy a home.

Let's look at an example. If you bought a $650,000 home in Ottawa with 10 percent down, a 1.6 percent mortgage, and a mortgage you'll take 25 years to pay off, your monthly payment would be $2,439 a month, according to the mortgage payment calculator on Ratehub.ca. On top of that, the tool estimates you'd likely pay $542 a month in property taxes, $135 in utilities, and $50 for home insurance. That's a massive $727 coming out of your bank account every single month in addition to the $2,439 mortgage payment. (You don't generally have to pay property taxes every month, but it's a good idea to set aside money for it monthly since it can be such a big bill.)

There's also the cost of property upkeep. As I quickly learned after we bought our home, houses are money pits. Every single year, there's probably going to be something that needs fixing or that you want to upgrade. One general rule for estimating these costs says you should set aside the equivalent of 1 percent of the purchase price of your home every year for maintenance. But I find that's a pretty rough rule. In Vancouver, you can spend more than $2.5 million to buy a bungalow, but it won't cost you $25,000 a year to keep it in decent shape. A more useful starting point is calculating $1 per square foot, which is directly related to the size of your home. Still, keep in mind that costs can vary significantly based on the characteristics of your property and what contractors and tradespeople charge in your area.

If you're buying a condo, your upkeep costs may be a lot lower, but you'll have to pay condo fees, part of which will fund the maintenance of your building's common areas. Keep in mind that both property taxes and condo fees can — and generally do — go up. Another cost you should watch out for as a condo or townhouse owner is condo insurance. You can read up on that in chapter 7.

No matter what kind of home you buy, the money-bucket system we talked about in chapter 1 can help you manage the costs. See the box for details on how this works.

HOW TO MANAGE THE COST OF HOME OWNERSHIP WITH MONEY BUCKETS

Are you worried about — or, shall I say, daunted by — the unending expenses that await you now that you've bought a home? Fear not, my friend, the money-bucket system was made for this.

Here's how my husband and I handle it. We have two hefty house-related bills that hit us a few times a year instead of monthly. The first is property taxes, which is the really big one — we're talking thousands of dollars per year. Then we have the city's utility bill for water usage and solid waste. That's a much smaller amount, but still hundreds of dollars per year. Since we have a pretty good idea of how much we're going to pay every year, we treat both as a monthly expense with automatic transfers to accounts where the money accumulates until it's time to pay. Another solution, if you have the option, is to sign up for monthly billing.

We have another money bucket for home repairs and upgrades. By now we know, roughly how much we're likely to spend every year just to fix stuff that will break (our house is in good shape and yet, as of year five, we've had something break *every single year*). We top that up with savings for whatever small upgrade we have planned for the year. And then, for bigger, urgent expenses we didn't see coming, we have our emergency fund.

The carrying costs of a home can be crushing if you buy more than you can truly afford. Lenders usually will happily give you the green light if your annual mortgage payments, heating costs, and property taxes (plus 50 percent of condo fees, if applicable) amount to 32 percent or less of your annual before-tax income. Similarly, they'll be content if your housing expenses and non-mortgage debt payments add up to 40 percent or less of your income.

But there's a lot this kind of financial vetting doesn't take into account. "The bank doesn't necessarily look at whether you've got four kids or whether you're kidless. They also don't care whether you're pursuing FIRE" — the financial independence, retire early plan discussed in chapter 1 — "or you go on four vacations a year," says Jason Heath, a fee-for-service financial planner and managing director at Objective Financial Partners.

Lenders want to know that you'll be able to keep up with your mortgage payments and other essential costs. They aren't budgeting to make sure you'll also have enough money to pay for the rest of your life. Doing that kind of math is up to you.

• • •

Should You Rent Instead? Buying versus Renting

Some people rent because it suits their lifestyle; they like or need the flexibility to easily relocate. Many others are taking a harder look at this other, forever-shunned housing option because they can't afford to buy a house in the city they'd like to live in. If you're facing the familiar buy-versus-rent dilemma, you may have heard what sounds like common-sense advice in support of both options.

On the one hand, the received wisdom about housing in Canada is that you should always buy. Renting, countless parents have explained at the dinner table, is paying someone else's mortgage. You aren't building equity, and your housing costs will never go down. On the other hand, in the increasingly vocal pro-rent camp, people argue that what you pay to the landlord is usually much lower than the carrying costs of owning a comparable home.

Instead of wasting money on repairs and property taxes, you can build wealth by investing what you're saving in housing costs.

Unfortunately, both of these persuasive lines of reasoning can be wrong, depending on your individual situation and the conditions of the market. To help you figure out whether you should be buying or renting, you can follow a three-step process. Whip out your calculator and let's crunch some numbers. As I describe in more detail below, the first step is to figure out whether you'd actually be financially better off renting instead of buying where you currently want to live. You may find that renting isn't the cheaper option. However, if your math turns out in favour of renting, the second step is to look at whether you can actually afford to rent — in big cities this isn't necessarily a given. Finally, if the math shows you *can* comfortably carry the rent, the third step is to look at whether being a tenant will actually fit your life.

STEP ONE: THE 5 PERCENT RULE

There's a useful rule for the buy-versus-rent math: If a year's worth of rent adds up to less than 5 percent of the market value of a similar home, renting is an attractive option. Vice versa, if rent works out to more than 5 percent, buying may make more sense financially. This kind of math is all about comparing the rent to the unrecoverable costs of owning a home. Yep, you heard that right. You may be used to your parents saying renting is throwing money out of the window, but as we've seen, homeowners also spend a significant amount of cash every year that does not build equity. The 5 percent rule estimates that those unrecoverable costs of home ownership are equal to 5 percent of the value of the property. For a much more detailed explanation of what's behind the rule, you can read the article "Rent or Own Your Home? A Handy 5% Percent Rule," by Benjamin Felix, a certified financial planner and portfolio manager at PWL Capital. (Felix also breaks this down in one of his popular YouTube videos.)

So how do you use the rule in practice? Let's say you'd like to live in a three-bedroom, two-bathroom home and buying that kind of property costs around $650,000 in your city. If you became a homeowner, your annual unrecoverable costs would be 5 percent of $650,000, or $32,500, which works out to just over $2,700 a month. If you can rent the same kind of home for less than that, you might want to take a serious look at renting. The rule works the other way, too. If you are paying $2,700 a month in rent for that three-bedroom, two-bathroom house, how can you tell whether you'd be better off buying? Multiply your rent by 12 months of the year and then divide that by 0.05 (or 5 percent), which gives you roughly $650,000. If a three-bed, two-bath home in your area is selling for significantly more than that, you may want to keep renting.

Of course, the 5 percent rule has many limitations. For starters, it is based on the assumption that, as a tenant, you're going to be a disciplined saver and investor. Renters can build up wealth by growing their money in the financial market. But if you aren't squirrelling away your cash as a renter, you'll be in trouble. As a homeowner, even if you weren't saving a penny, at least you'd be building up equity in your home and would have an asset you could sell for hundreds of thousands of dollars once the mortgage was paid off. That's why financial planners often talk about home ownership as a form of forced savings. You have to pay your mortgage every month, and part of that money goes toward your home equity, which increases your wealth. If you're renting, it is entirely up to you to set aside some money every month to grow your wealth.

Also, the 5 percent rule assumes you're going to be a pretty aggressive investor — someone comfortable putting a good share of their savings into stocks — to keep up with the long-term wealth growth a homeowner might see. I'll have much more to say about investing, risk, and reward in chapter 6, but for now suffice it to say that if you have most of your savings tied up in low-risk investments that barely keep up with inflation, there's a good chance you'll end up considerably worse off as a renter.

On the other hand, some caveats work in favour of renting. Paying the mortgage may be easier than summoning the willpower to save money as a renter, but owning a home these days is also a constant temptation to borrow against your home equity. You won't build much wealth if you keep tapping your home-equity line of credit, notes Jason Heath of Objective Financial Partners. And if you have a generous pension plan at work where your employer matches your contributions, that's a vote in favour of renting and being able to make bigger monthly deposits to that group retirement plan, Heath also notes.

STEP TWO: CAN YOU REALLY AFFORD TO RENT?

The 5 percent rule is a useful starting point for figuring out whether you live in a renter's or homeowner's market. But it doesn't tell you whether you can afford to rent in the first place. If rent is eating up such a big chunk of your monthly income that you aren't able to save, being a tenant for life isn't a good option. It really doesn't matter whether buying would be even more expensive.

"It's really tricky," Heath says. "Some people should neither rent nor buy in certain cities. They may need to change professions or change locations to be able to balance their short- and long-term financial goals."

If you love living in a big city and also happen to be passionate about a job that doesn't pay enough, this can be an incredibly difficult decision. Some are able to avoid this dilemma thanks to significant financial help from parents and grandparents. Others have turned to co-ownership — buying a property with relatives, friends, or like-minded strangers. You can skip to chapter 9 for a discussion about accepting money from family and co-ownership.

STEP THREE: SET THE MATH ASIDE

Maybe the numbers will show that you can easily afford to rent and would save money doing so. That's great news, but there's more to the decision than what your calculator says. Are you actually going to be happy renting?

Don't get me wrong. I am in no way suggesting that home ownership buys happiness or that you need to buy a house to be a fully functioning adult. Growing up in Italy, I had no concept that renting was inherently bad, as many Canadians do. In Milan, my hometown, everyone lives in apartments, and there's no way to tell whether someone rents or buys based on their address. I know doctors and lawyers who've happily raised their families in the same beautiful homes they've been renting for decades. I also lived in Germany, where more than half of the population rents.

When I moved across the pond, the whole notion that one *had* to buy a house just seemed bizarre. But after spending the better part of a decade renting in both Canada and the U.S., where cultural attitudes toward home ownership are similar, I've actually grown a little wary of renting in North America. For one, renting often means living in a shoebox-sized condo unit with zero storage space and paper-thin walls that will turn you into an unwitting eavesdropper of your neighbour's romantic life. If you want to have children, having a place to rent big enough for a family can be a challenge. Tenants often face sudden rent increases and landlords who will do only the bare minimum in terms of repairs and upkeep, not to mention the risk of having to move out on short notice, which can be logistically complicated if you have little ones in tow and can also affect which schools your kids can attend.

You can contrast that with Germany, where renters can easily get indefinite rental agreements that virtually eliminate the threat of being kicked out (although they still have to move out if they break their contract or if their landlord needs the place for themselves or their immediate family). There are also significant financial incentives for landlords to pay for property upkeep, such as the ability to sell a rental property without paying taxes on the profits if they've owned the house for more than 10 years, just like homeowners.

These policies aren't a magic bullet — Germany, and particularly Berlin, is dealing with its own rental-market challenges — but there's a lot Canada could do to make renting more attractive. That doesn't mean renting in this country is never a good idea. You may very well find the perfect solution in the rental market — I know people who have. Just keep in mind there's a lot in the buy-versus-rent debate that the math just doesn't capture.

Finally, if you're thinking about renting from a friend or renting to a friend to help pay the mortgage, check out the box on those kinds of arrangements. They can be a win-win but there are caveats.

BUYING A HOUSE AND RENTING OUT PART OF IT TO A FRIEND

Here's a housing hack that can work well for both homeowners and renters: one friend buys a house, and another friend rents out part of it. I've heard from homeowners and renters who've described this as a win-win.

If you're the home buyer, having a renter will help you with the carrying costs of home ownership. And it may be easier to share your living space with someone you know and trust.

A legal secondary suite also makes it easier to qualify for financing — it isn't for nothing that these units are known as mortgage helpers. The idea is that the rental income lowers your debt service ratios, which lenders use to vet you as a potential borrower (more on that later in this chapter). Lenders typically allow 50 percent to 100 percent of the rental income to be used in your mortgage application, says Robert McLister mortgage editor at RATESDOTCA.

However, for rental income to help you qualify for a mortgage on your primary residence, you'll need an arm's-length rental agreement (lease), McLister says. "You can't just say your mother-in-law pays you $500 a month to rent a room in your house." Mainstream lenders will only take into account rental income coming from a self-contained suite that conforms with zoning and regulations or one that was grandfathered in because it was built before those rules were put in place, McLister adds.

Still, if you're the potential home buyer, beware that a house that comes with a rental suite may cost much more. In Toronto, I've seen bidding wars break out over properties with so-called income potential. Make sure to weigh any price premium against your expected income (minus expenses) as a landlord. Also, the sale of your primary home is normally exempt from tax, but it may not be completely so if you have a renter. If you sell the property for a higher price than you bought it at, you may have to pay taxes on the portion of the house you rented out.

Finally, if you're the renter, having someone you know well as your landlord may mean the security of knowing you can stay for the long term without having to worry about sudden, steep rental increases. But keep in mind that the arrangement may not be forever. Eventually, your friend may want the whole house for themselves.

• • •

Buying Somewhere Cheaper

The classic third option, if you can't afford to buy or rent where you work, is to "drive until you can afford to buy." In a 2021 study, CIBC economists Benjamin Tal and Royce Mendes found that beyond the first 50 kilometres outside Toronto "every 10 km drive further away from the city will buy you an extra $25,000 of house."[18]

Like generations before them, older millennials were packing up and moving to cheaper housing markets in the suburbs even before the pandemic. But there's little doubt that Covid-19 accelerated the trend. Between the second half of 2019 and the first six months of 2020, a period that includes the first three months of the health emergency, Toronto saw 50,375 more people relocate from the city to other parts of Ontario than move in the opposite direction. Montreal saw a net outflow of 24,880 people leaving for other areas of Quebec, although the city's overall population continued to grow, just like in Toronto, thanks to international immigration.

The burbs, meanwhile, were bursting. Some 50 kilometres east of Toronto, for example, the town of Oshawa saw the fastest population growth in all of Canada in those 12 months. Something similar happened in Farnham and Saint-Hippolyte near Montreal. Some went even farther afield — all the way to the Maritimes. Halifax, for example, saw a net influx of 1,584 people from other jurisdictions between late 2019 and early 2020.

Moving out of the city, or to a lower-cost city like Halifax, comes with well-known pros and cons. You'll be able to buy a bigger home, and life isn't quite so stupid expensive, including, crucially, when it comes to child care. You may find a slower pace and a greater sense of community. The cons have often traditionally included a soul-sucking commute or having to give up on a big-city job and the earnings and career potential that may go with it.

But did the pandemic fundamentally change that? As I write, it's hard to say whether the rise of work-from-home has finally decoupled high-paying jobs from large and pricey cities. On the one hand, you have the likes of Nat Friedman, CEO of the software-development collaboration platform GitHub, saying that remote work is bringing opportunity "for productive people all around the world."[19] On the other hand, a number of employers are telling pollsters they want people mostly back in the office when we're all vaccinated. According to a Statistics Canada survey taken in the second half of 2020, less than 15 percent of businesses planned to have everyone continue to work from home after the pandemic.[20] Still, it seems safe to say the world isn't going to go back to what it was pre-virus. More people will likely keep doing at least some of their work, if not all of it, from home.

At the same time, though, the pandemic has also brought bidding wars and breakneck increases in the price of homes to smaller communities. In Oshawa, for example, the price of a typical two-storey home was nearly 20 percent higher at the end of 2020 compared to a year earlier, data from Royal LePage shows.[21] My reporting suggests urbanites flocking to nearby towns in turn have forced local home buyers and renters to move farther out in search of more affordable real estate, creating a domino effect.

In general, the pandemic seems to have been a double-edged sword for millennials thinking of ditching the city. While it has probably shrunk the potential earnings penalty of moving out, it has also reduced the discount on housing costs.

• • •

How to Get a Mortgage

You've done the math, examined your life, and now are sure of it: you're ready to buy a place — *and* you can afford it. That's fantastic — congratulations! Now, let's take a look at what's involved in securing what will likely be the biggest loan of your life: your mortgage.

In chapter 2 we talked about how to get a good deal on this super-sized debt you're about to take on. But as much as you should be shopping around and taking a hard look at what lenders are offering, they will also be taking a hard look at you. What they see will help determine whether they'll approve you for a mortgage, the maximum they'll be willing to lend, and at what interest rate. It's important to show up prepared.

HOW DOES A LENDER DECIDE ABOUT YOUR MORTGAGE?

Before you start house hunting in earnest, it's a good idea to get pre-approved for a mortgage. This is the lender saying, "I think I'm going to be able to lend you up to this much money at this interest rate." It's not a guarantee, but it will give you a good idea of what your mortgage payments are going to be. The process can also be an important reality check: you may find you don't qualify for as big a mortgage as you'd like, meaning you'll have to settle for a cheaper home, save up for a larger down payment, or work on improving your credit score. A pre-approval also allows you to secure a particular interest rate for a certain period of time — usually from three to four months, depending on the lender. This means you don't have to worry about interest rates rising while you're going to open houses. On the other hand, if interest rates decline, you'll be able to ask for a lower rate.

A number of variables affect a lender's pre-approval or mortgage offer. Many of them have to do with your financial situation, but the characteristics of the home you decide to buy and the state of the economy also play a role. Let's start with you. When examining your finances, the lender will look at four main factors: your credit profile, your down payment, your income, and your debt ratios, which measure the size of your debt and expenses compared to your income.

» *YOUR CREDIT PROFILE*

The better your credit score, the better your chances of accessing the lowest interest rates. Assuming you satisfy a number of other qualifying criteria, a score of 720 and up usually unlocks the lender's most competitive rates. As of February 2021, that might look like a five-year fixed rate of 1.64 percent for a mortgage that doesn't require default insurance, according to data provided by Robert McLister, mortgage editor at RATESDOTCA and founder of RateSpy.com, two rate-comparison sites. For the same mortgage type and term, someone with a score from 680 to 719 would likely get "closer to 1.79 percent," McLister told me via email. And an otherwise well-qualified borrower with a score of 650 "could potentially get 1.89 percent, give or take."

With a score of just 600, you probably wouldn't qualify for prime rates, which lenders reserve for their most creditworthy customers. In an environment of record-low rates such as that in early 2021, you might have to settle for rates around 3.5 percent or more and might have to pay lender and broker fees in addition to that, McLister says.

Before approaching lenders, make sure to get your credit score and your credit reports from both Equifax and TransUnion. Scan your credit history as reported by both credit bureaus and ask that it be updated or corrected if you find missing information or mistakes. Even if your lender has its own credit-scoring formula, what you get from Equifax and TransUnion will give you a good idea of where you stand. If your score isn't quite up to snuff, you may want to put the home-buying process on hold and work on building up your number — a higher score could save you a lot of money through a lower mortgage rate.

» YOUR INCOME

One of the first questions any lender will ask you is how much you make. Be prepared to back that up with evidence. If you have a job as an employee, this is usually pretty straightforward. Documents you should gather usually include pay slips, your T4, a letter from your employer confirming you still work there, and a notice of assessment from the Canada Revenue Agency. Keep in mind that if you just got a new job and are still in the probationary period, this could limit your lender options and access to best rates. If you're a freelancer or run your own business, you'll need a lot more paperwork. In addition to tax documents for the past two or three years, you may need contracts showing expected revenues, as well as proof that you own your company, are licensed to operate it, and have been in the same line of work for at least two years.

» YOUR DOWN PAYMENT

Another key question from your lender: How much have you saved up for the down payment? Mortgage advisers can calculate the maximum home purchase price you might qualify for based on that amount, your other qualifications, and current rates, among other things, says McLister. Once they know your target home price, they'll also be able to calculate your loan-to-value ratio, which measures the size of the mortgage you'll need compared to the value of the property you want to buy. For example, if the home value is $100,000 and your down payment is $20,000, the loan-to-value ratio is 80 percent. Another way to say this is that you have a down payment of 20 percent. As we've seen, if your down payment is less than 20 percent, you'll need mortgage default insurance unless you want to pay a drastically higher interest rate to a private lender.

» YOUR DEBT RATIOS

The home price and down payment determine the loan amount, a number your lender will use, along with your income and other monthly obligations, to calculate your debt service ratios. We've already touched on this briefly, but here's the deep dive. To check whether you'll be able to make your mortgage payments, lenders use two formulas. Both compare your monthly income to your monthly debt obligations and expenses. The first is called the gross debt service ratio — GDS for friends. This measures the percentage of income you'll need to cover your mortgage payments, property taxes, heating costs, and half of your condo fees, if applicable. The math looks like this, with the total of these expenses divided by your monthly pre-tax income:

GDS = (Monthly mortgage payment + Monthly property tax payment
+ Heating costs + 50% of condo fees) / Monthly pre-tax income

Next, a lender will rerun the formula adding in your other non-mortgage debt payments. This is called the total debt service ratio, or TDS:

TDS = (Monthly mortgage payment + Monthly property tax payment
+ Heating costs + 50% of condo fees
+ Other monthly debts) / Monthly pre-tax income

Traditionally, lenders have wanted to see a GDS ratio of 32 percent and a TDS ratio of around 40 percent, although you may still qualify if your ratios are slightly higher. For example, as of February 2021, on mortgages with default insurance, the maximum GDS ratio was 39 percent and the maximum TDS ratio was 44 percent, according to McLister. In general, federally regulated lenders must comply with their internal underwriting policies (as approved by the regulator) and with insurer guidelines.

This is where the uh-oh moment sometimes happens: a big car payment, for example, can bump you above your lender's TDS threshold. For credit cards and personal lines of credit, lenders usually factor in at least 3 percent of any outstanding balance (if you pay off your credit card in full every month, you don't have to worry about this). For home-equity lines of credit the math can be a bit more complicated.

In both the GDS and the TDS, a lot rides on what interest rate your lender uses for the calculation. This is where the mortgage stress test comes in. As I mentioned earlier in this chapter, with the stress test the feds upped the threshold to qualify for a mortgage, demanding that lenders use a higher interest rate in both formulas than the interest they're actually willing to offer you. This is meant to ensure you'd still be able to cover your housing and debt costs if interest rates rose in the future and you were faced with a bigger mortgage payment.

Another way to look at it is this: you're not allowed to borrow quite as much as you would if the bank tested your finances using only the actual interest rate you'll be paying. The stress test is mandatory for federally regulated lenders, which includes the big six banks, as well as lenders that sell mortgages that require default insurance.

That said, you won't have to pass the stress test again when you renew your mortgage if you stay with the same lender. This may come as a relief, but it might also keep you from shopping around for the best renewal rate, which can be a bummer.

Provincially regulated lenders like credit unions don't have to use the stress test if you're putting down 20 percent or more, although many do anyway, according to mortgage brokers I've spoken with. If you want to stress-test your finances to see if you might pass before heading to the bank, the Financial Consumer Agency of Canada has an easy-to-use online mortgage qualifier tool that will estimate your GDS and TDS using the federal government's stress-test rules.

The state of the economy also affects the mortgage rate you'll get. If you remember our short tour through economic history in chapter 1, the Bank of Canada may also adjust its benchmark interest rate up or down based on how the economy is doing. These rate changes often prompt lenders to raise or lower their variable-rate mortgages and can also sometimes affect the rate they charge on new or renewing borrowers with fixed-rate mortgages. What goes on in other economies also has an impact on mortgage rates, as Canadian banks borrow in the global financial market. With the economic crisis triggered by Covid-19, both variable and fixed mortgage rates dropped, which made it cheaper for people to borrow and easier for them to pass the mortgage stress test, contributing to the pandemic housing boom.

If you've applied for a mortgage pre-approval, once you put an offer on a place, the actual mortgage approval process will be very similar but even more thorough. The mortgage rate you'll actually get will also depend on the characteristics of the property you want to buy. After all, lenders keep their lowest rates for "marketable properties," which will be easy to liquidate should borrowers ever stop making their payments. "The last thing they want after default is a home sitting 180 days on market," McLister says.

What makes a home hard to market? There are "a million reasons," McLister says, but some examples include a remote location, knob and tube wiring, and the presence of asbestos in the insulation. A property that might be tricky to resell represents a higher risk for the lender — and that translates into a higher interest rate for you.

One important thing to remember is that a pre-approval doesn't include an appraisal, a professional assessment of the value of the property. (You can't estimate the value of a home you haven't found yet.) An appraisal that finds that the home has significant flaws or that you paid far more than the property is worth can cause the lender to deny you a mortgage even if you've been pre-approved. To play it safe, you can insert a financing condition in your purchase offer. That's a clause that allows you to withdraw the offer with no penalties if you can't get the mortgage.

Losing your job or taking on new debt can also cause your lender to walk back on the pre-approval. And keep in mind that some financial institutions won't check your qualifications when issuing a pre-approval. While they're holding a certain mortgage rate for a period of time, you have yet to be actually officially approved for the loan. Bottom line: a pre-approval isn't a guarantee you'll get a mortgage. That's another reason to include a financing condition in your purchase offer.

FIXED OR VARIABLE MORTGAGE?

When you're mortgage shopping, you'll also have to decide what type of interest rate you want. But before we delve into that, let's demystify a couple of terms you'll hear a lot as you start talking to lenders: *mortgage term* and *mortgage amortization*. A mortgage term is the duration of the contract with your lender. In Canada it can be as short as six months or as long as 10 years, though the standard choice is 5 years. At the end of the term, you must renew your mortgage based on your remaining loan balance. This is an opportunity to negotiate a new interest rate and mortgage conditions with either your existing lender or another institution. Usually people have to renew their mortgage contract a few times over the life of their mortgage, also known as the amortization period. This is the total length of time it will take you to completely pay off your mortgage. With a down payment of less than 20 percent, the longest you can take to repay your mortgage is 25 years. If you put down 20 percent or more, major banks will offer amortizations of up to 30 years.

Now let's go back to mortgage rates. With a fixed rate, your mortgage interest rate and payment will stay the same for the duration of your term.

With a variable rate, your interest rate can go up or down, usually based on whether the Bank of Canada is hiking or lowering its benchmark rate. Your monthly payment will increase or decrease along with your mortgage rate, although there is also the option of keeping your payments the same for the duration of the term. In the latter scenario, if interest rates rise, this means a bigger chunk of your money will go to pay interest charges and you'll usually face higher payments at renewal.

Most people like their mortgage rate to stay steady and predictable. As of 2020, 73 percent of Canadians with a mortgage had a fixed rate. What possessed the other 27 percent to gamble on a variable rate?[22] Intuitively, a floating rate is a good deal if interest rates decline during your mortgage term. If that happens, with a fixed rate you're stuck with whatever you agreed to with your lender. With a variable rate, your interest rate goes down and you save money. According to York University professor Moshe Milevsky, between 1965 and 2007, borrowers would have been better off with variable rates at least 77 percent of the time.[23]

Also, one important perk of variable-rate mortgages, as I mentioned in chapter 2, is that they usually come with lower penalties. If you think you might have to break your mortgage, doing so with a variable-rate contract won't cost you quite as much. Variable rates are also usually lower than the fixed rates you can get for the same mortgage term. That's because the security of knowing your mortgage rate won't change comes at a premium.

So, should you go fixed or variable? One thing is for sure: trying to divine the future of interest rates is *not* a wise way to choose. No one knows where interest rates are headed. I don't care if your neighbour or your uncle have strong opinions on the matter. *No one knows*, not even the Bank of Canada. It may get to set interest rates, but it adjusts those rates in response to economic conditions that can and have caught it off guard (the Covid-19 crisis being just one example).

The most important factor when deciding whether you should go fixed or variable is your risk tolerance. Would you be financially okay if interest rates rose significantly during your term? Would you keep sleeping soundly even if your interest costs or mortgage payments increased? If the answer is yes, maybe it's worth trying your luck with a variable rate, especially if it comes at a considerable discount on a comparable fixed rate.

• • •

Wrap-Up

And with this, you've come to the end of the whirlwind tour through the ins and outs of the question of how to afford a home where you can live and prosper. As you've probably surmised, there is no financial wizardry that will somehow bring housing within reach where prices and rents have ballooned. But what you can do in this unreal real estate market is stay cool, analyze your options, and choose the one that will benefit you the most in the long term. Now you have many of the tools to do just that.

Here are a few points that may help you decide on next steps:

» If you're in the very early stages of contemplating home ownership, start looking at local listings to get an idea of prices in your area. Then head over to the mortgage payment calculator at Ratehub.ca, or find a similar online tool that also estimates the monthly carrying costs of owning a home.

» If you're rocking it as a renter, don't let anyone tell you that you have to buy. There are good landlords and affordable rents out there.

» If home ownership seems within reach and is what you want, use a tool like the FCAC's mortgage qualifier tool to see if you can clear the mortgage stress test. Even if you do, remember there are so many — soooo many — monthly expenses the stress test does not consider.

Finally, a word about the meaning of housing affordability. *Affordable* is, of course, a relative concept. So far, we've talked at length about home prices, mortgage rates, and rents, all of which affect how much we can afford for housing. But we haven't talked about that other crucial variable: incomes. If you've been wondering what's been going on with our collective earning power and how you can individually boost your own, let's jump into chapter 4 for a no-nonsense discussion of how to make money.

CHAPTER 4

MAKING MONEY LIKE YOU MEAN IT

MOST OF US grew up with the notion that there is a fairly simple way to make a living: get a job and work hard. A lot of money-advice folklore rides on this notion. Finish school, get a job, and start saving up! What's so hard about that?

You've probably heard your uncle or another savvy relative wonder this aloud. But even in your uncle's generation, bringing home a decent paycheque wasn't nearly as straightforward as it's often made out to be around the dinner table at family gatherings. If you started working in the 1970s, you would have had to contend with stagflation — a dreadful combo of high unemployment and rising prices — which meant you either didn't have a job or had to constantly worry about your salary keeping up with the cost of living. And lots of our baby-boomer parents graduated in the early 1980s only to find an ugly economic downturn that would drag on for years.

The path to a decent living has never been as easy as the old-timey tales would have you believe. But today that path often looks more like an overgrown trail where it's easy to get stuck or hopelessly lost. This chapter will help you find your way forward. You'll learn how to better track your pay and hours and how to compare different kinds of work. You'll see why "Don't call us, we'll call you" isn't job flexibility; it's precarious, unpredictable work. We'll look at how to negotiate with employers and clients, and we'll bust some of the myths about job-hopping your way to a better paycheque.

But first, as in previous chapters, it helps to know how we got here in the first place.

• • •

What Really Happened to Middle-Class Incomes

For decades, middle-class incomes have been going nowhere fast. Dig up individual income data from Statistics Canada, plot it as shown in the chart, and here's what you'll see: back in 1976 the typical working Canadian between 25 and 54 was making what would amount to roughly $48,000 today. In 2019, that figure was — drum roll, please — a little less than: $47,800. Yep, you read that right. Once you adjust for inflation, the archetypal Canadian worker was making slightly better money some 45 years ago.

But middle-class earnings didn't exactly sit still for nearly half a century. As the chart on page 118 shows, they took a dive between the 1980s and the 1990s and then climbed back up, recouping most of the ground lost. What happened?

When you zoom in on the data, things become more complicated. It's a story about gender and about what happened in different areas of the country, says Tammy Schirle, a professor of economics at Wilfrid Laurier University. First of all, what's been going on with men's and women's earnings is very different.

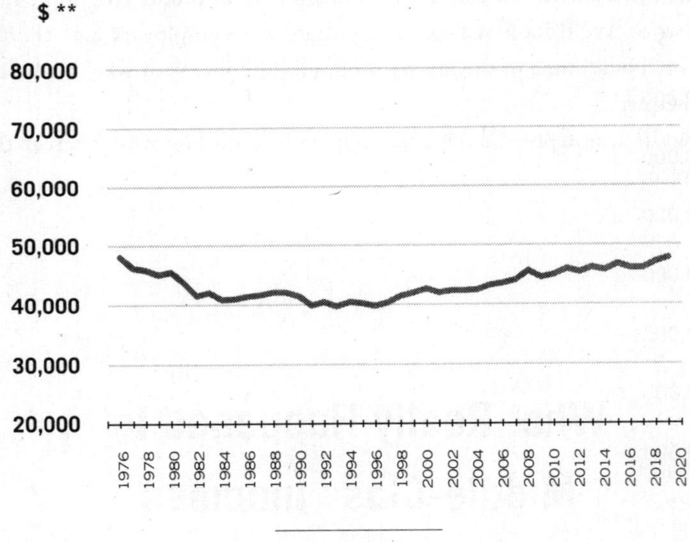

Source: Statistics Canada

*There are other possible sources of income beyond employment.

**2018 dollars

It is really men's incomes that took a hit, Schirle notes. "If you were a guy in the mid-1970s and you dropped out of high school, you had a really good chance of being able to find full-time employment with a decent wage," she says. But that changed in the 1980s and 1990s, as a number of stable, well-paying manufacturing jobs disappeared.

Something similar has happened in many rich countries, and economists have a pretty good idea why. Robots are one reason. Technological progress saw factories swap workers for machines that are both faster and cheaper than humans at, say, tightening screws on an assembly line. The lowly shipping container embodies another big change that has had a similar impact on manufacturing jobs: the rise of globalization and the corporate world's embrace of outsourcing. These giant metal boxes made it much quicker and

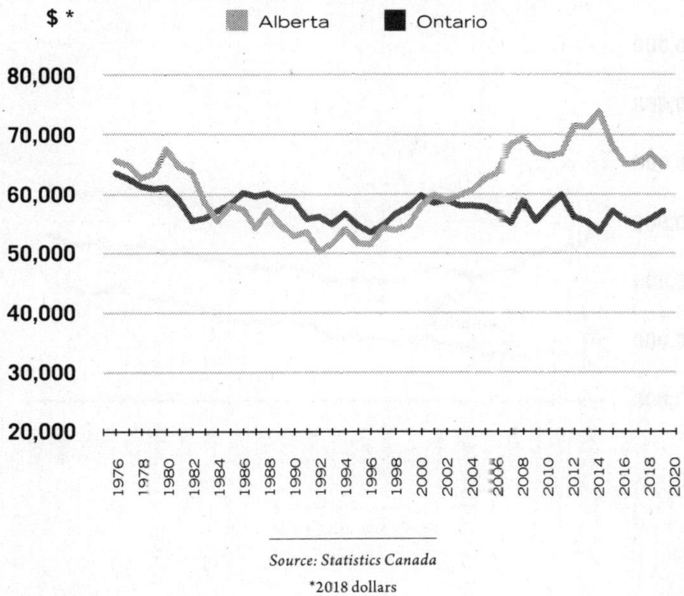

Source: Statistics Canada

*2018 dollars

cheaper to move merchandise from ships to trains and trucks and vice versa. Over time, this made it easier for companies to count on lower-cost suppliers in far-flung corners of the world to produce anything from toys to T-shirts. This likely meant lost jobs and lower pay for factory workers in rich countries who were competing with producers in poorer countries. It didn't help that the 1980s and 1990s also saw a steep decline in the share of unionized jobs, which used to be male dominated.

The decline of manufacturing jobs mostly hurt men, particularly young workers who'd left school early, Schirle says. The energy boom of the 2000s is also a story largely about men's jobs and paycheques but one mostly confined to oil-rich provinces. As oil prices climbed in the late 1990s, men saw huge income gains in Alberta, Saskatchewan, and Newfoundland. But in Ontario and

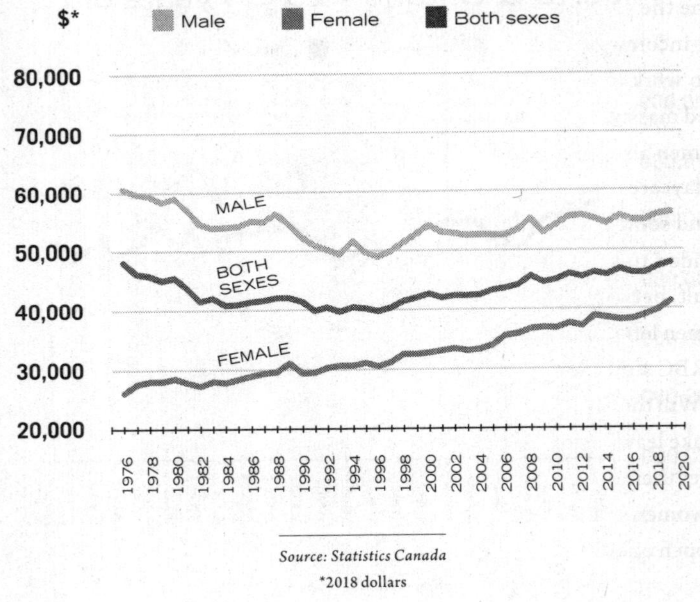

Source: Statistics Canada

*2018 dollars

Quebec, the heart of Canada's manufacturing sector, men's incomes have been stagnant. The chart on page 119 compares men's incomes in Ontario and Alberta.

When the energy boom went bust, so did the income of working men. "In Alberta, you see a huge decline in earnings after 2014. Between 2014 and 2017, earnings dropped to the same level that they would have seen around 2007, 2008," Schirle says.

A lot of what drives the conversation about middle-income Canadians is really about what happened for prime-age working men, Schirle says. As the chart on this page shows, although women were also affected by the decline in manufacturing and the energy boom, their earnings have been quietly and steadily rising through the decades as more and more of them have joined the labour force, graduated from university, and started working longer hours and advancing in their jobs.

But the upward-sloping line of women's earnings is a feel-good story only up to a point. Even in 2018, the latest available year when I retrieved the data, gender equality in terms of employment income remained a ways off. Then came the pandemic, which hit women — along with people of colour and low-income workers — disproportionately hard. Women were more likely to work in retail, hospitality, and personal services, all sectors that suffered massive job losses as the country went into various levels of lockdown. Women also shouldered the brunt of child care and home-schooling duties as daycares and schools shut down. Even when classes reopened, parents found some child-care centres had shuttered for good, while other parents decided to keep their kids at home to protect them from contagion. As a result, between February and October 2020, more than 20,000 Canadian women left the labour force, while nearly 68,000 men joined it, according to an RBC study.[1]

Will these women go back to work? Will working moms who were forced to take leave, cut back their hours, and trim their job responsibilities be able to get their careers back on track? Will the pandemic have a lasting impact on women's slow march toward higher earnings? As I write, all this remains an open question.

• • •

A Different Kind of Gig

When it comes to jobs, pay is only part of the package. And income trends tell only one aspect of how the job market has changed. Benefits are another important part of the story. Back in the late 1970s, 46 percent of employees had a pension plan. Today, that share has dropped to 37 percent, and most of the jobs with generous retirement benefits are in the public sector. We'll do a deep dive into pensions and retirement in the next chapter, but here I want to talk about a third big change in the world of jobs: the gig economy, in which people try to make a living by cobbling together a bunch of odd jobs.

There's a tendency to talk about the gig economy as if it were an entirely new, never-before-seen phenomenon, but gigs have been around for a very long time. Your parents probably mowed the lawn, raked the neighbours' leaves, or flipped burgers when they were young for a bit of spending money or to help pay tuition. When he was a schoolboy, my dad would deliver panettones — an Italian Christmas cake — around Milan on a bicycle during winter break (which is why he still has a cab-driver-like knowledge of city streets). And all the way back to the 1800s, women in working-class families often resorted to side gigs like washing clothes and turning part of their houses into boarding rooms to help beef up the household finances.

So what's changed? For one, the share of full-time, full-year jobs in Canada has been gradually declining since at least the late 1990s, especially for young people. This means gig-like work has been growing more common. For someone fresh out of school, "it used to be a quarter of all the job opportunities were temporary in nature, and now over a third are," says economist Armine Yalnizyan, Atkinson Fellow on the Future of Workers. She worries the economic ripple effects of Covid-19 will speed up the trend. "I fully expect that the pandemic will give rise to more demand for on-demand labour, because that's what happens in the wake of every recession," she says.

The shift toward more temporary jobs started well before most people had dial-up at home, but it was the internet that put a new spin on temp work and created what we now call the gig economy. On the one hand, the web has brought the gig to a whole new level. The age-old idea of having boarders to make some extra money, for example, has become Airbnb. From knitting to woodwork, monetizing hobbies has never been easier than with Etsy and Instagram. As any airbrushed social media influencer or charismatic TikTok creator will tell you, there are pretty much endless ways in which you can, theoretically, create a decent stream of money without ever leaving your house.

As we all know, this was an essential financial lifeline for many during the pandemic. People started selling handmade cloth masks online, personal trainers turned to YouTube fitness classes, and restaurant owners set up Zoom cooking classes and virtual tastings to try to stay afloat.

But of course, not everything about the gig economy is hunky-dory. Online job platforms like ride-sharing sites and freelance marketplaces have blurred the line between employment and self-employment. Like a self-employed worker, you get no benefits nor any guarantee of steady employment. But like an employee, you often don't get to cultivate your own clients or set your own prices, either. Even when you do have the ability to decide your own rate, you usually do so with the knowledge that potential customers can browse through the online profiles of dozens of other workers with similar experience and qualifications. Or you must bid against others to win a project.

Job apps have been a game changer, Yalnizyan says: "They reduce the workers' ability to control payment structures. There's no bargaining." And digital technology makes it easier to unbundle what used to be a single job into several separate tasks, just like assembly lines once did for manual labour. But while factories were, for a few decades, a source of dependable jobs that didn't require much education, digital technology is now, in some cases, making it possible to turn even high-level professional jobs into contract work.

Law firms, for example, can now hire junior lawyers for just a few days to help sift through tedious but important tasks such as sorting and tagging documents. Small businesses can grow their tech development team when needed by hiring freelance coders on Upstack. In any number of professional jobs, companies can now easily tap contractors for project-based work.

For some work that can be done remotely, online platforms may be doing to professionals like software engineers and graphic designers what containers did to factory workers. They've opened the jobs up to global competition. Need a simple business logo? There are plenty of talented designers in Bangladesh who can turn out something sleek for less than $30. How about turning your website into an app? Someone in Macedonia will nail the task for rates starting at less than $10.

• • •

Work-from-Home from Anywhere?

And one has to wonder — okay, *I* have to wonder — whether the work-from-home boom triggered by Covid-19 will accelerate the trend of companies' relying on just-in-time contract work and potentially sourcing freelancers all over the world. If employers have cozied up to the idea of us labouring away on laptops perched on the kitchen table, will it occur to them that someone else might be able to do the same job from a kitchen located in a place where living costs and wages are a lot lower?

I don't mean to spread doom and gloom here. I actually think many employers and workers will emerge from the pandemic with a renewed appreciation of the good old-fashioned office. For some jobs, says Wilfrid Laurier University's Schirle, there is value in in-person meetings and water-cooler conversations. But it does seem conceivable that more roles will become permanently remote and more companies will recruit around the world to fill them. "As people realize that you can do a lot of different types of jobs from home, you can imagine some of those services moving out of your standard offices," Schirle says. "And as soon as you move out of offices, then you can think about hiring people internationally." She adds, "Part of the job market might become more competitive."

To be sure, global competition can be great news for Canadian workers. The fact that Silicon Valley giants are after our tech talent, for example, helps raise the salaries of Canada-based data scientists and machine-learning engineers. But that's because there's huge demand for these jobs from deep-pocketed employers and only a very limited number of people with the right skills. When it comes to designing business logos and building simple websites, there's no shortage of qualified, talented people who can do the job for cheap.

• • •

Work Is Work Is Work

All this is to say that slashing your way through today's job-market jungle can be hard, sweaty, and precarious. But there is a way forward; the key is to have a good compass.

The first step is to dump old-fashioned ideas about "good jobs" versus freelancing and gigs. Yes, work that offers a good paycheque, stability, security, perks, a pension, and the potential for self-realization is great. But office jobs don't necessarily check all, or even most, of those boxes. Going freelance — by which I mean truly being your own boss, whether you start a business or work on your own — could be your ticket to a better income, better work, and ultimately a better life. And even gigs can come in handy. They can be a quick way to make a buck in a financial emergency or a means to turbocharging your income so you can reach your money goals faster. They're also a great way to gradually transition to a new career without having to leave the job that pays the bills or taking on tons of student debt.

The point is, it doesn't really matter whether you're working nine to five, stitching together a bunch of gigs, or running your very own company from your laptop. Work is work is work. What matters is making sure you're getting what you need out of your job and seeing clearly what's what. No matter where and how you earn your living, the driving, central question is this: Are you getting your work's worth?

Here's how to tackle that enigma and how to get to the answer you want.

• • •

How Much Money Are You Actually Making?

The very first thing you need to understand is how much you make. Now, I'm not trying to insult your intelligence by suggesting you don't know your salary, your hourly rate, or how much money lands in your bank account every month. Of course you do.

But knowing how much you get paid isn't the same as knowing how much money you're actually making. For example, even people with a regular paycheque sometimes misestimate their monthly income — it happened to me. I spent 24 full years living and breathing on this Earth before "discovering" there are, in fact, 52 weeks in a year. For example, if you get paid $2,000 every two weeks, I have good news: your monthly pay is more than $2,000 × 2 = $4,000. There are 26 two-week periods in a year, so your monthly income is $2,000 × 26 / 12 months of the year, which yields $4,333.

Of course, that's pretty basic stuff. An in-depth analysis of your earnings can lead to even more disconcerting discoveries.

TAXES

First of all, there's the question of taxes. After-tax pay is a rather straightforward matter when your employer takes care of calculating and withholding payroll taxes, contributions to employment insurance (EI) and the Canada Pension Plan (CPP) or the Quebec Pension Plan (QPP), union dues, and so on.

But figuring out your net pay gets more complicated if you're working for yourself or juggling more than one job. Forgetting to account for taxes is a rookie freelancer's mistake. Not only will you need to calculate and set aside your income tax, but if you start making serious money, you'll also have to pay sales taxes. If you don't have a good sense of what your freelance income will be for the year, setting aside 20 percent of every invoice for income taxes is usually a safe bet, says Gennaro De Luca, a certified financial planner and managing director of WEALTHplan Canada.

If you're side-gigging, keep in mind that your second job could bump you into a higher income-tax bracket, which could result in a surprise tax bill when you file your return. You can use an online tax calculator to roughly estimate your taxes.

You could also end up with an unexpected bill at tax time if you have multiple employers. That's because of what's called the basic personal amount, the amount of money you can earn tax-free every year. Unless you tell the payroll department that you have more than one job, each of your employers will factor in the basic personal amount when calculating your payroll tax. "I've seen this countless times," says De Luca.

EXPENSES AREN'T JUST FOR THE SELF-EMPLOYED

There are taxes, and then there are work-related costs. If you've been self-employed for a while, you are likely well versed in tracking your expenses, many of which are tax-deductible. But if you're a gig worker, it can be easy to forget about some of those costs. For example, if you're shuttling people around or delivering food for a ride-sharing company, you spend more on gas and possibly car maintenance than you otherwise would. It's important to track those expenses — not only for tax purposes, but also so you can evaluate your true take-home pay.

At tax time you may receive a handy statement showing your pre-tax pay and how many kilometres you covered while delivering passengers or meals. That's helpful, but it's not the whole story. You also need to account for the distance you travelled on your way to pick them up or while driving around waiting for a client request.

There may be other less obvious costs you're not thinking about. Rideshare apps, for instance, tend to use a lot of data. Don't forget to include part of your phone bill in your calculation. Good accountants who can help you think through all your out-of-pocket costs and make the most of tax credits and deductions are worth their weight in gold.

Even if you're working as an employee, you probably have some out-of-pocket expenses. The pandemic laid bare all the hidden costs of going to work that no one was thinking about, from commuting to buying expensive suits and shelling out for makeup and haircuts so you look presentable at the office. It was only during the big shift to work-from-home that many of us realized how much dough we were dropping every month just on showing up for work. If you're trying to estimate your real take-home pay, you need to factor in those expenses as well.

THE ILLUSION OF TIME

Figuring out how much you're actually making also means knowing how much *time* you're putting into your work. Let's say that, on paper, you make $35 an hour. There are two variables at play here. One is the dollar amount, which we just analyzed in detail. The other is the unit of time. Is it actually taking you an hour to earn that $35 pre-tax?

Underestimating how long it really takes you to do the job is another common mistake for freelancers, says Jackie Lam, an independent personal finance writer and business coach based in Los Angeles. If you're charging $35 an hour for tutoring but it takes you 30 minutes each way to get to your pupil's house, you're really making $17.50 an hour, not including the bus fare. Other time-consuming tasks for which you won't earn a cent include looking for new clients, bidding on projects, and financial housekeeping — from tallying up all those business expenses to chasing down customers who "forgot" to pay you. Freelancing comes with "lots of unpaid work," says Lam, and you should keep track of it.

Time is also critical to how you should charge your clients, Lam says. If a project is straightforward and you know exactly how long it will take you to complete it because you've worked on many similar jobs before, you can set a flat rate. But for something that feels like new territory or where you might run into unexpected problems, charge by the hour, Lam suggests.

The illusion of time can be an issue for people who work so-called regular hours as well. If you're being paid for 40 hours a week but you're actually putting in closer to 60 hours, your actual hourly rate is much lower than what shows on your paycheque. Similarly, make sure to include the time it takes you to get to the office when calculating your *real* pay per hour.

• • •

Employee versus Freelancer: Compare Apples to Apples

Suppose you're working at an office job making $35 an hour, but try your hand at freelancing and find out you can make $40 an hour. The freelance gig is more lucrative, right? Not so fast. You need to make an apples-to-apples comparison. De Luca, the financial planner, has a simple formula to help you do just that:

(Pre-tax employee pay + Dollar value of taxable employee benefits
+ Employer's share of CPP contribution)
/ [52 weeks of the year - (Vacation days + Sick days)]
/ Number of hours worked per week

Now, let's walk through an example. Let's say you work 40 hours a week at your steady job. If you multiply your rate of $35 an hour by 40 hours per week and then by the 52 weeks of the year, you get $72,800, your pre-tax pay. But you should also account for your employee benefits. Let's say you typically use $3,000 a year worth of health benefits and receive $6,000 annually in matching contributions from your employer to your pension plan. That's $9,000 no one will pay for you as a freelancer.

Also, when you're an employee, your employer pays for half of your CPP contributions, a cost you'd have to shoulder on your own if you became self-employed. As of 2021, to calculate your employer's share of CPP contributions, take your annual pre-tax pay or $61,600 (whichever is lower), subtract $3,500, and multiply by 0.0545. In our example: ($61,600 - $3,500) × 0.0545 = $3,166.45.

To recap: $72,800 pre-tax pay + $9,000 worth of benefits + $3,166.45 CPP contributions = $84,966.45. That's what you'd have to earn as a freelancer to match what you're currently making in that office job.

But, of course, as an employee you don't actually work 52 weeks a year. For example, let's say you get 3 weeks of paid vacation and 10 paid sick days. For a fair comparison, you should subtract those 5 weeks from 52, which leaves you with 47 weeks. You're effectively making the freelance equivalent of $84,966.45 in 47 weeks of work, or roughly $1,808 a week. Divide that by 40 hours of work per week and you get around $45. You'd need to earn at least $45 an hour as a freelancer working 40 hours a week to make something comparable to your employee pay. That's if you were able to work a steady 40 billable hours a week as a freelancer — which may be a big *if*. Finally, this calculation doesn't take into account any expenses and unpaid work you might face as a self-employed worker, De Luca warns, so keep our discussion in the previous section in mind, too.

Of course, this is back-of-the-napkin math. There are countless other possible nuances this short formula doesn't reflect. But it's a useful starting point. And the basic point is, $40 an hour as a freelancer isn't necessarily more than $35 as an employee. If you're contemplating a career change, it's worth taking some time to get a rough idea of how far your buck would really go.

• • •

Negotiating: How to Ask for What You Want

You won't get your work's worth unless you *ask* for it. But asking in itself is a complicated and nuanced art, one that requires training, practice, and refinement.

When I got my first real job offer, I had a vague notion that I should haggle a bit. I had just heard from a colleague my age who had bumped up her salary by several thousand dollars per year by negotiating with our mutual employer. So I requested a time to sit down with the managing editor and asked him if he could go a little higher. He looked at me, smiled, and said it was November; I'd be getting a cost-of-living increase in a couple of months. And with that, the conversation was over.

I knew I had to ask, but did not have a clue how to do it. In fact, I didn't even know *what* I wanted. Almost every negotiation requires some prep, and the place to start is figuring out what you want. What's the target you're aiming at?

This should not be conflated with your financial requirements. Calculating what you need to earn to make a living is important for your own consideration. But your target should be based on a clear idea of what's fair compensation for the work you're being asked to do and for the credentials, skills, and expertise you bring to the job. What's your market value?

This is a nebulous concept. It typically won't boil down to a specific figure but to a range, like mid-$60,000s to low $70,000s. To arrive at that range, you look at what other people with similar qualifications and job duties are making. Trying to look up that information on the web often isn't very helpful. The ranges you find online are often so wide they're useless, and many employers simply will not care about that kind of generic data, says career coach and human resources expert Allison Venditti, who runs Moms at Work and Ready to Return, organizations dedicated to creating equitable workplaces and supporting working women and parents.

Gathering your own on-the-ground intelligence yields far better results, according to Venditti. Talk to people in your industry. Ask your colleagues out for coffee (as long as we're not in a pandemic, of course). But discussing money is often awkward and delicate, especially in the workplace. How do you ask someone how much they make?

Venditti suggests playing what she calls the "over-under game." People won't tell you what they earn, but they will tell you whether they make more or less than a certain amount, she says. If you're a woman or have other reasons to suspect you're being underpaid, Venditti suggests adding 15 percent to the target pay you have in mind when playing the over-under game. Her clients — especially female ones — are constantly shocked to discover colleagues or others similarly qualified are making much more than they are, she says. "I had someone play the over-under game and find out she was being paid $40,000 less than her co-worker," Venditti says.

If you don't know anyone in the field you want to work in — because you're looking at your very first job or you're switching careers — it's worth checking out your school's alumni network. In my experience, LinkedIn is also a useful place to spot people in your area who have or have had the job you want. You may very well find someone you know or are somehow connected with.

The evidence you've gathered on your market value is what you should use to support your argument for higher pay — or a raise — in the negotiation. Your employer is not interested in your monthly budget and how expensive your rent is.

But don't wait for a company to come to you with an offer before you bring up pay, Venditti says. "The first thing you should do when applying for a job is ask them: Can you give me the pay range for this?" she says. If they say no or equivocate, ask to know at least the bottom of the range, Venditti continues. "Women are continuously blown away that even the bottom of the range is significantly more than what they were thinking."

Once you know a company's range or have your own target range in mind, it's time to focus on what negotiation experts call your reservation value and your anchor. Your reservation value is the absolute lowest offer you'd be willing to accept. Your anchor is your initial request, which should be higher than your actual target, which is what you are truly hoping for.

Anchoring in negotiations and other fields refers to our brain's tendency to get stuck focusing on the first number we hear about. That value often anchors the whole discussion, with negotiators unable to move very far from it. If your employer kicks off the conversation with a lowball offer, they've anchored the conversation at the bottom end of the range.

In that situation, you can say something like, "What I had in mind for the job was more along the lines of *X* amount." The *X* is *your* anchor, and it should be quite a bit higher than your target value so you have plenty of room to make concessions and still get what you want. Ideally, though, you want to go first so you can set a high anchor to begin with.

And don't let a prospective employer paint you into a corner by asking you to provide a range for your desired compensation on the job application. The temptation for every applicant is to write some lowball values because they're afraid they'll be weeded out from the start if they ask for too much, Venditti says. Those answers could very well limit your ability to negotiate something considerably higher if you do get the offer. Instead, Venditti suggests keeping your cards close to your chest by giving a wide range, with $15,000 to $30,000 between your low number and your higher one. And your bottom value should be 15 percent higher than your reservation value, she adds.

You also need to think about something negotiation pros call a BATNA, or best alternative to a negotiated agreement. In other words, what are you going to do if you don't get what you want? Can you comfortably continue on in your current job? Do you have a competing offer to turn to? Generally, the stronger your BATNA, the more bargaining power you have. In my first salary negotiation, for example, I didn't have much of a BATNA. At the time, the economy had just begun to crawl out of the financial crisis of 2007–2008 and the job market was nothing short of awful. I also happened to be an intern hire, the first in several years. I did not have another job to fall back on or a competing offer to turn to. *Of course* I was going to accept whatever they gave me.

Keep in mind, as well, that during salary or raise negotiations there's much more than pay to discuss. Here are some other requests to think about:

- Cash bonuses and stock options

  ____

- Changing your professional title

  ____

- Working arrangements (such as working from home, flexible hours, or an earlier or later start of the workday)

  ____

- Waiving waiting periods for health and retirement benefits

  ____

- A retirement payout; if your old job had a pension and your new one does not (or has a plan that isn't nearly as generous), you can ask for some compensation in the form of a one-time payment

Similarly, when you're negotiating a contract, there's usually much more to talk about than a rate or project price. A few examples of what to consider:

- Delivery timeline

  ____

- When you'll get paid and how, including any down payments or deposits

  ____

- What happens if you don't get paid in a timely manner (this may include ceasing work or charging interest)

  ____

- Reimbursement of certain expenses (and whether that will happen upfront)

  ____

» Contingency clauses (for example, what happens if you're delayed delivering the work because of circumstances outside your control? And what if the project requires more time or equipment than originally estimated?)

Going back, once again, to my first, stumbling foray into salary negotiations, even if there truly had been zero wiggle room on pay, I could have at least attempted to ask for other things. For example, I could have inquired about working remotely a couple of weeks a year so I could stretch out my annual stay in Italy visiting my parents. I've successfully asked for this in later negotiations.

You should also make sure that whatever you eventually settle on is recorded in writing. Not just your pay — everything. Don't go for off-the-books arrangements, Venditti says.

Still, keep in mind that, even with all the prep in the world and the most pragmatic, problem-solving, can-do attitude, those who ask the right way shall not always receive. Sometimes the outcome depends on factors entirely outside of your control. Research from PayScale, for example, indicates white men are more likely to get a raise when they ask compared to people of colour and women.[2]

If you don't get what you want, ask what you can do to get there and request that your boss sit down to revisit the issue in a few months. After, you might want to send your manager an email summation of the discussion, which will be a written record of your informal agreement. And if you keep asking and not getting, it's time to take the leap to a better job.

"This is like dating someone," Venditti says. "If you were with someone who stopped returning your calls, would you still be in a relationship?"

• • •

Does Job-Hopping Work?

If you're stuck in a job where you're not growing, don't get bogged down by notions of loyalty to your employer, Venditti says. This isn't the era when "you worked 30 years for the same company, got the gold watch, and walked away," she says.

But does that mean you should change employers as often as you can?

Job-hopping hype is pervasive online, with tales that sound more or less like this: Once upon a time, Jane (a fictional character) was barely a year into her first job when she switched over to another company. Three years later, she had hopped through two more jobs. She is now making double her original salary and will live happily ever after.

I've heard this story. You've heard this story. Bloggers, self-help gurus, and millennial money mentors often swear by this: switching jobs is the way to climb the earnings ladder faster.

I have no reason to doubt the many accounts of successful job-hopping. The idea makes sense to me. Frequent job changes mean more opportunities to negotiate your salary from a position of relative strength, as the candidate who's emerged victorious after a gruelling selection process.

But does job-hopping work for everyone or even in most cases? There isn't much hard evidence out there to support or contradict the success stories, but one of the best datasets I've come across is from the Federal Reserve Bank of Atlanta. Its wage-growth tracker uses data from the U.S. Census Bureau to, among other things, show the wage growth of people who've switched employers or job duties over the past year and those who haven't. The data goes back to 1998 and is pretty striking.

As of February 2021, the median wage of what the Federal Reserve Bank calls job switchers was around 4 percent higher than their pay 12 months prior. The average job stayer, by comparison, was making about 3 percent more.

This looks like a ringing endorsement of job-hopping. But look at what happens in the chart on page 137 in the years immediately after an economic recession: the gap between job switchers and job stayers virtually disappears for a while. This makes intuitive sense. Job-hopping works best when the

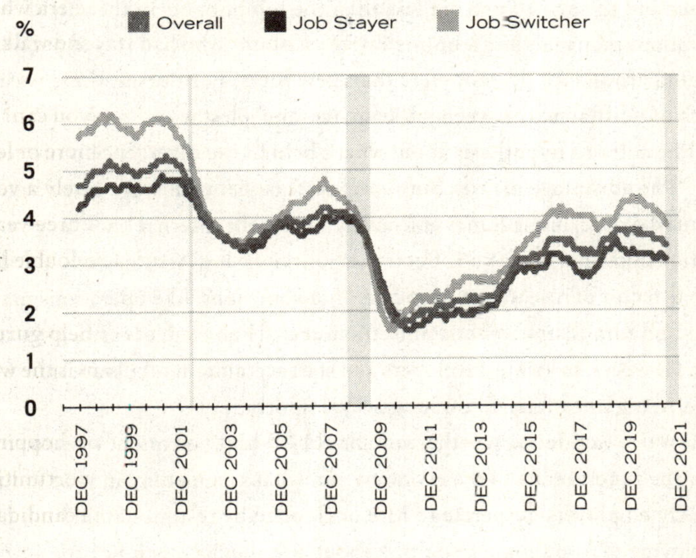

Sources: Current Population Survey, Bureau of Labor Statistics, and Federal Reserve Bank of Atlanta Calculations; 12-month moving average of monthly median wage growth; hourly data

economy is strong and there are plenty of job vacancies employers need to fill. That isn't to say you can't hop your way to better pay in an economic downturn — I've seen it happen many times. But, generally speaking, you're likely to have less negotiating power in a job market with high unemployment and few openings.

But there's another important question to address: Even in good times, does job-hopping lead to better pay in every industry? The answer may be no.

A 2018 study by salary-comparison site PayScale found that frequent job-switching could backfire in certain roles.[3] The analysis used more than 300,000 salary profiles to compare similarly experienced employees who had been in their current job for less than a year to those who'd worked at one company for 9 to 10 years. The data showed very different trends for different jobs. Software developers and staff accountants who'd never quit turned out to earn 10 percent less than the job-hoppers in their field. But operations managers and administrative assistants who had stayed put were earning around 20 percent *more* than new hires. For nurses, there wasn't much of a difference between job switchers and job stayers.

The author's hypothesis about what's behind the divergence is interesting. "The advantage of switching employers is that your wage gets reset to the market rate, but it comes at a cost: you lose the internal knowledge and relationships that make you effective *at your company*," wrote Chris Martin, then director of research at PayScale. "For some jobs, like operations managers and administrative assistants, this internal knowledge is critical to success. However, software developers and staff accountants skills are transferrable, so organizational know how is less important."

If you're wondering whether you should job-hop, you might want to consider the general state of the economy and what's happening in your industry. Are employers desperate to hire or flooded by resumés amid high unemployment? You should also think about how much — or how little — the organizational know-how Martin speaks about seems to matter for career progression in your role. Does it pay to be an insider?

• • •

When Is a Side Hustle Worth the Hassle?

There is a lot of side-hustle porn out there. Working a second job has become a status symbol, a mark of hard work, a can-do attitude, and kick-ass entrepreneurial spirit. *I can work my full-time job and then spend another three hours after dinner hustling to round up my income. Can you?*

But side hustles aren't a mandatory path to wealth and greatness. And life's not a pissing contest about who can work the hardest without dropping dead. Let's be clear about what side-hustling really is: working more than a full-time job. That comes at a cost.

I'm not here to defend the sanctity of the nine-to-five. I have no qualms working late on Friday evenings and the odd Saturday and Sunday when necessary. But there's a reason why labour unions on both sides of the border fought long and hard for an eight- or nine-hour workday, two days of weekend, and paid vacation.

As Jess Fickett (a.k.a. Piggy), co-author of the millennial money blog *Bitches Get Riches*, put it in one of my favourite posts: "If you work an eight-hour day only to come home and work another four hours on your side hustle before squeezing in a shower, a food, and a sleep, then at what point do you take a break? At what point do you read a book, catch up on the news, learn a new skill, clean your house, spend time with your family, walk your dog?"[4] If you're stuck working two jobs indefinitely just to make ends meet, you'll eventually burn out.

But side-hustling can be useful — extremely useful, in fact — when it's a time-limited effort to achieve a clear goal. You can afford to rev up your engine to the max for a little while to get where you're going faster.

SIDE-HUSTLE GOALS

A side hustle can be a good idea when it serves one of three purposes. First, it can be a way to temporarily boost your earnings to meet a specific financial target or make it through a rough patch. A side gig can be your ticket to an epic vacation or a way to turbocharge your savings for a down payment on a house. And if your employer trimmed back your hours, a second job can be a temporary hack to make ends meet or build up an emergency fund if you don't already have one.

Second, a side hustle can be a way to monetize something you enjoy doing. Do you spend your evenings baking to relieve stress? Why not try to sell some of those delicious creations? When your side hustle is also your hobby, you're killing two birds with one stone. You're getting your much-needed leisure time *and* you're bringing in some extra cash. The potential downside of this, though, is that it can be tricky to maintain the perfect balance between pastime and paid work. The moment you find yourself whipping eggs and flour in a frenzy at 10:00 p.m. to fulfill a last-minute order, you know you've officially crossed over from hobby into a second job.

The third and most powerful way to harness the potential of the side gig is to use it to eventually switch to a higher-paying or more fulfilling daytime job. If you're contemplating a new career, a side gig can be a way to explore something different, gradually build up new skills, and eventually make a name for yourself in another field.

For Canadian personal finance author Robb Engen, side-hustling hit all three sweet spots. Engen started blogging at *Boomer & Echo* in 2010. He had just turned 30 and become a father. But his wife had been diagnosed with multiple sclerosis a couple of years earlier, meaning the family was down to one income. "I really just spent a lot of that time, after our kid went to bed, reading other personal finance blogs and thinking about how I could improve on our financial situation and just learn as much as I could," he says.

Eventually, he started his own money blog with his mother, who had worked for years as a financial adviser. The name was inspired by David K. Foot and Daniel Stoffman's 1990s bestseller *Boom, Bust and Echo,* on Canada's demographic shift as baby boomers entered middle age. Engen's mother was the boomer, and he was the echo, part of the cohort born roughly between 1980 and 1995 (that's before *millennial* became the preferred term). Engen wanted to learn everything he could about money management and investing, help other people make better financial choices, and earn some money with ads and affiliate links to help with cash flow.

As it turned out, Engen was one heck of a writer. Soon, his money blog caught the eye of the *Toronto Star,* which asked him to become a contributing writer. That, in turn, led to more freelance writing gigs.

Engen, who ended up taking over the blog, was working evenings and weekends, putting in 15 or 20 hours on the blog, on top of his full-time job in the education sector. But helping Canadians with their saving and investing decisions and sharing his own was a labour of love, he says. "This was very much something that I started because I liked it, I have an interest in it. I was passionate about it," he says.

After a few years, Engen began to think of his side hustle as a way to slowly transition to working as a financial planner, a more lucrative career he also truly enjoys. He started by researching answers to readers' money questions, initially leaning on an experienced financial adviser for guidance.

Some 10 years after launching the blog, he figured he was ready to take the leap. "My 'a-ha' moment occurred to me … when I realized I was earning just under $50 an hour at my day job (37.5 hours a week) and just under $200 an hour working on my side gigs for 10 to 15 hours a week," he says.

In November 2019 he quit his job and he hasn't looked back.

PAYOFF VERSUS TRADE-OFF

What's a side hustle, anyway? There are gigs that pay the equivalent of minimum wage or less and those that pay hundreds of dollars per hour. Some you can pick up on the fly and start earning money with right away. Others require you to buy equipment, learn new skills, or spend a considerable amount of time hustling before any real cash starts coming in. And, of course, there's everything in between.

Asking what makes a side hustle worth your while may seem like an impossible question, but there's a simple framework you can use to tackle it: every gig has a payoff and a trade-off. The payoff includes your take-home pay, the enjoyment and mental benefit you'll draw from whatever you're doing, and any potential to improve your long-term financial situation or emotional well-being. The trade-off includes any barriers to entry you'll have to overcome to get going — money you'll need to set yourself up, time you'll have to spend on preliminary research or training — as well as a measure of how long it will take for your hustle to become profitable. You should also think about what you'll be giving up to pursue your gig: Is it aimless nighttime scrolling on your phone or storytime with the kids?

If the payoff you expect from the side gig is low, the trade-off must also be low for it to be worth your while. If the sole purpose of working more is to earn a few extra bucks for a short-term goal, the additional lift should be small. For example, if you're stuck working from home all day and need a stroll after lunch, dog walking could be a low-payoff, low-trade-off gig for you, says Jackie Lam, the L.A. personal finance writer. You're not going to make oodles of cash, but you need a breath of fresh air anyway, so why not turn your mental-health break into a money-making opportunity?

On the other hand, if the expected payoff of your side hustle is high, it may be worth it even if the trade-off is also high. That was the case for Engen. It took around six months before his blog started earning any money, and for a while it was just enough to pay his heating bill, he says. The time commitment was also a big trade-off. For nine years he took hardly any time off. He would keep writing blog posts through Christmas week. In the end, though, it paid off handsomely. The gig led to a higher income and a job he loves that he can do from wherever he wants. "Everything I do is just from my laptop and I can do it from anywhere," he says.

Engen thought his side gig had true potential, even before he started thinking about ditching his full-time job. He knew if his blog started attracting considerable traffic, some real money would be coming in from advertising deals. He had read about other personal finance authors who eventually sold their blogs for a tidy sum. And from the very beginning, there was also a big emotional payoff in writing.

Even if you're happy with the job you have, a gig can help you quietly hone some skills that might propel you up the corporate ladder. Just make sure your employer is okay with you working on the side.

The bottom line is, if your side hustle has a bigger purpose, it may be worth some significant hassle.

Online platforms, on the other hand, can land you in the low-payoff, high-trade-off zone. You'd think sites that connect freelancers with paying customers would be a slam dunk for making some extra cash fast. Often, though, you'll be wading into what Lam calls a "saturated market." If there are lots of people out there offering the same services you're trying to sell, you may find yourself competing against talented folks in places like India or Ukraine — or a small town in Middle America — who have 500 five-star reviews and seem to be able to somehow survive by charging ridiculously low fees. It may take you a while to break in, and even when you do, you may not bring in the kind of money you were hoping for.

If you're considering a side gig that comes with any meaningful barrier to entry or investment of time, take a long, hard look at the potential payoff first, Lam says. How are you going to make money? Who else has succeeded in doing what you're trying to do? How did they do it? How long did it take? How many others didn't make it? If you jump into a high-trade-off side gig without thinking things through, there's a danger you'll wind up sticking with it for far too long just because you need to justify the money and time you've already spent on it, Lam warns.

One of the advantages of low-trade-off, low-payoff gigs is "it's easier to give up," she says. "You can deliver food or you can walk a dog or something like that, then if it's not working out, you can always search for something new," she says. But if you've dropped $300 on a new piece of software and have yet to make that money back three months later or spent hours upon hours recording videos that just aren't catching on, it's going to be much more difficult to recognize that you need to pivot.

That's why Lam suggests setting out stepping stones. Perhaps the goal is to make enough money to pay for one utility bill within the first three months. If you're not at that stage by then, it's time to drop it. And maybe by year one the threshold is having enough cash saved up for a vacation — otherwise it's time to take a break from this particular side hustle. You get the idea.

A high-payoff, low-trade-off side gig sounds almost like a scam. *Yes, ma'am, easy work and make lots of money very fast. Great success!* That is, if you go work for Borat.

But this unicorn of the gig world does actually exist, says Lam. She recalls the story of a mover she once interviewed, who lived in New York City and started up a side business on TaskRabbit, the online marketplace that connects customers with people who can help with everyday tasks like cleaning, grocery shopping, raking the leaves, or moving. This mover cornered his market like a master, Lam says. He knew there was lots of demand out there from people who needed help dragging their belongings from one rental apartment to the next. "New York City is a very transient city," says Lam, and hardly anyone owns a car. But the mover also knew he had a key advantage over most of his competitors. Not only did he own a van, but he had all the equipment he used in his main job. The furniture blankets, the dollies, everything you could possibly need during a move. The mover did so well he eventually dropped his regular job and set up his own business, which he liked better because he could set his own schedule, Lam says.

The high-payoff, high-trade-off sweet spot often involves leveraging skills, experience, or equipment you already have and finding the perfect niche where what you're offering is rare but a lot of people need it. The secret sauce, in other words, is finding a way to use what you know or own in a market large enough where you have a competitive advantage. It ain't easy, but it's possible.

That said, if what you're doing in your side gig is very similar to what you do in your day job, watch out for two potential problems. First, your employer may not be pleased. If there's any doubt, always make sure you have a clear green light from your company to do whatever it is you want to do. Compromising your main source of income so you can make a few bucks on the side is definitely not worth it.

The second risk is burnout, Lam says. Doing the same type of work all the time can be exhausting, she warns. You may get to a point where you're super fast and earning a lot of money but you're also going on autopilot. Your brain never gets a chance to do something new and different.

Finally, allow me a word about income multipliers and passive income, for they are the Valyrian steel blades that can up your game from a regular Jon Snow to King in the North.

Income multipliers here have nothing to do with Keynesian economics (in case you just googled that). It's what happens when you find a way to grow your income for every given hour worked. Writing a newsletter that attracts an ever-larger number of paying subscribers is a good example of this. Your workload stays the same but if your fan base grows, so does your income.

Passive income is the powerful phenomenon by which your labour earns not one paycheque or invoice settlement but payment after payment after payment. Your work is done, but the money keeps coming in. It's when ad revenue flows into your account from people looking at a video you made two years ago. It's the cash that continues to grace your bank account from the affiliate marketing in your podcast. It's book and music royalties.

• • •

Wrap-Up

If you've been slaving away without much time to think about what you're getting in return — financially and emotionally — I hope this chapter gave you pause. It is so easy once you've climbed into the hamster wheel to just keep running because you're too busy, overwhelmed, and overworked all the time (I speak from experience). But you have to step down once in a while and take stock of what all that work is getting you. And if you don't like what you see, start plotting a different path.

Here are a few concrete steps to consider:

» Whether you're a nine-to-fiver or a freelancer or are holding down multiple gigs right now, it's a good idea to sit down at least once a year and analyze how much money you're *actually* making. Remember to account for all the money and time you're spending on your work.

» If you're an office worker contemplating the freelance life, or vice versa, you can use the apples-to-apples hourly-rate comparison formula to get an initial rough idea of how much money you'd have to make to maintain your lifestyle, if you take the leap.

» If you're wondering whether you're being paid fairly, you can try the over-under game with others in your field. You may be surprised by what you find.

» And if you have or are considering a side hustle, take a minute to think about your financial and career goals and evaluate the potential payoffs and trade-offs involved.

Finally, let's go back for a second to the concept of passive income. Of course, it's not just about royalties and ad revenue. Another way to generate passive income is to get your own money to make more money, also known as investing. That's the topic of the next couple of chapters.

CHAPTER 5

THE BIG FAT RETIREMENT MYTH

FOR DECADES, FACTORY and office workers alike believed in retirement with religious fervour. One day, they'd get to spend their Mondays through Fridays travelling, puttering around in the garden, or taking aquafit classes somewhere in Florida.

But if you're in your 20s or 30s and just starting to set money aside for your old age, you may be feeling skeptical about your own chances of ever reaching that stage. I'm here to say, it's not just you, it's everybody. Retirement has always been one of the trickiest parts of personal finance, and three big trends have only been making it more difficult over the years, especially for younger people. I'm talking about the gradual disappearance of employer pensions, the fact that we increasingly live longer but also take longer to land a decent job, and low interest rates (yes, that problem again).

We'll start with a quick look at how these three forces are likely complicating your efforts to build your own nest egg. Then we'll talk about what *retiring* actually means — because people have increasingly different ideas on the topic. Of course, we'll go over how much, when, and where to save for retirement and dispel all the jargon and mystery around registered retirement savings plans (RRSPs) and tax-free savings accounts (TFSAs). And finally, we'll discuss something I call nest-egg inequality, including why it matters and what you can do about it.

So, buckle up, put up your tray table, and forget your phone for the next little while. Here we go.

• • •

The Demise of Employer Pensions

Our collective faith in retirement is anchored in the idea of the good job with benefits and a pension. "That was always the thing that you were to strive for," remembers financial planner Alexandra Macqueen, one of Canada's top retirement experts.

Some 50 years ago, landing full-time employment often came with the promise that your employer would take care of you in retirement. This was usually in the form of a defined-benefit (DB) pension, which guarantees you receive a certain level of income in old age — often based on length of service and rank — for every year of retirement until death. It is a pretty sweet deal and one that, as of 1977, was part of the standard employment package for more than 40 percent of Canadian workers.

Today, if you're a millennial or Gen Zer working in the private sector, a DB pension has become a bit like a sasquatch: we've heard of them, but no one's actually seen one up close. In 2018, just 25 percent of working Canadians had a DB pension plan, and the vast majority of those were people in government jobs.

Private-sector companies often have something called a defined-contribution (DC) pension, where both you and your employer usually pay into the retirement plan. For example, you contribute 5 percent of your paycheque every month and your employer tops that up with a matching amount.

As the name suggests, what's defined — or guaranteed — here is the money that goes into the plan, not the money you'll get in retirement. Your retirement income from the plan will depend on things like how much you and your employer put in, how the plan was managed, and the performance of your investments. If you're wondering whether this sort of arrangement is even worthy of the name pension, you're not alone. "DC pensions, despite their name ... offer no promises of lifetime income," Macqueen and co-author Moshe Milevsky wrote in their book on retirement, *Pensionize Your Nest Egg.*[1]

And yet, DC plans where your employer puts in at least some of the money are still significantly better than having to save up for retirement all on your own. For example, a plan where you put in 5 percent of your monthly compensation and your company pitches in another 5 percent is like having a guaranteed 100 percent return, because the employer's contribution doubles your own. That's nothing to sneeze at.

There are also a handful of plans set up as hybrids between a DB and a DC plan, where the employer guarantees a minimum benefit and you add in the gravy with your own contributions. But the thing is, having *any* kind of workplace pension — DB, DC, or hybrid — is becoming rarer these days. Only around 37 percent of working Canadians have one today, down from 46 percent in 1977, according to data from Statistics Canada. And those numbers become even more striking when you look at the public versus private sectors. In 2018, a whopping 87 percent of public-sector workers had a pension, which is actually an increase from 1977, when around 75 percent of them did. In the private sector, by contrast, less than a quarter of workers were lucky enough to have an employer pension in 2018, down from around 35 percent in 1977.[2]

Even if you're one of the lucky private-sector workers with a DB pension, the promise of set payouts in retirement isn't exactly ironclad. You may remember what happened when Sears Canada went bankrupt in 2017: retirees eventually ended up having to take a significant haircut on their pensions. With company DB plans underfunded in Canada, it is entirely possible — and some would even say inevitable — that we'll see more of these pensions end up à la Sears. And if you're in the public sector with a pension, chances are you may not work for the government forever.

Bottom line: most of us will have to save our way to retirement by ourselves. This means figuring out how much to save and where to put the money — not to mention mastering the willpower and discipline to actually do it — and, last but not least, trying to grow our miserly savings into something that will fill in for a paycheque when we're no longer working.

• • •

Longer Lives and Slower Starts

Having to stitch together your own retirement with duct tape and paper clips like a money-minded MacGyver sounds challenging enough. But wait, it gets better (by which I really mean worse).

Also working against you are your increasingly good odds of becoming a centenarian. Today a healthy 30-year-old man in Canada has a 10 percent chance to make it to age 98. A healthy woman has the same probability of living to 101. And a heterosexual couple in good health faces the same odds that at least one of them will still be alive at age 102.[3] While I'm sure we're all strongly in favour of sticking around in this world for as long as possible, the scientific miracles that are lengthening our lifespans are also complicating the retirement equation. Living longer means more years to cover with your hard-earned savings and a higher chance of developing costly disabilities in old age.

Meanwhile, the official retirement age in Canada is still 65. If you take that as the goalpost, the problem isn't just that we're living longer and longer past that age and therefore have more retirement years to pay for. The issue is also that the length of time we spend working before hitting the big 6-5 is getting shorter, which means less time to save. Once upon a time, the idea was that most people would start working a full-time job at 22, if not earlier, and be able to hold it down until they didn't want to work that job anymore. People switched jobs because they wanted to. Even those who didn't have a company pension would have more than 40 years to save for retirement.

I don't need to tell you how far-fetched that scenario sounds to many of us who entered the job market between the financial meltdown of 2008 and the corona-mageddon of 2020. Of course, it is still possible to graduate from school debt-free and proceed to land a great job at 22. These people exist. If you studied computer science, engineering, or some such tech-related, math-heavy wizardry and did co-op work throughout school, you may well pull off the miracle of landing a well-paid, steady job in your early 20s with zero student debt. Training to be a plumber is another good way of doing that. But we can't all crunch code and clear clogs.

Higher education remains, for the most part, a worthy investment, but it increasingly demands more than a simple two- or four-year degree. And once you finally get out of school, your first few years after graduation are often a quagmire of barely paid internships, gigs, and contract work. It's not until the late 20s or early 30s that many of us (but not all) finally land a somewhat steady full-time job.

Now, if you're 30 and you're supposed to retire at 65, that leaves just 35 years to save up enough to sustain yourself for what potentially will be another 35 years of non-work. "You're going to have a retirement as long as your entire working life," Macqueen says. And that right there requires some math wizardry worthy of a computer engineer.

• • •

Low Interest Rates

You might be thinking you've got your work cut out for you at this point. But wait, there's more. In that rather short period in which you're supposed to save up for three decades plus of retirement, you're also going to have to think very carefully about what to do with the money you're painstakingly setting aside.

That's because interest rates have been stubbornly low for more than 20 years. This cuts two ways. On the one hand, as I've said before, they make it cheap to borrow. On the other hand, they make it hard to grow your savings. Back in the time when *E.T.* first hit the theatres (circa 1982), the classic thing to do with your retirement savings was to buy GICs, or guaranteed investment certificates. These investments work somewhat like putting money into a savings account. You lock up some of your savings with a financial institution for a set number of months or years and, at the end of the term, get it all back plus a certain amount of interest. Up to set limits, your deposit is protected by the federal government, which makes GICs super safe.

Basically, with GICs, "you just went to the bank and parked your money there," Macqueen says. When interest rates were in the double digits, that worked out just fine. In September of 1981 you would have been able to buy a one-year GIC with an eye-popping interest rate of 19 percent — *19 percent*! Today, you're lucky if your GIC earns more than the rate of inflation, which in recent history has been about 2 percent. Of course, inflation in the early 1980s was also quite high, but you could still get a nice investment return using GICs.

But with interest rates as low as they are today, many savers have to rely at least in part on the stock market to deliver the kind of returns needed for a halfway decent retirement. And while investing in the financial market these days isn't nearly as scary or complicated as many people think it is, it still requires a bit more initiative and awareness than just stashing all your cash in GICs. And, of course, investing in the stock market involves a higher risk that you won't get the returns you'd like (much more on all of this in the next chapter).

• • •

The Retirement Myth

Given the way these trends have evolved, chasing the traditional idea of retirement is starting to feel like trying to fit a square peg into a round hole. So part of the solution may be to let go of that old-fashioned concept.

The retirement ideal only really worked for a limited number of people during a limited period of time, anyway — and most of those people were men. While it's true that generous pensions used to be much more common than they are today, they were never all *that* common. Even going back to the late 1970s and early 1980s, more than half of the working population had no retirement benefits at all. In 1977, less than 36 percent of women had a pension, a smaller share than the coverage rate for both men and women today. "There's never been population-wide DB plan coverage," Macqueen says. "It's always been mostly limited to the old model of the workforce, which is a single individual, male, working over their career for a single employer."

Pretty much anybody working part-time, which was often women, didn't have a pension, Macqueen adds. Of course, many women — whether in the workforce or not — would be able to rely on their husband's retirement plan. But the point stands: the mythical golden age where every working Canadian had a pension never existed. A sizable share of the population always had to rely on themselves and government benefits for their retirement.

And what to make of the belief that life comes organized into three neat phases — school, work, and retirement? That's never been the case for working women. Their careers have always been stop and go, with periods of unemployment or scaled-back work to care for young children or aging family members, and sometimes the need to switch to a different line of work after a long employment gap.

Today, life is becoming more fluid and messier for everybody. Going back to school mid-career or having to regularly update and upgrade your skills, for example, is becoming more common, even though our school system still presumes we need education only before entering the workforce.

On the plus side, life doesn't have to switch to retirement mode at 65, either. It's easier to keep working beyond that age, which prolongs your earning years and shrinks the no-income period. This isn't to say we should all happily work a 40-hour week well into our 70s. But it's time to stop treating not being able to retire at 65 as an unimaginable hardship or the ultimate financial failure. Unless your job is physically taxing or you started working in your early 20s, there's nothing wrong with retiring a few years later. In fact, as we all live longer and healthier lives, many countries have already pushed back the official retirement age to 67 or 68.

Besides, retirement is becoming less and less of a black-and-white pivot from work to non-work. Increasingly, retirement is more of a slow and gradual downshifting from working all the time to working less. Perhaps that means trading the office for some freelance consulting, giving you longer vacations and more time to smell the roses while still earning an income. Even if you don't like your job or it doesn't easily convert into a freelance gig, there are more and more ways nowadays for semi-retirees to make an extra buck to supplement their lifestyles. People put their basements on Airbnb or rent out their parking spots. And some find ways to monetize their hobbies, whether it's selling their crochet work on Etsy or teaching yoga classes.

• • •

Financial Independence

The classic idea of retirement may seem increasingly unattainable. But for a growing number of people it's also becoming undesirable. Many boomers are opting for semi-retirement, often striking out as independent professionals after a lifetime in the office — not because they need the money, but because they like working on their own terms.

And many millennials have taken to the financial independence, retire early movement. You've heard me mention FIRE a few times in this book already. As I said in chapter 1, FIRE has a powerful vision: "retiring" super early, usually in your 30s or 40s. You may have read of people who managed to build a retirement fund of $1 million or more by the time most common mortals are just starting to climb the first rungs of the office ladder. That usually involves spending very little and saving 50 percent or more of their after-tax income for years. It also often requires a very well-paying job or moving abroad to a low-cost country where even a middling paycheque will go a lot further. But what many FIRE fans really mean by *retirement* is achieving the financial freedom of leaving the corporate rat race and being able to earn money when and how they want. Basically, a kind of very long semi-retirement.

And then there are those people who love their jobs and think the concept of retirement should itself be retired. These are usually healthy people who earn well and really like what they do for a living. They see absolutely no reason why they shouldn't keep doing it for as long as they possibly can.

Where do you stand in all this? Are you aiming for old-fashioned retirement in your 60s, are you ready to work — at least part-time — for years after that, or are you hoping to reach financial freedom early on?

Regardless of what the word *retirement* means to you, I hope we can all agree that having the *ability* to stop working or to scale back at some point in your life, if you so choose, is as important as it's ever been. And that, really, is what financial independence is all about. Pursuing this FIRE-style is its own thing, and there are plenty of books out there on how to do it. But if you're happy, as I am, to aim for financial independence at some point further off into the future, here are the basics to set you on the right track.

• • •

The Road to Financial Independence

Now that you are fully aware of the challenges ahead and unencumbered by outdated beliefs about retirement, let us embark on the road to financial independence with a fighting spirit and a peaceful mind. You can stand strong in the knowledge that many of the big financial independence questions actually have answers.

HOW MUCH SHOULD I SAVE?

How much money are you going to need to be able to get by without working when you're older? That's the mother of all retirement questions, and there are a number of answers a quick web search will turn up.

One is that you should aim for a retirement income target equal to around 70 percent of your pre-tax income in the last years of your career. This is a common piece of advice but doesn't actually work that well for many people. If you were making good money, for example, targeting 70 percent of your paycheque could actually be way more than you need. Think about it: when people are in their 40s and 50s, their income likely goes to things like the mortgage and kids. But by the time they're ready to leave full-time work, they probably won't have most of those expenses, meaning that their routine costs will be greatly reduced. Frederick Vettese, a former actuary and one of Canada's most influential authors on retirement, estimates homeowners may only need the equivalent of 50 percent of their pre-retirement earnings.[4]

On the other hand, if your income isn't that high or you're renting, you may need to aim for more than 70 percent. If your paycheque was barely enough to cover essential costs, it's risky to assume you'll be able to get by on less when you're not working. And if you're a renter, your housing costs will likely remain steady throughout your life. On yet another hand, Macqueen points out that many low-income Canadians will have stabler and higher income in retirement than during their working years because the CPP will cover more of their retirement income, proportionally, than it does for

CALCULATING YOUR RETIREMENT SAVINGS GOAL LATER ON

Once you start to have an idea of what kind of retirement you want, you can follow these steps to estimate how much you might need to save, Engen says:

1. Estimate your yearly expenses in retirement. To do this, I take my current expenses as a starting point and then think about how my life is likely to be different once I cross over into retirement. For example, my mortgage will be paid off (I sure hope) and I won't have commuting costs. On the other hand, I would really like to go back to globe-trotting before I'm too old, so my annual travel budget will need a big boost. There's much more to think about, but you get the idea.

2. Multiply your annual retirement expenses by the number of years you think you're going to spend in retirement.

3. Subtract a conservative estimate of the government retirement benefits you'll be receiving, such as CPP and OAS. It's important to include this step because CPP and OAS can make a big difference to your bottom line in retirement. Your savings target will likely look significantly smaller and more achievable when you take these benefits into account. But don't make the mistake of assuming you'll get the maximum CPP payout. A safer bet may be to use the average amount going out to retirees, which you can find on the government's CPP overview page.

   Calculate how much you need to save every year to reach your retirement savings goal. At the end of step three, you'll have your overall savings target; now you need to calculate how much you need to save every year to get there. You can use an online calculator like the Savings Goal Solver on the website The Measure of a Plan.

higher-income earners. When Old Age Security (OAS) is added to CPP, income security and stability increases further for low-income Canadians, Macqueen adds.

Another popular type of catch-all savings target is based on your age and income. For example, by 30 you should have the equivalent of one year's worth of salary saved up; by 40 the equivalent of three years of salary; by 50 the equivalent of five years of salary; and so on. If you've ever googled *how much to save for retirement*, you've come across this kind of advice. If you have, you can also forget about it, says Robb Engen, the financial planner and author of *Boomer & Echo*. "I don't think those benchmarks are all that useful. We all come out of the starting gate at different ages and with different circumstances," Engen says.

The same goes for most calculators you're likely to find on one of those Google searches. "I remember using one of those online retirement calculators when I was younger and feeling pretty depressed when it told me I needed to save thousands of dollars a month to reach my retirement goals," Engen says.

The thing is, the starting point for any kind of customized retirement math is an estimate of how much you'll need to live on and for how many years. But even a rough guess about your retirement expenses is usually a pretty useless exercise when you're in your 20s or early 30s, Engen says. "We don't really know what our life will look like 5, 10, or 20 years down the road," he says.

The only thing that really matters is figuring out how much you can afford to save for retirement and setting up automatic contributions to a long-term investment fund (more details on this later in this chapter and in chapter 6). "It's about making it automatic and just establishing that savings habit early rather than focusing on 'I need to save 10 percent, I need to save 50 percent or whatever,'" Engen says. It's fine if all you can spare at the beginning is just 2 or 3 percent of your paycheque, he adds. For example, it doesn't make sense to put all your extra cash into a retirement fund when you have student loans to pay off, plan to buy a car, or are getting married in a couple of years, he says.

Instead, figure out how much you need to set aside for short-term savings goals and how much you can truly afford to save for retirement. Then set up those automatic transfers to your financial independence fund "and just give yourself raises every year in terms of adding to your retirement savings," Engen says. When you're a bit older and better able to envision what retirement might look like, you can try some back-of-the-napkin calculations to get a rough idea of your savings target. See the box for more on this.

Keep in mind, though, that you may not be able to hit your savings target every year, so plan to revise your basic retirement math once in a while as your circumstances change. And, needless to say, a financial planner can come up with a much more detailed and nuanced retirement road map for you.

WHEN SHOULD I START SAVING?

As retirement questions go, this one is easy peasy. The answer is *now*. The sooner you start, the easier it's going to be to reach financial independence. And by easier, I mean exponentially easier.

I'm not talking about the simple adding up of your savings over time. It's pretty obvious that if you're putting away $500 a month, or $6,000 a year, for 30 years, you'll have more money by retirement than if you'd been doing it for only 20 years. To be precise, you'd be looking at $180,000 versus $120,000. But the difference between saving for 30 versus 20 years becomes much bigger if you take into account compound interest, the ability to earn interest on interest. Albert Einstein is said to have called compound interest "the eighth wonder of the world" — and whether or not the quote actually comes from him, it is absolutely accurate.

Here's how compound interest works in practice. For simplicity's sake, let's say you're depositing $6,000 at the end of the year instead of $500 every month. And let's also imagine you're putting your money into a fictional savings account that earns a fantastical interest rate of 5 percent per year. For now, let's look at what would happen if you simply put in $6,000 and then stopped. After 12 months, your $6,000 has earned $300 in interest. That's an extra $300 right there just because you left your money untouched for a year. But it gets better the following year. You will earn another 5 percent, except this time it's 5 percent of $6,300, or $315. In total, you now have $6,615. The year after that, your money grows by 5 percent of $6,615 to $6,946, and so on.

This is powerful stuff. The longer you leave your money in your account, the mightier the effect of compound interest becomes. And if you keep adding to your savings, the impact will be greater still. Over 30 years, your annual deposits of $6,000 will grow to nearly $400,000, of which almost $220,000 is the interest you've earned. That's right, your $180,000 in deposits over 30 years would turn into more than twice as much, thanks to the magic of compound interest.

But that same mathematical spell isn't quite so impressive when you save for only 20 years. Your $120,000 in deposits grow to just under $200,000 over two decades. That's *half* what you'd get if you'd had 10 more years to save. Thanks to compound interest, the $60,000 difference between what you put in over 20 years and over 30 years has grown to a more than $200,000 difference in what you end up with. (If you're curious about what compound interest can do for you, you can try the compound interest calculator featured on GetSmarterAboutMoney.ca, a handy informational website brought to you by the Ontario Securities Commission.)

Now, sadly, this example also illustrates why low interest rates are such a problem for retirement. No real-life savings account these days bears an interest of 5 percent per year. In fact, it's not uncommon to see savings accounts offering a pitiful 0.01 percent, which makes them only marginally preferable to your mattress as a receptacle for your money. Even some of the most competitive savings accounts in Canada had to trim their annual interest rates to less than 2 percent because of the economic downturn triggered by Covid-19 — and it doesn't get much better with GICs.

The good news is that you can get higher rates of return by investing in the stock market. Of course, the tricky part about this is that stocks are notoriously volatile. We'll get into this in the next chapter, but for now, suffice it to say that when you smooth out those ups and downs over many years, most major stock markets have produced solid annual average returns for the past several decades.

The moral of the story here is that compound interest is a formidable weapon when you're fighting to secure your financial independence. And time is what supercharges that weapon. The earlier you start to save and invest, the more compound interest will do the heavy lifting for you. For example, if you wanted to retire with, say, $500,000 by 65 — assuming our usual average return of 5 percent per year — you'd only have to save $337 per month if you started at 25. But if you began only five years later, at 30, you'd have to sock away $451. (I've deliberately left inflation out of this. We'll get to that in the next chapter.)

But please don't feel like all is lost if you haven't started saving and investing yet. It is not — far from it. Not everyone has $337 a month to spare in their 20s — I certainly did not. Just because you didn't start putting money away for retirement fresh out of school doesn't mean you've missed the boat. You can still get on that boat. You can *always* get on that boat.

Of course, if you're starting at, say, 40, you'll have to be more aggressive. On the flip side, your income is now probably quite a bit higher and stabler. Also, it's not unreasonable to think you'll be retiring later than 65, which, as I said before, allows you to stretch out your time horizon. That said, it's important not to get carried away thinking you have decades and decades ahead of you. Aiming to work until 75 is an aspirational goal if you love your job, not something you'd want to use in your retirement calculations. Who knows how you'll be feeling, physically and mentally, by age 75? And, depending on your field of work, it may not be possible for you to keep going for that long even if you're able to.

That said, aiming for 67 or 68 seems like a realistic target date for a prudent retirement plan — and it can still make a difference. Assuming you're 40 and want to retire with half a million dollars, you'll need to save around $700 a month to get there by 68, versus around $850 per month by 65.

WHERE SHOULD I SAVE?

As we just saw, harnessing the power of compound interest is key to securing a comfortable future for Old You in the absence of a generous company pension. One way to do that is to start saving right away so compound interest will have the longest possible time to do its thing. Another way of taking advantage of compound interest is to ensure your savings actually earn a decent return. Money left in the cookie jar does not grow into more money. And savings left lingering in a savings account or GIC with a pitiful interest rate won't do much for you, either.

Taxes are also a big deal when it comes to compound interest. At whatever speed your savings are growing through compound interest, taxes slow it down. It's a bit like driving with the handbrake on.

To keep things simple, let's go back to our example of the fictional savings account with fantastical interest of 5 percent per year. It is, once again, the end of year two, and your $6,000 has turned into $6,300. Now, that $300 in interest, just like the rest of your income, is normally subject to tax. If the tax rate is, say, 20 percent, $60 of that $300 would go to the government, leaving you with $240. You now have $6,240 — instead of $6,300 — available to earn that five-per-cent interest in year three.

Over time, the impact of taxes can make a big difference. Over 30 years in our example you'd lose tens of thousands of dollars to taxes. Luckily, in Canada there are two great options to lessen the impact of taxes on your retirement savings: RRSPs and TFSAs.

» WHAT ARE RRSPs AND TFSAs?

In my job at Global News, I've often heard readers refer to RRSPs as if they were an investment, as in, "Where can I buy an RRSP?" Let's clear this up before I go any further: RRSPs — and TFSAs, for that matter — are *not* investments or something you need to buy. They are special kinds of accounts, similar to the chequing and savings accounts in which you keep your everyday money and short-term savings. Both RRSPs and TFSAs are registered with the federal government and come with certain tax advantages. You can open an RRSP or TFSA at financial institutions such as banks, credit unions, or insurance companies.

RRSPs and TFSAs have two main things in common. First, you can invest money you put into them. Second, the money you make on those investments isn't taxed while it's sitting inside those accounts, which is a big deal. RRSPs and TFSAs are a beautiful gift from the government — they're Ottawa's way of helping Canadians help themselves when it comes to growing their savings. And it is absolutely imperative to grab a hold of that helping hand.

Still, this being the government, there are a ton of rules around how much money you can put in or take out of either type of account. For example, you need to have earned income in order to contribute to an RRSP. The amount of money you can put in every year is capped at 18 percent of the income you declared on your tax return the previous year, up to a ceiling ($29,210 for tax year 2022). If you can't afford to contribute the maximum every year, you can save what you can, which is always better than nothing. With an RRSP, any unused contribution room carries forward to future years, but if you didn't earn any money in a particular year, you don't get any contribution room for that year. Also, you must close your RRSP by the end of the year in which your turn 71. When it's time to start taking money out in old age, you can convert your RRSP into a registered retirement income fund (RRIF), use it to buy an annuity (a financial product that provides guaranteed regular payments), or cash out your savings.

With a TFSA, you need to be at least 18 to open one. The annual contribution limit as of 2021 was $6,000, although in the past it's been as high as $10,000 and as low as $5,000. This also carries over, but you don't need to be earning money to earn your TFSA contribution room. This means, among other things, that the TFSA is a good place to stash any windfall money you might receive. If a mysterious aunt you never knew you had left you a small fortune or you stumbled upon a pot of gold at the end of the rainbow, nothing would prevent you from putting that money into a TFSA, provided you had enough room.

Is your head spinning yet? Not to worry, it takes a bit to familiarize yourself with all the rules (and what you've just read is only a partial list). But there is one big difference between RRSPs and TFSAs you should focus on: what happens tax-wise when you put money in and when you take money out.

» Putting money in: With an RRSP, there's no tax on money going into the account. That's why you can get a tax refund for deposits into an RRSP. The government is returning the tax you already paid on the money you used to make a contribution. Just remember you have 60 days after the end of the year (usually until March 1) to put money into an RRSP for the previous year. That means, for example, that you can make a contribution for tax year 2022 on February 25, 2023, and deduct that amount from the income you declare on your 2022 tax return in the spring, which will likely lower your tax owing or net you a nice refund. With a TFSA, on the other hand, there is no tax break on money going in, so there is no refund.

» Taking money out: In my experience, everyone knows that when you use an RRSP, withdrawals are taxed, but with a TFSA they are not. But the thing is, neither type of account is a free lunch. With an RRSP, you get dinged when taking money out because you skipped the tax when putting money in. With a TFSA, you get a free pass on withdrawals but you likely gave the government a share before putting money in.

In short, with an RRSP your cash is taxed on the way out. With a TFSA, this usually happens before the money even goes in. This may seem like a simple difference but has countless ramifications. And you need to have a good grasp of these to decide where to put your retirement savings.

» AN RRSP IS A TAX TEETER-TOTTER; A TFSA IS A TAX BENCH

The best explanation I've ever heard of the main difference between an RRSP and a TFSA goes like this: the RRSP is a tax teeter-totter; the TFSA is a tax bench.

An RRSP works best if you're in a higher tax bracket when you put money in than when you take money out. As we've seen, this turns out to be the case for many people who don't need as much income in retirement as they did during their working lives. For example, imagine that, based on your income, you get a 30 percent tax refund on your RRSP contributions. When you retire, your income is lower and your tax rate is now at 20 percent, which is what you'll have to pay on those withdrawals. Bingo! The government gave you a 30 percent tax break on the way in but is now taxing you just 20 percent on the way out. In this case, the RRSP tax teeter-totter is sloping downward, which is great news for you.

On the other hand, the TFSA, as I said, is a tax bench. If you're contributing with money from your paycheque, every dollar is taxed based on your income that year, and that's that.

» TEETER-TOTTER OR BENCH?

If, like many ordinary mortals, you don't have enough cash to fill up both your RRSP and your TFSA every year, you need to think about whether you'll be better off sitting on a bench or a teeter-totter. This will depend on your specific situation.

For example, let's say your tax rate stays the same before and after retirement. In this scenario your RRSP teeter-totter would be flat, looking pretty much like a bench and, the teeter-totter wouldn't give you a tax advantage compared to a TFSA. In fact, using an RRSP to save for retirement could leave you worse off. That's because money withdrawn from an RRSP is income you have to report on your tax return. Those withdrawals could push up your taxable income, impacting your eligibility for government benefits such as OAS and the Guaranteed Income Supplement. On the other hand, withdrawals from your TFSA aren't taxable income. That money doesn't show up anywhere on your tax return and doesn't affect your benefits.

It's also good to keep in mind that the RRSP tax teeter-totter can end up sloping upward in some scenarios. For example, you're planning to rent out your basement to supplement your retirement. That extra income could push you into a higher tax bracket in retirement than you were during your working life, meaning the tax rate on your withdrawals will be higher than the rate at which you got your tax refunds on your contributions. The same thing could happen if you had other types of taxable income in retirement. With a TFSA, any withdrawals would have zero impact on the tax rate you would end up paying with that additional retirement income.

» *WHAT TO DO WITH YOUR TFSA*

In general, taking money out of a TFSA isn't just tax-free, it's also hassle-free.

When you withdraw from an RRSP before you close it, no later than age 71, you're not only subject to tax but you also lose the contribution room you used making the deposits you are now withdrawing. While nothing prevents you from maximizing your contributions every year after, you'll never be able to put back the money you took out. And when you close your RRSP and turn it into an RRIF or annuity, you have to start drawing down on your savings. RRIFs, for example, come with minimum annual withdrawals.

None of that holds for a TFSA. When you take funds out, you free up room for future deposits. You can recontribute the money in the following year, in addition to the contribution room for that year. And there is no obligation to start making withdrawals at a particular age.

Still, be careful about taking money out of your TFSA and then adding to it in the same year. While it's true that TFSA withdrawals free up contribution room, that room isn't added to your account until the following year. If you recontribute too soon and don't have enough room, you'll be dinged for having exceeded the yearly maximum. I know your eyes are probably glazing over reading this, so here's an example.

Say you've always contributed the maximum to your TFSA ever since you became eligible to have one. This year, you make your usual $6,000 deposit but then decide to take out $3,000 for a small reno project. But then you watch some DIY YouTube videos, read some home improvement blogs, and realize you can actually come up with a decent hack that won't cost you anything at all. What do you do with that $3,000 you no longer need? You need to wait until next year before putting that money back into your TFSA. Otherwise, the government will deem you to have overcontributed and will charge you a tax equal to 1 percent of the excess amount for each month that money remains in your account. All you need to do to avoid that is to sit still until January 1 rolls around. Then you'll be able to recontribute the $3,000 plus your usual annual $6,000 with zero consequences.

Overcontribution traps aside, though, the TFSA is more versatile than the RRSP. That's because the RRSP, which has been around since 1957, was designed specifically for retirement. The government wanted to help people save up for it but also wanted to make sure they'd use the money in old age. By contrast, the TFSA, which was first made available in 2009, works well for any number of things. Saving up in a TFSA helps you reach a short-term goal faster. And there are pluses to using it for your rainy-day fund, as well. The money is there for you to access at any point

But the bummer with using your TFSA for short-term savings is that you won't be earning much interest on that money, since it makes sense to keep things like your down payment, emergency money, and vacation slush fund in cash. That means you're not taking full advantage of the power of compound interest inside a TFSA.

Here's one way to look at it: using a TFSA for short-term savings makes the most of the account's flexibility. Using it for retirement— saving and investing for decades — maximizes its potential for tax-free growth.

A good starting point for solving this dilemma is to think about your present and likely future income and ask yourself whether you'd be better off saving in a tax teeter-totter like the RRSP or a tax bench like the TFSA. If the answer is the latter, you may want to use your TFSA for retirement first and foremost. That said, you can have more than one TFSA account as long as the total amount you contribute doesn't go over the annual maximum. One more point to consider, though, is that because RRSP withdrawals are such a pain to make, this can help you stay disciplined and not eat into your retirement fund ahead of time.

• • •

Nest-Egg Inequality

We've talked about why saving for retirement feels like swimming upstream. For every stroke you take toward financial independence, powerful currents are working against you: the slim chances of a proper pension, longer lifespans, later career starts, and low interest rates. But if you happen to be a woman, chances are you're facing an even stronger countercurrent.

Before I go any further, it's important to acknowledge that women are now more likely than men to have a defined-benefit pension plan in Canada because they're more likely to work in the public sector. Still, the numbers aren't high. In 2018, less than 3 in 10 female workers had a DB pension compared to 2 in 10 for men.[5]

But whatever you do for a living, if you're a woman, your retirement math is likely to get more complicated for two main reasons: one is biology, and the other is the fact that we're still a ways away from gender equality in the workplace.

Let's start with biology. Women usually live longer than men. This means that, all else being equal, they will likely have more retirement years to cover with their hard-saved money. Then there's the issue of how women's work is paid. When you look at the average hourly pay of both full-time and part-time workers in Canada, women earn just 87 cents for every dollar earned by men on average. Some of that difference is due to men and women concentrating in different occupations and female workers being more likely to be employed part-time. But nearly two-thirds of the gap remains, as Statistics Canada politely puts it, "unexplained."[6]

People of colour are likely to face an even wider wage gap. One 2018 Ontario study, for example, found that racialized men on average made just 76 cents for every dollar earned by their white peers. For women of colour the gap was larger still, with racialized female workers making only 58 cents for every dollar earned by white men.[7] An income gap exists among men and women with disabilities as well, although, as with race, the data we have on this is limited. The point here is that women still earn less than men, which means they have less money to save and invest to cover what will likely be a longer retirement.

And if you're a woman who has or plans to have kids, biology and social norms will likely combine to create yet another drag on your retirement savings. Maternity leave, for example, generally shaves off one or more of a woman's prime earning years, shortening the amount of time she has to work up to financial independence. Similarly, when women decide to switch to part-time work or a less demanding career after having kids, their earnings potential and ability to save for retirement usually take a hit. And while I know there's a growing number of dads sharing equally in the burden of raising tiny humans, the pandemic made this much clear: moms are still far more likely to be the ones faced with tough decisions about family versus work.

When you add up a longer life span, lower pay, and fewer years or hours of work, the result is that women can end up with considerably lower retirement savings. I'll show you what that looks like with a made-up example of a fictional Canadian couple, Joe and Jasmine, with help from Ilana Schonwetter, an investment adviser at B.C.–based credit union BlueShore Financial.

I'm going to use Joe and Jasmine, a heterosexual couple, to highlight the common retirements savings gap between men and women. However, the takeaways are relevant in other scenarios, too. If you're the lower-earning half of a same-sex couple, or if you've taken the lead in caring for children or older parents, you're likely in a retirement-saving conundrum similar to Jasmine's. Similarly, if you're single and have experienced pay disparity, you're at a disadvantage in saving for retirement, much like Jasmine. And if you're a single parent, you may be confronted with all of these issues, with little help or support from anyone else. Later in this chapter, we'll go over some advanced retirement-planning tactics that can help you bridge the gap. But first, let me introduce you to Joe and Jasmine.

MEET JOE AND JASMINE

Let's pretend Joe and Jasmine are two average Canadians who embark on their saving-for-retirement journey at the age of 30. Joe and Jasmine are pretty serious savers: every year, they manage to squirrel away 10 percent of their pre-tax pay. But Joe makes $80,000 a year and Jasmine only $69,600, which is the equivalent of 87 cents on Joe's dollar. This means that while Joe can stash away $667 a month, Jasmine can only save $580. If they invest the same way and retire at 68, how much money do they each end up with?

To keep things simple, we are going to forget about inflation and assume that Joe's and Jasmine's paycheques remain the same throughout their working lives. Now, let's fast forward to age 68. Both Joe and Jasmine have had the singular luck of enjoying uninterrupted employment for 38 years. But their fortunes are quite uneven when you look at the size of their nest eggs. With an average investment return of 5 percent per year, Joe's savings grow to an impressive $882,000, of which more than $577,000 comes from investment returns. Jasmine's retirement fund, on the other hand, ends up being just shy of $767,000, of which around $502,000 comes from investment returns.

Jasmine's nest egg is 87 percent of Joe's, which works out to a jaw-dropping difference of around $115,000.

But the gulf between the Joes and the Jasmines of this world can — and often does — quickly get even wider, according to Schonwetter. For one, if Jasmine had two kids and took two years off for maternity leave, she'd have to drastically scale back her contributions compared to Joe for two years. And those are years that occur fairly early on in Jasmine's working life, when her savings would have had lots of time to grow through compound interest. But the degree to which many working moms end up scaling back work goes well beyond maternity leave. It's also often a simple matter of family budget, Schonwetter says. With women more likely to be the lower earners in a dual-income household, "what ends up happening is that you end up paying more for child care for two kids than what you earn in the workplace."

This is a dynamic I saw at play during the pandemic when schools and daycares were shut down. In so many families, Mom had to drastically scale back her hours — or take leave or quit her job entirely — not because of some notion that Dad's job was more important, but simply because Dad made more money. So many couples with kids had to prioritize the job of the parent who came closest to paying all the bills. It was a rational decision, of course, but also a painful example of how the wage gap can become self-reinforcing.

And child care aside, women are also often dialing back or dropping out later in their work life as well, often in the crucial years just before retirement when many kid- and mortgage-free people manage to drastically ramp up their savings, Schonwetter says. That's because once the kids are (at least somewhat) independent, older parents start to require more and more help. Even when it's his parents who need assistance, it's almost always the woman who steps up, according to Schonwetter. "Out of the hundreds and hundreds of clients with whom I have worked over the years, I cannot think of a single example where the man has taken extended leave off work or has transitioned to part-time to take care of elderly parents," she says.

There's also another issue that tends to magnify the difference between Joe's and Jasmine's nest eggs even further. Women tend to be more risk averse with their investments than men, Schonwetter says. "When I talk to clients around their priorities — 'What's most important to you? Growth, stability, safety?' — for women usually the top priority is the safety and the low volatility of the portfolio," she says. But that, she adds, "comes at the price of a slightly lower rate of return."

I'll say much more about stocks, risk, and volatility in the next chapter. But here, let's look at how even the slightly lower rate of return Schonwetter mentions can affect Jasmine's retirement prospects. Let's rerun the example with a couple of tweaks. In addition to taking two years off work to have kids, Jasmine switched to part-time work at 60 percent of her usual hours for a year after the end of both of her maternity leaves. Also, as men generally take more risks with their savings, Joe's investments grew at an annual rate of 5.5 percent before retirement and 4.5 percent after. For Jasmine that was 5 percent before retirement and 4 percent after.

In this scenario, according to Schonwetter's calculations, Joe ends up with around $992,000 at age 68, Jasmine with $756,000. That's 76 cents on Joe's dollar for Jasmine. Now, let's imagine that Joe lives to be 95 and Jasmine 97. Joe's nest egg will yield a plush $5,273 per month in retirement income from his own savings. Jasmine's, on the other hand, will provide $3,660 — only 69 cents for every dollar Joe gets to enjoy in retirement.

HOW TO CRACK NEST-EGG INEQUALITY

If you're thinking that women ending up with fewer retirement savings is depressing, I'm here to say, it doesn't have to be so. You can scramble the nest-egg inequality math and eat it up for breakfast.

Let's focus on Jasmine first. Whether or not she has a Joe in her life, she needs to take a hard look at her investment decisions. When female clients tell Schonwetter their number one priority is the safety of their investments, she says she lays down the options. "If we are going to place this high importance on low volatility, it does mean that you have a lower rate of return and that we need to address that," Schonwetter says. And there are three ways to do so: "You can try to save a little more, you can retire a little later, or you can take on a little bit more risk."

Taking on more risk doesn't mean pushing yourself to do something you're uncomfortable with. It means learning more about investing. "Educate yourself on how money works," Schonwetter says. "Understand what different investment vehicles can do." The more people know about financial markets, the more likely they are to feel comfortable taking on a little more risk, she adds. But you need to get on it quickly. "Each year that you wait or kick the can down the road just means that there is so much more that you need to do to achieve the same result," Schonwetter notes.

Now let's look at Jasmine and Joe as a couple. There are a few simple hacks they can use to smooth out their nest-egg inequality. First, Joe could set up a spousal or common-law partner RRSP for Jasmine.[8] He could then start making regular contributions to top up Jasmine's own RRSP contributions. In the earlier example, Joe contributed $667 per month, or about $8,000 a year, to his RRSP. Instead, he could contribute $7,600 a year to his RRSP and $400 per year to Jasmine's, Schonwetter says. This, on top of Jasmine's $6,960 annual contribution ($580 per month for a year), would bring her annual retirement savings to $7,360. Joe should also ramp up his contributions to the spousal RRSP when Jasmine is on maternity leave and during her stretches of part-time work. On the flip side, if Jasmine happens to be out-earning Joe, the two should consider setting up a spousal RRSP for him.

The two may want to stop short of evening out their nest eggs perfectly, Schonwetter says. That's because if Joe passed away before Jasmine, she'd inherit any funds left in his retirement account. This would increase her monthly withdrawals and could put her in a higher tax bracket. If you open a spousal RRSP for your spouse or common-law partner, it is registered in their name. They're the only one who can withdraw money or make investment decisions, whoever puts the money in. Any contributions you make to a spousal RRSP reduce your contribution room for the year but not your partner's. On the other hand, you get the tax deduction for the contributions. By splitting your income more evenly in retirement, a spousal RRSP can result in a lower income-tax bill.

If Jasmine and Joe are using TFSAs to save for retirement, whoever makes more can gift some funds to the other every year to help them boost their contributions, Schonwetter says. This also holds if Joe and Jasmine happened to make enough money to save both into their RRSPs and their TFSAs.

And last, but certainly not least, there's a lot Joe can do to support Jasmine's career and earnings potential. For example, he can take more than a miserable two weeks of vacation after the birth of his children and share some of the parental leave to help Jasmine go back to work sooner, if that's important to her and her career prospects. I know dads still often face a stigma for taking extended periods off work to care for their own babies, but hopefully that will be less and less the case now that parents who share parental leave can receive several extra weeks of leave through employment insurance.

Joe can also act like the capable human being he is by *owning* several household and child-care tasks — from the planning stage to implementation. This means, for example, that he's not just getting the groceries but actually writing up a list after planning the week's meals. He can keep track of things like school supplies, pediatrician's appointments, and which kid needs a new pair of shoes. Sharing in the mental load[9] that comes with running a household will make it much easier for Jasmine to stay in her job full-time, if that's what she wants.

• • •

Wrap-Up

This chapter started with the familiar narrative that big trends are making it more complicated to save for retirement. By now, you've heard that refrain about a lot of run-of-the-mill financial goals in this book. But when it comes to retirement, there's a silver lining for Gen Z and millennials: time is on our side. If you've been following along, by now you know what a game changer it is to start preparing for retirement early on.

And that prep work goes far beyond squirrelling away a bit of money every month (although, of course, that's the all-important step one). So whether you've been saving for years or are just starting now, here are some things to think about:

» To save for retirement, you need to have a good handle on your cash flow. The money-bucket system from chapter 1 will help you do just that. Once you know how much you can set aside for retirement, see if you can set up automatic transfers to help you stay on track. And if you can, as Engen suggests, make sure to increase those contributions every year to keep up with inflation or pay raises.

» I hope this chapter has made it clear that *where* you put your retirement savings matters a great deal. RRSPs and TFSAs can give you a huge leg-up. Thinking about what tax bracket you're in now, how much your income is likely to increase through your career, and what level of income you can expect in retirement will help you figure out whether you'd be better off with a tax teeter-totter like the RRSP or a tax bench like the TFSA. But remember, taxes aren't the only consideration to choose between the two. Also, if you have money to fill up both, all the better.

» If you're in a couple that could end up with nest-egg inequality, consider spousal RRSP contributions or beefed-up transfers to the TFSA of the lower-earning partner to reduce the disparity.

Yes, we have time. But the ultimate magic combo to supercharge your retirement savings is time *plus* compound interest. In other words, you need to invest your money to make the most of your time. For that, let's head over to chapter 6.

CHAPTER 6

LEARNING ABOUT INVESTING: NOT OPTIONAL

LET'S START THIS chapter with a personality test. Imagine this is a glossy magazine you just bought because your tired eyeballs needed a break from all the computer screens, scrolling, and tablet reading. You lie down on the couch — if you have kids, let's pretend you have the time to do that — flip through the pages, and land on what looks like a fun quiz. The question is "What does *investing* make you think of?"

If the word itself makes you want to snap this book shut, I think I know what kinds of images are popping into your head: numbers, incomprehensible charts and jargon, and probably a few clips of Leonardo DiCaprio in *The Wolf of Wall Street*. You're one of those people who would rather have absolutely nothing to do with investing, thank you very much. Your instinct is to either stay the heck away from financial markets or pay someone else to take care of it for you. *Here, take all my money — do what you need to do with it but leave me out of it.*

I'm not here to tell you that you have to invest. But let me remind you of a not-so-fun fact we just went over in chapter 5: only 25 percent of Canadian employees these days have a workplace pension worthy of that name. And interest rates are hopelessly stuck in the muck. This means two things: First, most of us are on our own with prepping financially for our old age. Second, sticking your cash in a savings account or guaranteed investment certificate isn't going to cut it. (GICs, you'll remember from the last chapter, are like a locked-in deposit. You give money to the bank or financial institution for a set number of months or years and get it back, plus interest, at the end of the term.) With interest rates where they are now, if you put $1,000 in a high-interest savings account or GIC for a year, you'd be *lucky* to get $20, or 2 percent, in returns. That's peanuts — and peanuts is not what you use to build yourself a nice, or even a half-decent, retirement. If you want better returns, you'll very likely have to invest at least some of your money in the stock market.

What I *am* here to tell you is the idea that investing is only for dudes in suits is laughable. That's what some people in the industry would like you to believe to justify the hefty fees they want to charge you. It's also what has kept women from demanding a say in household investment decisions for decades. So let's crumple up all the scary stereotypes about investing into a tiny ball and give it a good flick, shall we?

In the world we live in, learning about investing is not optional. Having some basic understanding of how financial markets work and how they can work for you is an essential part of managing your money, just like knowing how much you can spend and how much life insurance you need. Thankfully if all you need to do is grow your savings for retirement or other far-off goals, it's not all that hard.

"Investing has become much more democratized," says financial planner Alexandra Macqueen. Back in the 1960s and 1970s, few people had stock accounts, she says. Saying that you had a stockbroker was a bit like saying you had a yacht — stuff for the very wealthy. Today, though, there are countless accessible, low-cost options for getting into the financial market. With some trading apps, you can start out with as little as $1 It's what Macqueen calls a "huge, positive step forward."

But there's a flip side to that. Let's go back to the glossy magazine and that question about investing. Maybe, as you've been reading up to now, you've been thinking none of what I just said applies to you. When you hear the word *investing* you think, *I got this*. You know a bit about stocks, bonds, and crypto (for everyone else: don't worry, we'll get to all that). You have your own trading account and have gotten the hang of buying and selling. Perhaps you've even made some money at it so far.

If this is your profile, my message to you is the same: you need to learn about investing. I'm not talking about reading up on exotic financial instruments or watching videos about how to get rich by trading options or buying up Bitcoin. I'm talking about learning some very basic, time-tested concepts about how you can use the financial market to grow your savings faster over several decades.

The democratization of investing has made it easier than ever to share in the returns of the stock market. But, for those who don't know what they're doing, it has also created loads of opportunities to make big mistakes with money they can't really afford to lose.

So however you feel about investing, here's a beginner's guide to making good decisions. In this chapter we'll go over the basics of different types of investments, what *risk* means when investing and how you can manage it, and different ways of investing and their associated fees. We'll also cover how you can invest in accordance with your values and — I know you were waiting for it — cryptocurrencies. Finally, we'll talk a bit more about how taxes can affect your investments.

• • •

Stocks and Bonds and All That

When financial planner Julia Chung of Spring Planning had to explain to her dad what a stock is, she started with Coca-Cola. "Do you think Coca-Cola is a good company?" she asked.

"For sure," her father said. "It's a great company." An entrepreneur, Chung's dad had investments in real estate but had thus far steered clear of the financial market, which seemed risky and hard to understand.

"Would you want to be an owner of Cola-Cola?" Chung continued.

"Of course," her father said. "That would be a fantastic opportunity."

"Well," Chung said, "all you need to do is buy a stock of Coca-Cola."

That's all stocks are: tiny slivers, or shares, of companies. Holding a company's stock makes you a part owner, also known as a shareholder.

Companies issue shares because it's a way to access the money they need to develop and grow. Investors give them a bit of their cash and in exchange become shareholders. If the company thrives, the value of its shares goes up, meaning investors can sell their allotment of shares for a higher price than they bought them for. Some shares also have dividends, an amount companies pay to their shareholders out of their profits on a regular basis. Those are called dividend stocks.

But shares aren't the only way in which companies like Coca-Cola can try to attract money from investors like me and you. Another option is good old-fashioned borrowing. You give them money, and they promise to return it after a certain amount of time with a certain amount of interest. That's what bonds are. These sorts of IOUs are also a common way to borrow for governments, public companies, and municipalities. Bonds issued by companies are known as corporate bonds as opposed to — you guessed it — government bonds.

Many bonds pay a fixed interest amount every year until their maturity date, when you get your principal back. For example, if you buy a five-year bond with a value of $1,000 and an interest rate of 5 percent, you'll get $50 a year. Your return over five years will be $250 on top of the $1,000 you put in, which you'll get back at maturity.

Both stocks and bonds are also called securities, which broadly indicates an easily tradable financial instrument that has some sort of monetary value. Bonds, specifically, are known as fixed-income securities, because you know exactly how much you're going to get in interest when you buy one.

Investors trade securities in the financial market. Think of it as your local farmer's market, Chung says. "A market is a market is a market," she says. "It really doesn't matter how big it is. It's just a market."

When you approach your neighbourhood farmers' market, you'll see a variety of sellers with their stands promoting their locally grown produce and other goodies, and a bunch of buyers walking around checking out what's on offer and the prices. It's the same in the financial market. The sellers can be companies or governments — when they issue new shares or bonds — or, more often, other investors looking for buyers for some of the securities they already own.

What's a bit different from filling your shopping bag at the local market is that prices in the financial market fluctuate all the time, often changing every few seconds. That's what's happening when you hear that a certain company's stock has gone up or down. Generally speaking, if there are more buyers for a certain stock than sellers, its price will go up. If there are more investors looking to sell than to buy, its value will go down. What investors want to buy and sell is influenced by many different factors, such as a company's profitability, the government's ability to repay their debts, economic conditions, and much more. And investors tend to be a forward-looking bunch, meaning the financial market prices tend to reflect what investors expect will happen in the future. That's why, in a recession, the stock market can bounce back much faster than the rest of the economy.

Securities change hands all the time, which makes for fluctuating prices. This holds for bonds as well. If the price of your bond rises above what you paid for it, you can make money by selling it before maturity (and you still get to keep whatever interest payments have been issued until that point). Bond prices can rise and fall for a variety of reasons. For example, say you have a bond paying 5 percent. If interest rates fall to 3 percent, your bond now looks very attractive. You will likely find a buyer willing to give you more than what you paid for it.

There is more you can trade in the financial market than tiny bits of companies and IOUs. You can also buy and sell financial instruments tied to the prices of commodities like gold, oil, and gas; livestock like beef; or agricultural products like coffee and wheat. There are also real estate investment trusts (or REITs), which invest in real estate properties such as apartment complexes and shopping malls. The list goes on.

For now, though, let's stay focused on stocks and bonds, the two types of investments you're most likely to deal with. Stocks usually trade on stock exchanges, like the Toronto Stock Exchange (TSX) in Canada, the New York Stock Exchange (NYSE) and the Nasdaq in the U.S., the London Stock Exchange (LSE) in the U.K., and so on. By *stock market*, people mean the buying and selling of stocks wherever it happens. Bonds, on the other hand, are mostly sold over the counter in what is known as the bond market. To zoom out even more, back to where we started, *financial market* is a catch-all term that refers to the buying and selling of securities in general: stocks, bonds, and more.

• • •

How Risky Is It to Invest in the Stock Market?

No matter how you do it, putting your money in the financial market involves risk. Now, I can hear the investment averse of you saying, "I knew it. *I knew it.*" But let me clarify. Whatever you do with your money involves some risk. Just to drive this point home, even stuffing your savings under the mattress or parking them in a low-interest bank account or GIC is risky. It carries the very real risk that you won't have enough money to comfortably live your life when you feel like you can't keep working anymore.

But just how risky it is to invest in the financial market depends on how you do it. Here's a look at what *risk* means when you're investing and how you can manage it.

RISK AND EGG BASKETS

Using all your cash to buy a single stock is pretty much as risky as it gets. It's really a bet. I don't care how much you've read up on that company or how well it has done in the past. Why? Let me give you a made-up but not entirely unrealistic example. Let's say you put all your money in Amazon. That's one bet that seems absolutely foolproof. Even the pandemic couldn't stop Amazon, so what could go wrong?

But suppose some day Americans became really concerned about how powerful Amazon has become. Let's say that surveys show the U.S. public wants the company broken up, and regulators oblige. The stock you own takes a hit and never recovers. To be perfectly clear, I am no stock analyst and have no special insight into the future of Amazon (nor am I trying to make an argument that the company should be broken up for real). But the general point stands: you never know what is going to happen.

So, if you're investing money you can't lose, you'll want to hedge your bets. This is what people mean when they talk about diversifying their investments. The idea is to spread your money across many different investments to reduce the risk tied to any single company, industry, or country. For example, holding stocks in both Hilton and Marriott is less risky than owning just one or the other. But both those stocks took a severe beating in the pandemic, along with the rest of the travel industry. Owning investments across different industries helps lower your risk. It's the same thing with countries: a deep recession in a major economy may drag down the stock of most companies that do a lot of business in that corner of the world. Holding investments from different parts of the globe helps you hedge that risk.

Putting all your proverbial eggs into a single investment or just a handful of investments is always a risky move — and not just in the financial market. Let's say, for example, that you're a real estate investor who owns a rental property in Toronto's trendy Distillery District. Who, at the end of 2019, would have ever thought that anything could go wrong with that? And yet, seven months into the pandemic, condo prices and rents were sinking across much of Canada. As my Global News colleague Sean O'Shea reported in the fall of 2020, downtown condos in Toronto had suddenly become "challenging" investments.[1] As I write, the Toronto condo market is once again heating up, and who knows what will be going on when this book comes out? But the bottom line is that investing in real estate has its own risks.

What's neat about investing in the financial market is that putting your eggs in many different baskets is way easier and cheaper than owning a bunch of rental properties across the world. With just $5,000, or even less, you can buy investments that spread your risk through a lot of different stocks and bonds.

Wait, you may be thinking, *how does this work?* I just gave you the example of a bond with a face value of $1,000. And as I'm writing this, buying a single share of Amazon would cost you almost $4,000. It doesn't exactly feel like you can go on much of a shopping spree with your puny $5,000.

Here's where investment funds come in. These are big baskets of investments like stocks and bonds owned by a group of investors. Basically, it's like teaming up with lots of other shoppers so you can pool your money and fill one giant collective cart with different investments. There are many types of funds — and funds of funds — out there, and I'll get to that later on in this chapter. For now, suffice it to say that funds make it easy and affordable to diversify even if you don't have a lot of money.

Another option is buying what are called fractional shares of a company through a stock trading platform. A fractional share is exactly what it sounds like: a tiny piece of a single share — a share of a share, if you will. Fractional shares allow you to buy into companies with pricey shares you wouldn't be able to afford otherwise. They became available only recently in Canada and, as I write, are offered for only a handful of companies.

RISK AND REWARD

We've talked about spreading your investments across many companies, industries, and countries. Another thing to think about is what mix of different types of investments you want to hold. For example, generally speaking, stocks tend to be riskier than bonds but also hold the potential for higher returns.

To understand why, let's go back to Coca-Cola, says Chung of Spring Planning. If you're simply lending money to them with a bond, the risk you're taking on is pretty low. Coca-Cola will pay you back what it promises unless it runs out of money entirely, which seems very unlikely. On the other hand, "if you become partners with them and now you own shares in Coca-Cola along with everybody else, then you're going to do as well as that business does," Chung says. But would you take on the bigger risk of being a shareholder if you could get the same return with a bond? You wouldn't. No one would.

In general, the riskier an investment is perceived to be, the bigger the potential reward needs to be for investors to buy in. This, of course, doesn't mean that riskier investments guarantee higher returns. But if you aren't willing to take on a bit of risk, you may be bound to have low returns.

As you think about what should be in your diversified basket of investments, you also need to think about risk and reward. Investing entirely in stocks, for example, may produce higher returns over the years but will also make for a bumpier ride, as the stock market goes up and down. Take the average annual return of the S&P 500 Index, a collection of around 500 of the largest companies traded on the U.S. stock market. Its average annual return for the past 60 years or so has been around 8 percent. That sounds really good compared to the return of 1 or 2 percent per year you can currently get on savings accounts deposits or GICs.

But even if you invested in the entire S&P 500 Index, you wouldn't earn 8 percent per year. In some years the index has produced very meh returns of 2 percent or less. On many occasions it closed the year more than 20 percent higher. And sometimes, in a recession or a financial crisis, it has sunk really low. In 2008, for example, it dropped more than 37 percent.

If that roller-coaster ride is too much for you, you can smooth it out by owning some bonds, which have lower returns but are also much less volatile. This will likely narrow down the range of possible outcomes for investment returns: the highs won't be as high, but the lows won't be as low. Over many years, your average returns may be something like 4 or 5 percent per year instead of 7 or 8 percent.

Usually, an investment basket made up of 50 percent stocks and 50 percent bonds is known as a balanced portfolio. You can think of this as being in the middle of the risk–reward continuum. Many investment pros also consider 60 percent stocks and 40 percent bonds to be a balanced portfolio. Aiming for the middle may sound like a good compromise, but it could actually yield a return that's too low to meet your goals or be too volatile a mix given your time horizon and risk tolerance.

RISK AND YOUR TIMELINE

How much risk you can afford to take on depends, in part, on how long you can hold your investments without touching them. The longer your timeline, the better you'll be able to ride out the market lows and wait for stocks to bounce back. For example, it took five years for the S&P 500 to climb back to where it was before the financial crisis of 2007–2008. A common piece of advice is to invest in stocks only if you have a time horizon of 10 years or longer. If you're saving up for a down payment on a house or a wedding and stocks are on a tear, it can be really tempting to give your hard-earned savings a much-needed lift by hitching a ride on the market. But what if there was a sudden crash? Are you going to postpone buying a house or tying the knot for five years (or more, potentially) so you can make your money back? That's a risk that simply isn't worth it.

In general, the longer your timeline, the higher the returns you can sensibly aim for. But as you get closer to your target, you may want to gradually downshift to a lower-risk, lower-return investment mix. One long-standing general rule for retirement holds that you should hold a percentage of stocks equal to 100 minus your age. For example, when you hit 40, your allocation should be 60 percent stocks and 40 percent bonds. But with people living longer and retiring later and returns from bonds very low, many investment advisers say the old guidelines aren't bold enough. Some suggest using 110 or even 120 minus your age to achieve the kinds of returns that will sustain you in retirement.

This kind of quick math, of course, is just a starting point. The right mix of stocks and bonds might depend on any number of circumstances specific to your situation and must also take into account your ability to stomach risk.

RISK AND YOUR GUT

Your gut is another important factor when you're trying to figure out what investments are right for you. How will you feel when the stock market crashes and your balance drops 30 percent, 40 percent, or even 50 percent in the span of a few months? It's important to think about this because, if you stay invested for decades, you *will* experience major stock market meltdowns. It's pretty much guaranteed — sooner or later it will happen to you.

Of course, history shows that, over and over again, the market eventually recovered and climbed to new heights. But even if you know this rationally, how you handle the ups and down emotionally matters. "If you can't sleep, I don't care what other people say about what's appropriate risk," says Chung. "It's too much."

Panicking and selling before stock prices have bounced back is one of the costliest mistakes you can make. And even if you manage to hold on tight, if the stress spoils your nights, it's just not worth it. So how can you figure out how much your gut can really take?

If you're letting someone else guide your investment decisions — whether it's a flesh-and-bone investment adviser or a robo advisor — they'll ask you some preliminary questions to assess your risk tolerance. If you're DIYing it, you can find similar self-assessment tools online. Vanguard, for example, one of the world's largest investment management companies, has an investor questionnaire that will recommend a stocks/bonds split based on your answers to multiple-choice questions. It will also show you how your suggested portfolio has performed in the past compared to others.

These sorts of Q&As are a good start, but you can never be sure how you'll feel about investing until you're actually doing it. If you start out at a point when stocks are going up and everything seems hunky-dory, it can be easy to overestimate your courage. And if you're starting out when the market is in the doldrums, you may be inclined to be too cautious.

This happened to me. When I started out, I took on a little too much risk. I got a relatively late start investing because I spent the first decade of my career hopping around the globe. When you're not quite sure which country you're going to be living in next year, your timeline is far too short to put money in the stock market. When I eventually settled down, I'd been writing about the economy for a while. I'd seen the market panic of 2008 and what had come after. I thought volatility — in a well-diversified investment portfolio — wouldn't bother me.

But it turns out ups and downs do bug me a bit Not a lot. But a bit. The first time the stock market tumbled when I had actual money in it, seeing the value of my hard-earned savings drop bothered me more than I thought it would. Clearly, I had overestimated my risk tolerance. I didn't do anything then and there, but when the market had recovered and all was well again, I trimmed my allocation of stocks slightly and bumped up my percentage of bonds. I've been happy ever since — including through the pandemic-linked crash of March 2020.

Keep in mind, also, that how you feel about risk may change over time. Perhaps as you understand more and more about financial markets — or after you've been through a serious downturn and recovered from it — you'll feel confident about taking on a bit more risk. Or maybe you'll find you need a smoother stock market ride. Either way, your risk tolerance is something that should be monitored on a regular basis. If your investment manager isn't checking in with you at least once a year about how you're feeling and what your reaction has been to the latest market developments — or if you don't have an investment manager to turn to — it's something you should be asking yourself.

Just to be clear, this isn't about ditching your riskier investments when the stock market drops. It's about scheduling time once a year to take a look at your investments and make sure everything still feels right. Any adjustments you make should be for the long term and done at a time when you are feeling calm. You can think of it as another form of self-care. Your body needs a bubble bath sometimes. Your mind needs me time. Your investments need your attention at least once a year.

• • •

Investment Fees

Let's say you have $5,000 set aside, your very first pot of money that you can afford not to touch for decades — decades! You've invested that cash inside a TFSA or RRSP, where your money will happily grow tax-free (see chapter 5 for TFSAs versus RRSPs). And let's also say you manage to add another $5,000 to that pot every single year. Congratulations!

Now here's a question. How much money will you have in 30 years if your investments grow by 5 percent per year on average?

The answer could be more than $330,000, or less than $250,000. And yes, we're talking about the same exact investments. The difference between the two scenarios stems simply from the fees you've been paying over the years. Specifically, that's the difference between annual fees of 0.25 percent per year — among the lowest in the industry — and fees of 2 percent per year, which would be on the high end.

Shopping around for investments is pretty much like shopping around for anything else. What you buy matters, but so does *where* you buy. Companies that allow you to invest in the market — like mutual fund dealers, robo advisors, and discount brokers — charge a fee for their services. Some are more expensive than others, and that can make a huge difference to your bottom line if you stay invested for a long period of time, because you pay those fees every year.

Contrary to what many Canadians assume, those fees are a percentage of your total investments, not your annual return. I received actual hate mail when I once talked about this on TV. Unlike other journalists, this doesn't happen very often to me. It's hard to get worked up about the topics I write about. But people do get emotional about investment fees, I quickly learned. I got emails accusing me of spreading fake news. How is it possible that you'd be paying fees even in a year when your investments have gone down on the whole? I understand the incredulity. And yet that is how investment fees work.

You can see now that whether you're paying a fee of 0.25 percent or 2 percent is a big deal. Let's look at year one. If your initial $5,000 grew by 5 percent, your return absent any fees would be $250. With a 0.25 percent fee, you'd pay something like $12, meaning the actual value of your investments after the first 12 months would be $5,238. With a 2 percent fee, you'd be paying something closer to $100. That's right! You'd end the year with just $5,150. The fee math is a bit complicated, so if you'd like to see for yourself, you can turn to a trusty online tool like the fee calculator on the GetSmarterAboutMoney.ca site made available by the Ontario Securities Commission.

Investment fees matter because they add up fast and diminish the awesome power of compounding returns. Remember how we talked about this in chapter 5? In year one your $5,000 grows 5 percent to $5,250. In year two, you're starting from $5,250, which grows 5 percent — or $262 — to $5,512. If you're contributing $5,000 per year, then at the end of year two you'll have $10,763. But fees are constantly shaving off a bit of your returns. With a 2 percent fee, you'd end year two with just $10,455. Depending on how large your investments are and how long you stay invested, high fees could mean tens of thousands — if not hundreds of thousands — of dollars less for your retirement and other long-term savings goals.

You may be wondering why certain investments come with much higher fees than others. In general, one big cost difference boils down to whether your investments are actively or passively managed. Active management means someone, known as an investment or portfolio manager, actively buys and sells investments for you based on your timeline, goals, and risk tolerance. Passive management involves putting money in investments that track the performance of a certain benchmark or investment model. Index investing, which you may have heard about, is a popular form of passive investing that tracks market indexes like the U.S.'s S&P 500 or the S&P/TSX Composite Index, which is Canada's benchmark stock index. The idea is that you're putting your investments on autopilot, which requires less tinkering and therefore tends to cost less.

Choosing passive investing does not mean settling for less. For example, in a 2020 report, U.S. financial services firm Morningstar found that just 51 percent of all U.S. actively managed funds had beat the performance of their passive counterparts during the first six months of 2020. "The coronavirus sell-off and subsequent rebound tested the narrative that active funds are generally better able to navigate market volatility than their index peers. Active funds' performance through the first half of 2020 shows that there's little merit to this notion," the report reads.[2]

If you decide to have someone actively manage your investments, take a hard look at their track record. Of course, past performance does not guarantee future results, but, as a general rule, Jeremy Siegel, a finance professor at the University of Pennsylvania, says, portfolio managers must be able to show 10 years of market-beating results to make a persuasive case that they didn't just get lucky.[3] But keep in mind that there can also be big differences in the costs associated with passive investing. For example, even mutual funds that mirror the returns of a market index can be quite expensive in Canada.

Understanding how much different types of investments will cost you in fees isn't always easy. Some of the big financial firms selling expensive products have zero interest in advertising just how much they charge. If you're thinking of buying mutual funds (more on what those are in the next section), look online for a document called Fund Facts about the fund you're interested in. This is a user-friendly guide to a fund's fees and performance that every mutual fund company in Canada must provide to investors. There you'll find information on a wide range of fees the fund may be charging.

The management expense ratio (MER) is likely the most important one. This is the yearly cost of your fund — anything from investment management through marketing to administrative costs. It's written as a percentage of the fund's value. The MER doesn't show up as a charge but is taken out of your balance on a rolling basis, usually daily or monthly. There is also a trading expense ratio (TER), which measures the fund's costs for buying and selling securities. These are in addition to the MER. And you may also have to pay fees for things like buying and selling units of the fund or penalties for selling your investments within a certain number of years.

Exchange-traded funds (ETFs), which are usually much cheaper, have something similar, called ETF Facts, that will also show you MERs and other fees (don't worry if you don't know what ETFs are — we'll get to them later in this chapter).

Online brokerages, which let you buy and sell investments on your own, typically charge commissions for every transaction you make. This means that the more often you trade, the more you'll pay in commissions. Today, though, you can easily find discount brokers in Canada that offer commission-free trading or waive the commission in many scenarios. There may also be exchange-rate fees — for example, for trades in U.S. dollars — as well as fees for inactivity on small accounts and other administrative costs. You may also have to pay to access market data that will help you make decisions about your trades.

• • •

Three Low-Cost and Low-Effort Ways to Invest

My attitudes toward investing and food are pretty much the same. I love eating — I truly do. But I have neither a lot of money nor a lot of time to devote to it, so when it's my turn to take care of feeding the family in my house, my goal is to throw together good, healthy, and budget-friendly meals in the shortest amount of time possible. My ideal recipe involves a pressure cooker and basically zero prep: throw some ingredients in, give it a stir, press a button, and forget all about it until the thing beeps and all I have to do is spoon a delicious dinner onto three plates. Doing the same thing with your investments is even easier, thanks to index investing.

Index investing, as I've mentioned, means buying investments that track the ups and downs of financial indexes. The beauty of this approach is that it comes with low fees and often beats the returns of investments managed by the pros, when you look at performance averages over many years. Better still, these days index investing requires as little effort as an electric-pressure-cooked dinner.

The main options for pursuing low-cost, low-effort index investing are index mutual funds, all-in-one ETFs, and robo advisors. Here's a look at some of their pros and cons.

INDEX MUTUAL FUNDS

What we're talking about: Mutual funds have become synonymous with high-fee, actively managed investments in Canada, because that's what most of them are. But not all mutual funds are like that. Mutual funds are simply investment funds that pool investors' money to buy a broad collection of investments. It's possible to have passively managed mutual funds that hold or track all or almost all the components of a financial market index. And even in Canada these index mutual funds — often called simply index funds — come with low fees. You invest in a mutual fund by buying units of it. The price of a unit is known as the net asset value (NAV), which is calculated by adding up all the fund's assets (cash and investments), subtracting its liabilities (fees, expenses, and taxes), and dividing by the number of outstanding units. The NAV fluctuates along with the overall value of the investments held by the fund.

Pretty low fees: Some index funds you can buy in Canada have very low fees (less than 0.3 percent). However, as I'm writing this, your choices are limited, and if you're looking for an all-in-one, hands-off solution, you may have to settle for an MER of anywhere from 0.77 percent to around 1 percent, which is quite a bit higher than what you'd pay with all-in-one ETFs.

Minimal effort: You can buy index funds through a sales agent at a bank or online through what is usually a user-friendly interface. Another big advantage: it's easy to set up preauthorized contributions to your index fund.

ALL-IN-ONE ETFs

What we're talking about: An ETF is an investment fund that trades on a stock exchange. Instead of buying units of it, you purchase shares just like you would any other stock. ETFs tend to be passively managed — although there are also actively managed ETFs — and can track all sorts of things, including commodities and real estate investments. All-in-one ETFs, also called asset allocation ETFs, are the lowest-effort way to invest in ETFs. They are funds of funds, or collections of several ETFs that track Canadian, U.S., and international investments. As with mutual funds, all-in-one ETFs give you the ability to get exposure to both stocks and bonds by buying a single investment. For example, a low-risk all-in-one ETF may be made up of 80 percent bonds-tracking ETFs and 20 percent stocks-tracking ETFs. A higher-risk all-in-one ETF with higher growth potential could have the opposite makeup: 80 percent stocks and 20 percent bonds. As is the case if you buy a single index mutual fund, with all-in-one ETFs you don't have to worry about realigning your portfolio to keep your desired value split among different types of investments despite price fluctuations. All-in-one ETFs rebalance automatically.

Minimal fees: All-in-one ETFs typically have very low fees (easily 0.25 percent or less). Since you buy and sell them like stocks, you do have to be mindful of transaction fees charged by online brokers. This could be an issue if you're hoping to make regular contributions to your account, which would require buying more ETF shares. That said, some self-directed trading platforms allow users to do this for free and others charge no commission for at least a selection of funds.

Pretty low effort: ETF investing used to mean having to build your own portfolio of many ETFs and tinkering with it on a regular basis to rebalance your investments. Putting all your money into a single all-in-one ETF is a lot less work but still slightly more labour intensive than using an index fund or robo advisor. To invest in one of these big ETFs, you'll need to know how to buy a stock. This isn't rocket science, but you may have to whip out a calculator to figure out how many shares you can afford to buy. And you may have some leftover cash if the price of the shares doesn't match exactly the amount of your savings.

ROBO ADVISORS

What we're talking about: A robo advisor is an online service that professionally invests your money for fees that are usually much lower than what a traditional portfolio manager would charge. Robo advisors usually keep their costs low by using portfolios of inexpensive mutual funds and ETFs. And instead of hand-picking investments just for you, they often have a range of pre-made portfolios. When you sign up with a robo advisor, you will generally have to answer an online questionnaire about things like your financial goals and how queasy you get when you see the stock market go down. The robo advisor will then slot you into the pre-made portfolio that best suits your needs. Some robo advisors also offer a bit more hand-holding than you'd get buying ETFs on your own through an online trading platform. For example, if the stock market is tumbling, your robo advisor may check in with a quick (mass) email reminding everyone that market crashes happen from time to time and the best thing to do is to take a deep breath and carry on.

Pretty low fees: You'll be paying the robo advisor in addition to the underlying fees tied to the low-cost mutual funds and ETFs in your portfolio. For example, the robo advisor may charge 0.5 percent per year in addition to around 0.2 percent for your ETFs. A 0.7 percent fee is higher than you'd likely pay with an all-in-one ETF but cheaper than some of the index mutual fund portfolios you can buy elsewhere, and far cheaper than investing with a dedicated portfolio manager.

Minimal effort: Robo advisors are a truly hands-off investment option. You do the initial on-boarding, set up automatic contributions, and that's about it. But you should still review your investments once or twice a year to make sure they continue to meet your needs.

If you're considering investing through index funds, all-in-one ETFs, or robo advisors just remember that fees, while important, aren't everything. Paying a slightly higher commission may be worth it if it helps you stay on track with your savings and stick to your investment choices. On the other hand, if a bit more financial housekeeping doesn't faze you, then there's no reason to forego the cost savings of all-in-one ETFs.

• • •

DIY Investing for Retirement and for Fun

You know where I stand on investing and cooking. But what if you're not like that? Lots of people love cooking. Making wonderful food can be an art form, a hobby, a way to get your creative juices going, or a stress release after a tough day at work. Honestly, even I enjoy cooking when I have the time.

Similarly, lots of people actually like fiddling with their investments. If you prefer a more hands-on approach to managing your own money, you can do what savvy Canadians used to do before all-in-one ETFs came along: assemble your very own DIY portfolio of index ETFs and mutual funds. Sites like Canadian Couch Potato provide model portfolios for self-directed investors. This investing route is undoubtedly more time consuming, as you'll have to worry about rebalancing your portfolio on a regular basis, among other things. Still, it's another way to go about index investing. You're putting your money in investments that track big financial indexes and you're letting the market do its thing.

This is very different than trying to choose winning investments, or buying and selling based on where you think the market is going. That kind of investing is very risky. But is there anything wrong with using a small pot of money for this sort of stock picking if you're also sticking to index investing with your retirement savings? I've heard several people talk about stock trading with their "fun money" during the earlier days of the pandemic, when discount brokers and robo advisors saw double-digit growth in new users, especially among millennials and the older Gen Zers.

There's nothing wrong with carving a bit of fun money out of your budget, if you can afford it. And, of course, you're free to do whatever you choose with that cash. You can spend it at the races, drop it in a slot machine, cr get yourself some stocks. I'm not here to judge. But I do worry about how you'll feel if you happen to win big. If you bought a stock whose price rose by 700 percent in a year, like Tesla shares did in 2020, would you be itching to buy more of it with money that should go into your long-term savings? And what if you placed a bad bet? Or suppose you bought into GameStop, the video game retailer at the centre of the WallStreetBets subreddit mania in early 2021, at U.S. $300 a share, only to panic and sell it shortly after when it temporarily collapsed to around $45 a share? Would you consider pillaging your retirement fund to replenish your fun money? I'm not saying you would. But we're all human, and our emotions can trick us into bad decisions.

Finally, one last word of warning about fun money: you may not want to hold it in your TFSA. One important perk of these accounts is that your contribution room grows along with your investments. For example, let's say you've contributed $10,000 in deposits to your TFSA. And let's imagine you've invested the money, which has now grown to $15,000. If you were to withdraw it all today, next year you'll be able to recontribute $15,000, not $10,000. But this very feature of TFSAs can turn against you when you have investment losses. If your investments dropped to $5,000 and you withdrew the money, you'd be able to recontribute just $5,000. That's one powerful argument for avoiding risky bets with the money in your TFSA.

• • •

Investing and Your Values

Investing in big market indexes means you may be benefitting financially from the growth of companies that don't align with your values. Luckily, you don't have to give up on low-cost, low-effort investing to do something about it. ETFs and robo advisors all offer options to invest in broadly diversified, passively managed portfolios that meet ethical, social, and sustainability standards.

The idea of keeping your investments in line with your values isn't new, and there are a few ways to go about it. Religious investors are widely credited for pioneering what's called negative screening, by excluding so-called sin stocks from companies involved in things like tobacco, alcohol, gambling, weapons, and pornography. Now many investors are doing the same with carbon-intensive energy producers or corporations with a spotty human rights record.

There is also positive screening, which means going "out of your way to invest in things you believe in," says Tim Nash, founder of Good Investing. If negative screening means, say, dropping a coal producer from your portfolio, positive screening may mean adding a wind farm.

Socially responsible investing, or SRI, may use both negative and positive screens. Halal investing applies a similar screening process that selects investments that comply with Islamic principles.

To create sustainable and socially conscious investment products, the industry often relies on ESG criteria. The *E* stands for *environmental*, which looks at corporate practices on issues such as carbon emissions and water pollution. *S* is for *social,* which focuses on things like treatment of a company's own workers and working conditions in its supply chain. The *G* stands for *governance,* or how a company governs itself, which includes issues such as who sits on the board of directors and how executives are compensated.

Financial firms use ESG metrics to create various financial indexes. For example, Canadian investment research firm Sustainalytics, now owned by Morningstar, created the Jantzi Social Index, made up of 50 Canadian companies trading on the Toronto Stock Exchange that pass a broad set of ESG criteria. MSCI, a U.S. financial firm, provides several stocks and fixed-income indexes that incorporate ESG metrics. Other financial firms, in turn, provide investment funds that track these ESG indexes. And many robo advisors choose from various ESG funds to craft their own socially responsible investment portfolios, although sometimes they may create their own funds.

While opting for value-conscious investing limits the number of companies and investment products you get to pick from, a portfolio of well-diversified ESG funds will still spread your eggs across many different baskets. Many investors believe sustainable investing is good for both your conscience and your wallet. Some, for example, point to the Jantzi Social Index, which, for 20-some years, has performed roughly as well or better than the S&P/TSX Composite and the S&P/TSX 60 (which tracks 60 large companies listed on the Toronto Stock Exchange).

Still, socially responsible investing does usually come with a bit of a price premium. Even funds that simply track ESG indexes tend to have slightly higher fees than their non-ESG peers. It's a bit like buying organic at the grocery store. Many sustainably minded investors are happy to foot that extra cost. But before you reach out for pricier ESG investments, it's worth doing what you likely already do at the supermarket: flip around that can of organic tomato sauce and look at what actually went into the product. The tomatoes will be organically grown, but is the second listed ingredient sugar?

Shopping for ESG investments can be even trickier. While the organic label comes with a clear set of standards in Canada (even though lots of people have quibbles with those standards), that's not true of ESG metrics. There is no agreed-upon methodology for quantifying a company's sustainability. Different financial firms follow different ESG criteria or may apply those metrics in different ways, although the industry is working toward standardization, Nash says. This can lead to surprising results. One example? Investment products labelled as sustainable may include exposure to the oil and gas industry. So before you buy, sift through the list of fund holdings and read the fine print to make sure you're buying an investment that truly reflects your values.

• • •

Cryptocurrencies

"What's a cryptocurrency and should I invest in it?" I got this question a lot in late 2017, when the value of Bitcoin rose to dizzying heights before crashing, and again in late 2020 and early 2021, as it reached a new record (before yet another crash).

Let's start with the basics. Before we get into cryptocurrencies, we need to talk about blockchain, the technology behind digital coins. Blockchain is a new way to store data that makes it difficult to tamper with the recorded information. Experts say this lends itself to all kinds of potential applications. Blockchain could be used for anything like setting up financial contracts, lending, or conducting an auction.

However, the first popular use of blockchain was to power digital tokens like Bitcoin, Ether, Litecoin, and — how could I forget — Dogecoin. (If you're wondering about non-fungible tokens, or NFTs, see the box.) The blockchain records who owns what tokens and when that ownership is transferred. What Bitcoin and other similar crypto tokens are is arguably in the eye of the beholder. If you use them to buy and sell stuff, then you're treating them like currencies. If you're buying them because you think they'll go up in value, you're treating them as an investment.

WHAT IN THE WORLD ARE NFTs?

NFTs — or non-fungible tokens — are another type of token made possible by blockchain. But unlike cryptocurrency, NFTs represent ownership of unique assets. As their name says, they are non-fungible, meaning they aren't interchangeable with other identical items. A Bitcoin can replace or be replaced by any other Bitcoin, just as a dollar can with any other dollar. An NFT is for owning something unique, like a piece of art or a valuable baseball card. You've probably heard that Beeple sold an NFT of his work for U.S. $69 million through the auction house Christie's. Some people see NFTs as a way for artists to sell their work without relying on intermediaries such as art galleries, record companies, or streaming platforms. But NFTs could one day be used to buy physical assets like a house or a car, too. That said, critics point out that NFTs in their current form still present significant risks for buyers.[4]

While there's a broad consensus that blockchain technology is a big deal, opinions about cryptocurrencies vary widely, as I'm sure you're aware. There's no agreement in the financial world on whether they should even be considered an investment.

Here's what we do know for sure: cryptocurrencies are extremely volatile, which makes them very, very risky. Another potential risk comes from relying on intermediaries such as crypto exchanges to hold your digital tokens. While it's difficult to delete or alter transaction records on the blockchain, it's entirely possible for hackers and fraudsters to separate cryptocurrency owners from the digital accounts that hold them. For example, Japan's Mt. Gox crypto-trading platform declared bankruptcy in 2014 after saying it had lost track of more than 850,000 Bitcoins belonging to customers amid allegations of hacking, theft, and fraud.[5] And here in Canada, the now-defunct crypto exchange QuadrigaCX turned out to be operating like a Ponzi scheme, according to the Ontario Securities Commission.[6] When the exchange filed for creditor protection in 2019, it owed its clients assets collectively worth $215 million. As I write, just $46 million of those funds have been recovered.

Since the Quadriga affair, Canada has adopted rules that require crypto exchanges that handle digital currencies like securities to register with the same securities regulators that oversee exchanges like the Toronto Stock Exchange. However, "many crypto asset trading platforms are not registered and have taken the position that they are not required to register with securities regulators," the Ontario Securities Commission noted in a 2020 report.[7] If you decide to invest in crypto, it's a good idea to check whether your crypto-trading platform is registered with securities regulators. You can now also buy cryptocurrency ETFs, which trade on regular stock exchanges.

• • •

Investments and Taxes

There's inflation, there are fees — and then there's tax. That's the third money-eating rodent that can gnaw away at your investments. Luckily, if you're a young Canadian with a middling income, there are some easy ways to tackle this issue. All it takes is putting your savings into registered accounts or plans — so called because they are registered with the federal government — where your money receives special tax treatment. Usually, while your investments sit inside one of these accounts, you won't have to pay tax on any returns you earn. RRSPs, TFSAs, and registered education savings plans (RESPs) are all examples of that. We've gone over RRSPs and TFSAs in some detail in chapter 5, and you'll get a deep dive into RESPs in chapter 8. In short, though, RRSPs allow you to defer taxes. You don't pay taxes on money you put into the account (which means there's more of it to invest), but withdrawals are taxable. With TFSAs you don't have to pay taxes to take money out, but you don't get a tax break on contributions.

The government created these accounts to help people like you and me grow our savings — and they are a big help. Remember the snowball effect that happens with compound interest when you start to earn returns on your previous investment returns as well as on the money you originally invested? Paying taxes on your investment gains is like shaving layers off your snowball as it rolls down the hill. The end result is the same as with investment fees: the snowball won't grow as big as it otherwise would. Over many years, being able to let your investments grow tax-free can make a huge difference.

The annual limit on RRSP contributions is 18 percent of your earned income for the year, up to a certain dollar ceiling that the CRA adjusts every year; in 2021 it was $27,830. Just keep in mind that if you have an employer-sponsored pension plan, your RRSP contribution limit is lower. The maximum you can contribute is reduced by the so-called pension adjustment. You can find your pension adjustment on your T4 slip every year.

For TFSAs, as of 2021, the contribution cap was $6,000 a year. If you have a middle-class income, that's a lot of money you can stash into RRSPs and TFSAs every year. And for both account types, unused contribution room adds up year over year. RESPs, which help families save up for their children's education, have a lifetime contribution limit of $50,000 per beneficiary and also allow you to catch up on missed contributions (more on RESPs in chapter 8).

But what if you have savings outside of a registered account? Then your returns are taxable. I know, many of us will never have to worry about investing in non-registered accounts because we just don't have enough dough to fill up our RRSPs and TFSAs *and* invest somewhere else. But we very likely have at least a puny savings account somewhere earning a little bit of interest, am I right? Well, that interest is taxable. Let's take a look at how taxes work outside tax-sheltered accounts.

DIFFERENT INVESTMENTS = DIFFERENT TAX RULES

Here's the thing: outside of RRSPs, TFSAs, and the like, the government taxes different types of investments in different ways. It pays to know how. Here's how it works:

» Taxes on interest income: This is the interest you receive from money sitting in your savings accounts, GICs, and bonds. From a tax standpoint, interest is treated exactly like your regular income. So if you made $50,000 a year from your job and received $500 in interest the same year, you'd be taxed as if you made $50,500.

» Taxes on capital gains: Capital gain is the profit you make from the sale of an investment or other asset. For example, let's say you bought $1,000 worth of stocks at the beginning of the year in a non-registered account and you sold them before the end of the year for $1,500. That $500 difference is your capital gain. The neat thing about capital gains is you get taxed on just half of them. Going back to our previous example, if your extra $500 came from capital gains, the government would tax you as if you made $50,250 ($50,000 + half of $500).

» Taxes on dividend income: Dividends are payments that some companies make to their shareholders out of their profits. That's what people are talking about when they use the term *dividend-paying stocks*. Dividends from shares of taxable Canadian corporations — called eligible dividends — get a preferential tax treatment. How it works is a bit complex, but to keep it simple, the tax rate for eligible dividends is usually lower than that applied to interest income and, depending on your total taxable income, may also be lower than that applied to capital gains, Chung, the financial planner, says.

Capital gains and dividends "both get special tax treatment from the government because they're trying to encourage investment," Chung says. But there's no VIP tax handling for your basic savings account interest.

There are two important takeaways from all this. First, if you ever find yourself investing in a non-registered account, mind the tax. Taxes shouldn't dictate how or where you invest but should be part of your math. Second, I hope this has helped you realize that the undersized interest Canadians can earn on safer investments might be even smaller than it looks. I've already mentioned how the interest rate on most savings accounts doesn't even keep up with inflation. And we've talked about how holding a well-diversified portfolio of stocks for a long time tends to yield much higher returns than bonds or GICs. But that spread could well become even larger when you consider after-tax returns.

Of course, we all need a savings account. But maybe the knowledge of just what a rough deal you're getting tax-wise will be extra motivation to take the time to look around for a savings account with a more competitive interest rate.

AN IMPORTANT ASTERISK ABOUT FOREIGN DIVIDEND INCOME IN A TFSA

Remember when I said investment returns earned by money lying inside an RRSP or TFSA are exempt from tax? That only goes for Canadian taxes. Generally speaking, if you're thinking of buying foreign investments, you should look into whether they would be subject to income tax abroad.

In practice, this issue usually comes up when Canadians invest in U.S. dividend stocks. Thanks to the tax treaty between Canada and the U.S., Uncle Sam will refrain from taxing U.S. dividend income received inside an RRSP (or RRIF, for that matter). But that doesn't extend to TFSAs. You'll be dinged with a 15 percent tax deducted at source for dividends paid on U.S. stocks held in a TFSA.

You don't have to worry about interest income or capital gains from U.S. stocks, though. The tax treaty guarantees those are only taxable in Canada, which means they're tax-free in a TFSA.

• • •

Wrap-Up

We started out this chapter with a personality test. Maybe you identified with the extremely risk-averse saver who'd rather stash the money in a pillowcase than put a dollar into the financial market. Or perhaps you saw yourself in the uber-confident investor who knows all about how to buy a stock with a couple of thumb scrolls. But wherever you landed on that imaginary magazine quiz, I hope you're coming out of this confident in the notion that (a) investing is really important; (b) getting started is easier than is has ever been; and (c) as easy as it is these days to buy investments, making informed decisions about investing requires some background knowledge.

Happily, that background knowledge has nothing to do with numbers or complicated investment strategies and schemes. This chapter touches on a lot of what you need to know, but it's just an introduction. If you're wondering what to do next, here are a few ideas:

» For much more information about investing, head over to the Ontario Securities Commission's GetSmarterAboutMoney.ca and the British Columbia Securities Commission's InvestRight.org websites.

» If you're wondering about how you should divide your money between investments like stocks and bonds, you could take the Vanguard investor questionnaire as a start.

» Investigate your investing options. On the web, you'll find several independent rankings of robo advisors and online brokerages. Once you've narrowed down a few potential options, make sure to also check out the investing platforms you're considering.

» If you decide to invest with an investment adviser, make sure to ask questions about their past performance and fees. If you don't get a straight answer you can understand, walk away.

And that's a wrap for investing and what you should know about the risk that comes with it and how to manage it. Now let's take a look at other risks we all have to contend with and what you can do to keep those puppies from potentially undermining your financial security or that of the people you love.

CHAPTER 7

PREPPING FOR LIFE'S CURVEBALLS

LIFE IS FULL of curveballs, and when one of those suckers comes flying your way at 150 kilometres an hour, you need to have a bat ready for it. I'm talking about insurance, of course, but also about having a will or power of attorney (not to worry, I'll explain what both of those are). Many people start thinking about these things when they have a partner or little humans who depend on them financially. But carving yourself a beautiful, shiny bat for those dreadful benders can be just as important if you're single and fending for yourself.

You're probably well acquainted with some forms of insurance. If you own a vehicle, you must have auto insurance — it's mandatory everywhere in Canada. If you own a house, home insurance isn't required by law, but I have yet to meet a homeowner who doesn't have coverage. If you're renting, hopefully you have renters insurance, which covers your belongings from common risks like fire and theft (more on that in a second). But the question is, do you have enough home or renters insurance? A plain-vanilla policy may not include all you need.

And what if something were to happen to *you* rather than to the stuff you own? You, and your ability to earn money, may be your greatest asset. An emergency fund can help soften the blow from a spell of unemployment, but in the event of death or disability, you may need insurance. Most people know about life insurance, which pays a tax-free, lump sum of money upon your death. But significantly fewer Canadians, in my experience, know much about disability insurance, which covers a portion of your income if you become unable to work, or critical illness insurance, which offers coverage even if you don't work.

It's also a good idea to have a plan for how you want your affairs handled — and by whom — should you become unable to make your own decisions, even if only temporarily. That's what a power of attorney is for.

And finally, there's the ultimate curveball none of us can dodge. I don't mean to be morbid, but what do you want to happen when you die? If you don't want the courts to decide for you, which can get costly and messy, you need a will.

In this chapter, we're going to learn about home, condo, and renters insurance and why you may need to beef up the coverage you already have. We'll also cover life insurance, disability and critical illness insurance, and something called mortgage life and disability insurance (confusing, I know, but I'll explain). Finally, I'll talk about wills and powers of attorney.

• • •

Home Insurance

As we've seen in chapter 3, whether you're a buyer or a renter, finding the perfect place — or, let's face it, a decent place — is hard enough. Once you've found it, make sure you're protected. Getting home or condo insurance as a homeowner is a no-brainer, and buying renters insurance, which covers your personal belongings, should be. But just because you have insurance doesn't mean you have enough coverage. As we'll see later in this section, climate change is, increasingly, a reason why Canadians need to boost their plain-vanilla insurance policies. But first, a look at the basics.

HOMEOWNERS, CONDO, AND RENTERS INSURANCE

Homeowners insurance typically protects you in case of theft, loss, or damage to the inside or outside of your home, to its contents (furniture, TV, appliances, clothing, etc.), and to any detached structures on the property (for example, a garage). It also usually helps you cover extra costs if you're temporarily unable to live in your own home. This may include, for example, the cost of living in a short-term rental while your house is being repaired or rebuilt after a fire. Finally, it usually protects you from lawsuits arising from accidental damage or injury linked to your property (like if someone slips and falls on your icy driveway, or your home catches fire and burns down your neighbour's property, too).

Condo insurance is similar to homeowners insurance but limited to your unit and your storage locker. Condo insurance typically covers your belongings, upgrades done by you or previous owners to the unit, and at least part of the expenses of living elsewhere if your unit becomes temporarily inhabitable. It also protects you financially if you accidentally cause injury or damage to others (think: your shower leaks on your downstairs neighbour). Your condo corporation also has a master insurance that covers the condo building structure and common areas. As a condo owner, you pay for a portion of the building's insurance policy through condo fees.

Renters or tenant insurance covers your belongings in case the contents of your rental are destroyed or stolen. It's important to know that your landlord's insurance does *not* cover the cost of repairing or replacing your stuff. Similar to homeowners insurance, renters insurance will also typically help pay for costs like hotel bills and restaurant meals if you're temporarily unable to live in your own home. And renters insurance usually includes liability coverage for any accidental harm caused to others who live in or visit the property.

HOME INSURANCE AND CLIMATE CHANGE

Home insurance was invented because of fires. In England, modern property insurance made its first appearance after the Great Fire of London in 1666, which destroyed some 13,000 homes. In the U.S., it was the risk of fires that Benjamin Franklin had in mind when he created the Philadelphia Contributionship, the oldest home insurance company in the country. But in much of 21st-century Canada, water has become the new fire.

As I write, there are more than 250 wildfires burning in British Columbia. We don't know yet what the financial tally will be of the inferno that followed the record heat wave of the summer of 2021. Still, when you look at the statistics we currently have, water has long surpassed fire as the number one source of home insurance claims, according to the Insurance Bureau of Canada. Around 1.7 million Canadian households — or just under 20 percent of the population — are exposed to some kind of water-related risk, whether it's from overflowing rivers and lakes, backed-up sewers, or melting snow and ice, according to a 2019 report by researchers at the University of Waterloo.[1] And water damage is expensive. In Toronto, homeowners affected by a flood face, on average, costs of more than $40,000.[2]

Climate change is a big reason for this. A warming planet means extreme weather events are becoming both more frequent and more extreme. Rain now often comes as flash storms, and in some parts of the country, once-in-a-century floods now seem to happen every few years. Between 2009 and 2017, the insurance industry paid out an average of $1.8 billion a year for extreme-weather-related claims, more than four times the average annual payout in the period between 1983 and 2008. Water-related losses are behind more than 50 percent of that increase.[3]

It doesn't help that we've been building in places we perhaps shouldn't have or without properly upgrading the sewer and drainage systems. Across

Canada, provincial and municipal governments have allowed people to build and buy homes on flood plains. And in cities, old pipes often can't handle stormwater in densely built areas. Plus, more and more of us now have finished basements. While having an additional floor for a man cave, a play space for the kids, or a home gym is great, it raises the cost of basement flooding.

Here's the thing: a plain-vanilla home insurance policy likely won't cover that kind of damage. A standard policy is good for accidents like a burst pipe in your bathroom or a broken washing machine. But if your water damage is caused by a backed-up sewer or an overflowing river or lake, you may be on your own.

Thankfully, in the last four years "the insurance industry has made great strides with respect to coverage for water damage," says Anne Marie Thomas, who was an insurance expert at InsuranceHotline.com when I interviewed her for this book. Sewer-backup insurance, which covers damage from waste water flowing back into your house from the city's storm and sanitary sewers, has become more common. Meanwhile overland flood insurance — which deals with flooding caused by overflowing bodies of water and didn't really exist during the 2013 Alberta floods — is now a thing. Some insurers also offer comprehensive coverage that promises to protect you against all sudden and accidental water damage.

But these insurance options aren't mandatory. They're sold as add-ons to your policy — and it's up to you to know whether you need the extra coverage. If you're going to be living anywhere close to a river, a lake, a stream, or the sea, you should look into overland flooding, Thomas says. And older homes, properties located in downstream or low-lying areas, and those connected to sewer systems that carry sanitary and stormwater at the same time are also at higher risk of flooding.

It's also a good idea to practise prevention. While having coverage is always better than being uninsured, never having to file a claim is best. Installing sump pumps and backflow valves and placing window covers over your basement windows, for example, are all steps you or your landlord can take to lower the risk of serious flooding.

Extreme weather linked to climate change is also a factor behind skyrocketing insurance costs for some condo owners. In British Columbia, where the problem is especially acute, provincial regulators found that condo building insurance premiums increased by a jaw-dropping 40 percent on average between early 2019 and early 2020. This issue is also widespread in Alberta and becoming more common in Ontario, with higher costs passed on to condo owners.

If you live in a condo, townhouse, or duplex — also known as strata in B.C. — it's a good idea to review what is and isn't covered by your building insurance. Talk with an insurance broker about possibly boosting your own condo insurance to reduce the likelihood you'll have to foot big bills out of pocket for claims that aren't covered, or are only partially covered, by the building insurance.

If you're hoping to buy a condo, make sure the condo building insurance coverage is adequate and the condo contingency fund, which is meant to pay for repairs, is well funded. Keep in mind that larger buildings, older ones, and those that haven't been well-maintained are more likely to see higher insurance costs.

Finally, a quick word to say that flood insurance isn't the only type of insurance add-on you may need. Damage or loss caused by an earthquake, for example, is also typically something you need to buy optional coverage for. If you live in British Columbia, this is something you should look into, because there's a 30 percent chance of a significant quake in the next 50 years.

• • •

Life, Disability, and Critical Illness Insurance

In chapter 3, I talked about how buying a house is not the mandatory rite of passage into adulthood that many would have you believe. But you know what *is* a sign of adulting? Making sure you have the proper amount of insurance in case of death, disability, or critical illness. While you may not need all three kinds of coverage, you should know what they are and how they work. We're also going to talk about mortgage life or disability insurance and why you might want to tread carefully with that one.

So move the cat off the couch and make yourself comfortable. Here we go.

LIFE INSURANCE YOU CAN AFFORD

The first thing to ask yourself when pondering life insurance is this: What's that big cheque your family would receive upon your death for? Most of us would probably respond that the money would serve to help make up for your lost income and pay off the mortgage and other big debts. If that's the case, what you likely need is something called term life insurance, which provides coverage for a set number of years for a fixed payment. For example, you could take out a policy for 5, 10, or 20 years or until age 65. The idea here is that as you grow older, you won't need life insurance as much. Eventually, you'll pay off your mortgage, your kids will become financially independent (one hopes), and when you retire you'll be able to rely on your own savings, government benefits, and, if you're lucky, an employer pension to get by.

But life insurance can also serve to leave behind an inheritance or cover the costs associated with your death, such as your funeral and, say, the tax bill that would ensue from the family cottage passing on to the next generation. For this, you'll want a policy that gives out a payout even if you die old. This is what permanent life insurance does. Coverage lasts your entire life, no matter whether you pass away at 35, 75, or 110. Two common types of permanent life insurance are whole life insurance and universal life insurance. With permanent life insurance, part of your money goes to investments that provide the cash value of the policy. Depending on the kind of coverage you have, you may be able to use that to borrow or for withdrawals. And if you cancel the policy, you get some money back. But permanent life insurance often comes with much higher premiums.

To understand that pricing difference, let's take a quick look at how life insurance works. Your insurance payment — the premium — depends on your risk of dying. The higher that probability, the higher your premium. At any age, healthy people have a lower risk of dying than those who don't enjoy good health. But as we grow older, we're all more likely to pass away. With term life insurance, your premium stays constant for however many years of coverage you signed up for, but after that it resets at a higher rate if you decide to renew the policy. At older ages, term life insurance usually becomes prohibitively expensive. With whole life insurance your premium stays the same for — you guessed it — your whole life. This means you typically overpay for life insurance when you're younger but pay less than you would have with term insurance when you're older. How premiums work for universal life insurance is more complicated, but it's still expensive.

In a nutshell, term insurance is by far the cheaper option when you're young, which is also when you are usually cash strapped but need life insurance the most. To give you an idea, as a 36-year-old healthy female non-smoker, I could get a 20-year term policy with a $250,000 payout for just over $20 a month, according to life insurance quotes I got online. For the same death benefit, I get quotes starting at around $160 a month for a whole life insurance policy. If you have a tight budget and your main concern is making sure your family will be financially okay without you, term life insurance is the way to go.

That said, in some situations whole life insurance may make a lot of sense, even if you don't have a fancy cottage to pass on to your survivors. If you think you'll still have kids in school or a mortgage to pay off by 65, it may make sense to look into whole life insurance, if you can afford it, says Thomas.

But your premium, of course, also depends on the size of the payout your family would receive. So how much should you sign up for? A quarter of a million dollars, for example, may sound like a lot, but spread out over a decade it's just $25,000 a year. To evaluate your insurance needs, you need to think about the expenses your family would face and the financial shortfall your death would cause. If you're the breadwinner, no longer having your income will leave a big hole, but household expenses may go down, so you may not have to aim for replacing 100 percent of your paycheque. You can use an online calculator to help you estimate your insurance needs or have an insurance broker walk you through it.

If you have life insurance coverage through your employer, book some time to go through the details of your benefits package. You may need to supplement it with your own policy.

DISABILITY INSURANCE

Most people know about life insurance. But what if you got into a car accident or got a concussion from slipping on ice and had to take time off work? What if you became *permanently* unable to work? If you need your paycheque to pay the bills, you need to think about disability insurance.

Canada's social safety net, I'm sorry to say, is full of holes when it comes to long-term disability. If you're self-employed, there isn't much of a net to speak of. But even if you have a "regular" job, long-term disability can be a formidable financial blow.

Provincial workers' compensation boards provide disability benefits to sick or injured workers, but only for work-related accidents or illness and only if you happen to work for a member employer. Employment insurance covers only a portion of your earnings for up to 15 weeks (to be extended to 26 weeks under 2021 federal budget legislation) and only if you've made enough contributions. And don't expect much from the disability benefits of CPP or QPP, which kick in after three months. The maximum benefit as of 2021 was just over $1,400 a month, and you must have paid enough into either CPP or QPP to qualify.

Your employer disability benefits, if you're lucky enough to have any, may not be enough, either. These days group long-term-disability plans may cover you for only 5 to 10 years. And even if your benefits extend to age 65, maintaining eligibility may get harder after the first two years on disability. That's because many employer-sponsored plans apply two eligibility tests. At first you qualify for long-term disability if the insurance company determines you're unable to perform your regular job, something known as the regular-occupation or own-occupation test. But after a period of time — usually two to five years — the criteria for eligibility become more stringent. You may be allowed to keep your benefits only if the insurer deems you incapable of performing *any* job for which you may reasonably qualify, something called the any-occupation test. To say that's a high bar to clear would be an understatement.

If you want proper coverage, you may have to DIY it. The good news is you can take out individual disability insurance, which provides a monthly cash benefit to replace a portion of your lost employment or self-employment income (you can buy disability insurance only if you work). The bad news is it's usually pretty pricey. For example, let's look at a plan for Mitra, a 30-year-old female non-smoker who makes $75,000 a year working as an office manager, a low-risk occupation. According to a sample insurance quote provided to me by Lorne Marr, director of business development at HUB Financial and founder of LSM Insurance, Mitra might pay $166 a month for a long-term-disability plan that starts after 90 days and pays $4,000 a month (or 64 percent of her before-tax income) until age 65 if she becomes unable to perform her regular occupation.

Not everyone can afford disability insurance, but there are a few strategies that might help you get the coverage you need without breaking the bank. First, you should know that if you make a disability insurance claim, the payments you receive are taxable only if your employer pays all or part the premiums. Generally, if you're paying 100 percent of the premiums out of pocket, those benefits are tax-free. This means a benefit that covers 65 percent of your pre-tax paycheque will actually come quite close to your after-tax income. Even with a 50 percent payout, you may still get more than half of your take-home pay. Needless to say, a smaller benefit comes with lower premiums.

Another way to lower your premiums is to stretch out what's known as the elimination period, the time you'll have to wait before receiving the benefit. For example, instead of 90 days you could consider a two-year waiting period if you have a group plan that applies the any-occupation test at the two-year mark.

Going back to Mitra, if she opted for a benefit of $3,000 a month until age 65 with a waiting period of two years, her monthly premium would be $102, according to a second sample quote provided by Marr. That's considerably less than the $166 of the first example.

Note that Mitra didn't try to save money by shortening her benefit period but stuck with a policy that would cover her until age 65, which would protect her from the risk of developing a permanent disability. Likewise, Mitra chose a policy that provides a payout for a disability that prevents her from doing her regular job — as opposed to any job. While own-occupation or regular-occupation coverage comes with more expensive premiums, you're more likely to actually be able to get a payout if you ever become disabled. You may also want to look into partial or residual disability coverage, which guarantees you'll get some cash even if you can only do part of your job or have lost only part of your earnings because of a disability. Another feature to consider: you may be able to add the option to increase your benefits at roughly the pace of inflation. This ensures your payouts keep up with rising living costs if your disability lasts many years.

CRITICAL ILLNESS INSURANCE

Critical illness insurance is somewhat similar to disability insurance but with several key differences. First, while disability insurance is only available if you earn an income, you can buy critical illness insurance even if you don't work (for example, if you're a stay-at-home parent). Critical illness insurance can also be a good option if you have a high-risk occupation for which disability coverage is unaffordable or unavailable altogether, Marr says.

While disability insurance pays a monthly benefit, critical illness policies provide a tax-free lump sum of money. If you qualify, you'll get the payout even if you can continue to work — and you'll be able to use the cash as you see fit. It can help you cover many of the added costs that often come with a disability, such as hiring a nurse or paying for treatment outside Canada. Critical illness insurance also provides a payout if you receive a medical diagnosis like cancer, heart attack, or multiple sclerosis, conditions that are usually covered by disability insurance as well if they cause you to become unable to work. But critical illness insurance tends to be expensive and often comes with very strict definitions of what diseases are covered. In general, if you work for a living and have a limited budget, getting disability insurance is the clear priority.

WHAT THE HECK IS MORTGAGE LIFE OR DISABILITY INSURANCE?

If you're taking out or renewing a mortgage, the bank may ask you whether you'd like mortgage life insurance or mortgage disability insurance — often referred to under the umbrella term *mortgage protection insurance* — to go with your big loan. This isn't the mortgage default insurance we talked about in chapter 3, which pays your lender if you can't keep up with your payments and is mandatory if you have a down payment of less than 20 percent of the value of your home. Mortgage life or disability insurance are optional products that cover or reduce your mortgage debt if you pass away or become disabled, so your family doesn't have to worry about making the mortgage payments without your income. And the bank will seamlessly add the insurance premiums to your monthly mortgage payments. Sensible and simple, right?

Well, not quite. If you read through the policy, you may find a lot you don't like. Possibly the biggest issue with these policies is that your family may find out only after they file a claim that there will be no payout. With mortgage protection insurance, the process of determining whether you're actually eligible for coverage typically happens only *after* your death or disability. And if there's something in your circumstances that voids the policy, your family will be left without coverage.

Even if your claim does go through, the money goes to your lender, not your family. In the case of death, the insurance will provide a lump-sum payout that will take care of your remaining mortgage balance. In the case of disability, the policy usually covers your monthly payments. Either way, your beneficiaries don't get to decide what to do with the money. Maybe they would have preferred to use the funds for other purposes or sell the home to pay back the mortgage.

Another not-so-great feature: your insurance payout may shrink as you pay off the mortgage. These policies are meant to cover only your outstanding mortgage balance, which will get smaller as you make your monthly payments. Your insurance premium, on the other hand, usually stays the same throughout the mortgage term. And if you switch mortgage providers, you may lose coverage and need to apply with the new lender.

• • •

Wills and Powers of Attorney

We've talked about floods, earthquakes, death, disability, and critical illness. But wait — we're not done. We need to talk about death and illness a bit more. (This is a good time to go grab a coffee or tea, and maybe add a snack as a pick-me-up.)

Every adult, regardless of relationship status, should have a will, which is a legal document that sets out what should happen to your estate.

"Nobody knows what an estate is. They think it's something huge with a moat around it," says Edward Olkovich, a lawyer, author, and Ontario-certified specialist in estates and trusts law. Essentially, your estate is the stuff you'd leave behind if you died, including your property and your liabilities, such as unpaid bills, debts, expenses, and taxes. Even if you don't own — or owe — much, dying without a will often means leaving a financial and legal mess behind for your loved ones to sort out.

For example, if you're single and didn't appoint an executor — somebody to manage your estate — no one's authorized to walk into your apartment to empty the fridge or pay your credit card bills until the courts appoint someone, a process that can take months, according to Olkovich, who writes an estate blog at MrWills.com. If you're in a common-law relationship, in some provinces dying without a will may mean your partner isn't automatically entitled to any part of your estate. Even if you're married with most assets in both your and your spouse's names, dying without a will can create huge headaches for your family. "Go to the bank and try to get $50,000 dollars out of your spouse's bank account and they won't give it to you," Olkovich says.

While you're at it, consider also preparing instructions in case you become mentally incapacitated, even temporarily. Who do you want in charge of making decisions on your behalf? A power of attorney is a legal document that gives one or more individuals the authority to manage your money and property. Without it, a court would have to appoint someone to manage your affairs, a process that can cost thousands of dollars and take months to accomplish, Olkovich warns.

You can also draft a similar document to put another person in charge of making health and non-financial decisions for you if you're no longer able to. These are sometimes called powers of attorney for health, personal or health directives, or representation agreements or mandates. People sometimes also call these living wills, although that's a U.S. term.

A lawyer can prepare a will and powers of attorney for financial and health matters for anywhere from a few hundred to several thousand dollars. And now some provinces allow remote or virtual signing of these documents, provided that one witness is a licensed lawyer, Olkovich notes. Just watch out for scams by unlicensed operators, he adds.

If you have a simple situation, you could also prepare these documents online. There are at least a couple of websites in Canada that will guide you through the process of drafting your own legal documents with an interactive, user-friendly interface — a bit like online tax software. These sites also let you easily update your documents when your circumstances change. Be aware, though, that DIY wills that simply consist of a blank form for you to print and fill in have quickly gained a reputation for dubious quality and low value for the money.

• • •

Wrap-Up

Do you need insurance? Yes, you do. I don't care if you're the person who never gets sick, always finds parking right away, and keeps spotting $5 bills on the street. Life happens — to everyone. Don't let it catch you unprepared.

That said, it *is* possible to buy too much insurance. I've made that mistake. Years ago, when my husband was a university lecturer in the U.S., we chose the slightly cheaper health-care option and then had a health scare that resulted in an even scarier health-care bill. After that, I loaded up on too much insurance when we came back to Canada. I have since realized we were overinsured and have trimmed back a bit.

If you're wondering whether you have too little or too much insurance, here are some steps to find out:

» If you have dependents and don't have life insurance, get it — and do it now. If you're young and healthy, term life insurance costs so little that it's a no-brainer. You may be able to take out a policy online and without a medical exam.

» Shop around. This holds for any kind of insurance. Just like with mortgage rates or credit cards, there are loads of financial-product comparison sites that can help you find the most competitive insurance. Just remember that the premium isn't the only thing that matters. Make sure to check how much you'd have to pay out of pocket after a claim and what's included — and excluded — from coverage

---

» Whether you rent or own, think about whether you need to boost your home insurance with optional coverage for things like water damage or earthquakes. You can use FloodSmart

Canada to see whether you live in a flood zone. The Institute for Catastrophic Loss Reduction has a similar earthquake risk tool and an interactive quiz to help you assess your risk of basement flooding, along with a slew of free resources to help you mitigate a variety of risks posed by extreme weather events and natural disasters.

» It's a good idea to review your insurance policies every year before they renew or whenever your circumstances change significantly. Your insurance needs may have changed, meaning you may need more or less coverage than you currently have. It's also worth looking around to see whether you could get equivalent coverage for less money.

As I mentioned, many people start to seriously think about insurance only when they have a spouse or common-law partner or kids. I hope this chapter has made it clear that you don't need to have dependents to need more insurance than the mandatory policy on your car. That said, the financial implications of being a couple or a parent go far beyond insurance. And that's what we'll talk about in chapter 8.

CHAPTER 8

SHARING MONEY AND PAYING FOR BABIES

ONCE UPON A TIME, there were simple rules for married couples to manage their money. The man of the house would make all the money and take all the big financial decisions. The woman, usually in charge of day-to-day admin, tried to make the most of whatever came in. In a slightly different twist on this basic arrangement, the man would hand over his whole paycheque to the wife, who would then give him an allowance, money that — as the stereotype goes — would help keep the local pub in business. Either way, it was simple — and it was dreadful.

Today, thankfully, it is widely accepted wisdom that both partners in a couple are functioning adults capable of handling the full array of money-management decisions that life presents. This isn't yet a universally held belief, and it's astonishing how long it's taken society to come this far. In 1965 women in Canada could run for office, but they still couldn't get a mortgage without a male guarantor. But allow me to relish, for a moment, the fact that we *have* managed to put the worst of gendered preconceptions around money behind us.

Still, whether you're in a heterosexual or same-sex couple, combining the finances of two independent, confident, and complex human beings comes with a host of thorny issues that the olde household economic textbooks could blissfully ignore. How do you share your money with someone who makes significantly more — or less — than you? And what if you have student debt and they don't? What if you like to spend and they like to save? How do you bring together two people who will invariably have their own particular hang-ups about money?

There is no simple script that will work for every couple. But there are some common-sense principles for arriving at a fair and practical arrangement. Having those conversations soon after you've decided you're in the relationship for the long haul will likely make you stronger as a couple. For you shall be tested, and likely sooner than you think. If you live in a big city, the issue of whether to rent or buy — and, if the latter, how much you can afford — has become one of the most stressful financial decisions of our times. If you're hoping to have or adopt kids in the future, brace yourselves for the cash crunch of your lives. You may find yourselves surrounded on three sides as you try to wrestle with (a) your mortgage payments, (b) your lingering student loans, and (c) a reduced income on parental leave, at first, and then child-care costs equivalent to a second mortgage. It's enough to shake even the most solid of relationships.

In this chapter, we'll go over how to tackle this financial obstacle course as a team, how to plan for a baby, and how to save for your kids' education.

• • •

Money for Two

In chapter 1, we went over how the money-bucket system can help you manage your money without collecting receipts and stressing out over spreadsheets. But how does that work when you're a couple? Now there are two of you spending and, often, earning. You have individual and shared saving goals, and you may each have debts that predate the relationship. I'm not going to lie; it can feel daunting. But let's take it one step at a time. First up: how to organize your bank accounts.

BANK ACCOUNTS: SHARED, SEPARATE, OR A BIT OF BOTH?

There is no right or wrong answer as to how couples should organize their bank accounts, says Sandi Martin, a certified financial planner and partner at Spring Planning. Some people are happy to keep almost everything separated, many others share every single bank account, and still others adopt a mixed approach. Where you and your partner feel most comfortable on that continuum depends on your personal preferences and couple dynamic, Martin says.

Some couples like the autonomy of separate bank accounts. "I do know married couples who love each other very much, who organize their finances like that," Martin says. Some even buy groceries separately. The only expenses they share are household bills and, if applicable, the cost of raising children — that's it. Even in this scenario, it probably makes sense to have at least one joint account for sharing routine expenses, Martin adds. Also, keep in mind that this set-up, while perfectly suited to some couples, comes with very little transparency. You'll have close to zero insight into what your other half is doing with their money unless they volunteer those details. So if you're taking this route, it might help to have a written agreement spelling out what the joint account is for, Martin says. You have to agree on what's shared spending, what's autonomous, and how you'll decide in the future where new kinds of expenses will fall.

At the opposite end of the spectrum, you can blend everything together by sharing all your bank accounts. My husband and I do something similar. We have access to each other's bank accounts, and I can attest it has some practical advantages. For example, since he's a freelancer who gets paid per project and I have a steady paycheque, being able to look at each other's bank account balances helps us smooth out our respective cash flows. I'll transfer money to his account if I see it's running low and, if he gets several payments at once, he'll use the surplus to pay some of the bigger one-off expenses. Since everything is in common, we don't have to constantly track who paid for what and who owes money to whom. The downside of total transparency, though, is that you get to see every single thing your partner spent money on. If this becomes an excuse to police each other's every small indulgence, it's not going to work, Martin warns. It's always going to be easier to justify your own small splurges compared to your partner's, but you have to be able to keep an open mind and refrain from judgment, she says.

This certainly resonates with my experience. For example, one of the things that used to drive me up the wall about my husband's spending habits was the number of books — and Amazon boxes — that would end up at our doorstep on a regular basis. Couldn't he just get himself an e-reader and save money and space — not to mention reduce our recycling waste — by buying ebooks instead? But the thing is, he can't. He loves his paper books and scribbling notes on the margin as he reads — and that's okay. For my part, when the pandemic hit and we all got stuck at home, I felt I needed to substitute machines for my own domestic labour as much as possible. I already had an electronic pressure cooker and now I wanted a robot vacuum cleaner. My husband had been an Instant Pot skeptic and now had his doubts about the expensive vacuum cleaner. Wouldn't it just be faster if I did the job myself with an old-fashioned vacuum? Wouldn't the stupid thing get hopelessly stuck under the couch in our cluttered house anyway? In the end, though, he accepted that I'd done my research and that the purchase would have a high emotional return for me. And let me tell you, being able to set up the little robot floor-sweeper, go for a walk, and return to a crumbs-free house is one of the things that helped me maintain my sanity during the lockdowns. (Also, for the record, my husband would like you to know that while I'm in charge of cleaning the floors and dusting in our house, he does the kitchen and bathrooms.)

Still, sharing all your bank accounts isn't for everyone. Many couples find their happy place somewhere in the middle of the spectrum, Martin says. One popular approach is to share most bank accounts but give each of you a monthly allowance you are free to spend as you want, no questions asked.

Money-Bucket System for Two

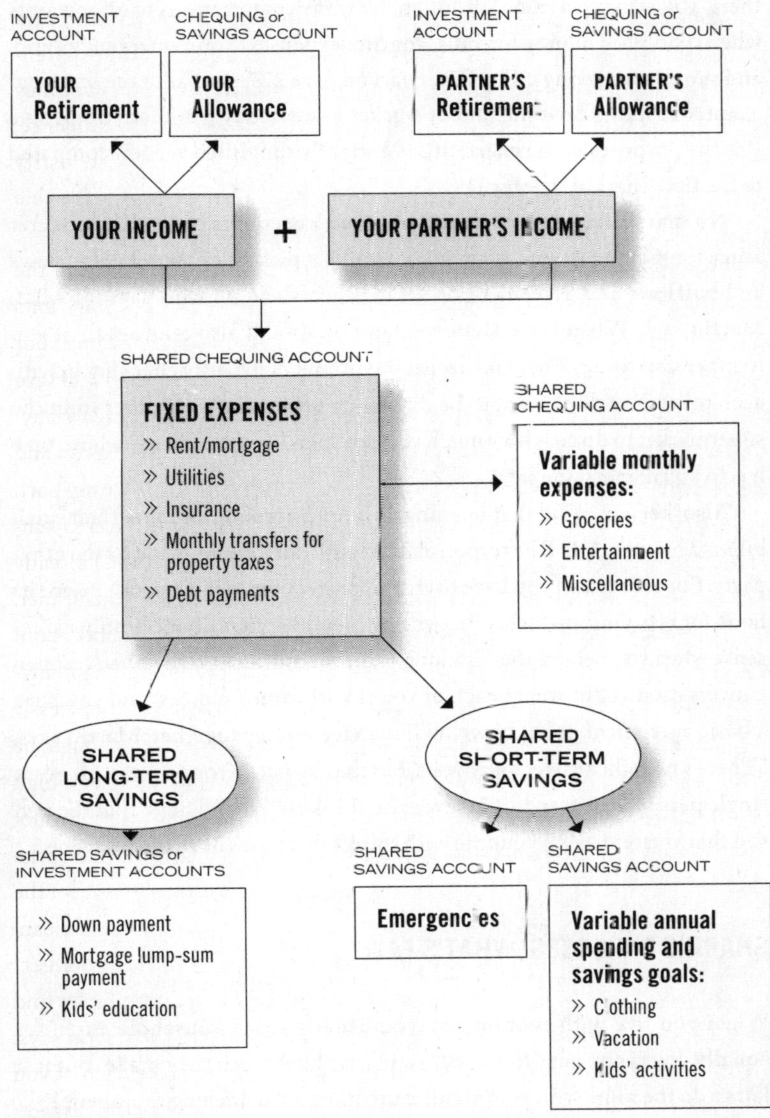

A similar approach that preserves a bit more autonomy is to maintain separate individual accounts where your respective paycheques land. From there, you set up a number of automatic transfers to various bank accounts where you pool money for bills, routine expenses, your emergency fund, and short-term savings. The flow chart on page 227, similar to the one from chapter 1, shows how the money-bucket system may work for two people (for the purposes of the chart, this is a slightly simplified version compared to the flow chart in chapter 1).

No matter how you organize your bank accounts, though, the secret sauce for making it work is having a complete picture of household inflows and outflows and agreement on savings goals and on who pays for what, Martin says. Whatever system you land on should also allow each of you to make day-to-day financial decisions without constantly checking in with each other. You don't want to be dialing up your significant other from the supermarket to discuss how much you can spend on groceries or whose turn it is to buy diapers, she says.

Also, keep in mind that opening up a joint account for more than small bills is a big step. You'll be responsible for any transactions made by the other party. For example, if you have overdraft protection, you may both be on the hook for repaying any debts. In general, blending your finances only makes sense when you believe there's a long-term commitment, you've had an open conversation about where each of you is with your finances, and you have a basic agreement about how you'll manage money together, Martin says. "There's no right answer for anyone, but the absolute wrong answer for every single person is just to do whatever you think is best and hope that the person that you're sharing your life with thinks that that's okay for everyone."

SHARING EXPENSES: WHAT'S FAIR?

When you live with roommates, you usually share household expenses equally. Everyone pays the same, no matter how much they make. But is it fair to do the same with your significant other, a.k.a. lifelong roommate?

If you both have roughly the same income, a 50/50 split seems the obvious way to go. But if one of you makes significantly more than the other, this can create problems. One of you will inevitably have to save less, spend less on themselves, or potentially put less money toward paying off their personal debt so they can keep up with their share of household expenses. "A strict adherence to 50/50 is actually not equitable," Martin says. "It might be equal, it might seem fair on the surface, but it's not equitable."

Splitting common expenses in half may make sense in the early stages of a relationship, when you're still figuring out whether you really want to make a long-term commitment. But even then it's important to look at your full financial picture and assess what's fair. For example, if your partner has a significantly lower income and moves in with you, will your more expensive lifestyle affect their ability to save enough or attack their debt as aggressively as they'd like?

Even when you both start out with paycheques of the same size, there's a chance the 50/50 split will eventually cause friction. What if one of you gets a raise? What if your partner loses their job? And what happens if you become parents and one of you sees their income drop through one or more years of parental leave? I've heard a few times of young moms who had to put their retirement savings on pause while their partner continued to save because they were expected to keep contributing 50 percent of the household expenses.

Many couples choose to share expenses proportionally to their income, which usually requires regular adjustments to adapt to your changing circumstances. It takes a little bit of work and a willingness to adapt, Martin says. And even if you put everything together and adopt a my-money-is-your-money approach, you'll need to have frequent conversations to make sure you remain on the same page about spending, saving, and borrowing.

OLD DEBT, NEW DEBT, AND SAVINGS

Income isn't the only source of financial inequality in a couple. The debt each of you brings into the relationship will also affect the lifestyle you can afford and your ability to share expenses. And let's be clear, the moment you start to seriously consider moving in together, you need to talk about debt. This isn't just about finding out whether the other person has been running up credit card bills with abandon. It's also about recognizing whether you come from different financial backgrounds. Maybe your partner has student loans and you don't because your parents were able to pay for your education. You may decide to help them pay off that debt, or they may want to tackle it on their own. But those loans need to be part of the conversation, because you need to agree on a lifestyle and expense levels that will work for both of you.

In general, any conversation about splitting expenses beyond the very early stages of a relationship must include old debt, new debt you and your partner may want to take on individually or together, and savings, Martin says. Whether you're saying, "My funding my own retirement is going to cost this much, and it means I have to save this much personally" or "We as a couple need to reach *X* amount per year of savings in order to reach our joint retirement," those savings goals are part of the household financial flow and will affect everything else, Martin says.

PRENUPS

If you've always thought of prenups as a mood killer, I'm not going to argue with you. Thinking about who gets what if we split up is pretty unromantic stuff. And whenever you hear about a prenuptial agreement in the news, it usually involves someone rich and famous trying to exclude the other party from much of their wealth in a divorce. Why would you want to do that to your significant other?

But hear me out: prenups — or similar contracts — can make a lot of sense even for common mortals like you and me who don't have a château in France to worry about. Edward Olkovich, the lawyer and certified specialist in estates and trusts law, names a few examples of common scenarios in which prenups can come in handy: you participate in a family business, you're involved in a tech start-up, or your family has a cottage that will one day pass on to you and several other relatives. Other people who share an interest in the business, start-up, or property may be entitled to insist you have a prenup, says Olkovich. Or you may want to protect what you bring into a second marriage for your children's inheritance, he adds.

But prenups don't have to be about ensuring the other person doesn't get certain things like family assets. That's not how Martin talks about them. The point, she says, is to map out what should happen in the unlikely event of a breakup so that the process is as painless as possible and everyone is treated fairly. When this is the spirit, prenups can actually be a way of showing one another that you truly care.

Prenup isn't quite the right word in every case. Similar agreements may be called marriage or domestic contracts. They are known as cohabitation agreements, if you're a common-law couple, but the basic idea is the same: they usually set out how you want to divide your property and debts and handle any spousal support. Depending on where you live, a lawyer or notary public can prepare these agreements for you, and it's generally a good idea for each of you to get your own legal advice as you decide what should be in the contract.

I'm not suggesting here that you absolutely need to have a prenup. But at least having a discussion about it is a good idea. As we just saw, there is lots to talk about.

RECOGNIZING FINANCIAL ABUSE

Earlier on in this chapter I mentioned the word *allowance* a couple of times. Couples can agree together to give each other an allowance — money each partner can spend however they want worry-free. But in the olden days, an allowance was the product of a one-way decision. It was what one adult in the relationship would "allow" the other adult to spend. Today, this kind of allowance arrangement should raise red flags.

Money and power have always been closely intertwined — and intimate relationships are no exception. Using the family finances to exercise control is known as financial abuse, a widespread issue on which we're just starting to gather data in Canada. Financial extortion or coercion very often overlaps with intimate partner violence, 80 percent of the victims of which are women in Canada.[1] But financial abuse doesn't always happen alongside physical violence, and men can also experience it.

Some instances of financial abuse are striking. Abusers have been known to steal money from their partners, prevent them from opening their own bank accounts, or force them to write bad cheques. But other examples of money-related abuse may be subtler and hard to recognize. Here are some common signs of financial abuse, according to the U.S.-based National Network to End Domestic Violence:

» Controlling how all the money is spent

» Demanding that the other partner stay at home instead of working or furthering their education, or, vice versa, refusing to contribute to the family income

» Hiding information about family assets

» Racking up debt in joint accounts

» Forcing the other partner to work in the family business for no pay (or, I would add, for less than minimum wage)

When one partner monopolizes the family's financial flows, it often deprives the other of their financial independence, which can make it much harder to leave an abusive relationship. This can happen at any income level. A 2019 report by the Woman Abuse Council of Toronto, for example, found that survivors of financial abuse came from households with incomes ranging from under $25,000 to $150,000 a year.[2]

If you're experiencing financial abuse, you can learn online about setting up a financial safety plan. This may include steps like gathering evidence of the family's assets and liabilities and building up your own savings — for example, by setting aside spare change from purchases in a safe place or by having raises and bonuses at work wired directly into a bank account the abuser doesn't know about. Women's and men's shelters and non-profits that help survivors of domestic abuse can help. However, as you search the web, make sure to use a safe computer your abusive partner can't access to check your browsing history.

• • •

Babies and How to Pay for Them

Children, if you want them, are wonderful. Even when the baby's poop somehow finds its way out of the diaper and all the way down to the toes (true story). Even when they wake you up at six o'clock sharp every single weekend morning. At the end of the day, there's just something about giggles, hearing little footsteps running to your bedroom, and raising tiny humans in general that makes it all worth it to parents.

These little bundles of joy, though, are *expensive*. In North America, raising a child until age 17 or 18 typically costs around a quarter of a million dollars, several Canadian and U.S. estimates show. Those figures are enough to give any prospective parent pause, not to mention that they don't include the cost of higher education. But if you want to have children, the question isn't *Can I afford to have a baby?* but *How can I afford to have a baby?* Let's take a deep breath here. Finances should not dictate whether or not you get to have a family. If you believe having children will bring you meaning and fulfillment, then there's no point in depriving yourself of that. We make and save money to live, not the other way around.

Here's a look at how to add babies to your budget and what you should know about saving for your kids' education.

THE TRIPLE MONEY CHALLENGE OF PARENTHOOD

Kids cost money, but it's in the first three years that parents often face the ultimate cash crunch. Here's a scenario that will likely be familiar to many: You just took out a mortgage together but are still paying off your student loans, so now there are at least two debt payments coming out of your bank accounts. Then comes baby. For the first year, one of you goes on mat/pat leave, which means one income is greatly reduced (or perhaps you each take some time off to care for your little one, but you still have less money coming in than you used to). Then, when both of you are back to work, your now one-year-old is off to daycare, which adds another monthly payment of mortgage-like size. Here in Toronto, for example, it's common to pay $1,800 or more a month for a spot for kids under 18 months. It gets a bit less expensive as you move up to older age groups, but you won't see a significant cost reduction until your child hits kindergarten (all this, of course, with the glaring exception of Quebec — blessed be universal child care).

It took a pandemic for affordable child care to become a national priority. In its 2021 budget, the Trudeau government promised $10-a-day child care. The plan has its critics, and even fans acknowledge the road to creating a nationwide child-care system is still long and fraught with federal-provincial negotiation death traps. So until we get there, countless new parents will have to contend with the money challenge that often comes with starting a family in this day and age.

With a new mortgage, student loans, and first a reduced income and then crushingly expensive child-care fees, you'll feel the squeeze on three sides. Needless to say, that squeeze can be even tighter if you're a single parent fending (financially and otherwise) for yourself and your child. How do you manage these three money suckers without running up huge debts?

The good news is that a little prep work can go a long way. Kids aren't always planned, of course, but if you do have some time to plan ahead, you can start by estimating the financial shortfall you'll be facing while on leave and possibly through the daycare years. "Is there a gap between the income that we're going to have and the life that we want to have? And how big is that gap?" Martin, the financial planner we met earlier, asks.

Then take a look at your current budget. If you have any room to save, you can start building up a cash reserve that will help you bridge that gap when baby comes. On the debt side, remember that government student loans come with repayment assistance options. In general, though, if you have debt you can pay off before the baby's arrival and if eliminating those monthly payments would bridge your gap, that's an "equally valid" strategy, Martin says.

Burning your non-mortgage debt ahead of your leave means you've essentially taken down one of the three money suckers. Another option is not buying a house — or at least postponing it. The notion that we need to be homeowners before starting a family is deeply ingrained for most of us, but babies don't actually know the difference. If you're worried about being forced to move on short notice, Martin suggests inquiring about signing a multi-year lease once you've found the perfect place. "Your landlord might be supremely delighted to sign a longer-term lease."

SAVING FOR HIGHER EDUCATION

You don't need me to tell you that higher education is expensive. Around half of university students in Canada graduate with debt — and those who do so owe a massive $28,000 on average. That's a formidable financial load to carry when you're just starting out in the job market. It's a weight that drags you down just as you're trying to take off in life. If you've been paying off your own student loans for years, you know the struggle. So what can you do to avoid or minimize this burden for your children?

Registered education savings plans (RESPs) are arguably the most powerful tool available to Canadian families to save for their kids' education. Like RRSPs and TFSAs, RESPs are registered accounts that allow your investments to grow tax-free. But unlike RRSPs and TFSAs, RESPs come with an extra bonus: free money from the government. For every dollar you put into an RESP, the feds pitch in an extra 20 percent, up to $500 per year per child, through the Canada Education Savings Grant (CESG). Depending on your family income, the government may throw in another 10 percent or 20 percent of the first $500 contributed every year (something called the Additional Canada Education Savings Grant or A-CESG). However, the maximum amount of CESG a child can receive is $7,200, and that includes any additional amounts.

There is another $2,000 per child available in federal dollars for low-income families through the Canada Learning Bond. Note that there is no need to make a contribution to receive a Canada Learning Bond. If your child is eligible, this is money the government will pitch in just for opening an RESP. Finally, in some provinces, you may also be eligible for provincial grants. You can keep putting money into an RESP until 31 years after you first opened it, for a lifetime maximum contribution of $50,000 per child.

To get the full $500 a year in CESG money, you'd have to contribute $2,500 a year per child, which works out to $208.33 per month. If that's more than you can afford, keep in mind that grandparents can also open an RESP for your kids, although opening multiple plans for the same child can get tricky. If you want to pool family resources, a simpler way to do so is to ask relatives and friends for some RESP cash contributions instead of gifts for birthdays or other occasions.

If you get a late start on RESP contributions or couldn't max out your contributions every year — which happens often, given how busy and cash strapped many new parents are — catching up is relatively easy. The unused grant room piles up and carries forward until the year your kid turns 17. Until then, you can make up for missed contributions one year at a time. In other words, you can deposit up to $5,000 a year and receive up to $1,000 in federal grants. Keep in mind, however, that the annual maximum CESG is $1,000, meaning you won't earn grant money for any catch-up contributions in excess of $5,000 in a given year.

RESPs are also more flexible than many people think. A common concern is what happens if your kid doesn't go to university. But RESPs are good to pay for a variety of other educational programs after high school, including colleges, trade schools, and apprenticeships. Your kids may even be able to use the money to bankroll their studies at a number of foreign schools. Even if your child doesn't continue their education after high school, it won't be the end of the world. Any CESG and Canada Learning Bond money goes back to the government, but your own contributions go back to you tax-free. The bummer is that any interest or investment returns the money earned over the years is taxable to you, at your marginal tax rate. In addition, you'll also face a steep penalty tax of 20 percent. But you may be able to transfer the money tax-free (up to a limit of $50,000) to your or your spouse's RRSP, provided there's enough contribution room.

All in all, RESPs are a pretty sweet deal. And sure, if you're thinking it would be better if higher education were cheaper, or free, to begin with, I'd say you have a point. But in the imperfect world we live in, RESPs are as good as it gets.

That said, not all RESPs are created equal. There are individual, family, and group RESPs. All the good stuff you've heard about RESPs so far applies primarily to the first two. An individual plan is meant to fund the education of one beneficiary. If you have more than one kid, you can opt for a family plan.

With group RESPs, however, tread carefully. A group plan, offered by so-called group plan dealers or scholarship plan dealers, combines your savings with those of other families with children of the same age and invests that larger pool of money. The plan matures on a certain date when the children are expected to start their post-secondary studies. A group RESP spares you the effort of investing your child's education savings yourself. However, you may pay a high price for that convenience. For one, these plans often have steep sales charges that come out of your contributions in the first few years. But for all the fees you'll be paying, your money may not earn much in investment returns. Group plans often invest in lower-risk investments like bonds, GICs, and mortgages, according to the Ontario Securities Commission's GetSmarterAboutMoney.ca. Also, you're usually expected to make contributions on a set schedule. If you miss one or more payments, you could face penalties and interest. If you leave the plan early, you may lose much of what you put in due to those steep sales charges I mentioned earlier, which are often non-refundable, and any investment returns go to the families who are still in. At maturity, what your child gets depends on how much money is in the plan and the number of families among whom the funds must be distributed. Keep in mind that group plans may have their own additional rules about which educational programs are eligible.

Finally, as I and many others have reported, group RESP dealers often employ aggressive sales tactics. While they must hand out a prospectus that describes how the plan works, they often pitch their product to exhausted, sleep-deprived new parents who don't have the energy or the time to read through the fine print. Newcomers to Canada who don't speak English or French well are also a frequent target, with dealers sometimes employing salespeople who speak their native language to gain their trust. It's good to know you have 60 days from signing to cancel the contract and get any money back without penalty.

• • •

Wrap-Up

Money quarrels can break up a relationship. And babies can break the bank. But it doesn't have to be that way. Whether you're pondering how to share finances with your significant other or wondering how you're going to pay for the baby, here are a few suggestions to help move forward:

» Have a frank conversation with your other half about money. Are there debts you or they don't know about? How do you both go about spending your money? What's the state of your respective savings? And what are your goals for the future?

» The next step is to come up with — you guessed it — a money system for sharing your finances. It may take some trial and error before you land on something that works, but that's okay.

» Whatever system you choose, never cede control of your finances to anyone else. It's fine to let your partner take care of financial chores you find boring, but you should always know where the money is going. And only you decide what happens with your money.

» If you're going to be a parent soon, start reading up on RESPs — you won't have the time or the energy to do that after the baby comes. And remember: RESPs come with free money from the government even if you can't contribute much or, sometimes, anything at all.

» You can save a lot of money on baby-related costs by buying second-hand or joining a group where members share or pass on what they no longer need. Buy-and-sell sites or buy-nothing Facebook groups can be great resources for finding gently used baby wear and gear. Remember: the baby won't know the difference between a $80 onesie and a $15 quality hand-me-down — and will spit up on it regardless.

We've talked about romantic relationships and babies. But what about the relationship with your own parents? That's the subject of the next chapter. I'm talking, of course, about the Bank of Mom and Dad.

CHAPTER 9

ALL IN THE FAMILY

AISHWARYA RAI, the Indian actress of Bollywood and Hollywood fame, was on the *Late Show with David Letterman* promoting what was then her latest movie, *Bride and Prejudice*, a modern twist on the Jane Austen classic. The year was 2005, and Letterman started by asking a few run-of-the-mill questions meant to bring the audience up to speed. Rai, already one of Asia's biggest stars, had recently burst onto the Western scene. Based in Mumbai, she'd been in about two dozen movies, one of which premiered at the Cannes Film Festival, "and that kind of got people talking and noticing me," Rai helpfully explained.

Then Letterman tossed her one of his signature curveballs: "By the way, do you live with your parents, is that true?"

"Yeees," Rai replied slowly, leaning on her armrest and fixing her famous, radiant blue-green eyes on the late-night show host.

"And is that common in India for older children to live with their parents?" Letterman continued.

Rai was ready. "It's fine to live with your parents," she said with a shrug and a benevolent smirk, "because, um, it's also common in India that we don't have to take appointments with our parents to meet for dinner."

Her answer drew roaring applause.

More than 15 years later, many of us could benefit from channelling some Aishwarya Rai. Today nearly 25 percent of men and 20 percent of women between the ages of 25 and 34 are living with their parents, according to Statistics Canada. When you look at older adults as well, 1.9 million people aged 25 to 64, or 9 percent of Canadians in that age range, share a roof with one or more of their parents.[1] That number has more than doubled from less than a million in 1995. Millennials are also much more likely to still be receiving financial help from family. One RBC survey from 2019, for example, found that around half of parents of 30- to 35-year-olds were still providing support to their children.[2]

The Covid-19 pandemic also brought adults and their parents back together. Gen Z students were forced to retreat to their childhood bedrooms as campuses across Canada shut down and summer job opportunities dried up in 2020. And many young millennials who lost their jobs in the pandemic had to make similar choices (as of January 2021, 15- to 24-year-olds accounted for fully 45 percent of net employment losses since the start of the pandemic, according to Statistics Canada).

But the fact that more people are doing it has hardly washed away the stigma. There's plenty of shame to go around for both young people and their folks. Living at home past your school-age years is still labelled "failure to launch." And parents who provide financial help to their adult children — whether it's cash or room and board — are invariably portrayed as the Bank of Mom and Dad (BOMAD), enablers of a spineless generation at best and unwitting destroyers of their own retirement security at worst.

And what do people do when they're embarrassed about something? They don't talk about it. They don't think about it. In fact, they pretend it's not happening at all. In a 2014 article for *Toronto Life* magazine, writer Leah McLaren noted how every 30-something middle-class professional in the city seemed to have an awkward financial secret: their boomer parents were beefing up their down payments, covering their mortgages, and even paying for child-care costs.[3] McLaren described a couple, Erica and Gavin — who were reportedly too embarrassed to use their real names — who'd spent three years looking for a home to buy with a $100,000 down payment only to watch property values skyrocket and the relative size of their cash deposit shrink. Eventually, Erica's dad offered to triple their down payment, something that allowed them to buy a $661,000 home with a manageable mortgage. "The 'velvet handshake' — an early inheritance from a relative before said relative dies — was once only common in wealthy circles. Now it's the secret force powering the city's middle-class downtown economy," McLaren wrote.

But that kind of guilt-driven secrecy is damaging. The shame so many of us feel about receiving — and giving — family help is not only deeply unfair, it can lead to bad financial decisions.

• • •

BOMAD and Bootstraps

The idea that everyone is supposed to strike out on their own by their early to mid-20s is worth examining. The concept is steeped in North America's mythology about rugged individualism and pulling yourself up by your bootstraps. But if you look around the world, the expectation that young adults should move out and stop needing help as soon as they graduate — if not earlier — is not widely shared. And within Canada, immigrant families are increasingly pushing back against this notion. Around 20 percent of Canadians of South Asian and Chinese descent who are between 25 and 64 years old live with their parents, compared to 9 percent of the total Canadian population in the same age group.[4] And in 2017 almost one in 10 foreign-born grandparents in Canada lived in multi-generational homes with their grandchildren, more than twice the share of Canadian-born grandmas and grandpas.[5]

Living with your extended family doesn't have to be about money. For many, it's a lifestyle choice. In a multi-generational home, everyone contributes. It's the proverbial small village it takes to raise a new generation and care for an aging one.

Even in North America, larger families living together is hardly an unprecedented phenomenon. At the turn of the 20th century, it was common for Canadian homes to include a variety of extended relatives — the 1901 census lists "stepdaughter-in-law," "half sister," "great nephew," and "goddaughter," among others. And in the U.S., fully 30 percent of 18- to 34-year-olds were living with their parents in 1880, according to a study by the Pew Research Center.[6] There were cultural reasons for young people to room with Mom and Dad for longer. For one, grown children — and especially women — were expected to live with their parents until marriage, says Nora Spinks, CEO at the Vanier Institute of the Family. But sharing the same roof also made good financial sense, whether it was about bringing in additional income or pooling resources to care for children and the elderly or working the farm, Spinks adds.

Today, as many young people contend with student loans, unfathomably high housing prices, massive child-care costs, and uncertain job prospects, families are banding together again.

For a while, the world chronicled millennials' journey into adulthood in the same tone in which Sir David Attenborough narrated *Planet Earth*. Twenty- and thirtysomethings, it was believed, were a new species of human who didn't care about the life milestones of previous generations. They didn't want to drive cars, own homes, or make babies, it seemed. That was the conventional wisdom circa 2010. But a few years later, older millennials started doing all of those things. It's not that we didn't want them — we just took far longer to get there.

And let's face it, the window of opportunity to hit those traditional targets — if those are what you want — is getting narrower. It takes years to pay off your student loans and save up for a down payment before you're struck with the double-whammy of parental leave and child-care costs. Getting all those ducks in a row with zero help is quite the feat. And in an increasing number of housing markets, the idea that you'll be able to buy a home on your own has become nothing short of ludicrous for most of us.

That's why scores of concerned parents and grandparents have stepped in to help, creating a family economy that is both a return to the past and a whole new reality.

For many couples in Vancouver, the attempt to buy their first home has become a group effort, with cash often coming from both sides of the family. "There's a fear of missing out factor, that's for sure," says Chris Catliff, president and CEO of BlueShore Financial. "But there's also the fear of losing touch with your grandchildren and your great grandkids," he adds. If the parents and grandparents live in Vancouver and the kids have to move to Chilliwack — a 100-kilometre drive away — to afford a home, the little ones may not get much of a chance to see their grandma, Catliff says.

It's a similar story in Toronto. Real estate broker John Pasalis estimates that around three-quarters of the first-time buyers he sees have help from family. The cash infusions have grown considerably in size over the years. When he started out some 15 years ago, the gifts from parents were around $20,000 to $30,000. "And now it's like $100,000 or $150,000," he says. The math of it is simple, he adds. Home prices are around 10 times those incomes or more, so "you need a huge down payment to get into the market," he says.

At the same time, real estate is often the source of wealth that enables parents and grandparents to come to the financial rescue. For example, Vancouver homeowners with kids in their late 20s or early 30s have likely seen their home value go up from three to five times, says Catliff, an increase he calls "staggering."

That's what's new about family help these days. While families have always shared resources in times of need, the ability to make gifts or loans in the hundreds of thousands of dollars — the true BOMAD — is no longer the purview of the wealthy, Spinks says. Middle-class families and sometimes even lower-income ones will have money to distribute if, say, Grandma leaves behind a $1.4-million home.

Another important difference comes from the fact that Canadians have been having fewer children. This has transformed the dynamic of intergenerational transfers, Spinks says. Think about a rural family in the olden days, for example. If a couple had four boys and four girls, the property would often be split among the male heirs, which made for four smaller farms (the girls would hope to marry someone with their own plot of land). Today, says Spinks, you often have four grandparents and only a couple of grandchildren. The statistics show that Canada has a record 7.5 million grandparents, but the average number of grandkids has declined to four, down from five in 1995.[7] As Spinks puts it, while once the transfer of money and assets from one generation to the next would dilute a family's wealth, these days it often concentrates it.

• • •

Stop Feeling Ashamed and Make a Plan

Parents and grandparents have increasingly stepped in to help, but, as I mentioned, the all-around awkwardness about family financial aid hasn't gone away. If you're on the receiving end, there's that feeling in the pit of your stomach that you should be able to stand on your own two feet — that somehow you did something wrong. And the parents and grandparents who are giving often worry that the kids are just financially clueless. Even for those who trust their progeny and understand just how much the economy has changed, there's a lingering shame about having to prop up grown adults.

All this means the topic is usually taboo. Silence, in turn, breeds misunderstandings, resentment, and family drama. When no one talks about money, feuds and bad financial decisions often ensue, even when everyone has the best intentions.

It's time to stop feeling ashamed and have a frank conversation. I'll go first. My husband and I have received financial assistance from both my parents and his — loads of it, in fact. I'm a journalist, as you know. He is a recovering academic, as they say, who is now self-employed. We have a small house in Toronto, where we can be close to my in-laws and there are lots of job opportunities for both of us. There isn't a chance we would have been able to buy even a shoebox in the city on our own. Some things we talked out with our parents; others we didn't to the extent that we should have, which I regret.

Based on my experience and research on the issue, here's a road map for discussing family financial help.

STEP ONE: A FINANCIAL STRESS TEST FOR PARENTS AND GRANDPARENTS

The first step for everyone involved is to verify whether those willing to provide the help can actually afford to give. I think we can all agree that parents and grandparents should not jeopardize their financial security and retirement. But figuring out how much older generations can safely give or loan is trickier than it may seem. It requires running through some worst-case scenarios like home prices falling (you never know) or significant long-term care needs in old age. The cost of the latter can vary widely and reach exorbitant levels. To give you an idea, while government-run nursing homes can cost between $25,000 and $40,000 a year, assisted living in a private facility can cost $100,000, and a full year of 24-7 care by professionals an astonishing $200,000 a year.[8] "You've got to start with the longevity risk ... and set up a bundle of money that takes care of that," Catliff says, ideally by sitting down with a financial planner.

Now, the adult kids who'd be receiving the helpful cash injections don't need to be part of these conversations. Your parents or grandparents may not want to discuss the ins and outs of their finances with you — nor should they have to. But if you're lining up for a big donation or extended support, you owe it to them to at least ask whether they've considered expenses like long-term care and suggest they get financial advice if they haven't.

Keep in mind that parents can overstretch themselves even if they have no cash to spare. For example, if money is tight, they may not really be in a position to provide free room and board, even if they offer — you should pay at least your share of groceries and utilities.

STEP TWO: WHAT ARE THE SHARED GOALS?

The ultimate goal of any significant or prolonged financial aid from family should be to make it easier for you to achieve financial independence. It's that starting push that makes it so much easier to get going on your bike, especially when the road ahead is uphill.

"It should be money that you use to grow your own net worth, whether that is to eliminate debt, invest in real estate, invest in the stock market, or invest in your education to improve your income," says Calgary-based Bridget Casey, a millennial money expert and founder of the popular blog *Money after Graduation*. Those funds are not meant to subsidize your lifestyle.

But when talking shared goals, the devil is in the details. Parents want the best for their kids, but you may not agree on what *best* looks like. What are your family's expectations? Often, larger financial gifts come with significant strings, Casey warns. "Like they'll help you pay for school, but only if you study certain things," she says of friends who were told they had to become lawyers and doctors, or else. Accepting financial help should never mean handing over the reins of your life to someone else. If that's the condition, you may want to bow out.

Often, though, the strings aren't quite so suffocating. For example, Mom and Dad will help you buy a house, but only if it's a property they like in a neighbourhood they approve. Or perhaps they'll pay for your wedding, but only if they get to be part of the planning. Maybe you can live with that — or maybe not. Either way, it's best to be clear on these sorts of issues from the get-go.

It's also crucial to agree on priorities. What is the money for, first and foremost? Both Catliff and Casey say the number one priority should be paying for higher education. "I think post-secondary education is the most important investment because that gives the person the ability to go earn at a higher level later on in life," Catliff says. But that doesn't mean that parents and grandparents need to shell out to send you to an expensive U.S. university, he adds.

And Casey says she's not sure she'd be ready to beef up a down payment if her daughter ever wanted to buy a house. "That one might be the one that I don't help with, to be honest ... because I don't think home ownership is essential to building wealth," she says.

STEP THREE: HOW MUCH HELP CAN YOU AFFORD TO RECEIVE?

You read that right. Your parents and grandparents must make sure they can really afford to help you, but you also need to take a hard look at your own finances to ensure they don't unwittingly set you on a path you can't afford.

I've seen this happen with home buying. Deep-pocketed parents help their kids get into a lovely home that is far too expensive for them. Even if the mortgage payments are manageable, the property taxes and general cost of upkeep are not. Don't let a generous gift leave you house-poor.

STEP FOUR: HOW ARE YOU GOING TO DO YOUR PART?

Some of this is obvious. First of all, don't be lazy. Your parents may give you a push, but you've got to pedal. Second, don't be reckless. Case in point: Casey recalls a friend who bought a house with a gifted down payment and then took out a home-equity line of credit to invest in Bitcoin. "I'm not even joking about that," she says. "[People] take bigger risks because the money came in so easy." Gambling with your parents' money is the best way to lose the financial privilege your parents worked so hard to give you, she adds.

If you're living at home, talking about how you're going to do your part may also involve discussing whether you should pay rent. Even if your parents can get by without it, it may be a good idea to pay a little something as "a way of acknowledging that they're really giving you a gift and you're going to help out," Casey says. And who knows, maybe Mom and Dad will give you that money when you eventually buy a house, she says. That's what some of her aunts and uncles did with her cousins. "It usually wasn't enough for a down payment to matter a lot," she says, "but it could furnish their new place."

At the same time, it's important to set realistic expectations about just how soon you might be able to take off on your own. If you're saving for a down payment, it could take you years to reach your target even if you're squirrelling away two-thirds of your pay. It's a good idea to share your timeline and any possible setbacks with your parents.

STEP FIVE: WHAT'S THE BEST WAY TO ACHIEVE YOUR SHARED GOALS?

If you and your folks are on the same page, it's time to discuss the best way for them to provide that lifeline. When it comes to family financial help, the *how* can be just as important as the *how much*.

• • •

When Your Family Helps You Afford a House

Giving money can be tricky and full of unintended consequences on both ends of the transaction. Often, getting advice from a financial planner or estate lawyer is well worth the time and fees. For example, there are many ways in which parents or grandparents can help you afford a home, each with a number of pros and cons. Here are some of them.

YOUR FAMILY GIVES YOU A GIFT OF CASH

One of the big perks of receiving a pile of money is that there is no tax on gifts of cash in Canada, unlike in the U.S. But keep in mind that if your parents or grandparents have to sell a second home or investments that have appreciated to free up said cash, they will have to pay capital gains taxes, Catliff notes.

Be aware, too, that one of the tricky things about using gifted money to buy a house is that, if you're married and your marriage falls apart, your ex would be entitled to half the property regardless of who financed the home purchase. Your family may want to speak to a lawyer about prenuptial and other possible ways to protect their investment.

Also, most lenders will consider cash from BOMAD as a loan unless your parents or grandparents sign a letter indicating the money is a gift, says mortgage expert Robert McLister.

YOUR FAMILY GIVES YOU A LOAN

If your family can't afford to — or doesn't want to — gift you tens or hundreds of thousands of dollars, they may be able to provide a loan. The potential upside for you is that your parents could make the loan interest-free or eventually forgive it. (If they do charge interest, it will count as taxable income for them.) This arrangement can work well if you have siblings or cousins who also need help and BOMAD is providing loans of different sizes to each of you, Catliff says. For example, if one kid gets $50,000, another gets $100,000, and a third gets $200,000 and you all repay the money, your parents or grandparents can redistribute some of the cash to equalize things.

A loan can also help ensure that the money will stay in the family in case of a divorce, although, again, talk to a lawyer about this.

On the downside, a mainstream lender may not allow you to use a family loan as part of your down payment, leaving you with a smaller selection of financial institutions to borrow from and fewer chances to get a really competitive mortgage rate, McLister warns. And, he adds, borrowed down payments, when they are allowed, will count as debt in the lender's total debt service ratio (remember, from chapter 3?), which could mean you won't qualify for the mortgage you need. The bank may not be persuaded to lend to you even if Mom and Dad don't demand regular payments. "Lenders commonly impute a payment, even if the loan terms require no payment until after the end of the mortgage term," McLister says.

YOUR PARENTS CO-SIGN OR GUARANTEE YOUR MORTGAGE

One of the obvious upsides of this arrangement for your folks is that — if you keep up with your payments — they can help you get a home without actually giving you any money. Co-signing usually means they own the home with you, typically because you don't have enough income on your own to qualify for a mortgage. They'll also be equally responsible for the mortgage, McLister says. Having them guarantee your mortgage usually helps when you have sufficient income but your credit score isn't great. A guarantor is liable only if the primary borrower defaults, McLister adds.

There are countless other financial, tax, and estate considerations to keep in mind if you're considering co-ownership, which a lawyer can help you navigate. (Also, more on co-owning a home in a few paragraphs.)

YOUR PARENTS OWN; YOU RENT

The first thing to consider is this: How comfortable would you be having your parents as landlords?

Second, if the end goal is for your parents to eventually pass ownership of the house to you, the obvious catch is the capital gains tax. The government will consider the transfer to be a sale at fair market value, and if the value of the property has increased a lot, your parents could face a steep tax bill.

YOU CO-OWN THE HOUSE

This may become an increasingly popular option. Multi-generational homes — which include at least three generations of the same family — are the fastest-growing type of household in Canada. More than two million Canadians these days have chosen that living arrangement. There are big potential perks for both the young and the old. Free child care courtesy of the grandparents is one example. At the same time, Grandma and Grandpa won't get lonely, and it will be easier for you to care for them when they get older. But the potential for family drama is significant.

Regardless of whether you're actually living with your extended family or their name is simply on the title, how you co-own a home matters. In most provinces in Canada there are two main types of shared ownership: joint tenancy with right of survivorship and tenancy in common. (The exception is in Quebec, where you only find the latter.)

Don't be confused by the word *tenancy*; in this case it has nothing to do with tenants and landlords. Joint tenants own the property together, and if one of them dies their share automatically passes to the surviving owners, says Tim Brisibe, director of tax and estate planning at Mackenzie Investments. This is often the way couples own a home together, but parents and children can also be joint tenants. This set-up may allow you to avoid probate tax, the fee provinces charge for the mandatory process of having the courts either legally validate your will or handle an estate when there is no will. The cost can be negligible or quite high, depending on where you live. Avoiding probate means saving not just money, but time. The probate process can last anywhere from several weeks to several years if the estate becomes the subject of litigation, Brisibe says. But true joint tenancy may also come with several potential pitfalls, depending on your situation and your plans. For example, you wouldn't be able to sell the property without your parents' consent.

With tenancy in common, on the other hand, co-owners may own unequal shares of the property and there is no right to survivorship. If one of the co-owners dies, their share becomes part of the estate and is distributed according to their will or the default rules that apply when someone doesn't have a will. There is no avoiding probate, but having clearly delineated ownership lines could come in handy.

If you're considering owning a home with your parents it's a good idea to sit down with an estate lawyer who has experience in real estate transactions to spell out your intentions, Brisibe says.

Finally, if your parents co-own the home but their primary residence is elsewhere, capital gains tax is another big consideration. An eventual transfer of their ownership share to you could generate a huge tax liability.

• • •

Mom and Dad May Need Help, Too

Canada's housing crisis has been a major reason why house-rich parents and grandparents have come to the rescue of millennials, many of whom would have otherwise been shut out of home ownership (and it will soon be Gen Z's turn to contend with that issue). But there's another crisis experts say is looming on the horizon, and it may soon see family help flow the other way: long-term care.

In a little more than a decade, a sizable minority of Canada's oldest boomers will reach the age when they will start needing considerable looking after, whether it's medical care or help around the house. By 2050, the number of seniors over the age of 85 is expected to more than triple. And who's going to care for them? For many families, most of the heavy lifting will have to come from younger family members, a.k.a. millennials.

Long-term care provided outside of hospitals isn't considered an insured service under the Canada Health Act. Instead, provinces and territories have their own standards for what is publicly funded and what isn't, which makes for a patchwork system with a number of gaping holes. Right now, much of the work of taking care of ailing seniors falls to family members, who put in an estimated five and a half hours of unpaid work every week, according to a 2019 report by the National Institute on Ageing at Ryerson University.[9]

But because of Canada's declining fertility rate, millennial caregivers may face an even greater load. We can only hope that the long-term-care-home scandals linked to Covid-19 will give the government the jolt it needs to start fixing this issue. But if nothing changes, the average family caregiver may have to put in nearly eight hours of unpaid work per week, the Ryerson researchers predicted (well before the pandemic). And it's hard not to worry that the job of helping with groceries and cleaning, tracking prescriptions, and shuttling older relatives to medical appointments will fall disproportionately on women.

But the main point here is that millennials will soon get their chance to return the favour to their parents.

• • •

The Real Trouble with BOMAD

In the grand scheme of things, BOMAD is quietly recalibrating some of the generational wealth imbalance between boomer and Gen X parents and their millennial and Gen Z adult children. But in another and very important way, it's making wealth inequality worse. If you're not among the lucky ones with parents willing and able to pave the way with dollar bills, it's hard not to feel like you're being left behind.

Casey, who put herself through undergrad and an MBA in finance with no parental support and then paid her way through an unexpected pregnancy as a single mother, says the financial gulf between millennials with access to BOMAD and those without has been widening. "I do notice — especially now, because now I'm in my mid-30s — how big that gap has widened between my friends and me, the ones who didn't have to take out student loans and those that did."

Casey has a pull-yourself-up-by-your-bootstraps story as great as any. *Money after Graduation,* which she started by chronicling her fight against student debt, is now one of the most recognized personal finance brands in Canada and a thriving business. In 2019, she bought her first Louis Vuitton bag and told the rest of the internet how to afford one, too (hint: prerequisites include having an emergency fund, automatic savings contributions, and zero consumer debt). And yet, the difference between her net worth and that of her fellow MBA grads who received generous BOMAD funding and didn't have children is "multi–six figures," she says.

Capable and hard-working as they may be, young adults who didn't get that initial financial oomph from their family may never catch up. This is something we should all be very worried about. But it doesn't mean you should refuse money from your family on principle. "I wish I had had all the financial help," Casey says.

That's especially the case when it comes to her student debt. Even if interest rates on student loans are low, it's still interest compounding in the wrong direction, she says. Instead, "if I had had more cash flow, I could have started investing sooner, I could have started investing more, and it would have compounded the other way on my net-worth sheet."

That's why Casey is adamant she'll be as generous as she can possibly be with her daughter without compromising her own finances. "I will absolutely pay for her entire education — no matter how much she studies, no matter what school she goes to," she told me. "I'll probably help her if she ever wants to start a business. And I think I'll give her her first TFSA contribution right out of the gate when she turns 18."

Casey says she would not bail out her daughter if she ended up racking up, say, credit card debt. But that's because she's going to make sure her girl is never in a position to have to use debt to pay for necessities. "My child should have no reason to ever go into debt — ever."

I know I feel the same way about my son. And here lies the great Catch-22 of wealth inequality: the more unequal a society becomes, the greater the incentive for parents to try to preserve their kids' advantage. I'm not here to wag my finger at anybody. As I've said before, there is no shame in helping those you love or gratefully grabbing that stretched-out hand.

But the least you can do if you're among the financially privileged is recognize just what a huge leg-up you have. This doesn't mean you have to spill your guts; exactly how much Mom and Dad gave you is nobody's business. But you do owe it to your friends to be open about how you financed your education, bought your house, or got to be debt-free. Even if your parents didn't have much to give but let you live in the basement for free or now watch your toddler every single day while you're at work, don't hide it — that also makes a significant difference to your bottom line.

Growing inequality is a problem far bigger than you or me or our respective families. It's a problem we have to tackle as a society. It requires political courage and smart, well-thought-out policies. So take the money, if it's offered, and use it wisely. Give to charity. Be an informed citizen, vote, and help build a world in which we all get a fair shake.

CONCLUSION

GO GET YOUR ACORNS

THIS BOOK HAS been waiting to happen since the financial crisis of 2007–2008. The fully formed idea for it wouldn't come to me for another 10 years or so, but the *need* for a book that put common personal financial challenges in their larger economic context was there for me all along.

Because things clearly aren't what they used to be. The economy is changing all the time. In many ways, it has made it harder to become a financially functioning adult. And it has been steadily moving away from the reality that shaped many public policies and much of our social safety net decades ago. That goes for anything from housing policy to employment insurance. This major tectonic shift has been happening slowly, over generations, with the gap between policy and reality getting wider and wider.

Meanwhile, many of us millennials and Gen Zers chasing after middle-class financial goals are looking increasingly like Scrat, the sabre-toothed critter from *Ice Age*. We're working hard to get and keep our little acorn, but the seismic convulsions of the Earth are — how shall I say it? — turning our modest pursuit into what feels like a battle for survival. (And yes, if you're wondering, we watch far too much *Ice Age* at my house.)

I hope this book has helped you understand why it sometimes feels so hard to achieve financial goals that our parents' generation largely took for granted. And I hope this helps you set aside any shame, guilt, or self-blame.

Instead, I want you to embrace the challenge and fight back. You're going to hop over the cracking ice, dodge falling boulders, escape avalanches, and get your flipping acorns. As your situation changes, you'll face different financial priorities. I'd like this to be your financial survival manual, a resource you can go back to whenever you need it, whether you're weighing your housing options, getting a car loan, or buying life insurance.

As I set out to write *Money Like You Mean It*, I would never have imagined that the world would go through yet another massive economic earthquake. For a while, the downturn triggered by the pandemic felt a lot like déjà vu. While the magnitude and speed of the job losses in the spring of 2020 were unprecedented in postwar times, younger workers were, once again, among the hardest hit and will likely feel the impact of the downturn for longer, as often happens with recessions. On the housing market the pandemic had the opposite impact of the financial crisis. Instead of falling, home prices soared. But the end result is that home ownership in Canada is now further out of reach for many millennials and Gen Zers than it was before Covid-19.

Still, for all the pain and suffering it caused, the health emergency also forced a long-overdue reckoning. When millions of Canadians lost their incomes, some of the gaping holes in our unemployment benefit system were quickly patched up — if only temporarily. When scores of working parents — and especially moms — had to trim their hours or leave their jobs entirely as schools and daycares shut down, the need for affordable child care became a top political issue. And as thousands of Covid-19 survivors live with debilitating long-term symptoms, we're finally thinking harder about how to financially support people with chronic and long-term disabilities who may not have, or be able to access, workplace insurance.

The good news is that we can keep that momentum going. Because, unlike Scrat, we *can* both chase after our little acorn and shape the world around us. Building a better post-pandemic economy will require bold ideas, fierce debate, and, probably, a good dose of trial and error. It's totally worth it.

ACKNOWLEDGEMENTS

IT TAKES A VILLAGE. This is true no less of writing books than it is of raising children.

My village starts with Chris, who never called himself a feminist but always acts like one. Thank you for bending over backward so I could finish this book despite the pandemic, school shutdowns, and everything else the past year and a half has thrown at us. And *grazie mille* also to my parents, who flew all the way from Italy and braved a hotel quarantine, among other Covid hassles, to come to the rescue in the latter stages of book editing.

A very big thank you to Kathryn Lane at Dundurn Press for convincing me to focus *Money Like You Mean It* squarely on millennials and Gen. Zers and their struggles. (That was just one of her many key editorial insights.)

Susan Fitzgerald was a kind, thoughtful, and eagle-eyed copy editor. Patricia Treble probed the manuscript from start to finish and cheered me on — reconnecting with her has been an unexpected treat. Working with Susan and Patricia was so nice that, as gruelling as the process was, I couldn't help feeling sad when it was all over.

Special thanks also to Jane Gerster and Jason Kirby, who provided crucial feedback early on. My literary consultant, Sally Keefe-Cohen, along with Kate Henderson, generously swooped in to help when I was just getting started and didn't know what was what.

And of course, this book would not exist without its sources, who liberally donated their expertise and time: Allison Venditti of Moms at Work and Ready to Return; Anne Marie Thomas, who was at InsuranceHotline .com when she spoke with me; economist Armine Yalnizyan of the Atkinson

Foundation; Brian Murphy, who was at Canadian Black Book when I interviewed him; Bridget Casey of *Money after Graduation*; Chris Catliff and Ilana Schonwetter at BlueShore Financial; Christopher Ragan at McGill University; David Larock of Integrated Mortgage Planners; Diana Petramala at Ryerson University; Douglas Hoyes and Scott Terrio at Hoyes, Michalos and Associates; Edward Olkovich at Edward Olkovich Law; Gennaro De Luca at WEALTHplan Canada; George Iny of the Automobile Protection Association; personal finance writer Jackie Lam; Jason Heath of Objective Financial Partners; John Pasalis of Realosophy Realty; Julia Chung and Sandi Martin of Spring Planning; Julie Kuzmic at Equifax Canada; Lorne Marr at HUB Financial; Mariel Beasley at Duke University; Nora Spinks of the Vanier Institute of the Family; financial planner Robb Engen of Boomer and Echo; Robert McLister at RATESDOTCA; mortgage broker Sean Cooper, who wrote *Burn Your Mortgage*; Tammy Schirle at Wilfrid Laurier University; Tim Brisibe at Mackenzie Investments; and Tim Nash of Good Investing. And I would like to send a special shout-out to financial planner Alexandra Macqueen, who provided invaluable help both on and off the record.

I have Elena Radic and the rest of the team at Dundurn to thank for how fine the final product turned out. And finally, I am very grateful to my employer, Global News, for its unwavering support throughout.

NOTES

CHAPTER 1: *MIND OVER MONEY*

1. Gerard Walsh, *The Cost of Credentials: The Shifting Burden of Post-Secondary Tuition in Canada*, Royal Bank of Canada, June 2018, rbc.com/economics/economic-reports/pdf/other-reports/Tuition_June2018.pdf.
2. Kyle Dahms and Camille Baillargeon, "Rising Home Prices Posing a Challenge for Affordability," *Housing Affordability Monitor*, National Bank of Canada, February 3, 2021, housepriceindex.ca/wp-content/uploads/2021/02/housing-affordability-q4.pdf.
3. Ran Kivetz, Oleg Urminsky, and Yuhuang Zheng,"The Goal-Gradient Hypothesis Resurrected: Purchase Acceleration, Illusionary Goal Progress, and Customer Retention," *Journal of Marketing Research* 43, no. 1 (2006): 39–58.
4. Lauren Torres (Kitty), "Share My Horror at the World's Worst Debt Visualization," *Bitches Get Riches*, November 13, 2017, bitchesgetriches.com/debt-visualization.
5. Abigail B. Sussman and Adam L. Alter, "The Exception Is the Rule: Underestimating and Overspending on Exceptional Expenses," *Journal of Consumer Research* 39, no. 4 (2012): 800–814, doi.org/10.1086/665833.
6. Nicole Lyn Pesce, "You're Spending More on Your Subscription Services Than You Think," *MarketWatch*, July 25, 2018, marketwatch.com/story/youre-spending-more-on-your-subscription-services-than-you-think-2018-07-25.
7. Nava Ashraf, Dean Karlan, and Wesley Yin, "Tying Odysseus to the Mast: Evidence from a Commitment Savings Product in the Philippines," *Quarterly Journal of Economics* 121, no. 2 (May 2006): 635–72, doi.org/10.1162/qjec.2006.121.2.635.
8. Nina Mazar et al., "Pain of Paying? — A Metaphor Gone Literal: Evidence from Neural and Behavioral Science" (working paper no. 2901808, Rotman School of Management; working paper no. 2017/06/MKT, INSTEAD, April 16, 2017). dx.doi.org/10.2139/ssrn.2901808.

9. Moty Amar et al., "Winning the Battle but Losing the War: The Psychology of Debt Management," *Journal of Marketing Research* 48, SPL (2011): S38–S50, doi.org/10.1509/jmkr.48.SPL.S38.

CHAPTER 2: *KNOW YOUR ENEMY: DEBT IS NOT CREATED EQUAL*

1. Financial Consumer Agency of Canada, *Home Equity Lines of Credit: Consumer Knowledge and Behaviour,* January 15, 2019, canada.ca/content/dam/fcac-acfc/documents/programs/research-surveys-studies-reports/home-equity-lines-credit-consumer-knowledge-behaviour.pdf.
2. Will Dunning, *Annual State of the Residential Mortgage Market in Canada, Year End 2018,* Mortgage Professionals Canada, January 2019, mortgageproscan.ca/docs/default-source/membership/annual-state-of-res-mtge-mkt-2018.pdf
3. Lance J. Lochner, Todd R. Stinebrickner, and Utku Suleymanoglu, "2013-3 Analysis of the CSLP Student Loan Defaulter Survey and Client Satisfaction Surveys," (working paper, Centre for Human Capital and Productivity, Western University, London, Ontario, 2013), ir.lib.uwo.ca/cgi/viewcontent.cgi?article=1092&context=economicscibc.
4. Cameron Yee, "Are the Costs of Owning a Car Worth It for Students?," *MoneySense,* May 29, 2020, moneysense.ca/save/budgeting/are-the-costs-of-owning-a-car-worth-it-for-students.
5. Canadian Mortgage and Housing Corporation, *The State of Homebuying in Canada: 2019 CMHC Mortgage Consumer Survey,* 2019, assets.cmhc-schl.gc.ca/sites/cmhc/data-research/consumer-surveys/consumer-mortgage-survey-results-2019-en.pdf.

CHAPTER 3: *EVERYTHING STARTS WITH HOUSING*

1. Paul Kershaw and Sutton Eaves, "Straddling the Gap: A Troubling Portrait of Home Prices, Earnings and Affordability for Younger Canadians," Generation Squeeze, June 2019, d3n8a8pro7vhmx.cloudfront.net/gensqueeze/pages/5293/attachments/original/1611267353/Straddling-the-Gap-2019_final.pdf.
2. Sal Guatieri, "Your House Makes More Than You Do," Bank of Montreal, February 25, 2021, commercial.bmo.com/en/resources/commercial-real-estate/economic-insights/your-house-makes-more-you-do.
3. *Global Financial Stability Report, April 2018: A Bumpy Road Ahead* (Washington, DC: International Monetary Fund, 2018), doi.org/10.5089/9781484338292.082.
4. As cited in Natalie Obiko Pearson, "Vancouver's Empty Mansions Highlight Middle-Class Housing Woes," Bloomberg, February 9, 2017, bloomberg.com/news/articles/2017-02-10/vancouver-s-empty-mansions-highlight-middle-class-housing-woes.

5. For more on this you can read Cooper's book *Willful Blindness: How a Network of Narcos, Tycoons and CCP Agents Infiltrated the West* (Toronto: Optimum Publishing, 2021).
6. Royal LePage, "New OSFI Stress Test Set to Limit National Home Price Appreciation to 4.9% in 2018," Cision Canada, December 13, 2017, newswire .ca/news-releases/new-osfi-stress-test-set-to-limit-national-home-price -appreciation-to-49-in-2018-663856403.html.
7. Canadian Real Estate Association, "Canadian Home Sales Inch Lower in December," January 15, 2020, crea.ca/news/canadian-home-sales-inch -lower-in-december/.
8. Twinkle Ghosh, "How the Pandemic Pushed Canadian Millennials to Home Ownership," Global News, February 25, 2021, globalnews.ca/news/7662252 /cda-millennials-homes-real-estate-pandemic/.
9. Bank of Canada, *Financial System Review, 2021*, May 17, 2021, bankofcanada .ca/2021/05/financial-system-review-2021.
10. Canada Mortgage and Housing Corporation, *Examining Escalating House Prices in Large Canadian Cities*, 2018, assets.cmhc-schl.gc.ca/sf/project/cmhc /pdfs/content/en/69262.pdf
11. Housing Market Information Portal, Canada Mortgage and Housing Corporation, www03.cmhc-schl.gc.ca/hmip-pimh/en#TableMapChart/1/1/Canada.
12. Jennifer Combs, Danielle Kerrigan, and David Wachsmuth, "Short-Term Rentals in Canada: Uneven Growth, Uneven Impacts" (forthcoming paper, School of Urban Planning, McGill University, Montreal, June 14, 2019), upgo.lab.mcgill.ca/publication/short-term-rentals-in-canada/short -term-rentals-in-canada.pdf.
13. Tom Cardoso and Matt Lundy, "Airbnb Likely Removed 31,000 Homes from Canada's Rental Market, Study Finds," *Globe and Mail*, June 21, 2019, theglobeandmail.com/canada/article-airbnb-likely-removed-31000-homes -from-canadas-rental-market-study.
14. Shaun Hildebrand, "GTA Rental Market Slows in Post-COVID-19 Period," Urbanation, July 15, 2020, urbanation.ca/news/284-gta-rental-market-slows -post-covid-19-period.
15. Shaun Hildebrand, "GTA Rental Vacancy Rate Rises in Q2," Urbanation, April 17, 2020, urbanation.ca/news/291-gta-rental-vacancy-rate-rises-q2.
16. Ben Myers, "Rentals.ca July 2021 Rent Report," Rentals.ca, July 2021, rentals .ca/national-rent-report.

overview.

Too Far?," *In Focus*, February 4, 2021, Canadian Imperial Bank of Commerce, economics.cibccm.com/cds?id=55d4e0a3-bdb8-426a-bf62-331015ce64c9&flag=E

New York Times, February 9, 2021, nytimes.com/2021/02/09/business/dealbook/cryptocurrency-bitcoin-tesla.html.

2020, www150.statcan.gc.ca/n1/daily-quotidien/201113/dq201113a-eng.htm.

n.d., docs.rlpnetwork.com/Communications/Royal_LePage_HPS_Chart_Q42020.pdf.

Annual State of the Residential Housing Market in Canada from Mortgage Professionals Canada, 22 percent of mortgage holders have floating rates and 5 percent have "combination" mortgages, in which part of the payment is based on a fixed rate and part is based on a variable rate.

about the Merits of Variable-Rate Home Loans," *Advisor's Edge*, February 2008, 25–39, advisor.ca/wp-content/uploads/sites/5/2018/09/AE02_2008 .pdf.

CHAPTER 4: *MAKING MONEY LIKE YOU MEAN IT*

1. Dawn Desjardins and Carrie Freestone, "Canadian Women Continue to Exit the Labour Force," Royal Bank of Canada, November 19, 2020, thoughtleadership.rbc.com/canadian-women-continue-to-exit-the-labour-force.
2. As cited in Rachel Siegel, "How to Get a Raise: Be a White Man," *Washington Post*, June 6, 2018, link.gale.com/apps/doc/A541556778/STND?u=tplmain&sid=bookmark-STND&xid=bab68394.
3. Chris Martin, "Can You Quit Your Way to Higher Pay?," PayScale, January 19, 2018, payscale.com/data/quit-way-higher-pay.
4. Jess Fickett (Piggy), "Romanticizing the Side Hustle: When 1 Job Isn't Enough," *Bitches Get Riches*, April 17, 2017, bitchesgetriches.com/romanticizing-side-hustle.

CHAPTER 5: *THE BIG FAT RETIREMENT MYTH*

1. Moshe A. Milevsky and Alexandra C. Macqueen, *Pensionize Your Nest Egg: How to Use Product Allocation to Create a Guaranteed Income for Life* (Hoboken, NJ: Wiley, 2015), 15–16.
2. Data from a custom table provided to me by Statistics Canada based on their Pension Plan in Canada and Labour Force Survey.
3. Nathalie Bachand et al., *Projection Assumption Guidelines*, FP Canada Standards Council, April 30, 2020, fpcanada.ca/docs/default-source/standards/2020-pag---english.pdf.

4. Frederick Vettese, *The Essential Retirement Guide: A Contrarian's Perspective* (Hoboken, NJ: Wiley, 2015), 39.
5. Data from a custom table provided to me by Statistics Canada based on their Pension Plan in Canada and Labour Force Survey.
6. Rachelle Pelletier, Martha Patterson, and Melissa Moyser, "The Gender Wage Gap in Canada: 1998 to 2018," Statistics Canada, October 11, 2019, www150.statcan.gc.ca/n1/pub/75-004-m/75-004-m2019004-eng.htm.
7. Sheila Block and Grace-Edward Galabuzi, *Persistent Inequality: Ontario's Colour-Coded Labour Market* (Ottawa: Canadian Centre for Policy Alternatives, December 11, 2018), policyalternatives.ca/publications/reports/persistent-inequality.
8. Learn more about spousal RRSPs and spousal contributions by reading "Tax Planning: Should I contribute to a spousal RRSP?" on RBC's website: www.rbcroyalbank.com/healthcare/en/advice-learning/article/?title=tax-planning-should-i-contribute-to-a-spousal-rrsp.
9. French comic artist Emma has illustrated this concept in her graphic novel *The Mental Load: A Feminist Comic* (New York: Seven Stories Press, 2018).

CHAPTER 6: *LEARNING ABOUT INVESTING: NOT OPTIONAL*

1. Sean O'Shea, "How the Pandemic Has Turned Downtown Toronto Condos into 'Challenging' Investments," Global News, November 4, 2020, globalnews.ca/news/7440669/toronto-downtown-condo-investments-pandemic.
2. Ben Johnson, *Morningstar's Active/Passive Barometer*, Morningstar, August 2020. © [2021] Morningstar, Inc. All Rights Reserved. The information contained herein: (1) is proprietary to Morningstar and/or its content providers; (2) may not be copied or distributed; (3) does not constitute investment advice offered by Morningstar; and (4) is not warranted to be accurate, complete or timely. Neither Morningstar nor its content providers are responsible for any damages or losses arising from any use of this information. Past performance is no guarantee of future results. Use of information from Morningstar does not necessarily constitute agreement by Morningstar, Inc. of any investment philosophy or strategy presented in this publication. (Source: © [2021] Morningstar, Inc. All Rights Reserved. Reproduced with permission.)
3. As cited in "Active vs. Passive Investing: Which Approach Offers Better Returns?" Wharton Executive Education, n.d., executiveeducation.wharton.upenn.edu/thought-leadership/wharton-wealth-management-initiative/wmi-thought-leadership/active-vs-passive-investing-which-approach-offers-better-returns.
4. Jacob Kastrenakes, "Your Million-Dollar NFT Can Break Tomorrow If You're Not Careful," The Verge, March 25, 2021, theverge.com/2021/3/25/22349242.

5. Ben Dooley, "Bitcoin Tycoon Who Oversaw Mt. Gox Implosion Gets Suspended Sentence," *New York Times*, March 15, 2009, nytimes.com/2019/03/15/business/bitcoin-mt-gox-mark-karpeles-sentence.html.
6. *QuadrigaCX: A Review by Staff of the Ontario Securities Commission*, Ontario Securities Commission, April 14, 2020, osc.ca/quadrigacxreport/web/files/QuadrigaCX-A-Review-by-Staff-of-the-Ontario-Securities-Commission.pdf.
7. *QuadrigaCX: A Review*, 4.

CHAPTER 7: *PREPPING FOR LIFE'S CURVEBALLS*

1. Natalia Moudrak and Blair Feltmate, *Weathering the Storm: Developing a Canadian Standard for Flood-Resilient Existing Communities* (Intact Centre on Climate Adaptation, University of Waterloo, Waterloo, 2019), intactcentreclimateadaptation.ca/wp-content/uploads/2019/01/Weathering-the-Storm.pdf.
2. Moudrak and Feltmate, *Weathering the Storm*, 10.
3. Moudrak and Feltmate, *Weathering the Storm*, 9.

CHAPTER 8: *SHARING MONEY AND PAYING FOR BABIES*

1. Maire Sinha, "Section 3: Intimate Partner Violence," Statistics Canada, November 30, 2015, www150.statcan.gc.ca/n1/pub/85-002-x/2013001/article/11805/11805-3-eng.htm.
2. Lieran Docherty et al., *Hidden in the Everyday: Financial Abuse as a Form of Intimate Partner Violence*, Woman Abuse Council of Toronto, 2019, womanact.ca/wp-content/uploads/2020/11/WomanACT_Hidden-in-the-everyday_Financial-Abuse-Report.pdf.

CHAPTER 9: *ALL IN THE FAMILY*

1. "Family Matters: Adults Living with Their Parents," Statistics Canada, February 20, 2019, www150.statcan.gc.ca/n1/daily-quotidien/190215/dq190215a-eng.htm.
2. Sylvia Stewart, "A New Age of Parenting: Supporting Adult Children," Royal Bank of Canada, June 19, 2019, www6.royalbank.com/en/di/hubs/now-and-noteworthy/article/a-new-age-of-parenting-supporting-adult-children/jx0r1ylj.
3. Leah McLaren, "The Bank of Mom and Dad: Confessions of a Propped Up Generation," *Toronto Life*, November 4, 2014, torontolife.com/life/the-bank-of-mom-and-dad.
4. "Family Matters: Adults Living with Their Parents."
5. "Family Matters: Grandparents in Canada," Statistics Canada, February 7, 2019, www150.statcan.gc.ca/n1/daily-quotidien/190207/dq190207a-eng.htm.

6. Richard Fry, "For First Time in Modern Era, Living With Parents Edges Out Other Living Arrangements for 18- to 34-Year-Olds," Pew Research Center, May 24, 2016, pewresearch.org/social-trends/2016/05/24/for-first-time-in-modern-era-living-with-parents-edges-out-other-living-arrangements-for-18-to-34-year-olds.
7. "Family Matters: Grandparents in Canada."
8. *The Cost of Long-Term Care: Canada's Retirement Savings Blind Spot* (Healthcare of Ontario Pension Plan, 2018), hoopp.com/docs/default-source/about-hoopp-library/advocacy/retirementsecurity-longtermcare-feb2018.pdf.
9. Bonnie-Jeanne MacDonald, Michael Wolfson, and John P. Hirdes, *The Future Co$t of Long-Term Care in Canada* (National Institute on Ageing, Ryerson University, Toronto, 2019), static1.squarespace.com/static/5c2fa7b03917eed9b5a436d8/t/5dbadf6ce6598c340ee6978f/1572527988847/The+Future+Cost+of+Long-Term+Care+in+Canada.pdf.

CHASING THE HORIZON

With Best wishes,
Sundeep

CHASING THE HORIZON

A TRUE STORY OF GRIT, HOPE AND PERSEVERANCE

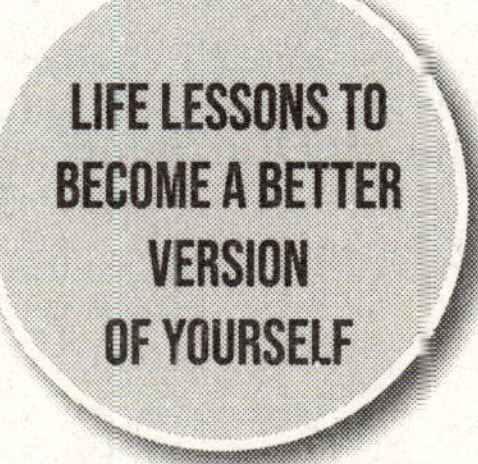

SUNDEEP SINGH

An imprint of
Srishti Publishers & Distributors

Srishti Publishers & Distributors
A unit of AJR Publishing LLP
212A, Peacock Lane
Shahpur Jat, New Delhi – 110 049

editorial@srishtipublishers.com

First published by Bold,
an imprint of Srishti Publishers & Distributors in 2023

10 9 8 7 6 5 4 3 2 1

This is a work of non-fiction based on the author's life and experiences. While due care has been taken by the author and publisher to verify content at press time, any inadvertent miss that is brought to their notice shall be duly verified and updated subsequently. Actual names of people and places have been changed for storytelling purpose.

Printed and bound in India

Praise for the author and his work

I regularly interact with youngsters from varied backgrounds, all trying to search their own path to success, dealing with their own fears & insecurities. There is no magic wand to navigate this journey, but there are some simple mantras that all successful people adhere to. This book does a remarkable job of laying these out through a beautifully narrated story – a simple, fast-paced and captivating story that finds you cheering and praying for the protagonist as he undertakes his pursuit of success. This is one book that you would want to read over and over again.

– Professor Amit Gupta
Mechanical Engineering, IIT Delhi

Life's most enduring and timeless lessons illustrated through the lens of a young boy struggling to come to terms with the real-life pressures. The author not only lays bare his shortcomings but does a remarkable job of celebrating the role these shortcomings have played in shaping his personality. I particularly loved the key messages section at the end of each chapter. It's a fantastic reference point – just adhering to the simple principles laid out here can have a transformative impact on one's life. A truly roller-coaster ride!

– Dr. Bhaskar Chatterjee
CEO, Anil Agarwal Foundation – Vedanta
Ex–Secretary General, Indian Steel Association

If only we could cut the noise all-around and focus…if only we could choose the right path…if only we could realize our true potential… Chasing the Horizon *is the story of a young boy who did all this with incredible hope and patience. Through his debut novel, Sundeep has done a fantastic job of bringing out some powerful messages, which are much needed in the world full of distractions today. He does it through a simple relatable story that takes you along a nostalgic wave of emotions – it's an absolute must read!*

– Chhavi Rajawat
India's youngest & first woman MBA Sarpanch (Soda, Rajasthan)
Member of WEF's Young Global Leaders community

Chasing the Horizon *is an impressive and reflective debut novel by Sundeep Singh. It tells the story of the relentless pursuit of academic and corporate success - that will resonate with millions of professionals across "middle-India" from the post liberalization generation. The metaphor of the Horizon for success rings true - enticing, visible within grasping distance - but never really there and ever changing. A sincere attempt by the author to share a legacy of learning and values for the next generation, so they can navigate the pulls and pressures of an increasingly competitive, changing and stressful world.*

– Deepak Malkani
Co-Founder, IndusGuru Network Partners

An absolute masterpiece! Chasing the Horizon *is Sundeep Singh's honest yet unapologetic account of his vulnerabilities as a student, and the way he discovers simple life principles to overcome any obstacle. While the story is set-up in an academic context, the messages highlighted here are relevant for one and all - this book should feature on top of everyone's reading list.*

– Dilip Chenoy
Chairman, Bharat Web3 Association
Ex-Secretary General, FICCI

Chasing the Horizon *is a heartfelt and non-judgmental account of the joys and struggles of growing up. Sundeep Singh's powerful storytelling unfolds real-life situations to help the reader discover insights by offering questions rather than providing answers. I'd highly recommend the book not just to youngsters preparing for life beyond school, but also to professionals looking to keep the child inside alive.*

– Gagandeep Bhullar
Founder, SuperHumanRace
(a NITI Aayog incubated startup)

Simple yet hard-hitting – Chasing the Horizon *is an inspiring story underpinning the power of patience and perseverance - the ability to hang-in there against all odds. The story brings to life powerful life messages through the story of a young boy undergoing a journey of self-discovery. Compliments to Sundeep for bringing out this inspiring story. A must-read for one and all.*

– Ganesan Ramachandran
Managing Director, Accenture

If you've ever wondered what it takes to achieve success in a holistic sense, then you've laid your hands on a delightful treat. Sundeep, in his inimitable style, delivers life lessons distilled with precision from personal experience. From conquering self-doubt, to avoiding negative self-talk, to staying laser focused on goals. Having watched Sundeep's journey from afar, I can say with confidence that ordinary people can do extraordinary things. This is a veritable "how to" compendium.

– Himanshu Tambe
CEO, Cosmode Consultants
Faculty (part–time), ISB / Singapore University of Social Sciences

Sundeep is an outstanding individual of good character, with a passion to change the world for the better and an incredible ability to get things done. Over the 15 years we have worked together, I always wondered how he manages to do so much, so fast. Having read this remarkable account of his foundational years, I now know the answer. This book is an excellent articulation of what it takes to succeed in life. It's an absolute must-read for all youngsters.

– Justin Keeble
Managing Director, Google Cloud

Sundeep has crafted a wonderful account of the rites of passage that millions of young people go through in their school-leaving years in India. Yet, the lessons he draws are meaningful for adults of all ages. His inspirational story will warm your heart.

– Mukund Govind Rajan
Chairman, ECube Investment Advisors
Former Brand Custodian, Tata Group

Sometimes the most powerful messages are hidden in our daily incidents. All it takes to bring it out is some introspection and the art of storytelling. Sundeep through his debut novel, brings it out through a simple and engrossing narrative that immediately strikes a chord through the nostalgic account which is very relatable. It subtly reinforces the fact that stepping out of one's comfort zone is the first step towards success.

– Ruchi Kalra
Cofounder & CFO, OfBusiness
Ex-Partner, McKinsey & Company

Here is the story of a man who realized that 'Profundity lies in simplicity' and lived his life on his terms to come to terms with life. As Frank Sinatra sang - 'I did it My way...' Insightful, engaging and knocks on life's door.

– Ms. Rupa Chakravarty
Director, Suncity Schools

Sundeep Singh's Chasing the Horizon *is all about hope. The book beautifully narrates the story of a young boy navigating a rocky phase of his life. The silver lining to the cloud is the way he overcomes his challenges, with dogged resilience and perseverance. Kudos to the way the book also sketches out the role of parents in extending unconditional support to children. It's a must read for both youngsters and parents. Congratulations to Sundeep for his outstanding compilation with his debut novel.*

– Sanjay Dawar
Managing Director, Accenture

People spend a lifetime chasing big goals, but sometimes miss out on the joy of small moments along the way. Chasing the Horizon *by Sundeep Singh is a refreshing reminder of the magnificence of these small moments. The small things, the ups & downs, make the journey worth remembering in hindsight. It is the culmination of these moments that leads us into the future and becomes the foundation for success. Kudos to Sundeep for beautifully penning this thoughtful message and richly overlaying very pragmatic tips he has acquired over the years. I strongly recommend this book, particularly to those looking for motivation to overcome obstacles.*

– Scott H. Pharr
Senior Managing Director, Accenture

We often read about success stories and heroes from different fields of life. They are all inspiring, but sometimes limit our definition of what success means. To me, Sundeep's Chasing the Horizon *is a tribute to countless inspiring people all around us, all fighting their own mini-battles in their own sweet way, every single day, shaping their own pursuit of success. The story nicely outlines the art of becoming a better version of ourselves through commitment, passion and hard work – something that we all can learn from. Simple, straight from the heart, and truly very inspirational. A must-read.*

– Vaishali Nigam Sinha
Co-Founder and Chairperson Sustainability, ReNew

To my loving parents,
who always support me.
Unconditionally.

Note from the author

I stood at the start line of Tata Mumbai Marathon, thinking it was a mistake to not carry my iPod for the run. It was the first time I was going to run a full marathon without music. Even if I ran well, I was looking ahead at a good three and a half hours by myself. I was thinking how I'd keep myself distracted. Then, I decided to do something unusual. I decided that at each kilometre mark, I would think what life used to be at that numerical age. I thought the strategy would keep me distracted for the first 36 kilometres, and then I would figure something out for the last six kilometres.

The plan worked. Riding the tide of emotions, I reached the 36-km mark. It was during that state of fatigue that I made three promises to myself – one of those was to write a book about the emotions that I felt most strongly during the run.

This is that book. Through this book, I intend to share the roller-coaster ride that I went through during the last two years of my schooling. I intend to express my deepest love and gratitude for my parents and sister, who stood by me unconditionally, always. I wouldn't be here today, had it not been for their commitment and care over the past three decades.

Life seems to have come full circle. In a few years from now, my son would undertake his own journey, a journey of transition from being the most adorable kid to a man ready to face the challenges of the world. I find myself at a similar juncture where my parents once were, possessed with the desire to shape a peaceful, successful and enriching life for my son. Through this book, I intend to share with my son that things won't always be easy. As he grows, he is bound to face his share of hardships and disappointments. But even when he navigates the most testing times, we would be there by his side, showering our unconditional love and support.

Lastly, through this book I intend to thank my lovely wife, who has been a partner in crime for over fourteen years. She completes me in every sense, and without her unconditional love and support, I could not have completed this book.

Sundeep

Sundeep Singh

July 2021
Current day

> Deep within, there are nostalgic memories, comfortably placed beneath the layer of consciousness. We may have long forgotten about their existence, but once in a while, these memories get nudged, perhaps inadvertently, triggering a realization of the path we have taken to reach where we are.

I, me, and my million dollars

It was a frustrating Saturday night. I had been completely hooked on to my laptop for over four hours. Every few minutes, I firmly straightened my back. My face must have looked like I was on the verge of a breakthrough for the entire world. In reality, though, I was working on a usual project report, not very different from dozens of similar reports I had done in the past. After reviewing every slide, I casually reclined back in the chair to view the progress. It was shaping up nicely. My concentration was broken as my wife Mehr entered the room.

"Dinner is ready, Aman," she said softly.

"I don't feel like eating."

"That's not good. It is bad to skip meals, and worse when you have to do it over the weekends."

"If I feel hungry, I will have something later, but don't need anything for now," I offered my usual response.

"Take a short break and have something to eat. Sit with Ekkam... he has been waiting for you."

I was tempted to offer an excuse, but the fact that my two-and-a-half-year-old kid had been waiting was difficult to condone.

"Give me a moment. I will come in a few minutes."

Seeing me in the living room, Ekkam shouted cheerfully, and rushed towards me. He went up on his toes to add an additional inch to his height and managed to hug my thigh.

"Papa!" Ekkam exclaimed with kiddish exuberance.

"Ekkam!" I replied in just the same way.

We were halfway into the meal, and I hadn't spoken a word. It had just been the baby talk between Mehr and Ekkam. It wasn't the first time I was having such a quiet dinner. I had this knack of conveniently isolating myself in a shell.

"How is your report coming along, Aman? Are you anywhere close to wrapping it up?" asked Mehr.

"I am comfortable with the storyline. But there are a few sections that need to be better represented. I think it will take me a few more hours to finalize."

"When you say a few hours, do you mean a couple of hours, or is it significantly more than that?" Mehr asked, looking expectantly at me. "I am asking because I might require some help tomorrow evening."

"What is it regarding?" I asked.

"Ekkam's play school is re-opening on Monday and there is a lot of homework to be completed."

"Homework? You can't be serious! He doesn't even know how to hold a pencil properly."

"These are actually fun activities designed to introduce new concepts. For example, things like using wastepaper to build paper planes and imprinting poster colours over a white shirt."

"Oh okay!"

"So, back to my question. Would you have some time tomorrow to help us wrap up the remaining activities?"

"I wish I could, but as it stands right now, it looks difficult. These reports can take forever."

"...even when it looks just a few hours away from completion?"

"I guess, yes. The client paid us a million dollars for this project!" I coldly replied to close the discussion. Without saying anything further, I picked up my empty plate and got ready to move. "I think I should get back to my work before it gets too late."

Just as I walked out, I felt I shouldn't have used the word 'my'. It just felt too conspicuous.

After entering the study room, I quickly created a list of pending items with a clear priority order. I started working through the list, hoping to strike out most before hitting the bed. Even after an hour, I had hardly made any progress. Physically, I was at work, but my mind seemed to be wandering. I reclined back in the chair and tried to fathom the reason for my distraction. I wondered if it was the fact that I had refused to help with my son's homework that was troubling me.

Maybe it was, or maybe it was something more than that. Perhaps, the discussion at dinner was just a trigger to something much more profound. I could not immediately define what it was.

I gently closed my eyes, put my right forearm on the eyes and started thinking about the final two years of my schooling days. Those days did not seem too long ago, at least not till the conscious mind reminded me that it had been well over twenty years!

March 1998
The uncertain pathways

> Every moment, every interaction, every experience is nudging us along a pathway - towards an unknown destination. This subtle yet strong steer is so self-organized that its occurrence often goes unnoticed. It is happening, nonetheless, continually steering us along the path to our changed version, that we will meet one day, years down the line.

Life is beautiful

It was a pleasant spring afternoon. I took the window seat at the rear end of the bus, lazily enjoying the gentle breeze. I was sitting alone but had a beaming smile across my face. The Pragati Vihar bus stop was still a few blocks away, but I decided to move to the front door anyway. I stood near the driver's seat, casually holding a support rod with one hand and the school bag in the other. I leaned forward to see where the bus had reached. I was in a hurry to reach home.

"Please stop the bus there," I said pointing towards the bus stop ahead.

The bus driver lazily turned around to stare at me, as he slowed the bus down.

I quickly jumped from the bus, even before it had completely halted. As I hurriedly walked home, I looked up at the balcony to see if my mother and sister were standing there. I was disappointed to not find anyone there. I hopped through the stairs to reach the top floor. Unlike other days, I could feel an unusual spring in my step. I pressed the doorbell once and then a few more times in quick succession.

Mama opened the door with a broad smile. A short lady in her early forties, she had always been a lively and energetic person. During her college days, she had once been suspended for a week for registering herself as the band lead for two separate events scheduled at the same time. She used to be a teacher, but quit long time back to spend time with her kids. Over the past decade, her routine had revolved around the whims and fancies of her two children – me and Pooja – and she was happy about it.

"Mama, board exams over. Vacation time!" I exclaimed excitedly.

"How was your exam?" asked Mama.

"It was okay."

"Was it okay, or was it good?"

"It's over," I replied without revealing that I had done very well. It always helped to set the expectations low and conveniently exceed them later.

"Don't worry Mama. His okay means he has done well," Didi said in an assuring tone. She was three years elder to me. She had completed her twelfth board exams a year ago and was preparing for her medical entrance tests. She had always been an over-protective sister, never hesitant to pick up fights for me. Not long ago, she had ferociously argued with a group of college boys, when she felt that I was not getting my fair share of batting during the routine evening games.

"Let's just have lunch quickly. I want to go out and play with my friends."

"Don't be stupid. No one plays at this time of the day. Wait for a few hours for the sun to settle down. Also, call Papa to tell him about your exam. He called up some time back," said Mama.

"Okay!" I replied with a bit of disappointment.

"And by the way, when I bat later today, please don't keep observing me from the corridor. I have requested you many times. It makes me conscious. Plus, it's so awkward to have your mother watching over for two hours. I am not a kid anymore," I continued, seizing the opportunity to convince her on a long-standing open point between us.

"Yes, I know you are not a kid. But these college boys have a bad reputation. So, it's important for me to keep an eye," she reproduced the same old answer.

"Mama, I never see anyone else's mom watching over like that. Anyway, I don't want you standing there at least when it's my turn to bat," I retorted knowing fully well that she would not budge.

I ambled into my room, which was small yet spacious. The bed was neatly aligned to one of the walls and a sleek little study table stood opposite to it. The wall adjacent to the study table sported a large-sized Tendulkar poster.

It was still not dark when Papa returned home. Like most Sikhs, he had a tall, well-built body structure. But in many other aspects, he was different from other men in his community. He was a rare vegetarian in the family. Also, he was a man of very few words. He would keenly observe things and form an opinion, but would rarely bother sharing it. During the occasional family get-togethers, he would easily win the award for the quietest member if there was one. However, when he did say something, it carried weight and people often regarded it as the opinion that mattered.

Hearing the doorbell, Didi and I rushed to the door. We knew Papa would bring home patties and pastries. He had always done that on any special occasion. He looked at me and smiled heartily, his eyes congratulating me on completing the tenth-standard board exams.

"Thank you, Papa. It is a relief," I said to answer his implied message.

Papa raised his right hand and pointed to the snacks he was carrying. "I got something to celebrate."

"We knew you would, and that's why we didn't let Mama prepare any snacks," replied Didi as she went to the kitchen to grab four plates.

"If you wish, we can also play chess today," Papa said, looking at me.

"Fantastic!" I was excited.

Our house resembled a very different ecosystem than what it had a day ago. After a gap of a few months, Mama had played her favourite music at a volume that was comfortably audible to a human ear. Didi comfortably sank in the rocking chair, browsing through news channels. Papa and I occupied opposite seats on the dining table and played chess, something that we had not done for over two months. The entire house had looked like a library till a day before, but now it looked like a happy house that inhabited humans who interacted, laughed and enjoyed.

✩✩

The soothing warm breeze

It was almost half past eleven when I finally got up. I went to the living room to grab the sports section of the newspaper.

"Mama, I am hungry. Can I get an omelette and a banana shake?" I shouted, gradually settling into the rocking chair. Didi was already sitting there, working on her physics assignments.

"Welcome! I am privileged to have the opportunity to wish you good morning today. Thank you," she said contemptuously staring at her watch.

I took an intense yawn, rubbed my eyes and considered answering her. After a brief pause, I replied, "Don't thank me, thank BCCI. There is a day-night match today, so I got up early. Rest assured, this won't happen tomorrow."

I didn't pursue the discussion any further. I turned my attention to the last page of the newspaper lying on the dining table, a habit I had developed ever since I fell in love with Tendulkar.

After a few minutes, she asked, "How's your vacation coming along?"

"Just the kind of break I was hoping for. Very relaxing and full of fun."

"What are you doing these days?"

"Nothing!"

"Despite that it is fun?" asked my workaholic sister.

"Precisely because of that," I replied with a wry smile.

"I hope you recognize that these are golden days. Don't waste this time. Try to build some good habits during this vacation."

"Like? Any suggestions?"

"It could be simple things. The paper you are holding has fifteen other pages. You would read each word on the sports page twice, and if it relates to Tendulkar, then many more times. But you would not bother reading a single word on the other pages. May be this is one habit you could change."

"I couldn't care less about what's brewing up between Clinton and Lewinsky. Suggest something else."

"Umm, stop reading those stupid diamond comics. Pick something more intellectual. If nothing else, at least start reading the English version of those same comics."

"That won't happen. We have already discussed it. Let's not get started all over again. Any other bright idea?"

After thinking for a few seconds, Didi replied, "You could develop the habit of getting up early."

"Don't I anyway get up early every afternoon?" I asked.

"Stop wasting my time. Just get lost and do whatever you want."

By that time, Mama had joined us at the dining table with the breakfast tray in her hands. I pounced on the banana shake. Mama delicately balanced the tray and asked an unrelated question, "When do you want to visit Jalandhar?"

Visiting Jalandhar after the exams had been an annual ritual. It used to be the get-together time of the year. My grandparents and two maternal uncles were based there as a joint family. Our and my maternal aunt's family were based in Delhi and we visited Jalandhar around the same time. In all, it meant seven cousins converging under one roof to have loads of fun and we all eagerly looked forward to that time of the year.

"Let me call Nancy to check if they have planned anything. If not, maybe we can go together like last year. What do you think?" I replied.

"Yes, that's fine. I spoke to them a few days back, but they hadn't firmed up their plans. If you get a chance, speak with her," said Mama.

Later that day, I called up my cousin sister.

"Hello, who's this?"

"Hey Nancy, this is Aman. How are you?"

"Hey, I am good. You are calling after ages. Where have you been?"

"I was tied up with my tenth standard board exams."

"I am sure you would have done very well, as always."

"It wasn't as bad as I had expected. You tell me, what have you been doing?"

"I was solving a crossword puzzle right now and have been stuck at a point for quite some time now. You called up at a good time actually. Maybe I could use some help from you."

"My vocabulary is not that great. I am sure any word that I can come up with, you would have already thought about it. I could help you with math puzzles," the last sentence had inadvertently popped out as a balm to the hurt self-worth.

"Okay, before I forget, I actually called up to check something. When are you planning to go to Jalandhar? Like last year, we could book our train tickets together," I asked. I was conscious that the call had been made by me and didn't want to make it a long one.

"We have already booked our tickets. Anyway, we are travelling by AC coach this year, so..." Nancy abruptly cut short her sentence and after an awkward pause added "...we will meet directly in Jalandhar."

I took a brief pause as I tried to comprehend the remark. "No problem. For now, please get back to your crossword puzzle," I replied with a fake smile.

"Sure, take care. Bye."

"Bye." I continued holding the phone receiver for a few seconds. I wondered how much extra an AC coach charged anyway.

✩✩

It was barely six in the morning when we reached the New Delhi railway station. It was a nice, soothing morning. The sun was yet to assume its full effect. Papa and Mama hurriedly walked through the overhead bridge to reach the platform. Didi and I had to jog to keep up with their brisk pace. The station looked busy, crowded with people from diverse backgrounds moving in all directions. The men in red looked particularly active.

Once inside the train, Papa moved a few bags beneath the seat to adjust the luggage. He carefully looked around the cabin to ensure everything was fine. He had always been an overprotective family head and went about performing his duties with minimal fuss.

"Tickets are in your purse. Keep them carefully," Papa told Mama.

I giggled.

"What?" Papa asked quizzically.

"She is not a kid. Of course, she will keep be careful."

"Okay."

"Train might start anytime. Please get down now," said Mama.

"Alright," said Papa as he got ready to leave.

I had a habit of kissing Papa's hand whenever we left. I did that even while leaving for school. I did the same on the train as well. Didi had often nudged me to develop a more subtle way, especially when in public space. But I never paid heed to her suggestions.

Shortly after the train left, I climbed the support rods mounted next to the aisle and comfortably slept on the top berth. I guess Mama and Didi too dozed off in a sitting posture. By the time I came down, we had covered over half the distance. I occupied the window seat adjacent to Didi. She seemed immersed in her favourite music, oblivious to the surroundings. Out of sheer boredom, I pulled out her earplugs with a jerk.

Didi angrily stared at me and shouted, "Idiot, are you crazy? What do you want?"

It was a soft shout as she intentionally tried to avoid attention from the fellow passengers.

"Good morning," I said with an impish smile.

Didi frowned.

"Is that what you pulled out my ear plug for?" She looked annoyed.

"Yes."

"Idiot!" She almost whispered.

"What are you listening to? I hope not those boring *ghazals*."

"Of course, I am," she replied.

"I really can't imagine why one would willfully listen to that crap. It's ok if that is a punishment, but why otherwise?" I had this knack of identifying what would irk others, especially those close to me, the most. I often did exactly that and derived immense pleasure out of it.

"Stop irritating me," she said, putting the earplugs back in her ears.

My attempt to induce a gossip conversation had failed. I was getting bored and was hoping that the conversation would last a little longer. But that was not to be.

I quietly sat beside the window, staring at the vast fallow land outside, enjoying the breeze on my face. Despite the warm air, the breeze was soothing. The last thought crossing my mind before reaching Jalandhar was that Nancy would not have experienced it, as she was travelling by an AC coach. I wasn't sure whether I felt good or bad about it, but I did feel a sense of discomfort recollecting my last conversation with her.

Everyone came rushing out when we reached. Cheerful and excited faces greeted us. I was particularly pleased to see my cousin brothers – Gagan, Vikram and Kabir. Gagan was holding two bats, one in each hand. Vikram was holding a cricket ball and had three more in his pockets. The one in the shirt pocket looked a bit obscene. Kabir, the youngest of all, was barely managing to hold on to the stumps loosely clinched under his right arm.

After a quick exchange of hugs and high-fives, we disappeared for a long-extended play.

The exchange of pleasantries for the girls was a bit more prolonged and conspicuous, especially for the younger members - Nancy, Neeti and Pooja. They all possessed strong distinct personalities. Pooja was the eldest in the group. She had always been a studious kid with a strong aspiration of becoming a doctor. Neeti was the most authoritative. A simple stare from her was usually enough to intimidate us. She was also the one who had a distinct flair for acting. Nancy was the most fashion conscious in the group. She was admired by one and all for her creativity. She sometimes misused her creativity to come up with mischievous pranks.

For the next two weeks, the seven siblings – four boys and three girls – were all going to be under one roof. It was all set for an exciting summer vacation ahead.

Grapes are sour

It was a hot summer afternoon. We had done well to continue playing for over three hours under the sun. After returning home, we stealthily slipped through the side passage to reach the verandah on the first floor. We were conscious not to make any noise as it carried the risk of us being forced to the confines of a closed AC room for the rest of the afternoon. The verandah was a spacious porch with plenty of green plants on one side. The bunch of ripe grapes hanging from the finely rolled vines around the wall railing looked serene. We comfortably laid down on the floor, enjoying the soothing shade.

"I am bored. Should we do something interesting?" I asked.

"I have an idea, if you guys are in for it," said Gagan.

No response.

Gagan continued, "These grapes are juicy and there are people on the street."

Gagan did not need to elaborate any further. Before Gagan could say anything else, Kabir replied with a bright sparkle in his eyes, "Brilliant!"

We hid behind the bushes and started throwing grape bunches at random passers-by on the road. We took care to drop the grape bunches a little away from the feet, just sufficient to make the juice splash onto the person's toes and momentarily scare the person. We noticed that on most occasions, the person donned a semi-confused-semi-annoyed expression. He would blankly look around to see where the grape bunch had come from. Then the person would walk off, making a futile attempt to regain composure.

"Ah, just missed."

"Watch out for that fat ass. That's my next target."

"Good shot."

"Get a little closer to the feet."

We continued the adventure for a while, thoroughly enjoying the timid reactions from people. Every time someone got scared, we crawled back and merrily shook hands. Our misdeed eventually ended when one of the bunches landed straight on a person's head.

"Oh damn!" I murmured.

The man on the scooter appeared to be in his mid-forties. He was wearing a nicely ironed maroon shirt casually tucked in his light-grey trousers. He was partially bald, but the brown hair on the remaining part of his head seemed well-combed. There was a helmet hanging with a knob on his scooter, which he surely repented not wearing in that moment. The grapes had landed on the bald part of his head, but the juice splashed all over. He furiously looked around to identify the felons.

"I think this guy will come and complain. What should we do?" asked Gagan.

"There is no one to validate his claim. Let him come. We will simply refuse," I replied.

"But ours is the only house with grapevines on the terrace. So..." said Vikram.

"Let's just slip into a room and pretend that we have been playing board games. That's our best chance," I suggested.

We all got into the room and anxiously waited for the drama to unfold. Within a few minutes, we heard the dreaded doorbell.

"We need to know his side of the story. One of us needs to step out and listen in. Who would be the one?" I asked nervously.

"Let's send Kabir. The cute little kid that he is, no one would suspect him," Vikram suggested.

We all nodded.

Almost instantly, Kabir got up and moved out of the room. He seemed happy with the additional responsibility entrusted on his young shoulders.

"Madam, I was passing through the road and some kids from this house hit me with a bunch of grapes from the balcony," said the stranger.

Before Kiran Mami could say anything, Kabir intervened, "But, we have been playing carrom board for the last two hours. If you want, you can come and see in the room."

It was a mistake to send our youngest partner to handle the tense situation. Our expectation of Kabir was to just listen in and update us before being questioned. But inadvertently, Kabir had almost confessed.

"Madam, if I am lying, what do you have to say about this?" retorted the stranger, lowering his head to show the juicy splash.

"It looks bad, but I am sure my kids didn't do it. It must be children from some other house. I know my kids very well."

It took Kiran Mami a while to pacify the stranger. But she was right in saying that she knew her kids very well. She knew exactly what had transpired.

After the stranger left, Kiran Mami came to our room and surprisingly didn't scold us. She instead chose to say the few words which she knew would hurt the most.

"From tomorrow, you all will sleep for two hours after lunch," she said and walked off.

Fine-dining – The new currency of social status

By the time it got dark, everyone was ready to leave for dinner. It was a celebratory dinner my aunts had organized to mark the completion of my board exams. My cousins had been quite vocal about the high standard of the new dining place we were heading to. They did not seem to get tired of talking about its ambience, supreme buffet, and its unmatched quality of service. So much so, that I was almost getting annoyed with the hype.

On reaching the restaurant named Maya, I partially understood the reason for all the excitement. The place had a royal reception with a refreshing lemon fragrance. The ambience and décor of the luxurious hotel was much better than any other place I had ever visited. The exotic moustache of the security-guard standing at the reception appeared apt for the place. Looking at the imperial ambience, I became conscious of my attire. I wondered if I had done the right thing by wearing slippers to that place.

We occupied a large oval table that could accommodate fifteen people. Once settled, folks started chit-chatting about the choicest fine dining places around the city. It seemed like a platform to brag one's awareness of high-profile places. Every time someone said something, they expected appreciation from others. I was becoming increasingly conspicuous by my silence. I considered mentioning a chowmein stall in Lodhi Road's Mehar-Chand market, not particularly because of the high regard I had for the place, but only to succumb to the pressure of contributing something.

"Damn it!" I faintly murmured after thinking about it for a few seconds.

As folks transitioned from starters to main course, the discussion shifted to the choice of food. The food in one's plate seemed like an important social status proxy.

"Aman, your plate looks bland. I can't see anything non-veg in your plate. Are you having an upset stomach?" asked one of the family members.

"I have given up eating non-veg food," I replied.

"What!!!" replied several family members together.

There was an exaggerated collective moan at the table as everyone reacted to the seemingly shocking piece of news. I was amused with the reaction. I had expected a surprised reaction, but what I witnessed seemed bizarre. It was as if I had announced an irrevocable decision to stand naked on one leg and fast until death.

There was an awkward silence for a few moments as everyone tried to come to terms with the betrayal. After a few uncomfortable moments, I got a rather solemn piece of unsolicited advice.

"It is difficult to understand why you should torture yourself with grass and straw for the rest of your life. You might want to reconsider your decision. Give it a thought."

"There is nothing to think about it. I am happy with what I am eating. Honestly, I don't think it's a big a deal."

"Really?"

"Yes, really! You eat what you like; I eat what I like. It's as simple as that."

I stayed quiet for the better part of the dinner from there on. I felt bad at having created a scene, more so at a dinner that was organized to celebrate the completion of my exams.

After clearing the bill, we all walked back towards the valet parking. Mama was walking alongside my aunts. Right behind that group, I casually walked alongside my cousins. I had a gut feel that I was the subject of the discussion in the group moving ahead of me. I made a concerted effort to overhear.

"If you don't mind, can I say something?" said one of the voices.

"Yes, please," Mama replied.

"I think you should take them out more often."

"What do you mean? Take them where?"

"Try and take them out to formal dinners and social gatherings more frequently. This will help them develop social etiquettes and confidence."

I didn't hear any response. Mama's silence was perhaps the response.

✩✩

Next evening, we all gathered around the front verandah.

Neeti was the first one to speak up. "Guys, do you want to play something?"

No one replied.

"I have a game in mind, it's called 'know yourself challenge'. I played it at a friend's birthday party. Anyone interested?" she continued.

"By the sound of it, feels like a boring game. How does it work?" asked Nancy nonchalantly.

"It works on the principle that your top of the mind thoughts are usually the most honest ones. It means that if you are put on the spot to comment on something instantly, you will tend to speak what you truly believe in. The more time you take, the more fake the responses. That's exactly what this game doesn't allow."

"Sounds interesting! So how do we play this?"

"It goes a bit like passing the parcel game. One of us will play the music and we will all keep passing a ball around. As soon as the music stops, everyone has to say a word or a phrase instantly to describe the person who is holding the ball. Speed is of essence here. It is a lot of fun."

"Honestly, sounds like a very boring game," I said jumping into the conversation out of nowhere.

After a bit of wheedling and cajoling, we all agreed. Nancy volunteered to play the music. The game finally began!

When the music stopped, it was Kabir who was holding the ball. Everyone looked at him and the adjectives started spurting out.

"Innocent."

"Cute."

"Sportsmanship."

"Charming."

"Stop guys! The first three I heard were innocent, cute and sportsmanship," intervened Neeti.

"Well, cute and innocent are no-brainers, but where did that sportsmanship thing come from. He is such a cheater when it comes to cricket. Even when the ball hits the middle stump, he tries to defend it, and worse still, often gets away with it!" exclaimed Vikram.

Kabir couldn't hide his typical blushing.

The next round started. This time the music stopped on me.

"Social embarrassment."

"Milk addict."

"Crazy."

"Rustic."

"Eccentric."

"Stop guys, stop! The first three I heard were social embarrassment, milk addict and crazy," Nancy said.

Neeti had a loud laugh. "I love the first one. Social embarrassment! It is so apt for him. I mean who wears bathroom slippers at Maya? And when everyone orders exotic dishes, you gulp milk shake, probably the only thing that you understand on the menu card."

The whole group, including me, laughed whole-heartedly. Just that mine was a fake one.

Out of sight, out of mind

The next evening, we all again converged at the front verandah. It took us good 15-20 minutes before we could all agree on a game. It was going to be hide and seek.

The game started. We explored the usual hiding spots – inside the kitchen, under the dining table, behind the sofa in the drawing room, under Grandma's bed, and behind the grapevines on the terrace. As the game progressed, we had to extend our imagination to come up with new hiding places. It was becoming increasingly difficult to stay hidden for long.

It was Nancy's turn to seek others. As she stepped away to allow others to hide, everyone hurriedly scampered in all directions. Kabir seemed to have run completely out of ideas.

"Where should I hide? Suggest something," he whispered to me.

"I have an idea. Hide inside the cupboard! You are small and you can easily get in there. All you need to do is keep the door a little open, so you don't feel suffocated. I am sure Nancy will never be able to figure it. What say?"

"Fantastic!" replied Kabir.

Gagan, Vikram and I helped Kabir sneak into the cupboard and scattered some clothes around him. Gagan carefully closed the cupboard door, leaving a little open gap to allow for enough breathing space.

"Bro, all good?" asked Vikram.

"Yes, it's fantastic in here," whispered Kabir from the confines of the cupboard.

"Awesome! You think can stay here for an hour?" I asked.

"Yes, I can go on for two hours, if that is what it takes to win today," replied Kabir.

"Awesome. If it gets too sweaty, just think of the grand victory in the end," I said.

"Don't worry. I am stronger than you think."

After the brief pep talk, we dispersed to find our own hiding places.

Soon, Nancy arrived. It didn't take her long to find us. Once Gagan, Vikram and I were found, we huddled together to discuss the next steps.

"What's the plan now?" asked Gagan.

"Let's play something else. Imagine how much fun it would be when Kabir comes out and finds that we are not even playing hide and seek anymore!" I suggested, giggling.

"Brilliant! For once, I will literally experience what it means to be rolling-on-the-floor-laughing," Vikram said.

"Done then."

We soon inter-mingled with the larger group to execute our wicked plan. After a bit of casual chit-chat, we decided to wrap up for the day and get back to the TV room. In the transition, everyone – except the three of us – forgot about Kabir.

After about half an hour of hiding, Kabir had started sweating profusely. But he was a tough kid. Instead of getting bogged down by the physical discomfort and giving into the temptation of stepping out, he tried to focus on the glory that lay ahead

It was almost 9 p.m., and Kabir had been in there for more than an hour now.

Kabir had started feeling terrible in there. He had done exceedingly well for a kid of his age. He recognized that he was close to the moment of glory. He finally decided to step out.

He carefully balanced his body weight and managed to step out without falling on the floor. He sheepishly moved out of the room, softly on his toes to not make any thumping noise. He was a little confused to not see anyone around in the lobby. He continued to search for others and checked out all the usual places. He was getting perplexed.

At last, he walked into the TV room.

He was shell-shocked to see all of us comfortably watching TV. Gagan, Vikram and I erupted with joy. On one side of the room, there was an innocent little kid standing with tears in his eyes, and on the other side there were the three of us, going wild with our celebrations.

"What's going on here?" asked Neeti with a stern voice.

"Guys, I am talking to you. What's happening here?" Neeti asked again, as our guffawing continued.

"Once upon a time, we were all playing hide & seek..." I couldn't complete the sentence and again started laughing.

"... And then, we all moved onto watching TV, but Kabir was enjoying the game so intensely that he continued to hide inside the almirah."

Kabir looked like he would kill me! The truth is, we had stepped the line that evening. But whatever it was, it was fun while it lasted.

The haunted soul

"Why are you scolding us?" asked Nancy.

"The boys did what they did, and I will get to them later. But I am amazed that for almost an hour, none of you realized that Kabir was missing. Nancy, you are the elder one in the group. I expected more responsibility from you. Please be more careful next time," said Kiran Mami as she walked out of the room.

Nancy wasn't amused to be at the receiving end for our misconduct.

"Because of the three of you, I had to put up with this unwarranted scolding," said Nancy.

"Thank you for that," replied Gagan.

"Damn it, what do you mean, thank you for that! I was expecting you to take responsibility. Why didn't you tell her that I had nothing to do with it?"

"But no one said that you had anything to do with it. She just said that as the elder one in the group, you need to be more vigilant."

"And how do you intend to help me do that?"

"That is your responsibility. Don't expect any help from us," Gagan replied and left the room.

Nancy, Kabir and I continued chit-chatting for some more time.

"It's time I taught him a lesson. I have an idea," said Nancy.

"You are still thinking about that! Let it go. It's okay," I replied.

"No. It's not."

"So, what's your idea?" I asked as a courtesy gesture.

"Have you guys noticed how terrified he is when we watch horror movies?"

"Yes, he is a coward," replied Kabir in a dismissive tone.

"Exactly! So tonight, we will play Darkroom..." replied Nancy, firming up her thoughts as she spoke. "...and I will dress like a vampire," she continued.

"Brilliant. It's the first time I am seeing you put your creativity to some good purpose," I egged her on.

"I will need some help from both of you. We need a script. Aman and I will work on it. I also need some make-up material. I need a face pack, an eyeliner, a foundation, some skin cream, a nail-polish, a lipstick, a hair straightener, some artificial jewelry, and a white saree."

"I don't understand most of these things," replied Kabir.

"Don't worry. I will arrange that with Neeti. You just need to meet everyone except Gagan and explain the plan to them. We don't want to create panic in the room, so everyone except Gagan should know about it in advance. Can you do that?"

"Yes certainly!" Kabir quickly got on.

We had an early dinner that night to quickly get to the game. It was a simple game, somewhat similar to hide and seek, with the key difference being that it was played in a dark room.

Everyone except Gagan was aware of the plan. As soon as Gagan stepped out of the room, Nancy put on her make up to creatively transform into a vampire. She spread the face-pack unevenly on her face, giving the impression of peeling skin on one side. She had creatively used a lipstick to put some red colour around her lips, which looked like blood. Her loosely hanging hair, untidily ruffled on all sides complemented the image of a haunted soul.

"Damn it!" exclaimed Kabir, tightly gripping my hand.

"Dude, you know that it's all fake, so stop giving me that look. By the way, how much more time do we have? I have a few more things to put up," asked Nancy.

"Sis, you are not going for a fancy-dress competition. What you have is more than enough. We are calling Gagan. You be ready to show up from behind the curtain in exactly ten minutes." I summed it up.

Shortly thereafter, Gagan entered the room and started searching for everyone.

Within a few minutes, Gagan identified everyone except Nancy. He desperately looked around to find her. He opened all the wardrobes. He looked around the metallic trunk. He even looked under the bed. No luck.

A few moments later, Gagan noticed that the quilts were lying on the floor instead of being on the metallic trunk. He latched onto our bogus cue, just as we wanted, and assumed that Nancy must have hidden inside the metallic trunk. He excitedly opened the trunk, putting his hand inside to look for Nancy. All he found inside the trunk was an old abandoned doll.

At exactly that point, Kabir and I walked up to him for a casual pre-planned conversation.

"Found her?" I asked.

"No. She is not here," replied Gagan.

Kabir and I looked at each other in bewilderment. The stare was subtle enough to not make things obvious, but still explicit enough for Gagan to notice. As Gagan continued to look around, Kabir and I started a soft chat. Again, the volume of our speech was cleverly orchestrated – soft enough to give the impression that we didn't intend for him to hear it, but loud enough for him to actually hear it with some effort.

"Dude, what the hell is going on here?" I whispered.

"That's exactly what I am thinking. I thought Nancy had hidden herself inside the trunk."

"Of course, she did."

"But where is she? And where the hell did that doll come from?"

"She must have changed her position to confuse Gagan."

"But that's not possible. Didn't we agree that she will bang the trunk from inside when she wants us to unlock it? She never banged it. At least I didn't hear anything," said Kabir.

"Or maybe she did, but we were all so engrossed that we missed it."

"Are you suggesting that she died inside because of suffocation?" asked Kabir with a trembling voice. All the cousins were surprised to notice the poise with which Kabir was enacting his part.

Gagan was keenly listening into all this whispering. He could feel a chill running down his spine.

"But even if she died, where is her dead body?" I asked.

"I have heard that when people die an unnatural death like this, their haunted soul wanders haplessly."

"Shut up and do me a favour. Just open the curtain a little bit. I want to look for her."

Kabir sheepishly walked up to the glass wall and carefully pulled the curtain to one side.

What we all saw was a sight that none of us would ever forget in our lifetimes. A lady wrapped in a white saree stood there with a candle in one hand and the other hand delicately resting behind her back. The scary face with its peeling skin, bloody mouth, ruffled hair and to make matters worse the candlelight held at just the right distance from the face to add to the gory effects. We all had goosebumps.

Gagan cringed.

"What the hell is that?" he murmured.

"What?" I replied calmly, pretending as if I didn't see anything unnatural.

At exactly that moment, Nancy opened the balcony door and started walking towards Gagan, ever so slowly. That was the tipping point for Gagan. He let his natural instincts take over. There was a loud prolonged hysterical shriek. We all panicked that the elders would hear that. Neeti tried to suppress the howling by tightly clasping her hand around Gagan's mouth.

Pin-drop silence.

No one knew how to react. The prank had worked well, perhaps too well for our comfort.

Gagan sat there quietly, unable to react to anything. He just sat there blankly. No movement, no blinking of eyes, nothing. He just kept staring at the wall. He looked terribly scared to turn around, lest he caught the ghostly visage again through the corner of his eye. It was hard to determine what was scarier – Nancy's get-up or Gagan's response.

Nancy went inside the washroom to clean off her make-up. A few moments later, when she came out, Gagan was still looking in the same direction, motionless.

"Bro, we are sorry. This was a prank. Yesterday you played a prank on Kabir. Today, we played a prank on you. It's all fun," said Nancy.

We all looked at each other helplessly. No one knew how to revive Gagan. After a few moments, it was Neeti's turn. She tightly slapped Gagan with all her might. Gagan immediately broke into tears and started shouting.

"Damn it. I hate you all. Go to hell. All of you. Just go to hell."

He continued to weep, letting those suppressed tears roll down his cheeks. We were all relieved to see some emotion. We all hugged him and profusely apologized. We kept chit-chatting for almost an hour thereafter to make sure that Gagan had completely overcome the horrible incident.

"How did that doll get inside the trunk?" asked Gagan.

"We kept it there," replied Nancy.

"How did you get the facial expression?"

"Little bit of make-up and loads of creativity."

"And what about all that talk about Nancy dying because of the suffocation and that crap?" Gagan asked me and Kabir.

"It was all pre-planned. She was never in there and we were just speaking out our part of the script."

"Damn you all. Seriously!" replied Gagan, continuing to shake his head in disbelief.

✩✩

It was all in good jest. It always is!

Few days later, we returned home. The visit to Jalandhar had been full of excitement and drama. As I laid down to sleep that night, I reflected upon the way things had unfolded in Jalandhar. I noticed that there were a few memories that brought a distinct sense of anxiety. I wondered what was bothering me. On introspecting for some time, I realized that I had started noticing things which had never crossed my mind earlier.

I had started comparing my material possessions with those of others. For the first time, I felt that all families in the extended family were different. The ability to spend on luxuries was not the same.

It was well past mid-night. To break my chain of thoughts, I went for the tactic that worked in similar situations – a Maggi break with Didi. I knew she would be awake as she had a routine of studying till late. I went to her room and sat there silently.

"What is it? Why haven't you slept?" she asked.

"Nothing. Some random thoughts troubling me."

"What random thoughts? Tell me."

I didn't say anything. "What is it?" Didi asked again.

"Nothing much. I have been thinking about some things that have never bothered me in the past, but have started playing on my mind of late."

"For example?"

"For example, the other day, when I had called up Nancy to check up on their program to visit Jalandhar, she had cut short the discussion by telling me that they were planning to go by an AC coach. I know for a fact that she didn't mean to offend, but still have been thinking about what exactly she said."

"Go on. I am listening."

"Then, Neeti called me a social embarrassment because I was wearing slippers at Maya. I didn't like that either."

"But it was all in good jest. You know that."

"Yes, I know. It always is. But..." I couldn't articulate my thoughts to complete the sentence.

"But what?"

"But nothing. Are you making some Maggi, or should I go to sleep?"

Didi reluctantly got up from her chair and went to the kitchen. In a few minutes she came back with two bowls of Maggi nicely balanced in a rectangular tray. As we started relishing our late-night meal, it was Didi's turn to speak.

"It's normal. Don't worry. Everyone has an inherent desire to be revered. We all want to be appreciated and perceived in a positive light. There's nothing wrong in it. It's normal human behaviour."

"Yes, I get it."

"Then what's the problem?"

"The problem is that I am unable to get it out of my head. It almost makes me feel like a loser. Worse still, I don't know which battle I lost to get that feeling. It just feels like there is a void. I guess I am getting excessively consumed by these petty thoughts."

"These are not petty in any way. There is a lot of power in these thoughts," replied Didi. She was just three years elder to me, but the way she said that felt like it was coming from years of wisdom and experience.

"What do you mean?" I asked.

"It all depends on how you channelize these thoughts. If you keep sulking over them, it will build negativity inside you. On the other hand, if you channelize them constructively it can push you on the right path – the path that leads you to become a better and evolved version of yourself one day, a path that leads to success and happiness."

IN HINDSIGHT

As I look back at this phase of my life, I think I was an energetic, happy-go-lucky kid who derived immense pleasure from typical kid activities – idling around with friends, playing outdoor games, unleashing mischievous pranks.

However, beneath that youthful exuberance lay a somewhat subdued Aman – the Aman that was full of insecurities, was often vulnerable, wanted to be revered, and badly wanted to win.

While it took me years to explicitly recognize that side of me, Didi had probably identified it very early. If I had the luxury of going back and reliving my childhood, I would probably want to meet and make friends with that side of me sooner rather than later.

KEY MESSAGES

- ✓ It is okay to feel insecure or vulnerable at times. All humans feel it in varying intensities; however, not many admit to it, given the associated stigma.
- ✓ So, what should you do about it? First things first – take the time to introspect and consciously identify your insecurities; it is a critical part of your personality.
- ✓ Never try to suppress or evade your insecurities. The world may or may not need to know about it, but you ought to know yourself fully.

April 1998-July 1998
The new beginnings

> As you wake up to new beginnings, you may find yourself in a very different world – a world where joy is scarce, with clouds of self-doubt, and ample temptations to take short cuts. If at any stage it gets too difficult to bear, just remind yourself – this too shall pass.

Mother giraffe kicks its new-born

We were all out in the park for a routine cricket game.

"Are we good to start now?" asked one of the boys.

"Well, almost."

"Why almost?"

"We still need to fix the height of the wicket. As always, Aman has engraved it too high," said Abhinav, pointing to the red line I had etched on the tree bark using a brick.

"Honestly, it looks fine to me, and I really don't see a need to adjust it," I retorted.

We started playing and went on till it got so dark that we could barely spot the ball. After closing for the day, we all broke into smaller sub-groups for relaxed chats.

Abhinav was the most conspicuous kid in the group. He was a short fellow donning a serious look with his thick, black-framed spectacles, which must have been at least minus five or six diopters in power. The size of his glasses appeared disproportionately big as compared to his small square-shaped face. His hair was always untidily ruffled and the guy was in desperate need of a haircut. He was usually quiet and reserved in those late evening group gossips. His distinctly studious personality suggested that he was on his way to becoming a great scientist.

Just before we wrapped up for the day, Abhinav stepped aside and asked me a rather unexpected question.

"Hey Aman, I am planning to opt for Engineering stream. Have you thought about your choice yet?"

"I haven't given it a thought. And I don't want to think about it till I really have to. I do know though that it won't be medical stream. I can't dissect rats. Other than that, I am fine to pitch-and-toss a coin to decide the stream," I coldly replied and waived him good-bye on the pretext of getting late for home.

Next morning, I got up at around noon. As I entered the living room, I had an uncanny intuition that I would be greeted with some unsolicited coaching that morning.

"You would soon be starting the last and perhaps the most important two years of your schooling. Have you thought about your plans?" asked Didi.

"No," I replied disinterestedly.

Didi was visibly annoyed at the indifference, but managed to retain her composure. She continued, "I have been talking to some friends about how you could make effective use of this vacation. There are two good coaching institutes for engineering entrance examinations - FIITJEE and Vidya Mandir. You should join one of these."

She continued, "Also, you should try and change your school. You should consider joining Shri Patel School (SPS). It's one of the better schools in Delhi and has some really distinguished alumni members. My friend Yamini joined this school three years back and she speaks very highly about the facilities."

"When did we decide that I am opting for engineering stream? Anyway, I think it's too early to be talking about this. I still have good two years to go before I start worrying about all of this. So, chill!"

"Listen, you need to be serious about this. You aren't inheriting some business or huge wealth. Are you?"

Didi took a pause to invite any reactions. I preferred not to react though.

She continued, "Most of your competitors would have already started preparing, while you are busy doing nothing."

"Bunch of losers, I guess. I hope they realize the price they are paying to get into this rat race so soon. As they say, you might win the rat race, but you will still be a rat. Anyway, they are free to choose their path," I replied.

"And what path do *you* intend to follow?"

"I haven't thought about it, but I'd much rather go for a crash course few months ahead of the entrance exams."

"That doesn't guarantee success."

"I guess nothing does."

"Precisely, and that's why it is important to do everything under your control to improve your chances. Starting early and making effective use of these two years is a proven way that works."

It was clear that Didi had been thinking about it and had come prepared with all the necessary arguments.

"Ok, let me think about it," I replied to bring the uncomfortable conversation to an end.

I had a quiet breakfast before heading out to meet my friends. I was worried that by the time I come back, Didi would have shared 101 reasons with Mama to have me join a coaching institute. I could sense my summer vacation plans slipping away, right under my nose.

☆☆

Our house had a small little balcony, with a few flowerpots on one side and a metallic swing on the other. Mama spent a disproportionately large amount of time in the balcony, given its size with respect to the overall house. That night I quietly occupied the vacant seat on the swing, right beside her. I was keen to figure out what had transpired between the ladies after I had left.

"What do you think about the idea of joining a coaching institute that Didi was mentioning?" I asked.

"I think you should join one at the earliest to make the best use of this vacation," Mama replied with a warm smile. It was evident that she was expecting the question.

"But then what happens to my vacation? I have been waiting for it for so long. Didn't you tell me that once the board exams get over, I would have all the time in the world to enjoy," I pleaded.

"Joining a coaching institute doesn't mean that you can't enjoy your vacation. A coaching institute is not like a regular school," Mama reassured me.

"Then what is it?"

"It is a two-year course that prepares you for engineering entrance exams. You would have three to four sessions in a week and each session would include four hours of tutoring."

"That sounds terrible! And then I am sure there would be assignments, tests and all that too."

By that time, Papa and Didi had also joined us in the balcony. It didn't come as a surprise when Didi jumped into the conversation. It was her stupid idea after all. "Assignments, quizzes, vacation, and enjoyment are trivial considerations. These things won't even matter few years down the line."

"May I know what would?" I asked, without attempting to hide the sarcasm in my tone.

"Your level of preparation on the day you write the entrance exam for the first time, whether you clear it in your first attempt or you sit at home for one full year and prepare all over again," said Didi in a frustrated tone, and after a brief pause added, "like me."

"What do you think?" Mama asked turning towards Papa.

"I think you should join a coaching institute and change your school too. You don't need to slog during the vacation, but at least get started. And I can always help you with your assignments, especially in math and physics," he said.

"...and I can help with chemistry assignments," Didi added excitedly as she knew the verdict was clear. Papa had expressed his view.

When Didi and I were chatting later, I asked exasperatedly, "Are you happy now?"

"Yes, I am."

"Everything was moving so smoothly. I have just written the board exams. I was so excited about the vacation. Life looked so beautiful. You just screwed it all! I can't understand why you did that to me?"

Didi took a pensive pause before responding. "Do you know what happens when a baby giraffe is born?"

"What kind of a stupid question is that?"

"No. Tell me. Do you know what happens?"

"No and I really don't care!"

"The mother giraffe kicks the baby giraffe."

"Kicks the baby giraffe! That's strange. That's the last thing I would have imagined. Why would she do that?"

"Go find it out for yourself. You will get the answer to your question too."

"I asked you a simple question. Can you please give a simple answer that an average human being like me can understand?"

"The simple answer is that whether you like it or not, soon you will have to go through the grind and compete in the entrance exams. The sooner you start preparing, the better your chances of winning. And if you are successful, I get to brag about your success."

"Crap! For some cheap bragging rights, you screwed my happiness. I can't believe it," I responded, shaking my head in disbelief.

"On a serious note, how bad is it?" I continued.

"It's not bad at all. You will have to write a small test to get selected in one of these coaching institutes. If you get in, they will coach you for the next two years".

"What non-sense are we talking about? You are telling me that I will take an exam to possibly get into a coaching institute. If I succeed in doing that then that coaching institute will train me for another exam, the actual entrance exam, which is two years away anyway!"

"Yes. That's your only route to success. Take it or leave it!" Didi replied without blinking an eye.

✩✩

One step forward, two steps backward

The next evening when Papa returned from office, he had a bunch of brochures in his hands. The brochures had a glossy shiny appearance which made it hard to miss. About an hour later, when I returned home after the usual evening playtime, I was intrigued to see them all engrossed.

"You all are playing something?" I asked inquisitively.

"Yes, we are playing an interesting game. It's called 'choose the right coaching institute'. Do you want to join us?" replied Didi.

"This might be interesting for you, not so much for me. You all carry on," I replied and headed straight into the kitchen.

Few days later, it was time to appear for the selection test for FIITJEE coaching institute. The first thing I noticed on reaching the venue was the sea of students who had come over to take the exam. For a moment I wondered if all the fuss I had been creating was really justified. I had been feeling victimized for being pushed into joining a coaching institute and here I was amidst countless aspirants. Had they all lost their mind? Or were they unfortunate to get a kick from their mother giraffe too.

When it was time to move in, Papa said, "I will meet you here after two hours."

Once inside, I had a eureka moment. I thought about deliberately leaving the answer sheet blank.

I felt a sense of pride for my last-minute creativity. However, there was also a sense of guilt underneath. I was feeling bad for my parents and Didi, who were putting in so much effort. While I did not agree with their ideology, it still did not take anything away from the fact that they were genuinely my well-wishers. It would have been terrible to have Papa wait outside the venue in hot sun, while I was busy not answering anything. I rubbished the idea and got on with answering the paper to the best of my ability.

Two weeks later

When the doorbell rang, I lazily opened the door.

"Yes?"

"Courier for Mr Aman Singh," replied the postman.

"Give me!" I replied with as bland an expression as I could possibly don.

I disinterestedly scanned the courier package. The FIITJEE logo at the bottom left corner was the first thing to catch my attention. I left the courier at the dining table without bothering to check the details inside. Papa noticed the envelope a few hours later. He curiously stared at the envelope, wondering why one would just keep it there without opening it, especially since they were all awaiting admission test results.

"When did this come?" he asked.

"Today afternoon."

He excitedly took the letter out and read through it. The smile on his face indicated that it was the bad news.

"Selected?" I asked to validate the bad news.

"Yes."

"When are the classes starting?"

"Very soon."

The smile had still not vanished. I wondered if there was something more to it. It was unusual for Papa to smile for that long in one go.

"Is there anything else?" I asked quizzically.

"Yes. You have been offered a scholarship worth 35% of the program fee on the basis of your performance."

That took me by surprise. Despite the distinct aversion I had for the program, I managed to smile on hearing the scholarship news. I momentarily even felt motivated to join, howsoever ephemeral that feeling may have been.

✩✩

While I was struggling to come to terms with the thought of joining FIITJEE, Didi had already seen it all. She had started preparing for medical entrance tests at the beginning of her eleventh standard and had taken her entrance examinations a year ago. Unfortunately, since she had missed securing a seat in the first attempt, she had taken the tough decision to drop a year and prepare all over again. I had seen her struggle very closely. She had literally shunned any kind of recreational activity

– no friends, no social life, no evening walks, nothing whatsoever. All I had seen her do over the past three years was slog it out with heavy books, books that could very well have been used for weightlifting. It was for this reason that I was so averse to the idea of joining a coaching institute. Ironically, it was precisely for that reason Didi wanted me to join coaching classes early to be fully prepared in my first attempt.

The months of April and May were extremely important for Didi. By around mid-May, she had written all her entrance tests. She was hopeful of securing a seat, but wasn't overly bullish about the prospects. The first few results turned out to be quite disappointing. She had missed securing a seat even in the test where she was most hopeful. The morale at home was quite low. To lighten things up, one fine Sunday morning, Papa offered to take us all out to the science museum at Pragati Maidan.

"I am in no mood to go to anywhere. You all continue please," said Didi.

"It would be a good break," said Mama.

"I just don't feel like going. Please go ahead if you want to."

I was closely following the conversation. I knew there was no way Mama-Papa would take me out for a picnic leaving Didi at home. I could sense the picnic opportunity slipping out fast, so I interjected.

"Maybe the ladies can stay home, and you and I can go," I said turning to Papa.

Papa just smiled. The smile meant that he was fine with my suggestion.

Papa and I spent a good day at the museum. Papa used it as an opportunity to teach me several new science concepts. Though the overall picnic construct was academic, I thoroughly enjoyed it. By evening we were both exhausted and decided to go back home. The same day, we were also expecting the result for yet another entrance test that Didi had taken. Just when we were about to leave for home, Papa broached the topic.

"I think today the result for CBSE pre-medical entrance tests will be announced," he said.

"I hope she gets selected in this one," I replied anxiously.

"If you want, we can check the result. The venue where the result has to be put up is on our way back."

"But do you remember the roll number?"

"I carry all roll numbers with me all the time."

"What will we say if she doesn't get selected?" I asked, more worried about how we will break the news at home.

"Don't think like that!" Papa instantly replied.

Within a few minutes, we reached the venue. I noticed a large white board outside the building where a handful of people had gathered in the hope to find their roll number in that list. As we walked towards the board, I saw Papa murmuring something ever so softly. He seemed to be saying some prayers silently, though I wasn't sure. It was an intense moment, so I didn't bother checking either.

"The list contains the roll numbers of the selected candidates arranged in ascending order. Our roll number is 2303755. See if you can find it in the list," he told me.

I started scanning the long list, and was surprised to see the big gaps between the roll numbers. There were jumps in hundreds between the roll numbers. I anxiously moved down through the list. It seemed increasingly improbable that I would eventually land on a number that would read 2303755. Few seconds later, Papa gingerly kept his finger at a spot on the white board and carefully looked back at the number that he was holding in his hand.

"This is it!" he said almost in disbelief.

"Check these two numbers," he said pointing to one in his hand and the other on the board.

"Yes, these two numbers are the same!" I exclaimed.

Didi had finally secured a seat in a medical college. Papa and I hugged each other a few times and jumped with joy. Papa looked genuinely happy.

Seeing the celebrations at home, I too felt mildly motivated to work hard for the coming two years for my own entrance exams. However, letting go of my summer vacation was a big price to pay, something that I was not mentally prepared for.

✩✩

I caught hold of Abhinav after the usual evening play.

"Hey scientist! I recently joined FIITJEE coaching institute. Do you know how it works? I mean, how will we manage these classes once the schools reopen?"

"The schools run from 8:00 a.m. to 2:00 p.m. Most of these coaching institutes have classes from 3:30 p.m. to 8:00 p.m. So, you are safe."

"Bloody hell! How do you call that safe? When do you get to play then? If you add the commute time to these timings, you are telling me that we leave home at 7:30 a.m. and come back home at around 8:30 p.m. And there would be some assignments from school too. When do you get to do that then? It just doesn't add up. Am I missing something?"

"No. This is exactly what it is. You do school homework after 8:30 p.m. and then you sleep. That's what it is going to be."

"This is bad."

"It's not bad at all. In fact, it's only going to get better from here. You will have more time to play," replied Abhinav with a mischievous smile.

"How?"

"Right now, does your mother allow you to step out of the house before 5:00 p.m.?"

"No!"

"But when you have a class at 3:30 p.m. you will have to leave home at 3:00 p.m. And then it is up to you. You decide whether you want to go to the coaching class or stop on the way to play or to do whatever you ever wanted to do!"

"Not bad! Just by saying that one sentence you made things so much easier. Thank you!" I replied, feeling somewhat relieved.

I continued to reflect upon Abhinav's suggestion for a few days. There was a wave of muddled thoughts, all seemingly contradicting each other, masking my ability to think rationally. I was increasingly attracted towards the option Abhinav had suggested, though I knew that was not the right thing to do. I didn't realize it back then, but it was probably the worst piece of advice I could have received just before the start of a new journey. If the scholarship grant at FIITJEE and Didi's selection had mildly propelled me forward one step, Abhinav's crappy advice hurled me two steps back.

✩✩

Limitless exasperation tending to infinity

I was all set to start the two-year training programme at FIITJEE.

On the first day, I reached the venue around thirty minutes ahead of the scheduled time. There were hundreds of students swarming the venue. I wondered if they were all serious about getting into IITs or were there a few others like me too.

On entering the class, I looked around to identify the least unfavourable seat. I walked through the class and occupied the corner seat in the last row. Geometrically, that was the farthest I could move away from the teacher while staying inside the class. I quietly sat there, observing the activities inside the class. I was becoming increasingly conscious of my presence in that group of largely active students. I wondered if I was appearing studious enough to be sitting in that room. I tried to don a serious look, pretending to be browsing through the course curriculum.

A student arrived and occupied the vacant seat next to me. He had a wheatish complexion, neatly combed hair, and donned a terribly serious look. If I had my way, I would have granted him a seat in the IITs just based on his looks.

"Hi, my name is Vipin. I am from DPS RK Puram school," he said.

"Hi, I am Aman."

At exactly 3:30 p.m., a simple looking gentleman entered the class. He was dressed casually for a professor. His trousers appeared a couple of inches shorter than what it should have been. Or maybe it looked short because he was wearing flip-flops. A loose fitting brown half-sleeve shirt, not tucked in, an expression that was bland, especially for the occasion of the first lecture in a two-year training program. He was not holding any books.

"Hello, my name is Sanjay Jha. I hold a B. Tech in computer science engineering from IIT Delhi. I am your mathematics professor. Since this is the first class, it would be good to do a quick round of introductions. Please keep your introductions brief. Let's keep it simple – your name and your professional aspiration. I love back benchers, so let's start from one of the back corners."

'Dammit! Who starts introductions from the back corner? Idiot!' I thought.

I nervously tried to think of a fake but intelligent sounding professional aspiration. Professor Sanjay pointed his hand towards the other corner in the last row and requested the person sitting there to start. It was a sigh of relief, as I was going to be the last person to speak. That gave me plenty of time to develop a professional aspiration.

When students ended their introductions, it was Professor Sanjay's turn to speak.

"I am happy to have you all here. Before we start, I want to convey an important point. In a few days, you would realize that this program is very different from your school courses. The most important difference here is that your evaluation is in relative terms and not absolute terms. The competition is tough. Every year, lakhs of aspirants appear for the IIT Joint Entrance Examination, but there are only about two thousand seats available across IITs. This means that for every 100 students appearing in the exam, only one will eventually make it. To succeed, you need to have single-minded focus and dedication. You should be willing to completely isolate yourself from the external world and work with razor sharp focus and determination.

"What is also critical for each of you to realize is that JEE is not a short distance sprint; it is a marathon. You cannot succeed in this competition by slogging for a few weeks or months, no matter how intensely you slog. Please internalize my words carefully. What I just said is as important as any of the concepts you would be learning here."

The professor took a brief pause to allow the students to assimilate his words of wisdom.

"Do you have any questions?"

Pin drop silence.

"If you have no questions, let us get started with the first concept. It is called Differential Calculus. It lays the foundation for a variety of topics that you would be learning later. To begin with, we will learn about the principles of limits and derivatives."

I tried to concentrate for some time, but given my short attention span and vulnerability to distractions, my thoughts soon swayed to irrelevant things. Though I was not following what professor was explaining, some conspicuous things caught my attention. I noticed that mathematics now looked more like English alphabets than digits and numbers. I also noticed that letter 'd' was used far more frequently than any other letter. Letters 'y' and 'x' had a life of their own and enjoyed good coverage on the board. Mid-way through the lecture, I was struggling to keep my eyes open. Even the novelty associated with those fancy Greek letters had faded away.

Just before the break-time, I stared at the board to comprehend what all I had missed during my sweet little nap. I glanced through all parts of the board.

We say f(x) tends to a real limit if and only if...

Limit x tending to infinity…

Limit of a function as x tends to minus infinity, Right hand limit and Left-hand limit…

There wasn't an inch worth of board space that made any sense. Something seemed to have changed since I fell asleep. Suddenly the words 'limit', 'tends', and 'infinity' had gained prominence. I haplessly scribbled in my notebook –

'Limitless exasperation tending to infinity…'

At around 5:30 p.m., we got our first 15-min break for the day. Outside the class, I met Abhinav, who looked as exhausted and lost as me.

"Hey Scientist, how are you doing?"

"Not good at all. I just can't stand this crap," replied Abhinav in a frustrated tone.

"Good to hear that. Clearly, I was not the only one struggling in there."

"We had a chemistry lecture. He taught us something by the name of stoichiometry."

"What is that?"

"I don't know, didn't pay attention to that part. My sole focus was to get the pronunciation of the word right," he replied with a sense of shared helplessness.

Shortly thereafter, a professor walked through the gallery, summoning all students still standing outside to get back to their classes. Once inside the class I tried to pay attention. The Greek letters got scarier as the lecture progressed. Towards the end of the lecture, Professor Sanjay wrote a problem on the board and asked for volunteers to solve it on the board.

For the following functions, find dy / dx from first principles.

"Let me pick someone," Professor Sanjay said.

Few hands went up.

"Don't worry if you think you can't get the right answer. I will help you through the steps wherever you get stuck," the professor encouraged.

I was not worried about my inability to get the right answer. My worry was that I did not even know what the question meant. I tried to don a relaxed look to evade professor's attention. The more I tried, the more obvious it became that I was clueless

Professor Sanjay eventually looked at the corner in which Vipin and I were sitting and signaled one of us to come forward. It was not clear who he had called. There was a moment of awkward silence as all three of us waited. Thankfully, despite my terrible attempt with the fake expression, it was Vipin whose expression had looked more stupid and obvious. Vipin got up with great effort. His confused facial expression and lethargic body language seemed to suggest that he had been summoned to attempt a problem standing nude in front of the class.

As Vipin walked to the board, I nervously looked at my watch. It was 7:39 p.m., another six minutes to go for the lecture to end. I prayed and hoped that Vipin would do something on the board to kill those remaining six minutes. Strangely, moments like those reinforce the importance of every second. The difference between 7:39 p.m. and 7:40 p.m. appeared stark.

Vipin looked at the problem on the board with immense concentration.

"Don't look so intensely at the board, it might set the board on fire," said Professor Sanjay.

Vipin looked visibly embarrassed by professor's remark.

Just then, an office boy entered the class with a huge carton of books in his hands. The carton contained books which had been compiled by FIITJEE professors for the two-year training course and were commonly referred to as FIITJEE packages. There were many students in the class, including me, who thanked their stars for the timely arrival of packages.

"These are FIITJEE packages. You would receive six such modules at appropriate times. Each module contains three packages, one each for physics, chemistry and mathematics. Make sure to treat each of these packages as your Bible for the next two years," Professor Sanjay told us all.

"So, back to you."

"Yes sir." Vipin again started blankly staring at the board.

"Ok Vipin, let's not hold the entire class for this. Think about this at home and in the next class, we will start with you solving this on the board for us."

"Yes sir, thank you!" Vipin was relieved.

I survived the first FIITJEE session, somehow.

X tan theta minus g x square u square cos square something

Two days later, it was time for the second session. After the first session, I was determined not to sleep shamelessly through the lecture. At least not in the first fifteen minutes, like I did in the mathematics lecture.

I noticed that some students were already discussing assignments from the first session, while I had still not figured the meaning of those cryptic deltas and limits. I was obviously not serious about the training programme, but seeing my fellow students moving ahead so fast did instill a sense of insecurity.

In a few minutes, a smartly dressed professor entered the class. He appeared far more formal and well-dressed as compared to Professor Sanjay. He had a fair complexion and a characteristic glow on his face. I noticed a brown-coloured mobile holder which was smartly clipped to his waist belt, something that I had never seen before.

"Good afternoon, everyone. My name is Rakesh Menon, and I am here to take care of your physics concepts. It is a pleasure to begin this two-year journey with you all. Before we get started, I want to ask you all something."

"What do you really think about the subject of physics?" he asked after a brief pause.

"It is one of the three subjects that I need to crack to get a good rank in JEE," said one of the students.

"I am sure it is. What else?"

"This is the most complex of the three subjects and hence often the deciding factor."

"It depends!" replied Professor Menon with a subtle wink, indicating that he was not convinced with the answer.

After a brief pause, Professor Menon said, "I don't think I articulated the question well. You are all thinking of physics in the context of JEE. What I meant was something more fundamental about the subject."

"Sir, physics is the subject that explains different physical phenomenon we observe around us," said Vipin.

"Give me an example."

"For example, when a stone is dropped from the top of a building, it falls down. The observation is so intuitive that the observer never bothers to think about the reason behind this. However, the phenomenon can be explained scientifically, and it is the subject of physics that can explain this."

I wasn't convinced with the answer. I casually nodded my head in refutation without intending for anyone to notice it. Professor Menon did notice it though.

"You don't seem to be convinced," he interjected.

"You are right, sir. I am not."

"Why?"

"Because I don't think anything can explain anything."

"What do you mean?"

"I mean there is no such thing as explaining observations. As humans, we want a reason for everything. This has led to several laws and theorems which apparently 'explain' things. When we speak of a falling stone, we may believe that the law of gravity explains it. However, if we really think of it, law of gravitation is just describing the motion a little more formally, a little more mathematically if you will, but it doesn't really explain why the stone falls. Nothing can explain that."

Professor Menon took a deep breath, making a prolonged eye contact. In fact, it was a bit more than an eye contact. It was almost a stare, indicating Professor Menon's irk at my stupid response.

"Howsoever stupid your response may have been, you actually touched upon an important aspect. That is the part about mathematical equations. Falling of stone is a very simple example, but when you get to solving complex JEE problems, it will often happen that your intuition will tell you something which is different from what the mathematical equations suggest. At such times, you should resist the urge to go by your gut feel. It is always a safer option to go by mathematical equations. With that, let us now start."

I was again not convinced with the answer, but this time checked the spontaneous nod of my head.

The class started.

For a change, I managed to keep aside all my mental distractions. I did manage to follow the lecture for a while, but as the lecture progressed, it kept becoming more and more complex. I didn't realize when but somewhere through the lecture, I got completely disconnected. By the time we got our first break at 5:30 p.m., I was completely lost. In mathematics lecture, I had not followed a single word from the beginning. But, in the physics lecture I grasped a few things initially, just the intensity kept fading gradually.

At break time, I strolled out of the class along with Vipin. The only reason why I chose Vipin's company was because I had no other friends in the class, and it felt awkward to be ambling alone amidst the large number of students. I was sure that Vipin too had a similar reason. Once outside the class, Vipin and I stood beside a pillar. We both were extremely uncomfortable and would have dearly loved to disappear at the first opportunity.

In a few minutes, Abhinav too joined us.

"Here comes the great scientist!" I said in a much more confident tone. The sight of my neighbourhood pal had temporarily raised my energy level.

"Stop calling me scientist."

"Why? I have been calling you that ever since we met two years back."

"Yes, it was all fine till FIITJEE opened my eyes and exposed my worthlessness."

I realized that Vipin and Abhinav did not know each other. I apologized and made quick introductions.

"So, which class did you have today, Abhinav?" Vipin asked.

"I had a mathematics lecture. Those Greek letters are completely esoteric, it just doesn't make any sense," Abhinav replied. "How was it for you guys today?" he continued.

"We had a physics lecture. It started off well actually, with both Aman and I getting some airtime in the first ten minutes. But then things started becoming complex and surprisingly those Greek letters came back to haunt us here too. Bizarre!" added Vipin, sounding like a five-year-old kid who was narrating the story of a ghost to his younger sibling.

There was a solemn silence. Shortly thereafter, we went back to our respective classes.

"I am now going to start a new topic, the projectile motion. For the part covered in the first half, go through the concepts once again tonight and try the assignment problems. We will discuss your doubts in the next lecture," said Professor Menon.

"Hey, what's wrong with him? Why is he in such a hurry?" I whispered in Vipin's ears.

"I think he is drunk," Vipin replied softly.

I couldn't help giggling at his response, which attracted Professor Menon's attention.

"Did I say something funny?" retorted Professor Menon looking at me. "I am talking to you. Can you explain what makes you giggle?"

I didn't utter a word. "Sorry, I forgot the wisdom you shared with us. Nothing can explain anything. Let me rephrase. Can you describe what makes you giggle?"

"Sorry sir."

"Let me make one thing clear. This is not your regular school lecture where you miss something and read it one day before the exam. This is serious competitive stuff. You need to concentrate hard here. Otherwise, it's going to be a struggle."

"It's already a struggle sir," I replied softly.

"Then get lost and let others concentrate!" Professor Menon turned back to the class.

"So, I was talking about the projectile motion. Technically speaking, a projectile is the trajectory of a body that has been thrown obliquely and it moves through a curved path under the influence of gravity. To relate to it, think of a fielder standing close to the boundary on a cricket field. When he throws the ball back to the wicketkeeper, the ball follows a curved path all the way back before landing in the keeper's gloves. The trajectory of the ball is nothing but a parabola."

"Finally, he is talking about something interesting. I mean the cricket part." I scribbled on Vipin's notebook. I was cautious not to make any more whispers.

Professor Menon continued, "What other examples of projectile motion can you think of from day-to-day experiences?"

"Sir, the trajectory of a javelin throw," – said one of the intelligent souls.

"Hmm, correct. What else?"

"Sir, the motion of a bullet fired from a gun," said another IITian in the making.

"Sure, that's a good one."

As an example hovering in my mind. I drew the schematic of a man peeing from the top of a building. Vipin spontaneously burst into laughter, which again attracted the professor's attention. He turned around to see where the noise came from and noticed me pulling back my notebook.

He was mad to see me creating nuisance again. He walked up to me with a frown on his face and snatched my notebook. The frown disappeared as soon as he looked at the last page of the notebook.

"At least you were listening to what was being discussed," said Professor Menon with an amused smile. After a few moments, he continued, "Do you want to share this with the class?"

I was not sure if he was being sarcastic or if he was serious. I assumed it to be the latter and tentatively replied, "Sure sir, if you feel that's appropriate".

"Forget it!" said Professor Menon as he ambled towards the board.

There was a brief murmur in the class. "Sir, you are making us curious now." – said one of the students.

"Don't bother. It's nothing important; just a dirty imagination of an example of a projectile motion from day-to-day experience."

After that brief distraction, Professor Menon went back to the board. He introduced several variables to describe the projectile motion, using complicated equations.

Just before the lecture ended, he casually walked up to me and softly whispered, "The next time you take a pee from the terrace, do think about that equation."

Y is equal to x tan theta minus g x square upon 2 u square cos square theta

"Sure sir," I replied sheepishly.

Harmless sulphuric acid attack

It was still early days in my FIITJEE journey, but I had already learned a few important lessons. I had learned the relationship between my level of sleepiness and my handwriting. It tended to start resembling a different script as my sleepiness quotient increased through the lecture.

As we waited for the chemistry professor to arrive, I casually skimmed through the study materials. Few moments later, a rather funny looking man entered the class. He was a short, bespectacled man with height no more than five feet. The man donned a thick long moustache, which appeared disproportionately big for his small round face. It seemed to cover a significant portion of the face, most of which was anyway hidden by the spectacles. I thought that if his moustache grew any further, there was a genuine risk that he might topple over under its weight.

"Good afternoon!"

Brief pause.

"Manoj Sharma."

Another brief pause and a smile.

"B. Tech and M. Tech, IIT Delhi, 1983 batch."

Another brief pause, a slightly broader smile, and a nod of head.

"Chemistry."

The man had delivered the most succinct and raw introduction that one could expect from a professor. It was a collection of the basic details interspersed with a few pauses and funny smiles. He surely appeared strange by his looks, but it was his communication style and body language that completed the image of a perfectly comical character. It was hard to imagine that the character could be a professor at a reputed coaching institute. We were about to witness that first appearances could be grossly misleading.

The funny smiles evaded as soon as the professor started talking about the stoichiometry concepts. The succinctness and rawness gave way to an animated body language. It was evident that Professor Manoj was intensely in love with his subject. Unlike Professor Sanjay and Professor Menon, here was a professor who did not believe in nudging the students or asking questions. He enjoyed teaching the subject so much that he tried to avoid any unnecessary distractions for himself. His only form of nudging the students was through his favourite sentence that he would say every ten minutes – 'this is the most critical point, it is covered beautifully in your packages, but you may still want to write it down if you are taking notes'. Every time he said that, I nodded my head in affirmation and pretended to write something in the notebook.

Unlike the previous two lectures, the chemistry lecture was slightly more bearable. There was an added fun element which came at no additional cost. It was the artist, Manoj Sharma, performing in front of the class.

I was staring at the board while thinking of Tendulkar's exemplary batting skills. It was 6:00 p.m. and I had done well to kill the first couple of hours rather conveniently. I continued to blankly stare out of the window, enjoying the soothing effect of gentle evening breeze from my window seat.

"Yes?"

No response.

"Yes please."

Again, no response and a gentle laughter in the class.

I felt a sudden gentle tap on my shoulder. It took me a moment to realize that Professor Manoj had been standing next to me and was trying to grab my attention.

"Sorry sir," I immediately responded.

"What for?"

"For staring outside and not responding to your call."

"That's okay. It happens with many of you in the first few lectures, but please make sure that this does not continue for long."

"Yes sir."

"I was trying to get your attention to let you know that there are two problems I have written on the board."

"Yes sir. Getting to it right away."

"Don't worry! You won't be able to solve it in today's class. I noticed you were busy staring outside the class for the last one hour. Go through the first 17 pages in the chemistry package and then try attempting these problems at home before you come for the next lecture."

"Okay sir," I replied and then quickly added, "Will be more attentive next class onwards, sir."

"That's fine. Don't worry," he said and gently ambled towards the board.

I was amazed at the professor's calmness. He deliberately had the conversation with me very softly so as to not grab everyone's attention. I stared at the board to see the questions the professor had written.

As we walked out at the end of the lecture, the emotion of the class resembled that of a cinema hall after an intensely emotional movie. There were students who stretched their bodies to get the blood circulation back. There were others who yawned shamelessly. Most students just appeared numb and speechless. I experienced a strange pleasure, a pleasure that emanated not from one's own success but from others' similar plight, a pleasure that all humans probably experience to varying degrees but not many admit to it.

✩✩

Lull before a gathering storm

My summer vacation was ending. The classes at the new school were commencing from 6th July. I sat alone in the balcony and wondered how quickly the three-month vacation had flown by. I felt a sense of anxiety and despair at the thought of getting into the same mundane cycle from the next day. I was still in deep thought when Mama came to the balcony.

"Is there something bothering you? You don't look happy," she asked.

"No. Nothing."

"There is something. What is it? Are you worried about the new school?"

"Not really. Just that I wanted to do a lot more in the vacation, but it went by so quickly. Plus, it's going to be the same monotonous routine from tomorrow."

"The next two years are going to be really important for you. There is no point getting sad about it. Just get on with it in a positive frame of mind."

"That's exactly what you said a year ago as well. Now I am being told that the next two years will be even more important. I am scared that this cycle of increasing importance will continue forever," I replied with a smirk.

Silence.

"Let's go to the park and play badminton? You will feel better," she said.

I always found playing badminton with Mama a good physical exercise – not because she was very agile, but due to something exactly opposite. She had an asthma condition and could not move around very fast or bend down too frequently. This meant that every time the shuttlecock fell, I had to move around the court to pick it up, even if it fell a few inches away from her. I think she deliberately made me move around a little more than usual that evening to break my chain of thoughts.

Next morning was supposedly an important day.

As always, Papa was the first one to get up. He switched on the lobby light and got started with his usual routine, which had been the same for several years. He would start the day by chanting a prayer while bathing. He had a peculiar habit of singing the prayer rapidly, as if someone had pressed the fast-forward button. The backdrop sound created by each mug of water provided a nice musical rhythm. By the time others in the house woke up, Papa completed several small but important household activities. As a kid, I had always wondered what motivated Papa to get up so early to do those same things day after day, year after year.

By around 7:15 a.m., I was ready. All four of us sat around the dining table and shared a few light moments. Mama and Didi were bombarding me with innocuous and seemingly useless suggestions. Didi's suggestions tended to be in the form of things that I should do. Among other things she asked me to sit in the first row, be alert, and concentrate hard. Mama's suggestions tended to be of the nature of things that I should not do. She advised me to not fight with anyone. I was not paying much heed to their suggestions, but some really silly ones did catch my attention.

As usual, Papa had been silent. A few moments later, Mama and Didi looked at Papa and almost instantly started giggling. Papa was not sure what he had done to elicit that reaction. He looked at his clothes to see if there was something amiss.

"What?" asked Papa as he failed to comprehend the joke.

"Your son is going to a new school and there are no taxes to be paid for any suggestions you may want to share," replied Mama.

Papa warmly smiled and nodded his head, suggesting that he had nothing to add. He picked up the scooter keys and waved at me to indicate that he would be waiting downstairs. Just as I got ready to leave, Mama offered me a spoon of curd.

On reaching the parking lot, I noticed that Papa had already turned the scooter. As always, he had left a few minutes earlier to be able to clean the scooter before I reached. I had often noticed from the balcony that Papa spent time cleaning the back seat of the scooter and then hurriedly wiped the rest of the scooter. He was extra cautious to ensure that there wasn't any visible dust mark on the backseat. That day was no exception. I silently wondered how love manifests in small ways, and one doesn't need big material possessions or eloquent words to express true love. We silently settled on the scooter and rode to the school.

On reaching the school, I kissed Papa's hand and got ready to enter the school. Just as I was about to leave, Papa did eventually share with me a parting thought. "You never get a second chance to make the first impression," said Papa as he waved goodbye.

✩✩

My new school building was set up amidst a beautiful lush green ambience. The first thing that caught my attention on entering the school was its simple yet elegant architecture. Right in front of the entrance gate was the school's proud auditorium. The large Konark wheel mounted on the front wall completed the perfect image of the school's guiding philosophy of harmony in all forms. On the left side from the entrance was the large sports facility. That was probably the only thing that excited me about my new school.

In class, the students had already started settling in. They all looked happy and comfortable. For most of them it was just about getting back to the school after a long vacation. For me, as for a few other students, it was also about adjusting into the new school environment. I occupied a seat in the second row from the front. Unlike the FIITJEE classes, I had no intention of sleeping shamelessly through the school classes.

Few minutes later, I noticed an anxious looking student standing at the class door. He donned a confused expression and looked uncertain about where to go next. Just before entering the class, he paused, stepped back, and rechecked the section name engraved on the door. He nodded his head in affirmation and then finally made a move in. He walked up to the empty seat next to me and gracefully occupied it. He took out his handkerchief, wiped his face, adjusted his hair with both hands and took a deep breath.

"Hi, my name is Paramjyot. People call me PJ," he introduced himself.

"Hi, I am Aman. Good to meet you."

"Are you new to this school?"

"Yes. Today is my first day. How about you? For how long you have been here?"

"A few minutes now. It is my first day too," replied PJ. "I usually don't like to reach late, but today was an exception."

"I don't think you are late. We still have a minute to go to 8:00 a.m."

"Yes, but I had reached the school at 7:30 a.m."

"Then? How did you get so late to get here?"

"I mistakenly went to the wrong classroom. I went to the biology section and made a friend too. It was only when we started talking that I realized that I was sitting in the wrong section."

"That explains the thoroughly confused expression you had when you walked into the class," I cheered him up.

Just then, an aged gentleman entered the class. He donned a warm and somewhat apologetic smile.

"On behalf of the SPS fraternity, I would like to welcome the new members of our family joining us today. I am also happy to welcome back the old students."

"Thank you, sir," murmured the class

"I am given to understand that we have a class of 35 students, of which 11 are new students. It is important that we make you feel comfortable. So, why don't we take a quick ten-minute tour around the school? Just be cautious that you don't whisper as we don't want to disturb other classes. Just follow me please."

We all organized ourselves in a small herd and followed the teacher. I noticed that the gentleman had a slight limp in his gait and used a supporting stick while walking. He also had a small hearing aid attached to one of the ears. It resembled a complete incarnation of a soft, warm-hearted, caring man who could never hurt anyone intentionally.

He took us around and showed us the stationery shop, physics lab, chemistry lab and computer lab. After that, we headed back towards our classroom.

By this time, some of the restless students had started giggling. I, of course, was one of them.

"I don't think he could become the most successful tour guide ever. What do you think?" I whispered softly in PJ's ears.

There was a little bit of a murmur which caught the teacher's attention. He turned around to see where the voice came from. He had that same warm apologetic smile on his face. He kept staring with an intensity that defied any purpose or motive. He quizzically raised his hand a little over waist height, palm facing upwards and held the hollow stare for a little longer.

Once inside the class, he kept his stick on the table, leaned against the table, and started addressing the class.

"As I said, I am happy to have you all here and once again welcome you to the SPS family. My name is PC Malik. People usually address me as Professor Malik."

There was a soft murmur from the back bench.

"He is lying. People usually address him as Mallu," an old student whispered softly.

Despite the faint articulation, I managed to catch the remark. I was happy to note that the class had other non-serious students like me.

Professor Malik continued, "Here at SPS, we follow a system of weekly evaluation tests. We firmly believe that there is no replacement for continuous practice and hard work. I would strongly urge each of you to imbibe this principle and prepare well for the weekly tests. Also, I am aware that some of you, the more ambitious ones, would have already joined coaching institutes. From experience I can tell you that these coaching institutes do more harm than any good to you."

He then delivered a well-rehearsed speech which he had used umpteen times in the past. Towards the end, he circulated the schedule for the weekly tests. I casually glanced through the test schedule and disinterestedly circled the date of the first weekly test with my ball point pen. It was going to be computer science.

"Sir, I have a question," erupted an inquisitive student sitting a couple of rows behind me. It was Abhinav, my neighbourhood friend.

"Sure Abhinav. Tell me, what is it?" asked Professor Malik.

"Sir, I am curious to know how these weekly test evaluations integrate into the overall evaluations. I mean, what is the weightage of these tests?" asked Abhinav.

"Son, at this stage you should not really be bothered about these things. First thing is to clear the basics. Let me reiterate – to succeed in today's competitive environment, you just need three things."

There was a dramatic pause, which Professor Malik deliberately introduced to make the delivery of his point impactful. A smile appeared on Professor Malik's face as he got ready to count the three gems on his fingertips.

"These are practice, practice and practice."

Most students pretended to have discovered the eternal truth. I could not help noticing that the student sitting in the first row frantically took notes as he wrote the word 'practice' three times on a fresh page.

"Wow!" I gently whispered to myself.

This was going to be a fun journey.

As I waited for the bus, I reflected upon the first day at the school. I particularly thought about the strong sentiment my school teachers had against coaching institutes. I wondered how people could have such divergent views about the same thing. The professors at FIITJEE and the teachers at school had completely opposite perspectives. I was in a state of haze and disillusionment.

I reached home at about 2:30 p.m. ready to crash after a seemingly long day. Mama and Didi were excitedly waiting for me.

"How was the first day?" asked Didi.

"It was good. I made some friends, met my new teachers, saw around the school, gathered some intelligence from the old students. Overall, felt like a day well spent," I replied somewhat disinterestedly.

"Intelligence! What kind of intelligence?" asked Didi quizzically.

"Intelligence about which teachers are strict that one cannot afford to mess with."

"You be sincere about your work, and you wouldn't need to use that intelligence."

I nodded my head while continuing to have food.

"By the way, you might need to hurry up. It's already 2:50 p.m. You should be leaving latest by 3:00 p.m. to make it in time for your FIITJEE class."

It took me by surprise. Amidst the new school routine, I had completely forgotten about the class that afternoon. It had momentarily slipped my mind, and the sudden reminder did shake me up a wee bit. I considered expressing resentment, but realized that playing the victim card would not have helped in any way. I quietly packed my bag, waved goodbye to the ladies and left for the class.

By the time the FIITJEE class ended at 7:45 p.m., my mind was numb. Abhinav also looked like a hapless chicken that had resigned to its fate and was about to be butchered. We both silently walked up to the bus stop. Conscious that we had both not spoken anything in a while, Abhinav was the first one to break the silence.

"This is tough."

"Sure, it is. I am already feeling drained and feel like I need a vacation to get over the fatigue I have accumulated since morning. I am finding it hard to digest that this is going to be the routine for the next two years."

"No, this is not the full picture. Today being the first day at school, it was light. The actual routine would be set in a few days, when there would be school homework to take care of after we reach back home."

"Damn it!" was all I could muster.

"I think we will need to unleash my plan very soon!"

"Which plan?"

"About bunking FIITJEE classes to play cricket at that time?"

I was not sure what to say to that. While I had expressed excitement about the idea when Abhinav had first mentioned it, I was not fully convinced if that was the right thing to do. I had contemplated the idea a few times since then. On each occasion, I was reminded of the advice Mama had once shared – 'If you ever get confused about whether something is right or wrong, apply the simple test – can you do it with our knowledge or do you need to hide something? If the answer is the latter, most likely that path will take you in the wrong direction.'

I had applied that simple test a few times to the choice of bunking FIITJEE classes. On each occasion, I got the same answer. It was not the right thing to do.

"Where are you lost? You agree with my plan?"

I waited for a few moments before responding with great effort, "May be."

IN HINDSIGHT

When we are in the middle of a journey, it is sometimes difficult to see the bigger picture. Things only become clear with the advantage of hindsight years down the line.

When I look back, I think I was standing at an interesting crossroad in life. The path ahead seemed full of choices and options – some coming from my near and dear ones, others from friends and acquaintances, still others from professors at school and FIITJEE. The ones coming from folks who genuinely cared appeared right, but hard to pursue, while others seemed wrong but highly tempting. It all seemed like a medley of shades, randomly thrown over a piece of canvas.

KEY MESSAGES

- ✓ Sometimes you may not have the wisdom or foresight to see the bigger picture. In such times, lean on the advice of your coaches and mentors to fully understand your choices. Do remember that your choices define your destiny. So evaluate them critically before committing to a particular choice.
- ✓ There is a saying that you are the average of the five people that you spend the most time with. An important corollary is that just by being mindful of who you decide to spend your maximum time with, you can evolve yourself. Surround yourself with people who talk about ideas and possibilities, rather than the ones who talk about obstacles and challenges.
- ✓ There will be temptations and distractions along the way, inhibiting your ability to think rationally. A simple rule can help – the choices requiring struggle and toil in the short-to-medium term are usually better compared to the ones that offer instant gratification.

August 1998-April 1999
The mess unfolds

> "Take the first step in faith. You don't have to see the whole staircase, just take the first step." – Martin Luther King Jr.

2 on 25 is 8 percent, I know!

I had always been a bright kid in school and had never worked too hard to achieve good results. My happy-go-lucky nature coupled with a reasonably good intellect had always helped me sail through quite easily. However, I found myself in a very different situation this time around. Things seemed to be moving very fast, right from the word go! I was struggling to balance two very divergent set of expectations – one from the school and another from the coaching institute. My happy-go-lucky nature was already beginning to wane, and my reasonably good intellect was beginning to get exposed as not good enough.

As I sat through the FIITJEE class that Monday evening, I remembered that on the following day I had my first weekly test at school. I was already feeling exhausted and had no clue about how I intended to cover the syllabus. I vaguely remembered school friends talking about two distinct types of questions – one based on facts and theory, and the other more application-based where one had to use logical thinking to build simple algorithms. I realized that it was too late to cover the whole syllabus. I took a smart punt. I decided to cover only the part involving logical thinking.

Later that night, I sat down with the computer book to skim through the C++ basics. I didn't realize when I fell asleep, but when Papa woke me up in the morning, I knew I had not been able to cover a lot of topics. I didn't know if the alarm had failed me, or had I just fallen asleep inadvertently the previous night. Either way, I had no option but to get up and face the music.

I tried to make the best use of limited time at hand in the bus and during the morning assembly. But that was not going to be of much use. Once inside the classroom, I nervously looked around, hoping to derive some inspiration from other unprepared students. I was hoping to see fidgety students looking tense and anxious. Unfortunately, for some reason, everyone looked comfortable. I overheard some of the group conversations. I had read about a few things I heard, but there were way too many terms that I had never heard or read about.

I didn't want to appear nervous, so I tried to don a composed expression. I realized I was screwed.

At exactly that moment, the bell rang. Our computer science teacher, Malvika Surmai Das, entered the classroom. Students often referred to her as MS Dos. It was a creatively manipulated name that aligned well with her subject. She distributed the question paper.

I quickly scanned through the question paper, desperately hoping to see a few familiar words. On the first glance, I couldn't find many. In fact, I didn't find any. I slowly scanned through the paper again.

I identified a few questions which I understood, but didn't know the answers to.

'Who is the father of C++ programming language and in which year did he develop the language?' I kept staring at the question, digging deep into my memory logs to come up with an answer. Guessing an answer to a question like that would have required more than a miracle.

'Build an algorithm using a do-while loop to generate a Fibonacci series.'

Again, I kept staring at the question.

'If only I knew what a do-while loop is and what a Fibonacci series is... I could have cracked this one.' I thought.

I kept staring at the paper for a long time, before beginning to put some ink to the answer sheet. Eventually when I did write, it felt more out of an obligation to write something rather than a genuine need to write. I did manage to fill a few pages during that one-hour humble attempt.

☆☆

I knew I had messed up badly in my first test. In the few days following the weekly test, I must have thought a zillion times about the fiasco. I was afraid of being embarrassed in front of everyone. I tried to convince myself that the test didn't really mean anything. It was just a set of questions that I didn't know proper answers for – and that's it. It was in no way a reflection of my ability or who I was as a person. But I also realized that howsoever worthless that small weekly test may have been, I would still have to face the ignominy of sharing my marks with friends and family. I remembered the words Papa had said while dropping me at school on the first day – 'You never get a second chance to make first impression'.

As much as I had been thinking about my own performance, I had also been thinking about how other students would fare in the test. I was hoping that everyone would get screwed, royally. It was easier to cope with 'the entire class, including me, got screwed' narrative compared to the simple 'I got screwed'. I had also silently wished that MS Dos would never return the test paper. All of it was just wishful thinking though.

The dreaded day arrived.

MS Dos had a bundle of papers in her hands. She announced, "I am going to distribute these. Two simple rules that I expect each one of you to follow – first, do not come to me unless there is a totaling mistake; second, I don't want to see any discussion on the marks."

She continued, "I like to distribute test copies in an open and transparent manner. I would call out each student's name and marks so there is no need to enquire marks amongst yourselves anyway."

"Damn you! Sadistic pleasure disguised as transparency," I murmured softly.

MS Dos started calling out each student's name and marks out of 25. I could feel my heart beating faster and louder with each passing name. I had always been an agnostic, but strangely, in such moments of stress, I often found myself saying silent prayers.

"Abhay 17.5, Nikhil 21, Amit 11.5, Saurabh 13…"

MS Dos went on for a while without looking up.

"Aman 2."

There was a pause as MS Dos lifted her face to see me.

"2 on 25! Do you know what that means in percentage terms?" she asked solemnly.

I sat speechless across the desk, my chin resting on my palms, eyes staring at nothing in particular, struggling to hold tears. I wanted to smash the board, but that wouldn't have helped in any way. I didn't want to think about how exactly at that moment in time all the students would have been staring at me, but the thought still flashed in my mind.

"Meet me after the class. Do you hear me?" asked MS Dos.

I realized that MS Dos was waiting for a response, and I was becoming conspicuous by my silence.

"Yes, ma'am," I replied sheepishly.

"Disgusting!" murmured MS Dos, and continued - "Anuradha 15, Arindam 16, Vaibhav 12, Paramjyot 11."

After distributing the sheets, MS Dos allowed students to go through their answer sheets for a few minutes. I didn't have the courage to look at my sheet. I was also conscious not to open my sheet in front of other students. I made several folds of the sheet and placed it beneath the other books inside my bag.

"You smashed it out of the park," quipped PJ, not understanding the terrible state I was in.

"Don't make me smash you out of the park now!" I retorted angrily.

When the day ended, I quickly packed my bag and hurriedly rushed to the washroom. I had a strange desire to meet my new self, a new version of me which felt anxious, miserable, and helpless. Once inside, I blankly stared at my marks at the top hand right corner of the answer sheet. A tear trickled down my cheek. I continued to stare at my marks for a few minutes.

On my way back home, I kept thinking about how to break the news at home. I didn't have a clue.

As usual, Mama opened the door with a pleasant smile.

"How was your day?" she asked.

No reply.

"What happened?"

No reply.

"Tell me what happened please."

"Nothing," I replied.

"Of course, there is something. Your ears are all red. Did someone scold you?"

"No."

"Did you fight with someone?"

"Did you get less marks in some test?" Mama continued.

I didn't speak, but nodded in affirmation.

"How many did you get? Zero?" she continued. "You are worried about such a petty thing?!"

She deliberately said that in a very casual tone, subtly suggesting that she couldn't care less for marks. Just by saying that one word, zero, Mama had made things infinitely easier for me. It gave me a strange confidence. My brooding shoulders instantly got back in shape. And why not? I had scored good two marks more than what would have qualified as a low score.

"No, not that bad. I scored two!" I replied.

"My god! You really scared me. I got unnecessarily worried. Come, let's have lunch," she replied and went to the kitchen to get food.

No one at home talked about that test again.

Later that night, when I sat alone in my room to complete the homework, I carefully scanned the answer sheet. I noticed that there was a totaling mistake. I discovered that I had scored half a mark in five distinct questions, which all added up to 2.5. I quickly turned the pages again to validate my observation. It indeed added up to 2.5. I wondered if that really made a difference and if it was worth getting corrected.

The next day, as soon as MS Dos entered the class, I approached her to raise the totaling mistake point.

"Good morning, ma'am. I need to speak with you for a minute."

"What is it about?" asked MS Dos, with a stern face.

"It's about my marks in the weekly test. There is a small totaling error," I replied extending my arm to handover the marksheet to MS Dos.

MS Dos flipped through the pages to make a quick mental calculation. It didn't take long as it was just five half marks.

"How much does it add up to?" asked MS Dos quizzically, sincerely hoping that she had missed something.

"2.5 ma'am."

MS Dos took a few seconds to consider the right response. She gracefully tore the answer sheet into two halves and extended her arm to hand it over back to me.

"Don't you dare talk to me ever again. Get lost!" she shouted with an expression that rolled anger, sarcasm and disgust, all into one.

Her loud reaction got the entire class interested.

"There was a totaling mistake in his answer sheet. I had mistakenly totaled his score to two," she continued. "Do you know how much it actually totaled to?"

A brief pause as the entire class waited for her to share the magical score. "2.5! ...and he has the audacity to come ask for correction!" she shouted angrily.

The entire class burst into laughter, a really loud laughter.

As I walked back to my seat, I could overhear some jibes.

"John Nash in the making."

"I have heard these people lose their mind at the magical hour. I am seeing it for the first time, though."

"Idiot!" said another one, a female this time.

I walked back to my seat. It was just two rows from the front but seemed like a really long walk back. I carefully caressed the torn answer sheet and kept it securely in the middle of a book, as if preserving a prized possession. I was not sure why I was doing that, but I wanted to do it, nonetheless.

Through a subtle stare, MS Dos noticed the act. I couldn't be sure, but I think she too felt that she had been a bit harsh on me.

It's not me, but my stars this time

After the computer test fiasco, my self-confidence had taken a serious beating. I was mindful that my grand performance in the test had already exposed my intellectual capabilities. To make matters worse, my seemingly innocuous request to get the totaling fixed had positioned me as a subject of mockery. I wondered if all the teachers knew about the incident, as I had often seen contempt even in the eyes of other teachers. I had become overly conscious about not saying or doing anything which might expose me any further.

In fact, several weeks passed by and I had not dared to utter a word to any teacher, no questions, no participation in class discussions, nothing. I used to keenly look at the elite students in the class, who would always be amongst the toppers. I silently observed their body language and the sense of confidence they exuded. They all just looked so happy and comfortable. I furtively examined their facial expressions when the teacher would explain things. I was amazed at how quickly they used to absorb new topics, almost giving the impression that they already knew it all.

I was conscious that my lack of communication could be perceived as my indifference. To address the risk, I often deployed fake body language and bogus facial expressions to connect with the teachers. When the teacher explained a new topic, every few moments I would gently nod my head with a sudden wink of eyes and a studious expression, suggesting that I was not only listening but also following the topic. It's a different matter that on most occasions I was doing neither. Those fake expressions were soon going to land me in trouble, this time with Professor David, our mathematics professor.

As Professor David entered the class, the students quickly settled into their seats and the noise decibels gradually dropped.

"I understand today we have two back-to-back classes, so we have good seventy minutes. We will continue with the trigonometric identities in the first half and in the second half we will practice some problems," he said.

He was so soft in his speech that it was difficult for students sitting beyond the first row from the front to follow anything.

"Any questions?" he continued.

"Dude, he does this all the time. Sometimes I wonder if he really means to check for questions or is it a subtle joke," said PJ.

"Hmm. The only question I can think of is to check if he can be a little louder?" I murmured.

"You can afford to speak a bit louder in his class. Even if he gets offended, he wouldn't bother scolding," replied PJ.

Professor turned to the board and started writing several trigonometric identities. When he reached the bottom of the board, he turned towards the students to check if it was all making sense.

"Fine?" he asked.

No one responded.

"Good," he replied and turned back towards the other half of the board.

Even the brightest students struggled to hold attention in Professor David's class. It was no surprise then that the likes of me used to just resign to their fate.

"Hell. This seems like a contest between him and me. If he manages to put me off to sleep, he wins. If I stay awake through the class, I win," said PJ in an exasperated tone.

"There is no shame in losing to a stronger opposition," – I replied softly.

"He is in the wrong profession. He could make millions as an infant caretaker. While all the nannies in the world would struggle to put the babies to sleep, our David will do it in a matter of seconds."

"Whatever!"

It had been a little over thirty minutes since the class started. We noticed that Professor David had comfortably settled in his chair, while the students seemed to be working in their notebooks.

"Why is he sitting like that? Can you check with Abhay what's going on?" asked PJ.

"What's up?" I whispered to Abhay.

"He has given ten problems on the board. We have to try these and then whoever is interested can present the solution on the board."

"Hmm. How long has it been since he gave these questions?"

"It's been about ten minutes. I am on to the seventh problem."

"Good going buddy!" I replied.

PJ and I continued to comfortably chit-chat. We were sure that there wasn't any risk from not attempting the questions. He was such a gentle soul that he would never make anyone uncomfortable by calling them to the board. At most, he would have asked if someone wanted to volunteer.

A few minutes later, Professor David and I happened to make an inadvertent eye contact. Professor David tilted his head slightly and moved right palm facing downwards. He seemed to be asking something, which I couldn't immediately fathom. I assumed that the Professor was asking his usual question 'All fine?' I too slightly nodded my head in affirmative to respond that everything was indeed fine.

As it turned out, it was one of those glorious uncertainties of life, that appear beautiful in hindsight, but quite embarrassing when they happen. On that occasion, Professor David was asking me if I wanted to solve the first question on the board. My unintended yet affirmative nod of the head suggested that I wanted to volunteer. Professor David gingerly got up from his seat and pointing towards a piece of chalk on the table welcomed me to get on the board. I realized that the speculative speechless conversation had created some confusion.

"Please come," said Professor David.

I didn't know what Professor David wanted of me exactly.

I sheepishly walked up to him and innocently asked, "Yes sir?"

"Please go ahead!" replied Professor David, pointing towards the board, not in any way intending to embarrass me. It was just a stupid miscommunication.

I remembered what Abhay had told me and connected the dots. I understood that the professor was expecting me to solve the problem on the board. I casually picked the chalk stick and moved towards the board. I read through the first question.

'If A + B + C = 180, prove that tan A + tan B + tan C = tan A tan B tan C'

I cursed my stars to have landed in that position. I just couldn't believe my luck. I continued to stare at the board for a while before beginning to write. I knew that I would not be able to solve the problem, but was determined to make a valiant effort. I started writing down all the trigonometric identities that could have been remotely related to that problem. The other students had already started making jeering remarks.

Professor David was too good a soul to trouble anyone like that deliberately. Seeing my fate on the board, he appeared more disturbed than me.

"Son, I thought you volunteered to solve the question on the board," asked Professor David, almost apologetically.

"No sir. There was some miscommunication. Sorry."

"Ok. No problem. Please go back," replied Professor David.

As I walked back to the seat, I could overhear various derisive remarks by my fellow students. The ones from the female voices annoyed me particularly.

"These two jokers are amazing. One is named PJ and the other is actually a PJ," said one of the girls.

✩✩

Neither mute nor deaf, I am dumb

Months seemed to be rolling by rather quickly. With every passing week, it felt like I was getting a step closer to a disaster. Howsoever hard I tried, nothing seemed to be going right. On the one hand, I had to deal with FIITJEE classes, which were nothing short of a mental torture. On the other hand, I had the teachers at school to deal with, who considered me nothing more than a clown. It almost seemed like they all needed a guinea pig to vent out their frustration and in me they had one such soft target. I was becoming increasingly disconnected and oblivious to my surroundings. I frequently missed important announcements at school, and I couldn't care less about it.

November 1998

In the previous chemistry class, Kavita ma'am had announced that she would be taking an extra lab session on the following day. We were supposed to be carrying our lab coats as we were not permitted to enter the lab without coats. As usual, I must have been dreaming away to glory when ma'am made that announcement in the class.

The shrilling sound of the bell marked the end of the lunch break. It was time for the chemistry class. I noticed an unusual hustle-bustle in the class. Everyone seemed to be heading out of the class.

"Where are they all going?" I asked PJ.

"They are heading to the lab."

"But why? Today is the theory class."

"We have an extra lab class today. She announced it in the class yesterday," PJ updated me.

"Did she?" I replied with a nervous chuckle.

"That means you are not carrying your lab coat. Get ready for the fun. You know how paranoid she gets when it comes to adhering to lab rules."

I followed the other students to reach the lab. Just as I was about to enter the lab, Kavita ma'am noticed me without my coat.

"Where is your coat?"

""Ma'am, I am sorry. I forgot."

"What kind of a crazy nut are you? Can you ever do anything right?" retorted Kavita ma'am angrily.

I looked down towards my shoes to avoid eye-contact.

"I am talking to you. Look at me!" She took a pause and continued, "I must have announced at least three times that we would be using today's theory class to cover lab activities. You still forgot?"

Pause.

"Now what do you want me to do? I cannot allow you to work inside the lab without a coat. It is unsafe."

"I understand ma'am. I am really sorry."

"If my memory serves me right, you are also preparing for your entrance examinations?"

'Now what does that have to do with my forgetting the lab coat!' I wondered.

"Cracking JEE exam is not a joke. It is meant for the brightest and sharpest minds, not for nuts like you. It requires aptitude, it requires hard work, it requires discipline. I am afraid you don't have any of this. On the contrary, you struggle with basic concepts. Why are you wasting your time and your parents' money?"

Silence.

"Anyway it's your life. You are free to screw it the way you want to. It is none of my business. For now, just please tell me what I should do to ensure that you don't forget to carry your lab coat ever again?"

I genuinely didn't know what to say. I couldn't think of anything that I could have said to pacify her. For a moment I wondered if she was really expecting an answer or was it just a general outburst.

"Are you deaf or mute? I mean, are you not answering because you cannot hear my question or is it that you hear my question but can't speak?" she retorted after she had asked me twice already.

Everyone has a tipping point. I was no exception.

I stared into her eyes, for the first time in that conversation, and allowed my natural instincts to take over.

"I am neither mute nor deaf. It's just that I don't understand your question. I guess I am dumb." I continued, "I am not carrying my coat. I cannot change that, but I said I am sorry. Now, to your question around what you can do to ensure that it doesn't happen again, I really don't know ma'am. Maybe you can consider punishing me, maybe ask me to stand outside the lab holding my ears, maybe ask me to clean the lab after the class is over, whatever you please. Really. Whatever."

Silence.

I stood there motionless, continuing to look into her eyes, not with arrogance but with indifference and helplessness.

I softly added after a few moments.

"Ma'am, failures are not natural. They are set-up systematically. It's a conspiracy."

"What is that supposed to mean?" she asked quizzically.

"Doesn't matter," I replied with a heavy voice.

I was expecting things to get bad after that outburst from me, but what happened next turned out to be a pleasant surprise.

"Get in and start the experiment. Be careful next time!" Kavita ma'am said softly.

It was not that I had planned that outburst, nor did I intend to do it ever again with any teacher. It was just a spontaneous eruption of the turbulence within. But I did feel great about squaring off. I felt good at the way I protected my self-respect and the way Kavita ma'am backed off thereafter.

I learned an important lesson that day – the world cannot intimidate you if you refuse to oblige. The world cannot belittle you without your consent.

✩✩

By the end of 1998, I found myself in a state of complete disorientation. I was beginning to slip into a state of depression, though I never discussed it with my parents explicitly. It was not that I feared lack of support, but just that I didn't know if anyone could do anything about it. The only good thing was that I was not the only one struggling. My close pal, Abhinav, was equally stressed out. We used to go to FIITJEE classes together in the afternoon. On the way we used to have all the time in the world to discuss. And discuss what? Not any concepts or problems, but our plight. We had started cherishing those discussions as it helped us derive a sense of comfort, similar to the one that one gets from seeing other co-passengers in a sinking ship.

December 1998

Abhinav and I were travelling in the bus to our FIITJEE class. I occupied a seat right next to the window and Abhinav was sitting beside me. Halfway through the distance, none of us had spoken a word. Abhinav seemed to be in a pensive mood, lost in his thoughts.

"Do you really want to attend the class today?" he asked, almost giving the impression that the question came up as a part of an ongoing conversation, a conversation that he may have been having in his mind perhaps.

"What do you mean?" I asked, somewhat surprised by that sudden out of context question.

"I mean, do we really need to attend this class? We both don't understand anything in the class anyway," asked Abhinav, carefully evaluating his words.

I didn't reply immediately.

After a brief pause, I asked him, "What could we possibly do at this time of the day?"

"I guess even if we don't do anything and just lay idle in the sun, it would be better than dozing off shamelessly in the class." He said. "On a slightly more positive note, I am carrying a Cosco ball in my bag. We could play catches."

Again, I didn't reply immediately, but was excited about what Abhinav had suggested. The prospect of missing the class was too tempting, but I was just not sure.

"What do you think?" he coaxed, desperate for me to say yes.

"Okay! Let's do it today, but only for today. Let's not make it a habit," I replied. What I had said to Kavita ma'am a few days back may have been in a fit of retaliation, but that response from me proved that inadvertently I had spoken nothing but the truth. I was indeed dumb.

"Great. Do you have a place in mind where we could go?" asked Abhinav.

"Yes, I think I do. I have never been to this ground, but I always watch kids playing here from my favourite window seat in the class. We might need to do a bit of searching though."

We went around the venue to roughly locate our classroom from a distance. We then made some directional assumptions to figure the ground location. It took us just around ten minutes to get to the ground.

"Scientist, our trigonometry concepts are not that bad, after all. We did manage to work out the directions in a three-dimensional space pretty comfortably," I exclaimed.

"It's 3:50 p.m. Professor Sanjay would be putting the class off to sleep with his deltas, cosines, discriminants and derivatives, while we merrily relax here under the sun. Not a bad trade-off, I say."

We both lay on the grass, staring at the bright sky, cherishing the soothing winter afternoon sun for a while. The instant gratification masked our ability to see the dark clouds looming large over our heads.

At around 4:30 p.m., a group of boys came over to the ground for their usual evening play. We both joined them. We were both conscious not to push too hard as we couldn't afford to sweat. That would have made our misdeed obvious to our family members. We continued our rendezvous till around 7:30 p.m. and then walked back to the bus stand to catch our usual evening bus. After a long time, it felt like a day well spent, though deep within, there was a sense of guilt.

Out of fear, Abhinav and I attended the next class, but bunked class a few days later again. Within a matter of few weeks, what had started off as a one-off exercise had become a habit. We started bunking a majority of our FIITJEE classes, offering ourselves the lame justification that we would anyway not follow anything in the class. The more we bunked, the harder we were making it for ourselves. By around the beginning of 1999, I was in a state of complete disarray. Worse still, I was staring straight into the annual exams, both at FIITJEE and at school, in just a few months.

Fantasies need not be rationalized

February 1999

As I switched off the lights, I thought about the mess I had created in my life. I thought about the computer science test disaster, the bunked classes, the jeering remarks of fellow students, the mockery at school –

it was all perfectly chaotic. I particularly thought about Kavita ma'am's words – *'Cracking JEE exam is not a joke. It is meant for the brightest and sharpest minds, not for nuts like you.'*

I wondered if there could possibly be a way for me to crack the JEE exam. It could have been the sweetest way to redeem my lost pride. I instantly rubbished the idea and dozed off.

The next morning, I got up early to assess the extent of syllabus I had missed by bunking the FIITJEE classes. It was a lot. I had missed several important topics in all the three subjects. I sat at my study chair, allowing my forehead to comfortably rest on my right hand. I continued to flip through the pages, feeling more intimidated with each passing page. I wanted to simply tear away those pages to eliminate them from the syllabus and from my life forever, but then my redemption depended on those pages.

I drew three columns on a piece of paper and labelled them as topics I understood well, topics for which I attended classes but didn't understand, and topics which I had completely bunked. I spent the next two hours meticulously putting all topics into one of those three columns. At the end of the exercise, I was disappointed to see the first column largely blank and most topics getting evenly distributed between the second and the third column.

Papa entered the room at the usual time to wake me up. He was surprised to see me already awake.

"What wakes you up so early? Do you have some test today?"

"No. It's just that there are a few topics that I don't understand well. I was making a list of all these topics."

"Which topics are these? Maybe I could help?"

"There are way too many and the challenge is that the pace of teaching at FIITJEE is so fast that if we miss one topic, it becomes very difficult to catch up."

"Don't worry. Just give me the names of the topics. I will read these up during the day today and will explain at night."

I smiled.

"This is not a one-day task. This will take many weeks to cover up. Each topic has new concepts, complex assignments, and quizzes."

Papa smiled back.

"Okay, then I will read up these topics one by one over the next many weeks. Let's spend an hour each night and I will help you cover these. Now tell me which topics are troubling you?"

'*Everything taught so far!*' I wanted to say, but that would have exposed me, so I started sharing the topics subtly. I positioned some of them as topics where I had conceptual clarifications, others as topics where I struggled to apply concepts, still others as topics where I tended to make mistakes so needed more practice. Through those vague classifications and a bit of beating around the bush, I effectively conveyed to Papa that I didn't understand differential calculus, trigonometry, complex numbers, quadratic equations, binomial theorem, kinematics, laws of motion, rotational motion, work and energy, thermodynamics, stoichiometry, chemical kinetics, atomic structure, and a few others.

Papa had always been a man of immense patience, but I was sure that I had stretched it a bit too far with that conspicuously long list of topics. I would not have been surprised if Papa had retorted asking, 'Is there anything that you understand?'

"Okay, good that you know which topics need more attention. That's the most difficult part. Rest is easy. We will take care of it together."

I considered replying, 'Really? Is that the most difficult part? Great! Then I am already on my way to cracking JEE. I am really doing well with the difficult part. It's only the easy part that we need to take care of now.'

But I just smiled warmly. I very well understood the intent behind Papa's remarks. I felt bad at having landed myself in that mess, despite a strong support system I had in the form of my parents.

"Now let's gets ready. Otherwise, you will get late for school," replied Papa as he headed out of the room.

✩✩

Papa spent a major part of the day at office studying the first topic on my list, the differential calculus. He meticulously made notes in a maroon-coloured diary, which was soon going to become our most trusted pal for months to come.

Later that night

"I studied the first topic today. I have not completed it yet, but if you want, we can spend some time on the part that I covered so far."

"Yes, certainly! What time can we sit?" I asked excitedly, as if someone had just offered me a lifeline.

"That you have to decide," replied Papa.

"Should we start at 11:00 p.m.?"

"Perfect."

Papa spent a couple of hours explaining the concepts to me. It was a completely new topic for me, though I could visually relate to the Greek symbols from Professor Sanjay's class. The good thing about studying with Papa was that I could ask any question – good question, bad question, stupid question, irrelevant question – they were all dealt with patience and compassion.

On a few occasions, I did tend to get distracted by the enormity of the syllabus, but Papa would calmly bring me back on each occasion. We continued studying till about 2:00 a.m. While I was thrilled that my learning curve had finally made a modest start, I was concerned that we had only managed to cover three pages in over three hours.

"You have to go to school tomorrow morning, so you should go to bed now," said Papa, conscious that I just had four hours to go before I would have to get up next morning for school.

"Okay, but this was a very useful session. I learned a lot of new things."

"We will do this every day if it's helpful."

"Much needed. By the way, how many days do you think it will take us to cover one topic?"

"May be 10-15 days for each topic, considering you also have other commitments. And then you will also have to spend some time practicing."

"This means that I will need almost a month to cover up each topic. In parallel, the FIITJEE curriculum will continue to move ahead at a rapid pace. It all feels so impossible."

"What is the rush? We will cover it all slowly but surely. It will take months of patience and perseverance, but as they say, all it takes is all you got, so get to ready to give it your all."

"The little bit of urgency is that I have the national Open Test coming up in about two months from now," I replied with a hint of despair underpinning my otherwise hopeful sentiment.

"What is an Open Test?"

"It's a test that FIITJEE conducts every year across the country. Based on the performance in this test, they give us a percentile score, that is what fraction of students have scored less marks than me. They also use this data to predict our actual rank in the JEE exam."

"Don't worry about predictions. Predictions are just predictions and can be wrong."

"Our professors tell us that it is important to perform well in this exam as historically their prediction accuracy has been almost 95 percent. 95 out of every 100 JEE rank predictions they make turn out to be accurate."

"Given where we are with our preparation right now, a good target to have would be to feature in those 5 percent incorrect predictions," replied Papa, trying his level best to not demoralize me.

In his words, I noticed how the same message could be conveyed in so many ways. Just a few days ago, Kavita ma'am had conveyed a similar message in such harsh words. Papa managed to convey the same with such positivity and grace that I felt motivated to work hard. I noticed that Papa used the phrase 'where we are' and not 'where you are'. Just by replacing a single word, he had made a world of difference.

As I lay in the bed that night, I again entertained the same thought I had the previous night. I wondered if there indeed was a way for me to crack the JEE exam. '*I would if I could, but...*' I thought to myself, but then abruptly and somewhat deliberately, cut short the thought. I realized that I didn't need to complete it. Fantasies don't need to be rationalized. A tear rolled down my cheek as I eventually fell asleep.

Over the coming weeks, the late-night study with Papa became a norm. Mama too adjusted her routine to ensure that the environment at home was vibrant and lively till late night, and on some days till early morning. On my part, I didn't bunk any FIITJEE classes thereafter. I also ceased to get those irresistible pangs of sleep during the FIITJEE classes. It was not that everything became fancy, but at least there was a direction. Despite the mess all around me, there was a sense of pride – the sort of pride that doesn't necessarily come from success, but from just being sincere.

I knew that I needed all the time in the world to cover the backlog. I started creating extra hours each day by adding up bits and pieces of unproductive time – by getting up early, by sleeping late, by reading up while commuting, by cutting down lunch time at school, by cutting down the gossip time with friends. My parents' love and support had transformed my mindset completely. I started finding positives even amidst all the mockery and embarrassment I had to deal with at school.

Student counseling! Counseling my foot

April 1999

The final exams of eleventh standard were around the corner. There was also the added pressure of FIITJEE Open Test, which was just a few days away. I had planned to spend all my efforts on the Open Test. However, I was conscious not to mess up at school as badly as I had done in the first computer test. I was willing to put in just the amount of effort needed to clear the exam, but nothing more than that.

Everyone had a different view about my approach – I thought of it as a smart strategy, my friends thought of it as a calculated gamble, my teachers at FIITJEE considered it the right thing to do, my teachers at school felt that I was being a fool, while my parents did not have any specific view, but were committed to support me unconditionally all the way. Whatever it may have been, it did lead to some embarrassing moments for me at school.

Few days later

In the computer science revision class at school, MS Dos asked us, "Build an algorithm to generate the list of all prime numbers less than 100. Who wants to take a stab at that on the board?"

Many hands went up.

"Vidit, do you want to try that?"

Vidit was a smart guy. It was easy for him.

"Ok next question. Build an algorithm to check if a number is a perfect cube. Who wants to try this?"

Again, several bright hands up. Abhay got a chance to solve that one. He too was a bright lad and cracked it comfortably.

"Ok, next question. Write an algorithm to check if a number is a palindrome."

This time fewer hands went up.

"Aman, why don't you try that on the board?" asked MS Dos.

My heart sank. I didn't know what a palindrome meant. Even if I knew, I would not have been able to solve that one. I stood there shamelessly staring at the board.

"Clearly, you don't know this one. Okay let me ask an easier question. Can you just tell us what a palindrome means?" asked MS Dos with a display of frustration that comes from giving up on someone after months of effort.

Silence.

"Okay, so you don't know that one too."

She turned towards the class. "Can someone please tell him what a palindrome means?"

"Ma'am, palindrome is a number which reads the same backward as forward. For example, 98789 is a palindrome, because even when we reverse it, we get the same number," answered Nikhil.

"Thank you," replied MS Dos. "Can you now write the algorithm?" she asked, turning her attention back to me.

No response.

"What should I do with you?" she asked exasperatedly. I couldn't help thinking about a similar question Kavita ma'am had asked me few weeks back. This time, I was quick to respond.

"Ma'am if you deem appropriate, you could ask me to get out of the class."

"Please get out," replied MS Dos in an unequivocal tone.

"Do you mind if I carry a book with me?"

"Not at all. Please do."

It all looked so graceful and uncomplicated that it hardly felt like a punishment being meted out. I took out one of the FIITJEE books and gracefully walked out of the class.

"We have always been very proud of our rigorous selection process. We are very choosy about the new students we pick each year. I am not sure how our school made this blunder," she quipped as I walked out of the class.

When the period ended, MS Dos stepped out. As she walked past me, she saw me reading the book in my hand. I wished her to just walk away, but was sure that she would have something to say.

"Stop that pretense. If only you could be half as sincere as that..." she said without bothering to complete the sentence. That sentence brought a smile to my face as I felt good about my ability to predict human behaviour.

✩✩

The night before the Open Test, I scanned through the list of topics for the test. It was a long list. Despite my best efforts, I had not been able to cover much ground. I was still reflecting upon my readiness for the next day when Papa entered the room at around 9:30 p.m.

"All set for tomorrow?"

"Not really. I have not been able to practice several topics," I replied with a nervous smile.

"Do not take tomorrow's exam too seriously. For all I care, it doesn't matter even if you tell me that you want to skip it. It just doesn't matter."

"I will go with it. If nothing else, I will use the time to get used to the exam environment."

The next day, I did take the Open Test. I struggled to attempt most of the questions. Even the few that I did, I wasn't confident if I had done those correctly. It had been a physically and mentally draining day.

At the end of the day, I quietly observed the conversations between fellow students. I noticed that there appeared a strong correlation between the decibel level and the intelligence level of students. The brightest and smartest students were always the loudest in the group. Those who had done well in the exam had an inherent need to show-off. The need seemed to amplify multi-fold if there were students of opposite sex around.

Over the next couple of weeks, I took the eleventh standard final exams at school too. Overall, it was a very humbling experience. It all served as a bitter reminder that there is no place for anything less than cent percent effort in the big wide competitive world.

It was no surprise, at least to me, to see the result. I scored around 62 percent marks on average in school, the highlight being my score in English where I managed just 44 percent. I couldn't help thinking that a few marks lesser and I would have achieved the dubious distinction that no one had ever managed in the family – of flunking in an exam. I fared equally miserably in the FIITJEE Open Test. I managed a modest percentile of around 65 percent. Based on my performance, FIITJEE predicted an All-India JEE rank in the range of 50 to 55 thousand, while the reality in those days was that IITs only had about two thousand seats.

About a week later, the school organized a special counseling session for select few students. The intent was to better understand the student concerns and explore ways to help them cope with the academic expectations. The session was organized completely in the spirit of making it valuable for the students. The students had been encouraged to come along with their parents, but the final choice was left to them. I did consider attending the session along with my parents. However, it was beneath my dignity to let them know that I was considered a worthy candidate for such a session.

The school auditorium appeared vibrant with the collective energies of teachers, students and parents. The animated interactions made up for a bright and cheerful Saturday morning, no matter how gloomy the context was. The teachers seated themselves well apart to ensure quiet ambience for the discussions. I occupied a seat ten rows opposite to where Professor Malik was seated. I patiently sat there waiting for other parents to leave before approaching Professor Malik. With my tightly folded arms, slightly hunched-up shoulders and shaking legs, I could have easily been mistaken for a convict waiting for his trial in the court.

After a wait of around twenty minutes, my turn arrived. I walked up to Professor Malik and sat opposite to him.

"Good morning, sir," I said.

"I wish it was a good morning, but I suspect it isn't really," replied Professor Malik with a subtle nod of head. He casually pulled out my report card from the bundle and continued, "physics 66, chemistry 68, mathematics 74, computer science 59. Overall, 62 percent. That doesn't sound like a good morning at all, my dear."

He breathed in a deep sigh and said, "Mr Singh, time and tide wait for none. Please wake up. Your time is running out. It feels like just yesterday when you joined this school. Unfortunately, my section. It has already been a year since then. The year seems to have passed in the blink of an eye. Do you realize that another blink and it would be time to write the board examinations?"

Silence.

"You know what worries me the most about you? It's not your marks, it's your attitude. When I see other struggling students, I at least see a sense of urgency, a sense of desperation. They at least have a plan. How well they execute that plan is a different matter, but there is a plan alright. In your case, I don't see that. There is a complete lack of intent."

Silence.

By that time, other teachers had become free as most of the students had left. They started to huddle behind me, though I did not notice it.

"I hear funny stories from other teachers about your heroics. You come unprepared to revision classes and still have the audacity to dare the teachers to punish you. And when they do punish you, you are shameless enough to ask them for permission to carry a book outside the class! Damn it, what's wrong with you? You score two out of 25 and are shameless enough to approach the teacher to fix the totaling mistake, only for the teacher to realize that it totals up to 2.5."

"That was a masterpiece. I still can't get that one out of my head," interjected MS Dos.

I was surprised to hear her voice. I turned around to notice all the teachers standing around me. It felt like a trial case where all the circumstantial evidence was against me, but I continued to make a humble attempt to plead innocence until proven guilty.

"Are you out of your mind or what? I mean what was going through your head when you requested her to fix the totaling to 2.5?" interrogated Professor Malik.

'So much for a counseling session. Counseling my foot!' I thought.

"I am waiting. Can you please say something?"

"When I got two out of 25 in the first test, I realized there was every chance that I would flunk in computer science at the end of the year. I wondered how costly that totaling error could turn out to be if I were to miss the passing cut-off by half a mark at the end of the year. That's what I had thought when I decided to approach ma'am to fix the error."

"It's funny that the only thing that you found erroneous was that half a mark gap. You have quite an attention to detail, I must say. But I wish you had the common sense to look at the bigger picture too," replied Professor Malik with a sense of exasperation.

It was Kala ma'am's turn to add fuel to the fire, "Talking about funny things, I have a fresh one for you all. In the English final exam, there were three long answer type questions from literature. Each question carried seven marks. I was perplexed to see that he wrote the same answer for all the three questions. I just couldn't fathom what could have been the possible reason behind that. I mean, why would one produce the same answer, an exact replica, for three different questions." She looked confused with an exaggerated shrug of shoulders and overly elevated eyebrows.

"Can you explain that please?"

"Yes ma'am. Based on last year's English exam pattern, I was expecting only 25 percent questions from literature."

"So?"

"So, I did not read a single story in the literature book. Unfortunately, as it turned out, almost half the paper was based on literature. Now that really put me in a difficult spot. I realized that I had to score a few in the literature part too, otherwise I would have struggled to clear the passing threshold."

I took a brief pause and continued, "Now coming to those three specific questions. As I said I had not read a single story, but I had some vague recollection of the character names and the plot from what I had heard in the class. Since it was all very hazy, I decided to write the same answer for all three questions, hoping that if it matches any of the questions correctly, I could fetch some valuable marks."

"You sure did fetch some valuable marks. You scored zero in two questions and five in one of those questions. Howsoever stupid that logic sounds, you would have missed the passing threshold by one mark if you had not done that. That said, please for heaven's sake, do not try such gimmicks in the board exams. More than anything else, it reflects badly on the school."

"Bizarre!" murmured Professor Malik with an exaggerated shake of his head. "Bizarre because you did something like that and managed to pull it off, but equally importantly you did not read a single story even one day before the exam! I mean who does that? Is it confidence? Apathy? Arrogance? What is it? I fail to understand you!"

"That's something I struggle with too. I mean, the part about understanding you. The other day when you stood outside the class, for a moment I genuinely thought that you were reading the book in all earnestness. But then I immediately abandoned the thought. Now when you tell us that you did not read a single story even one day before the exam, I just feel validated. It surely couldn't have been that you were reading the book seriously that day."

"I actually was. The only difference is that I was reading a FIITJEE book. But it was a book, alright. And I was reading it with complete attention," I replied.

"What's this joke about FIITJEE thing going on? I know it's fashionable to prepare for IITs, but come on, for god's sake, don't fool yourself," interjected Professor Malik.

"I am sorry, sir. I didn't get you," I replied.

"I mean you can't be serious about preparing for IIT. Are you?"

"Of course, sir. I am pursuing this ambition very seriously."

There were a few dismissive nods and a gentle collective laughter around me. I didn't bother looking around, though I did notice MS Dos intently staring at me. Unlike others, she was not amused. Maybe she was too annoyed to afford a smile, not even a mocking one. Or maybe it was something else, which I couldn't fathom. But there was something different about her expression in that moment.

"Then let me tell you - this is a wild goose chase. You are pursuing something that you are not made for, something that doesn't exist. It's a pursuit of void!" added Professor Malik, making a vain attempt to maintain his composure.

"Okay sir," I replied.

"What okay sir?" he retorted, this time not even attempting to hide his exasperation.

Silence.

Professor Malik took a deep breath to regain his composure. After a few awkward moments of silence, he calmly continued, "I really do want to know what's going through your mind because I am struggling to make sense of it. I have been in the field of teaching for over fifteen years. Every year I see new students, with widely varying capabilities and aspirations. None of them confounded me as much as you do. We are trying to help you secure passing marks in your twelfth standard board exams, and here you are talking about preparing for JEE exam. There is a huge disconnect. I am not sure if I find this fascinating or abnormal. For a moment, please be completely honest about it and tell me what you think about the way all of this looks from where we see it."

"If I have to be completely honest, I don't think about how it looks from where you see it," I replied with a stern stone-faced expression.

IN HINDSIGHT

I passionately recall the moment when MS Dos tore my answer sheet. It was a critical moment in my life. It may have lasted just a few minutes, but the impact it had on my psyche was long lasting. I will forever be grateful to MS Dos for the same.

As I look back at this phase of my life, I think I created a real mess for myself. I wasted a lot of precious time talking about problems, confronting people, finding ways to evade problems, and daydreaming. But I gradually recognized the futility of my actions.

KEY MESSAGES

- ✓ Sometimes stressful and uncomfortable moments turn out to be the most defining moments in life. Hold on to these moments as your prized possessions, for these are the moments that can help you unlock your true potential.
- ✓ We often get trapped in the vicious cycle of brooding over our problems and confronting people. All of that is a waste of time. The only way to solve a problem is to solve it; might as well quickly get on with it.
- ✓ It's human to make a mistake. But if you have made one, don't make the second mistake of covering it up. Two negatives don't make a positive.

May 1999-March 2000
The frantic scramble

"If you can't fly then run, if you can't run then walk, if you can't walk then crawl, but whatever you do you have to keep moving forward."- Martin Luther King Jr.

***

Time to unplug and unwind

It was the summer of 1999. Schools were closed for the annual summer break. Unlike the previous year, this time around it was going to be a somewhat shorter vacation as the school had planned to start extra classes earlier than usual for the twelfth standard students. At FIITJEE too, we were getting a mini break of two weeks. I was looking forward to the break, not so much for the usual fun that a vacation brings along, but more so for just switching off for a few days.

'Even machines and engines need to be periodically switched off to reboot, we humans are no exception!' I thought to myself.

Like previous years, there was a discussion about visiting Jalandhar. I wasn't overly excited about the idea. The past year had taken a toll, leaving me mentally and emotionally drained. I felt like I was on the verge of a mental breakdown. I was in no mood to meet anyone, not even my beloved cousins or friends. All I needed was peace and serenity for a few days, a few days with no scolding, no exam pressure, no mockery, no backlog, no pretense, just peace of mind.

At around the same time a year ago, I was making so much fuss about not being able to enjoy the vacation, and here I was a year down the line, happy at the prospect of isolating myself for a few days.

"I got a call from Kiran Mami last evening. They are all planning a short trip to Shimla. She wanted to know when we are visiting this year so we could all go together," Mama asked.

"I don't think I can afford a proper vacation. All I want to do is switch off for a few days and then use the time to organize myself for the storm ahead."

Papa had been keenly listening to the conversation. He had observed the mess I had created for myself very closely.

"Don't worry about the studies. You have been working very hard. You do need a break," he said.

"You say that despite knowing the state I am in?" I asked.

"I say that because I know the state you are in," he replied. "And I know which topics we need to cover. By the time you are back, I would be ready with those."

"There's a lot to be done on the other side of the vacation, so get yourself charged up for that," Mama added.

I reluctantly agreed.

☆☆

It was exhilarating for the cousins to be back together after a year. Excitement was in the air. The kids happily recollected the pranks they had unleashed a year ago. Nancy was the first one to brag about the one that was her brainchild.

"Guys, it is good to be back together. I do want to put in a word of caution, especially for the boys. Don't mess with me. You don't want me to pull off something similar to what I did to Gagan last year," she said.

"Don't you dare do anything like that again. I will kill you!" replied Gagan, managing a smile.

"That was so much fun. The poor guy almost peed in his trousers," added Kabir.

"Dude, I would prefer peeing in trousers any day over peeing inside a cupboard. I am sure you were not far from that when you waited inside the cupboard for two long hours," snapped Gagan.

"Are you sure about that?" asked Neeti.

"About what?"

"About your preference to pee in a cupboard over peeing in trousers. We could arrange for that tonight," replied Neeti.

Gagan just shook his head.

"Guys, my suggestion is that this year we don't screw each other. Let's focus on fun activities like smashing people on the road with grape bunches," I added.

"Good anti-social fun idea from none other than our very own social embarrassment," added Neeti.

We all continued to chit-chat through the afternoon, recollecting previous year's memories and excitedly looking forward to the days ahead. The plan was to leave for Shimla by road early morning the following day. Shimla had a special place in my heart as I had spent a good three years of my young childhood in that city. It was good to be going back to the place where I had spent beautiful carefree days of life, even if just for a few days.

As the car navigated through the narrow meandering lanes on the hill, I silently stared out from the window, keenly observing nature's might in the form of lush green mountain valleys. I allowed my mind to wildly sway across a time frame separated by almost a decade. I tried to compare everything I observed with the way it was during my childhood days. For a moment I felt everything was the same – it was the same aroma, same monkeys having fun in the mountains oblivious to the activities of the trespassers, same greenery all around, same invincibility of nature. I was about to conclude that nothing had changed. At exactly that instant, my chain of thoughts was broken by an abrupt recall of the year that had just elapsed. Maybe it was god's way of preventing me from jumping to a hasty conclusion. Because the last time I was there, I was a carefree kid free from any expectations or obligations. With the passage of time, things had become much more complicated.

I found myself in a state where I wanted to enjoy, but something was pressing me down. It felt like a split personality, wherein one part of me wanted to be happy and cheerful, while the other part, probably the more dominant part, constantly reminded me of the chaos that awaited me.

'Things have indeed changed. I have accumulated a lot of clutter over the years,' I thought continuing to stare out of the window.

☆☆

It was almost mid-day by the time we reached Shimla. Everyone was exhausted after a long road journey. Based on the itinerary, the rest of the day was reserved for rest and rejuvenation at the resort. After a lavish lunch buffet, folks lazily strolled back to their rooms to rest. I had a different plan though. I sneaked out to spend some time with myself on the familiar roads of Shimla.

It took me barely ten minutes to walk up to the famous Ridge Road. Back in the day, it used to be a daily routine for me to cross the Ridge to reach my school. I had never bothered to observe the beautiful panoramic view it offered, one of those things which one takes for granted when you have it. Almost a decade down the line, here I was! Carefully observing every nook and corner of the Ridge as if to ensure that all my childhood possessions were safe and secure.

I walked up to the Church on one side of the Ridge. I stood there motionless, observing its simple yet beautiful structure. I walked up to the other side of the Ridge and leaned on the road-side structure to view Lakkad Bazar, the beautiful wooden crafts market. I turned around to notice the horse-riding point on the other side.

Shortly thereafter, I took an uphill walk to my childhood school. It was quarter past two by the time I reached there, almost the time for the school to end. I stood there at the gate, carefully observing the hustle bustle inside the school premises. From the limited visibility I could gather, I observed a group of kids merrily playing hand-cricket in the ground. They all looked happy. On the other side of the school, a few teachers were making a humble attempt to organize kids in a queue. The sight of teachers instantly reminded me of my own teachers back home, who were waiting to pounce on me. I could particularly visualize Professor Malik waiting to mercilessly butcher me in a few weeks. The thought of my plight at school dampened the spirit a wee bit. I decided to walk back.

I took a long downhill stroll to walk up to my childhood residence, two kilometres further away from Lakkad Bazar. I had always enjoyed walking downhill, the natural springiness under the feet that downhill walk offered. There was something exhilarating and liberating about it. I felt the same excitement as I used to feel as a young kid. As I continued to cherish the walk, I wondered how Professor Menon at FIITJEE could conduct a long boring lecture describing the same downhill motion mathematically using obscure concepts – potential energy, kinetic energy, gravitational pull, acceleration due to gravity, frictional force, sines, cosines, tangents, free body diagrams, and much more. I consciously tried to control my thoughts. It was too precious a moment to be thrown away with academic distractions.

It took me around half an hour to reach my childhood residence. The house looked exactly the same as it once did over a decade ago. It was built over an elevated structure overseeing a vertical wall of around six feet opposite to it. I vividly remembered how Mama Papa had trained me to climb the wall directly, because it used to save me few precious minutes every morning when I would be getting late for the school. Didi always used to be dressed up well on time and had all the time in the world to walk up through the proper route. On the other hand, it always used to be a frantic scamper for Mama Papa to get me over the wall to meet Didi on the way. I stood next to the wall, overwhelmed.

There used to be two natural grooves on the wall at exactly the right positions which made it possible to climb the wall.

Left foot in the lower groove, right hand in the upper groove, a little push off the ground using the right foot, right hand on top of the wall, right foot in the upper groove, another little push and one reached the top of the wall.

I performed the drill without any discomfort; it had been well programmed into the muscle memory. I got down from the wall and then repeated the drill a few more times. There was something cathartic about climbing that wall. For a moment, howsoever short-lived it may have been, it helped me completely get over the stress I had been facing at school.

☆☆

The verdict is clear: Doomed

It was dark by the time I reached the resort. I went straight to the indoor games room. I was sure to find my cousins there.

It was a large spacious room with two table-tennis tables placed on one side. The other side of the room had a magnificent pool table. The sound of feet tapping on the lavish wooden flooring made up for a royal musical backdrop. The bright lighting in the room almost gave it the feel of an indoor stadium. I walked up to Vikram, who was keenly watching the contest between Gagan and Kabir.

"Who's winning?" I asked.

"13-10 in Gagan's favour," he replied "Where the hell have you been? You are missing all the fun," he continued.

"I had stepped out for a walk along the Ridge."

"Never mind. It's human to make mistakes."

"Shut up! When does this game end? I want to play the next one."

"This should end in a few minutes and then it is you versus me," replied Vikram.

A little later, a gentleman named Varun entered the room. The way he exchanged pleasantries with my cousins, it was evident that they had already met. There was something about Varun that made me uneasy. There was a sense of arrogance in the way he walked. His way of talking seemed condescending. I did not like the way he chewed gum while speaking either. It was a case of abhorrence at first sight.

As we started playing, I realized that Varun was way better than any of us. Maybe that's where his attitude was emanating from. He was beating us quite comfortably and with every game he won, his display of contempt became more evident. I wasn't sure how my cousins were putting up with it, but I was getting increasingly worked up with each passing moment. I was desperately looking forward to my next turn to play him. I wanted to thrash him hard.

The game started well. I did not allow him to run away with an early lead as he had been doing in most of the previous games. Ten minutes into the game, the score was almost levelled at 11-10 in Varun's favour. With each point I scored, my cousins cheered louder for me. I realized I was significantly more animated than what an inconsequential game like that warranted. But with all that adrenaline rush, I couldn't care less.

My animated play coupled with my cousins' cheering, sometimes anti-cheering, was getting under Varun's skin. He was losing the plot, despite his superior skills, and I was thoroughly loving it. The score now read 14-18 in my favour.

At exactly that moment, I felt I had my man. Little did I know that something very different awaited me.

In response to my service, Varun smashed the ball hard. In anticipation of the smash, I took the stance to move backwards. However, the ball hit the top of the net and fell right there on my side of the table. Amidst all my animated motion, I did try to check my initial backward movement to pick the ball, only to lose my balance and fall straight with my face on the table.

Bang!

What I observed next was a white shiny button sized object and a few red drops on the green tabletop.

"15-18!" I said wiping the red drops and quickly getting back to my position. In the heat of the moment, I hadn't realized what had happened. I was only worried about the point I had conceded.

"Oh damn!"

"Are you out of your mind?"

"Ouch!"

"Get some first aid fast!"

I heard simultaneous shouts from my cousins, making it difficult for me to ascertain who said what. It took me a few seconds to realize that the white shiny button sized object on the table was my tooth. The game was all over, and Varun did have the last laugh. I wasn't sure what I hated more – losing my tooth, or losing out on the opportunity to beat Varun. In hindsight, both suck!

Later that night, I had the first opportunity to lock myself inside the washroom and peacefully analyze my loss. I was horrified to look at my face in the mirror. I shivered with anxiety at the thought of looking like that for the rest of my life. The front tooth I lost may have been less than one-hundredth the size of my face. But it was still important. Without it, I looked like a clown. I practiced a few facial expressions to see if there was any that wouldn't expose its absence so bluntly. There was none. The option which hurt the least was that of a solemn dignified silence, an expression which required me to keep my mouth totally shut and lips tightly sealed. So much for all the hoopla I had created prior to the fall.

I visited a dentist first thing the following morning. The only question I had for him was if there would be some solution to fix my tooth loss. The dentist did alleviate my fear by sharing that it was easily addressable. However, he advised me to get the treatment done once back in Delhi as he was conscious that I was in Shimla for just a few more days and the treatment would take much longer. After a bit of deliberation, we decided to cut short the trip and Mama, Didi and I returned home the same day.

We took a bus from Shimla that afternoon. On the way back, I had all the time in the world to think about all that was happening in my life. As I pondered over, I had far more frowns than smiles on my face. I was performing poorly at school and was a no one at FIITJEE. And now, as if god's way of subtly reinforcing the verdict, I had even managed to lose my tooth. What is more, it didn't take me a sport involving a hard cricket ball, or a metallic tennis racquet or a wooden hockey stick to lose a tooth. All it took was a sport involving 2.7 grams of white spherical ball and a 150-gram racquet covered with rubber padding on both sides to reduce me to a toothless clown. That truly summed up my misery.

☆☆

A fresh lease of life

The FIITJEE classes were scheduled to reopen in a day and the extra classes at school too were planned to resume a week thereafter. The thought of the same cycle starting all over again was depressing. It had reached a stage where the signs of depression were visible, despite my best effort to don a fake cheerful mask. My erratic sleep pattern, cranky behaviour, abnormally low appetite, and general lethargy was too conspicuous to go unnoticed. It was a matter of time before the topic came up for a conversation at home. It was Mama who first broached the topic.

"Yesterday I met Abhinav. He was asking why you don't join them for evening play even when there are no classes these days."

"I just don't feel like stepping out. It feels like a waste of time."

"When did stepping out to play start feeling like waste of time to you? As much as I have known you, this is the only thing that really makes you happy," replied Mama.

Mama warmly held my hand and continued, "Nothing should stop you from enjoying things that you are so passionate about. You used to wait so restlessly to go out to play, to spend time with your friends."

Just then, Papa entered the house. Noticing the solemn ambience, he looked at Mama quizzically. I continued to stare out of the window.

"If you don't want to play with your friends, then let's go out for a walk," she offered.

"And what will we talk about? I don't want to talk about anything to do with school, FIITJEE or entrance examinations."

"Nor do I. In fact, I don't even want you to think about it and that's the reason I insist on going for a walk. There is no dearth of topics to talk about. If nothing else, we can always talk about Tendulkar's last century," she added.

Just as I started to put on my shoes, Papa quipped, "You can also discuss the soap operas that your Mama watches at night."

Mama and I started our stroll along a closed society loop. A short while later, some of Mama's friends met us along the route.

"You ditched us today for the evening walk!" said one of the women.

"Yes, we decided to have a mother-son walk today," replied Mama, merrily holding my hand.

"Okay. So, no fitting for you today, son?" replied aunty, looking towards me this time.

"Aunty, fitting? I didn't get it." I asked.

"She means no FIITJEE classes today?" Mama clarified quickly.

"Ah okay. Yes, I didn't have a class today," I answered.

"Is it her ignorance or pathetic sense of humour that made her frame the question the way she did?" I asked Mama a few minutes later.

"It's the latter. But you tell me the more important thing. What is it that's bothering you these days? I am sure there is something. Not stepping out to play is just a symptom?" asked Mama, suddenly shifting the topic.

"Nothing much. I am just too stressed with the school mess on one hand and the FIITJEE woes on the other. I am sandwiched in between," I replied.

"Let's talk about each of them separately. What about school?"

"I scored 89 percent in my tenth standard and 62 percent this year. That's too steep a fall and it's been playing on my mind."

"But you were never focusing on school marks this year. You clearly said a few months back that you will focus solely on FIITJEE syllabus. Then why bother about school marks?"

"That logic holds only if I had been doing well at FIITJEE. I am struggling there too."

"We will come to FIITJEE in a minute, but is there anything else at school that bothers you other than marks?"

"Umm, I guess the whole attitude of my teachers and fellow students. It seems very condescending. There isn't a day that goes by when I am not scolded or meted out some punishment. I spend more time standing outside the class than I do sitting inside. I am okay with that too, but what really irks me is the tone in which my teachers speak to me. It feels like they are always looking for a reason to pick on me."

"Why would they waste their time and energy picking on you? They have better things to do."

"Exactly my point. Don't they have better things to do than ridiculing me at every opportunity?"

"Sometimes things are more complex than what they look from just one person's perspective. Maybe they genuinely want you to do well and pick on you only to help you improve your marks at school? The simple point is that the teachers we are talking about are renowned teachers at a very reputed school. One of the reasons we shifted you to this school was precisely that. Now, there are reasons for the way things have shaped up between you and your teachers. That doesn't necessarily make your teachers bad."

"What am I supposed to do in that case? Continue to be mocked at every possible opportunity?"

"No, not at all. Just be firm, yet polite in all your interactions with them. Also, dont waste a minute of your mental space worrying about their attitude. You have so much more to focus on. Also, have the assurance that regardless of who's right or who's wrong, we will back you up all the way," she assured me.

"What about the fellow students who make jeering remarks?"

"Name a few students in your class who are doing very well."

"Why?"

"Just name them."

"Nikhil, Abhay, Neha, Arpit. But why? What's the point?"

"Do these kids ever make any of those jeering remarks?"

I thought for a few seconds and then replied, "No, never. They are always busy with more productive things."

"That's the point. Making jeering remarks doesn't elevate you. It's a characteristic of weak people, losers if you will. So, don't waste your time and energy thinking about those losers."

Pause.

"Now, let's turn our attention to FIITJEE. What's bothering you there?" she continued.

"At FIITJEE, things are very different. Teachers at FIITJEE don't really care about petty things. There is no attendance, no assignment submissions, nothing. Teachers don't even care whether we show up in the class or not. But the problem is, what they teach is much more complex than what I can handle."

"Are you sure it is really that complex? I ask that because Papa always tells me that he is confident of your ability to understand those concepts."

It felt great to get that validation of my ability. I pondered for a moment and then replied, "I guess I created the mess by not being regular in the first few months. I just didn't anticipate the pace correctly. Before I knew, the first topic was over. By the time I got a hang of how things work here, several topics were over. From there on, it was always a catch-up game. I am oscillating between the topics that were taught several months back and what is being currently taught, inhibiting my ability to master either."

"Great! You articulated the problem so clearly."

"Now you please articulate the solution equally clearly for me," I replied, somewhat sarcastically.

Mama pondered over it for a few minutes. "You cannot go back and change the first few months. So, there is no point dwelling upon it. You will have to think ahead."

"Easier said than done, Mama," I replied with a hint of disappointment. I was really hoping for a magic wand that would solve all my woes.

"You once told me that clearing JEE exam doesn't require scoring exceptionally high marks."

"Yes, I did. So?" I asked.

"So, maybe you don't need to master all the topics. I mean, could it be possible to achieve a winning score by just becoming very good at the topics which are yet to be covered? I am sure it is not as simple as I am making it out to be, because many topics are inter-related. But think about it!"

Mama did not have a magic wand for sure, but she had given me a lifeline. She didn't understand the content at all as that was Papa's department. But what she had said gave me a lot of hope.

"Maybe other students would need to put in ten hours. You may need to slog fourteen hours daily. But that's fine. I know you are not afraid of hardwork anyway. Isn't it?"

"Yes indeed," I said cheerfully.

The walk with Mama had been exceptionally helpful. It had cleared a lot of clutter in my mind. I could experience a fresh lease of life.

Next morning

Papa was already aware of all the troubles I was grappling with. Mama had also updated Papa about the long conversation we had the previous evening. When we met at the breakfast table, Papa had done a careful analysis of which topics carried maximum weightage in the JEE entrance examination. While I savoured my usual bread-omelette, it was Papa who brought up the topic.

"What's your plan for today?" he asked

"I am planning to cover the topic of complex numbers."

"I love that topic. Let's pack your bag and go to Lodhi garden. I have requested Mama to pack our lunch too. We can take a spot under a tree shade and spend some quality time out there, covering as much syllabus as possible."

"Fantastic!" I replied cheerfully.

By around 10 a.m. we were inside the Lodhi garden. We spent about ten minutes ambling around the park to choose a comfortable spot for us. Papa carefully unfolded the mat we were carrying and placed it beneath a tree in a quiet corner.

"I looked through the previous years' exam papers to see which topics are most important. In mathematics, I think calculus and coordinate geometry are the high value topics. Calculus is something that we have already been studying a lot. Let's just make sure that we master coordinate geometry too."

"But we have not started this topic at FIITJEE yet," I replied.

"That's even better. It just allows us to master this topic the way FIITJEE teachers have planned in their curriculum."

"That's great!" I replied. "This is the first time in over a year that we are talking about a topic which is yet to start. Of late, we have only been talking about backlog. That's a mini victory of sorts, if you ask me."

"Indeed, and it calls for a mini celebration too. You start working your way through the questions. I will be back in some time," said Papa and walked away.

He came back with two cups of vanilla ice cream. We spent good 4-5 hours under the shade that morning, practicing math assignments.

The spot was soon going to become our favourite weekend study corner for several months to come.

Few days later at a mathematics FIITJEE class

As I walked into the class, I decided to change my seat. I realized that the luxurious park view from my favourite corner seat did not help, as it offered an easy distraction for me. I changed my seat to the front row, moving from geometrically farthest I could be from the professor to the closest possible point. Professor Sanjay walked in at sharp 3:30 p.m. As always, he was casually dressed, holding two chalk-sticks gently clasped in his fingers.

"Today we are going to start a new topic, coordinate geometry. It entails studying geometric figures by plotting them on two coordinate axes – x-axis and y-axis. It is an important topic as it constitutes around 25% of the total marks in the main entrance exam," said Professor Sanjay.

I was intrigued to hear the last statement from the professor. It was the third time I was hearing a similar message in as many days. First it was Mama who had suggested identifying a few priority topics during our casual evening stroll. Then it was Papa who reinforced the message during our Lodhi Garden visit a day before. Here I was hearing a similar message from Professor Sanjay. I wondered if it was a sign from the higher power, a subtle message that I could get my preparation back on track by being smart about the choice of topics.

For the next two hours, Professor Sanjay took us through the concepts. He had a knack of coming up with elegant solutions, which often reduced seemingly complex questions to mere mental math problems. He used to label such proprietary tricks and solutions in his local Bihari dialect, something that made it impossible to forget even for seemingly distracted students like me. I made sure to concentrate hard and not doze off. It was not that I followed every single concept taught, but I at least knew my doubts.

Before the professor left the class, he walked up to me and slowly whispered something which made me rethink if I understood Professor Sanjay all that well.

"I could see a new spark in you today. Don't let it die down. If you face any problems with previous topics, feel free to clarify separately before or after the class," he said. It was probably the first time a teacher had spoken respectfully to me in over a year.

"Thank you very much sir. It means a lot to me," I gleefully replied.

There was clearly more to Professor Sanjay than just mathematical theorems and solutions. He became a trusted coach for me that day onwards.

✩✩

Theory is theory, practical is practical

As weeks progressed, my position in FIITJEE started to improve gradually. I was never a shining star, but I was no longer the bottom performer, and I was very happy with that. The discussions with Mama were helping me get my head in the right space. As a student of Arts from her own academic days, she did not understand my course. But she had a sound understanding of how things work, and I trusted her guidance blindly, especially where my own thinking capability ended.

Following her tips, I had somehow managed to reduce altercations with teachers at school. One thing that continued to worry me was the thought of practical exams. I knew that I could still cram theory on my own, but to clear the practical exam, I needed help from the fellow teachers and students. The practical exam for computer science and chemistry worried me a lot.

The curriculum for computer science gave 25% weightage to the practical exam. A major component of that comprised of an annual project where students had to develop an application using the C++ programming concepts. Students were expected to organize themselves in groups of two to develop the project. For me, that was a big task, probably as big as the project itself. With the reputation I had in the class, I was sure no one would want to pair up with me. It was PJ who approached me in one of the classes.

"Hey Aman, can we pair up for the computer science project?" he asked.

"Are you sure you want to do that?"

"Yes. Why do you say that?"

"I say that because we are both duds. If I remember correctly, you got eleven marks in the first computer science test last year, the second lowest in the class."

"Yes, the second lowest. Second only to the one and only who hit the ball out of the park with two marks."

"It was 2.5! But yes, that's me and things haven't improved much for either of us after that lethal performance. I wonder who will build the project if the two of us, the two grand failures, pair up? We need a partner who is good and can cover up for our lack of ability."

I had of course been thinking about it for quite some time. I felt Abhay could be a great student to partner with. He had a strong grasp of the subject. He liked to develop new programs during his spare time and preferred minimal interference while developing his programs. However, I was not sure if he would be willing to pair-up with me.

'I wouldn't know till I ask.' I thought and decided to approach him.

Few days later.

"Hi Abhay! Have you thought about the computer science project?" I asked.

"What about that? The internal submission for the project is due next month, isn't it?"

"Yes, that's correct. But have you paired up with someone?"

"No, not yet. I have thought about the program that I want to work on, though. I am planning to build an Electronic Voting program."

"Electronic Voting! Sounds interesting. What exactly is that?"

"It's a program that would enable electronic tamper-proof voting during the ballot process. It would use the concepts of C++ objects to capture a voter profile along with contesting candidates' party and their personal profiles. It would have an interface to facilitate voting. Finally, it would have various functions to run the analytics and a cool output interface to project the election results."

"Wow, you have thought it through. So, the million-dollar question. Who are you going to partner with?

"That's the part I am struggling with. In my zeal to build the program I have already covered significant ground. I am almost halfway through with the programming. Now, the challenge for me is to find someone who would accept the idea and be comfortable with all the work I have done so far," he replied.

He was godsend for me.

"Right here. I am the one you are looking for. I love your idea and have absolutely no qualms about the work you have completed so far. I have no problem even if you want to complete the remaining parts without involving me." I realized that I had said a bit more than I should have. But I was still hopeful.

Pause.

I told him further, "The only request I have is that once you are done with the program, please take an hour or two to explain the details to me. I too will have to answer the questions during the viva, so would need that little bit of help."

Abhay was happy with the proposition.

"Done deal!" he replied.

It was a win-win for both of us – zero interference for him from my side, zero work expectation of me from his side. Just made for each other.

Over the coming days, Abhay built out the complete program with top-notch analytics functionalities and a thoroughly impressive user interface. He excitedly showed me the full package in one of the computer science practical classes. I was speechless. I always wanted him to build a good program, but what he had built was outstanding. It was so good that I was worried about my ability to understand its underlying technical details.

"Your program looks outstanding," I said, somewhat mesmerized by what he showed me.

"Let's say our program," he generously replied.

"Oh yes, our program!" I corrected myself. "I am just worried if I would be able to understand the working details for this program. It is so good that I might just get exposed in the viva."

"Don't you worry about that. I will explain all the details. It will not take more than a few hours."

"When can we do that?" I asked.

"This Sunday, there is a friendly cricket match being played at Jawaharlal Nehru stadium. I was planning to go there for some time, as they don't have an entry fee for this charity match. If you are game, we can carry along the project report, a rough notebook, and a ball-point pen to the stadium. We can do a bit of multi-tasking to watch the match and cover the program simultaneously. What do you think?" asked Abhay.

"The best idea ever!"

I was in the computer science lab class a few days later. I felt a sudden tap on the shoulder. I turned around to see who it was. It was MS Dos. I immediately stood up in complete attention.

"Yes ma'am?"

"I have been calling your roll number for mock viva."

"Sorry ma'am. I got engrossed in the program and somehow missed it."

"Don't worry. It's good to see you engrossed in something that's not FIITJEE books," she replied staring at the electronic voting program functionalities that I was checking out on the screen.

"Thank you, ma'am."

"Come over to my desk for the mock viva," she said.

I followed her to the desk.

"So, tell me. What have you built for the project?"

"We have built an electronic voting program. It's a program that enables electronic voting during the secret ballot process. It uses the concepts of C++ objects to capture a voter profile along with contesting candidates' party and their personal profiles. The program also has an in-built user interface to facilitate the voting process. Lastly, we have built some analytics capabilities and an output dashboard to project the voting results." I reproduced a well-rehearsed answer based on what Abhay had told me.

MS Dos went on to ask a few more technical questions. Surprisingly, I was able to answer all of them. In addition to building a fantastic program, Abhay had also done a great job of bringing me up to speed with his work.

"Sometimes when you give answers like that, I get baffled. I mean why are you always in so much mess when you have that kind of clarity?" she asked in all earnestness.

"Ma'am, I am very happy to see that you found my viva preparation good, but I will be very honest with you. I haven't done much work on the project. I just spent some quality time with my partner to understand the program in minutest detail."

"That's fine. As long as you have understood the details and can explain it to the external invigilator intelligently, I am fine." Then she asked me, "How is your preparation for the overall syllabus coming along?"

"Not bad, ma'am. I have started devoting some time to revise the concepts, something I didn't do at all earlier."

"That has been consistently reflecting in your marks. How many did you score in your last computer test?"

"I didn't do well. I scored 14 on 25."

Not intending to dampen my spirit, she replied, "That's okay! It's moving in the right direction. A bit more effort and you will be right there."

"Thank you, ma'am. That means a lot to me."

It felt great to have a decent conversation with a schoolteacher, a conversation that didn't end with me apologizing or stepping out of the class as a punishment. I felt relieved. I was hoping for a similar turnaround of fortunes in the chemistry practical classes too.

✩✩

Chemistry Lab

"Today we are going to practice identifying the composition of a given salt mixture. You have all been given a salt mixture at your respective workstations in the lab. You will have to perform the tests we discussed in the class yesterday to systematically identify the salt given to you. Please remember, you are dealing with real chemicals here. Some of the acids are concentrated and you must be extra careful to not spill anything. It's important for your own safety and for your fellow students' safety," said Kavita ma'am.

"Does anyone have any questions?" she asked after a brief pause. "Okay, good. Then let's get started," she completed with a sense of urgency.

I had always found the chemistry practical classes the most difficult to deal with. I had always found these experiments challenging on two counts. One, we really needed to have those tests on our fingertips to be able to perform the experiment, something that was never the case with me. Second, it involved dealing with real chemicals. Any misadventure meant a mess in the form of undesirable fumes or flames or sometimes even broken apparatus.

I started the experiment with the hope to somehow find the salt composition assigned to me. I performed a few tests, but quickly landed in a position where I was clueless about what to do next. It wasn't the first time I found myself in that position. Just as I was wondering how to possibly proceed, Kavita ma'am walked up to my workstation to check the progress.

"How is it going?" she asked.

"I am on it, ma'am. I have done a few tests and have eliminated a few possibilities, but haven't been able to ascertain the salt name yet."

"What have you found so far?"

"Ma'am, I added a bit of warm concentrated acid to the salt and heated the test tube. I was expecting a colourless gas with a pungent smell, but somehow that did not happen. So, I am a bit stuck."

"Bit stuck?" she said with a sarcastic chuckle.

"Yes, ma'am," I replied.

"No, I don't think you are a bit stuck. I think you are very stuck. Not with this salt analysis, but with something much larger in life."

I didn't know what to respond.

With a bit of effort, I spoke up, "Okay ma'am, I will try to figure and fix that larger problem, but for now if you could give me some steer on what I should do next with this salt analysis..."

"I heard that this year there has been a change in the JEE entrance test pattern?" she asked.

That question took me by surprise.

"Yes ma'am. They have introduced a screening test in December. In the screening test, they will select around 15,000 students out of over 2.5 lakh aspiring candidates. Only the shortlisted 15,000 students will be allowed to take the main entrance exam in which around two thousand students will be finally selected."

"This is a good move by the IITs. It will help them separate wheat from chaff."

I didn't respond.

"This new screening test is good news and bad news for you at the same time. Isn't it?" she continued.

"In what sense ma'am?"

"Good news because you won't have to live in your virtual fantasy world all the way till May. You will take the test in December, get knocked out of the process and then can focus on the board exams. Had it not been for this new screening test, you would have continued chasing your hollow dream all the way till May, only to screw both the examinations."

"Indeed ma'am. But why bad news?" I asked, rather reluctantly.

"You see, we all know you are not IIT material. You would not be able to clear the test anyway, screening or no screening. Had it not been for this screening test, you could have claimed that you narrowly missed out. Since they don't publish the ranks of non-selected students, no one would have come to know the magnitude of your screw up. Now when you don't clear the screening, everyone would know that you weren't even in the top 15,000. So much for all the hype you created around your FIITJEE classes. That will be embarrassing for you. Isn't it?"

I continued staring at her blankly for a few seconds. "Yes ma'am. If I don't clear the screening test, it will surely be embarrassing."

Just before she moved ahead, I added, "However, after what you just said, it would be much more embarrassing for you if somehow, even if by fluke, I do manage to clear the screening test. Strange things happen, you see."

Kavita ma'am dismissively shook her head and moved to the next workstation.

I was really annoyed with the conversation, not so much because of its provocative nature but because I did get provoked despite my resolve to stay clear of it. I tried to get my mind back to work and focus on the experiment at hand. I didn't want to sweat over petty unproductive matters, not anymore.

As luck would have it, I ended up breaking a glass test-tube in the lab a little later. The timing was unfortunate as it gave Kavita ma'am another opportunity to have a go at me.

"Can you ever do anything right?" she shouted from three workstations away.

"Sorry ma'am."

"Why are you so distracted?"

'Because of the provocative conversation we had a short while back, which by the way you started.' – I wanted to say, but kept my mouth shut.

"Hope you didn't spill anything on yourself?" she checked.

'Do you really care?' I wanted to ask, but just replied, "No ma'am, nothing. I am good."

"Charu Lal ji, can you please help him?" she called out to the lab assistant.

I breathed a sigh of relief as I managed to get away without any major drama. All the students got back to their respective lab activities too.

"Why do you do these things son?" the lab assistant asked while clearing the mess I had created at my workstation.

"I didn't do it deliberately, Charu Lal ji. It just slipped out of my hand," I replied.

"You need to be more careful here. These are practical experiments, not your theory classes. Do you know what's the biggest difference between theory and practical classes?"

"I guess here we are dealing with real chemicals," I replied.

"Yes, that's right. Always remember theory is theory, and practical is practical," he replied.

"Sure. I will always remember that." I replied, somehow managing to suppress my laughter at that innocuous little senseless remark.

☆☆

The boolean athlete

November 1999

Our school had a unique philosophy for recognizing student efforts. It laid emphasis on appreciating as many good performances as possible, rather than restrictively felicitating the top three. It believed in keeping the top as broad as possible. To bring to life this philosophy, the school had adopted a unique reward system. The school had identified qualifying standards in various fields spanning across academics, arts, sports, amongst several others. Every performance over the qualifying standard in a particular field fetched the participant a merit card.

It was the winter of 1999. The school's annual sports week was round the corner. This was a much-awaited week-long event at our school. During that week, all academic activities were put aside for a few days and students were encouraged to participate in a variety of extra-curricular activities. To encourage the spirit of participation, the entire school, including teachers, used to assemble in the sports facilities to cheer the young participants.

I was not a big fan of extra-curricular activities. In fact, I hated it and had never participated in any extra-curricular activity ever in my life. However, for the upcoming sports week, I decided to participate in a few games. I thought it would help me refresh and rejuvenate ahead of the all-important screening test which was scheduled in two-weeks. I also felt it could help me mend my relationship with fellow students, something that I had failed to achieve through academics.

I just had to pick the right sport to participate in. I didn't want to pick anything that required too much coordination or teamwork. I couldn't have afforded much time for preparations. Hence, I ruled out the idea of participating in a cricket match. After a bit of thought, I decided to participate in two events – 800 metre race and badminton.

Day-1 of the sports week

As we walked out to the sports field, I could feel a sense of excitement in the air. There were students of all age-groups bubbling with energy. There were rolling mats put up all around the sports field to allow seating space for the spectators. There were meticulous track lines that had been put up in circles using field chalk. The bright sunshine amidst an otherwise cold winter morning provided perfect ambience for the athletes to perform. There was also a special guests' corner for the teachers to comfortably watch the proceedings. I noticed from a distance that all my teachers were there. I thought it was a great opportunity for me to perform well and demonstrate that I too could do something well. I felt a sudden rush of adrenaline.

After a bit of warm-up, I made it to the start-line of the race. One round corresponded to 200 metres. For the 800-metre run, we had to complete four rounds. In line with the school's reward philosophy, the race did not seek to find the top 3 contestants, but offered a merit card to anyone who completed the 800-metre run in under 3 minutes. It was all set.

On your marks.

Get set.

Go!

....and off I went like a bullet.

I ran as hard as I possibly could. Within a few seconds, I could sense that I had taken a huge lead over other runners. I accelerated further as I crossed the guests' corner, where my teachers were seated, as my subtle way of telling them – 'Don't you dare consider me a loser.'

I was comfortably in lead by the time I finished the first round.

'*200 metres complete, 600 metres more to go.*' I thought.

I felt like an invincible champion, amidst the rising crowd cheer. I continued to push hard. I was approaching the end of the second round. It was then for the first time that I felt like I was beginning to run out of ammunition.

'*400 metres complete, 400 metres more to go.*' I thought again, but this time with a bit of concern.

With my rapidly rising heart rate, I couldn't imagine going the same distance again. I continued to push along somehow, but the pace started to drop. I could feel the lead closing out on me as there were a few runners right behind me. It was around mid-way through the third round when the first runner overtook me, and then a few seconds later the second, and then the third and then I didn't care anymore. I somehow dragged along to complete the third round.

'600 metres complete...' I took a deep breath. *'...and to hell with the last 200 metres.'* I thought. I wanted to stop right there, but I continued to drag along. I had to complete the race under 3 minutes.

By the time I reached the mid of fourth round, I realized that every runner in the race had overtaken me. I looked at my watch with despair. It showed 2 minutes 53 seconds. I still had about 100 metres to go, but only about 7 seconds to complete that to earn the merit card. I was aware that the world record for a 100-metre dash back then was around 10 seconds. I decided to put an end to my agony. I stopped with a jerk, kicked the air, and disappointedly stepped out of the track.

I quietly had a sip of water at the drinks corner and furtively found my way back to the classroom. I had no energy to field the jeering remarks of fellow students. On the way back, I noticed the scoring key put up on the board. Some runners had a 'Q' against their name, indicating that they had qualified by completing the run within 3 minutes. There were others who had a tick mark against their name, indicating that they had completed the run, but couldn't qualify. I was the only one with the digit zero put against my name, probably because I didn't complete the race.

I was thoroughly disappointed.

Day-2 of the sports week

After the first day's fiasco, I was keen to do well on the second day. I had a badminton match in the afternoon. I was aware that twenty-four students had enrolled to participate. At around noon, all enrolled participants were required to check their pairings at the sports notice board. I was keen to see who I was playing that afternoon. Not that I had any preference, but just wanted to make sure that I wasn't paired against the player named Arun, who was a serious badminton player, aspiring to break into the state team. The probability of being paired with him was low, but it was possible.

I carefully looked through the list put up on the board.

I couldn't believe my stars. Based on the random pairings done for the first round, I was paired against Arun. I considered pulling out of the event, but opted against it, rationalizing that it's the spirit of participation that matters. The good part also was that no matter how badly I lost to Arun, I was sure no one would ridicule me. After all, Arun was recognized as a rising badminton star by one and all in the school. I decided to show up for the contest.

The game started at around 12:30 p.m.

I tried to move around the court with pace and agility. I wasn't really looking to beat Arun, but even a strong fight against him could fetch me significant bragging rights. The game started well. I wasn't getting any points, but I was in no mood to meekly surrender either. Around ten minutes into the game the score read as 4-0 in Arun's favour.

I continued to push hard. It was evident that Arun was having to fight for his points. There were no free gifts from me. The crowd was cheering the effort I was putting up. They all probably sympathized with me for having been paired with a much stronger player. Around fifteen minutes into the game, I ended up winning my first point.

The score now read 7-1.

There was a loud cheer from the crowd as no one expected me to win any point.

I continued to fight hard after that. But life is no fairy tale. As much as I wanted to put up a strong show, I ended up with a score of 1-21. That's all I had to show up for the effort. It looked bad, especially if someone had not seen the match. I obliquely stared at the score board. I had a 1 against my name that day, compared to the zero I had the day before.

As I disappointedly made my way back to the classroom, I heard a voice from behind.

"Aman!" It sounded like MS Dos.

'What could she possibly want from me at this point in time?' I wondered.

I turned around to see who it was. It was indeed MS Dos. "Yes ma'am?"

I was sure there would be some contemptuous remark at what I had done on the field.

"I saw your match a short while back, and I also saw your run yesterday," she said.

I considered cutting her short right there by saying, 'Sorry ma'am.'

She went on, "I thought you were fantastic on both occasions."

I was caught by surprise. Of all possible things that she could have said, that was the last thing I expected.

"Ma'am, I think you are mistaking me for someone else. Just for records, I had a zero against my name yesterday and I had a one against my name today."

"I exactly know what the scoreboard read against your name. Sometimes scores and marks don't tell the complete story," she said with a warm smile.

"Well, that's very kind of you, ma'am," I replied thinking that she was setting me up for a mega-mocking to follow.

"What do you think went wrong yesterday?"

"I guess it's simple. I was not good enough to complete the run in three minutes."

"No! I think you were great, and for quite some time looked like the strongest runner on the track. I think you hadn't practiced any mock run, so were not aware of how much to push in the initial parts of the race. Consequently, you ran out of steam while others continued to maintain their pace through the run."

"Yes ma'am. You are right. I hadn't done any practice run. In fact, it was the first time I did a timed run in my life yesterday."

"What do you think went wrong today?"

"I guess I just ran into a much stronger opponent."

"Yes, that's right, and there is no shame in losing to a stronger player. He has been practicing for the last five years."

"It was evident on the court."

"What's next for you?"

"Nothing ma'am. These were the only two events that I had enrolled for. But thank you so much for your kind words of appreciation. I honestly feel it's too generous of you to be appreciating a zero-performance and 1-point performance," I said somewhat overwhelmed with her kind gesture.

"I don't evaluate students based on their scores. It doesn't matter that you had scores of zero and one against your name. I saw a sincere effort on the field from you on both days and I wanted to congratulate you for that." She continued after a pause, "But mind you, the two marks you scored in my first weekly test last year did annoy me. Not so much for the score, but for the lack of effort," she said.

"It was 2.5 ma'am," I replied sheepishly.

She just nodded her head in good jest.

"When is your JEE screening test? It's not too far, isn't it?"

"It's scheduled for next Sunday."

"Well, that's the sport you have been practicing really hard for. Please do well," she said and walked away.

As she walked away, I had a flashback of the strange expression she had towards the end of the student counseling session a few months back. I felt it had a definite linkage to our short but rather intriguing conversation that day. I wondered if I really understood MS Dos well enough. Maybe she was genuinely a simple kind-hearted teacher who liked to see her students do well. Just that I hadn't given her any opportunity to rejoice with my petty performances.

I walked back to the classroom feeling overwhelmed. I wasn't expecting anyone there as most folks were still out there in the field. However, a few students, a bunch of losers, were already waiting for me inside the classroom. As soon as I entered, they greeted me with a strange title.

"Boolean!"

"Boolean!"

"Boolean!"

The roar went on for a few minutes.

"What's this thing with Boolean? Why are you guys shouting that?" I asked, perplexed.

"That's the new name we have given you," said one of the boys.

"Boolean! But why?" I asked unable to comprehend the joke.

"Yesterday you scored a zero and today you scored one. It is evident that you are a Boolean athlete, one who only deals in zeros and ones," clarified one of the boys.

Inspired by Boolean algebra, a branch of mathematics that deals with variables that can only take binary values zero and one, they had christened me a Boolean athlete.

I couldn't help nodding my head in amusement.

The silent fireworks

With every passing day, I was unconsciously pushing the body limits to try harder. The normal sleeping time at night had started extending closer to the dawn hours. On most days, Mama and Papa stayed up with me. While I was thoroughly enjoying the slogging, I probably stretched it too far one night. The momentum that night was with me as I was cracking tough questions with relative ease. In my quest to make the most of it, I stayed awake the whole night and left for school in the morning without sleeping at all.

It was the first time I had put in a complete night out. It didn't take me long to realize my mistake. As Professor Malik walked in, I could already feel my head spinning. There was no way I could escape the inevitable that day. Despite my sincere efforts, I struggled to keep my eyes open. I shook my face and tried sitting in an upright pose. It helped temporarily, but then again in a few minutes I had those irresistible pangs of sleep.

My nap was broken by a gentle tap on the shoulder. I nervously opened my eyes to see Professor Malik standing right next to me.

"Mr Singh, would you want me to arrange for any other comforts?"

I realized that my best chance of controlling the situation was by keeping silent. I made a conscious effort to don an apologetic expression.

"Please say something Mr Singh. I am keen to ensure that our best and brightest students get all the comfort they need in the class," continued Professor Malik.

"I am sorry," I replied, trying to deliver those three words in a pleading and apologetic tone.

"Can you do me a favour?"

"Yes sir, anything. Please tell me."

"Please tell your parents to meet me outside the library during the lunch break tomorrow. You should also come along."

"That won't be required sir. I assure you. This won't happen again."

"Since sleeping in class is fast turning into a habit for you, it might be good for us to discuss how we can make it more comfortable for you."

"But sir..."

My sentence was cut short, as Professor Malik interjected by saying – "Do you understand English?" I noticed Professor Malik's expression suddenly changed to reflect his true inner emotion – disgust.

'*Damn you!*' I wanted to say, but all I could mutter was a "Yes sir."

"Then do what I told you."

"All right everyone. Thanks to our dear friend Aman, we could not cover anything in the last ten minutes. Let us resume the discussion in tomorrow's class," he said addressing the class as he picked up his documents to leave.

Students were happy that the class effectively ended ten minutes before the scheduled time. After Professor Malik left, a group of smiling students gathered around me making several remarks, some thankful and others mocking.

"Dude, the only difference between you and me is that in the class I sleep with open eyes, you sleep with closed eyes," said PJ.

"You are our superhero. If you sleep like this in every class, we will have to bear him for ten less minutes every day," remarked another student, a female this time.

I laughed and raised my hands to acknowledge the applause. I also joined them in cracking jokes. From the look of it, no one could make out how annoyed I was. But that had always been the case. No one other than my mother could generally make out my true inner emotion. In my mind, I was only thinking about one question – '*How the hell am I going to get around this one?*'

I silently sat through the remaining periods in the day, trying hard to avoid any further mishaps. When the bell rang for the final period of the day, I felt relieved. I dejectedly walked to the nearby bus stop alongside Abhinav and Rohan. To my utter exasperation, they kept chit-chatting as if nothing had happened. I expected them to at least extend some courtesy support.

"Guys, can you both please shut up for some time?"

"What happened dude?" asked Abhinav.

"You don't know what happened?"

"No. What is it?" replied Abhinav, after thinking for a few seconds.

"I am worried about how to manage Professor Malik tomorrow. He is expecting my parents to come along."

"Hey, you are still thinking about that fun incident. Don't worry. He just said that in a fit of frustration. He would not even remember that by tomorrow."

"Asshole, what makes you call it a fun incident!" I retorted angrily. After a brief pause, I regained my composure and told them what I truly felt. "He is not the one to forget such things. Any bright ideas how I could get around this one?"

Abhinav thought for a few moments and then offered a solemn piece of advice, "Your best chance is to fall sick and then show-up in the school after a few days, coughing and sneezing. He would have certainly forgotten everything by then and even if not, you might likely get some sympathy points due to poor health, which might save you."

Prima facie, it did look like an idea worth building upon. But there was a part of me that shouted from within – *'Fuck it. You have already suffered enough following his stupid advice once.'*

I thought about it for a moment and firmed up my mind to simply confront the situation rather than messing it up any further.

On reaching home, I practiced smiling while waiting for Mama to open the door. I didn't want her to know that I was upset. Mama opened the door, and as I had feared, she instantly knew something was wrong.

"What's wrong?" she asked, as I hurriedly moved in, trying to evade eye contact.

"Nothing!" I replied.

"No, there is something. I can see it. Tell me what it is."

"I didn't realize when I fell asleep in one of the classes today and Professor Malik wasn't too happy about it."

"Did he scold you?"

"Not really. But he wants to meet you tomorrow."

There was a brief silence after which she replied, "Do you have FIITJEE class today?"

"Yes, I do."

"There isn't much time then. Come, have your lunch and get ready. Don't worry about Professor Malik. You were just sleeping, it's okay. Maybe he is not interesting enough to keep the students engaged. It actually reflects badly on him."

I had just been summoned to meet the professor along with my parents for sleeping in the class and all she had to say was that the professor may not be interesting enough. I couldn't help smiling. *'Moms will be moms.'* I thought.

"No. That's not the case actually. The thing is that I didn't sleep at all last night. I would have struggled to keep my eyes open even if Professor Malik had played highlights from Tendulkar's last century."

"Well, I am sure that wouldn't have been the case," she replied confidently and then asked me, "But you didn't sleep at all last night?"

"No, I just got carried away and overestimated my body limits. I studied through the night and left for the school in the morning."

"Do you want to skip the FIITJEE class today?" she asked.

"No. I will manage."

I had a quick lunch and left for the more interesting part of the day.

After returning from FIITJEE at night, I deliberately did not speak about the incident that had been bothering me so much. I did not have the energy to speak about it anyway. I was confident that Mama would have already shared it with Papa and Didi. I walked straight into my room to take the first break of the day.

It was Mama who brought up the topic at the dinner table, "What time does he want to meet us?"

"During the lunch break at 11:30 a.m."

"Is there anything else that he wants to talk about or is it just going to be about the sleeping incident?"

"I am not sure. He is too hard a person to read. All he said was that the best and brightest students should get all the comfort they deserve, but of course that was in a taunting tone."

Papa had been intently listening. He had never been an expressive person, but on that occasion, I could sense that he did not like professor's mocking remark. The sudden blinking of his eyes said it all. He announced, "Don't worry. I will talk to him tomorrow."

"I can accompany you, if you want," said Mama.

"No, I expect some fireworks. Let me handle it," he said and went to the other room.

Didi looked at us with an amused expression. "Fireworks!" she said, and we burst into laughter.

"Or shall we say silent fireworks!" added Mama as the laughter picked up.

Next day, Papa reached the school library few minutes ahead of the lunch break. I joined him immediately after the break started. Professor Malik arrived within a few minutes. He raised his hand as a greeting gesture. The smile on his face appeared genuine, but I knew better.

"Hello Mr Singh," he said.

I noted that Professor Malik addressed Papa the same way as he used to address me – 'Mr Singh' – only the connotation was slightly different.

"Thanks for coming Mr Singh."

"No problem," Papa replied.

"Why don't we grab a table in the library and talk comfortably."

"Sure."

We occupied a quiet corner in the library. I was feeling anxious about what lay ahead of us in a few minutes. I was especially worried about the word 'fireworks' that Papa had used the day before.

"Mr Singh, with grave disappointment, I have to inform you that your son is floundering. He is just a few months away from the board examination, the most important exam in a student's career, but he is just not prepared for it. What is more worrying is that he does not even realize the gravity of the problem. I can easily see that he is heading into a disaster, head on," Professor Malik took a pause to invite reaction.

"Go on, I am listening."

Professor Malik was slightly taken aback. He was not used to such blunt remarks.

"I have caught him napping so many times in the class. Yesterday, for instance, we were discussing the list of important questions for the exam. But this gentleman was comfortably dreaming away to glory."

"I see," Papa replied.

I noticed that on an average, for every three to four sentences Professor Malik spoke, Papa replied in one sentence. Moreover, that one sentence itself did not have too many words in it. I immediately remembered the phrase 'silent fireworks' that Mama had mentioned.

"At this point in time, he is the most unprepared student in all the three sections. I am genuinely concerned and feel that it is my moral obligation to ring the warning bells at the right time. I am here to help him, and I genuinely do want to help. However, you tell me how I can help him if he chooses to sleep in my class?"

"Don't wake him up the next time you find him sleeping," Papa replied, maintaining a calm and poised expression.

"Pardon me. Did I hear you correctly?" asked Professor Malik, struggling to hide his disbelief.

"Yes, you did. I see him working hard till late night, or should I say till early morning every day. I know for a fact that he is sincerely trying."

"But Mr Singh, banging his head over those FIITJEE problems won't help him in any way if he flunks in the board examination. If what you are saying is correct, then it is an even more worrisome situation. It means he is working hard to fail. As I keep telling him, it's nothing but a pursuit of void. Believe me, he needs help."

"I already told you what help he needs from you."

"But Mr Singh, my problem is that if a student fails, it is a spot on my reputation. I am answerable to the school authorities."

"I see, so it is your reputation that is bothering you. All this while, I was thinking that you were concerned about Aman. In that case, let me ask you if there is any help that I could extend?" asked Papa.

I had never seen Papa get so aggressive and I was enjoying it thoroughly. I was not sure what was pleasing me more in that moment – the silent fireworks from Papa or the timid reactions from Professor Malik.

"Why don't you give it to me in writing that you are responsible for your son's result as then I can comfortably stop bothering?" This was the last trump card Professor Malik tried to get the upper hand.

"Why don't you write whatever you want to write, anything for your comfort, on a piece of paper and I would sign it right now?" Papa replied.

The two of them continued to stare at each other, as if competing for the 'who blinks first' title. I noticed that the verbal exchange was uncomfortable, but it was the awkward silence that was more discomforting. The silence may have lasted a few seconds, but it felt like eternity. It was Professor Malik who yielded first.

"Well, Mr Singh, that's all I had to share. It was a pleasure meeting you," replied Professor Malik as he slowly got up to go back to the class.

The last few words made me wonder how adept he was at faking facial expressions. It came out so naturally, as if they had just concluded the most pleasing conversation ever. I was relieved that the discussion ended. Just as I was about to take a sigh of relief, I was surprised to see that it hadn't actually.

"By the way, there is one thing that we didn't talk about. I was hoping you would bring it up," said Papa as he continued to stare at Professor Malik.

Perplexed, Professor Malik asked, "What is it?"

"The point around arranging for comforts for your best and brightest students."

"What about that?"

"In future if you do need to interact with my son, I would appreciate you cutting out that sarcastic crap. We really don't need that, certainly not in the name of 'moral responsibility', 'trying to help my students' and all the other blah, blah that you wasted my time with."

No mincing of words. The meeting had well and truly ended.

Those fateful 105 dark shaded circles

December 1999

Days rolled by rather quickly. Before I knew, it was time for the all-important screening test. As an ardent cricket fan, the exam almost felt like a knock-out match.

'If I win, I move ahead to the main JEE exam; if I lose, it's over.' I thought.

I could feel a shiver running down my spine. It was not that I wasn't aware of the importance of the screening test earlier, but the enormity of the occasion was getting to me now. In the build-up to the screening test, I had committed a lot of mess-ups – in school tests, in practical exams, in FIITJEE tests, in mock open tests. Every time I botched up, I used to give myself a false sense of security that it was just a practice test and not a test that really mattered. The defense mechanism had become so entrenched in my psyche that I had almost forgotten that there would eventually come a day when I would have to appear for a test that mattered.

I had often heard wise men say that humans are creatures of habits. I had never bothered paying any heed to the wisdom behind that seemingly innocuous little sentence. But for the first time I started to wonder what it really meant. Were humans really creatures of habits? If yes, I wondered if it was possible to break away from those habits, for I had inadvertently picked up a bad habit over the year – the habit of losing and losing consistently at that. For the first time in two years, I wished I had done well somewhere, anywhere for that matter. It could have been a quiz, may be some school test or some exam at FIITJEE, or may be even the sports day event at school.

For as far back as I could think of, I could only remember losses and humiliation. For the first time I consciously recognized that I should have done well in school tests, not so much because the marks mattered, but because those losses were shaping my personality day after day. By choosing the comfortabie path of under-performing in those tests, I had created a mindset that found solace in hollow justifications, that settled for mediocrity rather than finding ways to pursue excellence.

Two days before the screening test

I had gone to bed early, but could not sleep till late night. The thought of the disaster that lay ahead was playing on my mind. I wondered what on earth was going through my mind when I had confronted Kavita ma'am a few weeks back.

'After what you just said, it would be much more embarrassing for you if somehow, even if by fluke, I do manage to clear the screening test. Strange things happen, you see.' I remembered my exact words.

It was completely unnecessary for me to raise the stakes. *'Empty vessels make the most noise,'* I thought.

I wondered how embarrassing it would be for me to face her after that big bold unwarranted statement. Thinking about facing her, what I did next was bizarre. I went to the washroom and practiced a few facial expressions that I could don during my eventual face-off with Kavita ma'am. I thought I was going insane. If failure ever had a face, it was right there in front of me in that moment.

Screening test morning

Once inside the examination center, I was visibly nervous. I looked around to see if it was just me. I saw cheerful and confident faces all around. Looking at their expressions, it was hard to tell if they were about to take the all-important screening test, or some regular practice test. I compared their comfort with my own plight, almost on the verge of peeing in my trousers. Fifteen minutes before the scheduled start-time, we were handed over the OMR answer sheets. I thought about the dos and don'ts Papa had asked me to take care of.

'Don't fold or crumple the answer sheet; always shade the correct circle properly; the circle should be fully shaded, but the shade should not extend outside the circle; most importantly, in your hurry to get on with the exam, don't mess up with your personal details on the answer sheet; always check, double check, triple check that you have put the roll number correctly; your roll number is your identity, one wrong digit and it's not you taking the exam thereafter....' – I remembered the wise words from Papa. I felt the point around being careful with the roll number was particularly important.

With trembling hands, I carefully put the six-digit roll number on the OMR sheet. I took a deep breath and compared the roll number on the admit card with what I had put on the OMR sheet. I went through the two numbers digit by digit, then went over it again, picking two digits at a time, and then the bell rang. Before I knew, the mad rush started. It was all happening very fast. I frantically browsed through the questions. The questions looked familiar.

Just as I started attempting the paper, I again remembered Papa's words, *'In your hurry to get on with the exam don't mess up with your personal details on the answer sheet...'*

I again looked at the admit card and compared it with the roll number I had put on the OMR sheet. It all looked in order. I was conscious that I had already wasted one valuable minute of the actual exam time in making the final checks.

'Enough of paranoia with the roll number. Time to get on with it!' I thought.

The paper had 105 questions, each carrying one mark, with questions evenly split across physics, chemistry and mathematics. I started attempting the questions, with my fingers trembling and heart pounding. Once I got the first few answers, I felt a bit more relaxed. I was pleased to note the watch still showing four minutes to go when I was done attempting all the 105 questions. I gingerly held the OMR sheet in my hand and looked at it for one last time. I carefully observed the way I had shaded the circles to mark my responses. There were 105 neatly shaded small circles on the sheet, each fully shaded, and none with shading extending outside.

Just before I handed over my sheet to the invigilator, I recalled Kavita ma'am's sarcastic words – *'It will help them separate wheat from chaff'*. If her words had any relevance, then those 105 neat little shaded circles were going to determine which category I eventually got labelled into, wheat or chaff.

I rubbished the thought, scanned the sheet one last time, kissed the OMR sheet, and handed it over to the invigilator. I wasn't sure why I kissed the answer sheet; I had never done that before.

As I walked out, my only concern was that it felt too easy. I didn't get stuck anywhere. I wondered if my level of preparation was that good or was it just a case of an easy paper. Maybe it was neither. Maybe it was a case of an overly tricky paper and with my terrible level of preparation I had failed to appreciate that. The more I thought about it, the more I felt that the last option looked most plausible. A part of me, the hopeful me, wanted to believe that I had indeed done a good job. The other part, the cynical me, was finding it hard to accept that as a possibility.

Later that afternoon, I decided to meet my professors at FIITJEE to check my answers. I thought that was the surest way of putting to rest all the speculation brewing up in my head. By the time I reached the FIITJEE office, the professors had already solved the question paper multiple times and were making a few phone calls to release the answer key in the following day's newspaper. It didn't take me long to figure that I had secured 93 correct answers from the 105 questions that I had attempted. The expert professors at FIITJEE predicted the cut-off to clear the exam to be in the range of mid-seventies. I was comfortably clearing that. I was ecstatic.

As I excitedly got ready to leave, Professor Sanjay called me into his cabin.

"So, Aman Singh! How did it go?" he asked.

"Sir, I got 93 correct," I replied in a jubilant tone.

"Never mind."

I was upset to hear that response. That was the last thing I expected after scoring 93.

"But sir… I thought the cut-off is expected to be 75," I murmured, confused.

"Clearing the cut-off in the screening test was never going to be difficult for our students. I am more worried about the 12 questions that you did not get right. Tell me, how is your mains preparation coming along."

"Sir, I have spent a lot of time on calculus and coordinate geometry. I think these are my strength areas. I really want to crack the questions from these topics."

"You sure will. But remember, mains test would feel very different than what you saw today. It will just have ten questions, each carrying ten marks. Don't expect to solve those so easily."

"Yes sir," I replied nervously.

"Are you in the mood to try two problems, one from calculus and one from coordinate geometry. It will give you an idea of what to expect in the final exam. I am sure you were planning to take it easy today, so might as well put this time to some good use."

"Indeed sir. I was planning to take it easy, but what you are suggesting sounds like a better idea."

Professor Sanjay carefully pulled out a few rough worksheets from his drawer and neatly put there two questions for me to try.

"Here you go! You can try these in my cabin. I might need to step out for some work, so if you don't find me around, we can discuss these when we next meet in the class," he said and walked out of his cabin.

Scoring 93 out of 105 in the screening test was no mean achievement, not for me certainly. My self-confidence was at a new high. After a long time, I was feeling good about myself. I started trying the questions with a lot of hope and expectations. After banging my head on those two problems for a little while, my self-confidence came crashing back to where it belonged. It seemed way above my capability. It felt like my seven generations couldn't have solved it, even if they were allowed to take a stab at it together. I kept trying, nonetheless.

In my quest to solve the questions, I completely lost track of time. It was well past eight in the evening when Professor Sanjay walked back into the room.

"Hey, you are still here?" he asked.

"Hello sir. Yes, I was trying the questions you gave me. I think I am close to cracking it, but not completely there yet."

He looked puzzled. It seemed like he had long forgotten about the questions.

"You have been trying these questions since the time we met in the afternoon?"

"Yes sir."

He took the sheets from me and carefully scanned through the content. There were lots of attempts and crosses I had put in there. I wasn't sure what he would think of my effort.

"Look, I will explain these questions in the class. But I do want to ask you something."

"Sure sir."

"Do you know what is that one attribute that differentiates successful people from the less successful ones?" I pondered over it for a moment. Before I could say anything, he continued, "It's the ability to hang in there. It's the ability to endure pain, to stay put when all seems lost."

"You have spent five hours on these questions. That's a lot of time. It takes a lot of mental discipline to do that. You have what it takes to succeed."

I was speechless, somewhat overwhelmed as he said, "On the final exam day, if at any stage you feel like it's all lost, just hang in there! That's your strength."

"Thank you, sir." I replied, probably with the brightest smile I had managed in two years.

"Now go home and we will discuss this in the next class."

The day had been an interesting one for me. In the first half I had solved 93 questions correctly in two hours. In the second half I had failed to solve two questions in over five hours and had still managed to get a compliment from Professor Sanjay, which I dearly treasured.

IN HINDSIGHT

We seldom undertake a solo journey in life. Invariably, our paths get intertwined with those of our family, friends, acquaintances, and even detractors. This is where it is important to be consciously aware of the ecosystem we operate in and actively lean on people who genuinely care.

In my case, I was blessed to have a super-strong support system in the form of my parents and sister. But I didn't do a good job recognizing some of my other well-wishers (Professor Sanjay and MS Dos, for instance), and continued to be sceptical of their inputs for a long time.

Also, I feel attributes such as talent and intellect are highly overrated. At the end of the day, it just boils down to how desperately you want something and how hard you are willing to work for it.

KEY MESSAGES

- ✓ There is immense power in positive thoughts. Never suppress a positive thought because of the enormity of the immediate challenges surrounding you.
- ✓ Nothing happens by chance; everything happens by design. If you are aspiring for something, make sure that all your thoughts and actions steer you in that direction.
- ✓ Be relentless in pursuit of your goals. Any step in the right direction is worth taking, howsoever small it might seem. Think about the woodpecker's pursuit – the little bird keeps hammering the hard tree trunk with its delicate beak, till it is able to drill a hole to find its food.

April 2000-June 2000
It's showtime

> You may be an expert, I may be a fledgling novice; you may be wise, I may be a moron; you may be right, I may be wrong. That still doesn't make you any greater or me any lesser. The fact remains that you are you, and I am me. I respect you for what you are, and am proud of what I am.

Countdown to D-Day

The JEE examination was just two weeks away. In the build-up to the D-Day, I had accumulated loads of physical, mental and emotional fatigue. The days were characterized by mood swings triggered without any apparent reasons. Cracking a tough question would elevate my happiness to unprecedented proportions. I would feel like an invincible warrior whose time had arrived. The very next moment, the euphoric feeling would come crashing down if I encountered a question that I couldn't solve. It would feel like the world was lost. I was conscious of the emotional turbulence I was going through, but could do nothing to control it.

That evening had been a particularly gloomy one. I didn't know for how long I had been staring at the question in the mock test paper I was holding. I thought hazily that I shouldn't allow myself to sit idle like that, but felt weak to change my coordinates. I thought I should close the notebook and take a nap, but a part of me made me believe that closing the notebook midway through a question would be akin to giving up. I wanted to smash the pen hard on the floor, but I needed that pen. Yes, I could still smash it on the ground, but that would not have helped. I wanted to tear the mock test paper I was staring at, but that wouldn't have changed anything either.

I was still evaluating my destructive options when Papa walked into the room. I suddenly became conscious of my existence in that gloomy set-up.

"When did you come?" I asked trying to look sharp and alert.

"Just now."

"It seems like you came early today."

"Not really. Its 6:15 p.m.," replied Papa.

I looked at the clock in disbelief. I couldn't believe that I had been sitting there for over four hours. I wondered why I couldn't snap out of my idleness to use the time more effectively. I let out a wide shameless yawn as if to formally succumb into the boredom.

"You look tired."

"Yes, I am tired of sitting idle. I have been sitting here since lunch. I think I need to be more mindful of my time, can't afford to just sit like this for hours two weeks before the D-Day."

"That's okay."

"I think it's not. It's happening quite a lot with me these days."

"Is something bothering you?"

"Nothing in particular. I guess I am just worried about what lays ahead. Almost half the time I am thinking about how things will shape up going forward."

"Never mind. Just make the most of the other half in that case," Papa said with a smile.

"The problem is that in the other half, I am thinking about how miserable the last two years have been."

"What about that?"

"Just the build-up. All the mess and humiliation I have been through, the interactions I have had with my teachers. It's all a bit overwhelming, both the journey till this point and the uncertainty around what lays ahead. I just wish I had made better use of time after the end of tenth boards examination. If only..."

"Don't think so much," interjected Papa. "How do you plan to spend the next few days?"

"I am trying to revise as much as possible. I am revisiting all concepts, formulae, and some of my favourite questions. Is there anything different that I can be doing at this stage?"

"Yes."

He slowly took a sip from the glass of water he was holding. He seemed to be carefully evaluating what he was going to suggest next. It seemed like an eternity before he finally spoke.

"Close all your books. Go out to the park in the evening. Meet your friends. Play cricket. Play chess. Sleep well. Eat well. Relax and rejuvenate."

"Good joke," I replied with a chuckle.

"I am serious!" Papa replied.

Despite those crisp three words, it took me a few moments to realize that he was actually serious.

"But why would you suggest that? I mean, what I do in the next two weeks could significantly determine my fate on the big day."

"Precisely! That's why I want you to feel fresh and at the peak of your energy levels. There is enough and more that you have imbibed. You just need to take it easy now and be in a good frame of mind."

"Are you sure this is the right approach?"

"Yes."

I was not completely convinced about the suggestion. I accepted it, nonetheless.

The D-Day was just a day away.

The night before the examination, I was visibly overwhelmed by the enormity of the occasion. I was trying to evade a direct eye-contact with Mama. I knew she would easily figure the turbulence that lay underneath. She eventually did.

"All set?" she asked.

"Would have an answer by this time tomorrow," I replied with an anxious smile.

I blankly stared out of the window, trying to condone the anxiousness I was feeling. Mama held my hand in her hands and said, "Whatever happens tomorrow, we will be proud of you. We know you have put in your heart and soul into this preparation for the past two years."

I did not respond. I just smiled. I was already struggling to hold back my tears. I turned towards Papa, trying to evade looking at Mama.

"Yes, that's correct," added Papa in his typical style. "Have you prepared the stationery for tomorrow?"

"No, not yet."

"Come, let's do it together".

Papa and I spent good thirty minutes carefully packing my bag. At the end of it, Papa pulled out a small little chit from his pocket.

"What's that? Some interesting physics problems that you found worth revising?" I asked.

"No, I don't intend to share any problems today. We have done enough of that. It's a list of things that you need to absolutely carry to the examination hall. I will go over the items one by one and keep crossing them once you tell me it is in the bag."

"Okay, but we have never done this for any exam earlier. This tells me that tomorrow is a big day. Isn't it?"

"Don't worry. It will pass and we will be playing chess the same time tomorrow," he said patting on my back.

"Okay, let's go over it," I replied with a smile.

"Roll number ticket, watch, five pens, five pencils, sharpener, two erasers, cardboard, water bottle…" Papa went on for a while, striking out things in his list as I kept confirming.

Shortly thereafter, I went for an early sleep. Time and again, my professors at FIITJEE had emphasized the importance of sleeping early before the exam day.

Once in bed, I tried hard to keep my mind free of any distracting thoughts. But that was not going to be easy. Before I realized, I was dreaming away to glory in my fantasy world. As was often the case, I created a larger-than-life image, visualizing myself as the super-hero taking the center stage. I imagined myself as the brightest student, for whom no question could be tough enough. I visualized other students revering me as the math wizard who only had to take the exam as a formality to adhere to the selection process. I continued to build upon my stupid fascinations for a little longer. I fantasized my teachers excitedly applauding me for my tremendous achievements. I visualized Professor Malik standing quietly in one of the corners with an apologetic smile to convey his regret for not spotting my intellect earlier.

It was already half past midnight, and I was still nowhere close to falling asleep. I continued to stay fidgety in the bed, restlessly moving from one side to another. After I had exhausted all possible super-hero fantasies, I thought about the potential realities that lay at the other end of the spectrum. I felt hollow. I particularly felt sad for my parents who had put in a lot of efforts in my preparation.

'This too shall pass.' I helplessly thought and tried to sleep.

☆☆

Mathematics exam – Calamity strikes

By around 7:35 a.m., I comfortably settled in the examination hall. I was extremely nervous and could feel my fingers trembling. I made a conscious effort to arrest the trembling of my fingers, but it seemed like a futile attempt. I anxiously looked around in the room to see how others were dealing with the pressure moment. The only person who looked calm in the room was probably the invigilator. He seemed relaxed and somewhat excited at the prospect of watching the drama unfold over the next two hours. I distinctly disliked him at the first sight. I continued staring at him a tad longer than necessary, not because I wanted to, but probably because there wasn't much to do in those seemingly difficult few minutes of wait time.

"I am going to distribute the question paper and answer sheets exactly ten minutes before the start time. You can fill in your personal details in the answer sheets, but do not look through the paper before I indicate. If I see anyone looking through the questions, I will immediately disqualify that student from taking the examination," he said in his screeching hoarse voice.

After a few minutes and some nervous nods, he placed the answer sheet and a pink-coloured printed question paper on my desk. I could feel my heart pounding. I had never been so consciously aware of my heartbeat. I could almost hear it, as if someone had plugged a stethoscope in my ears with the sensor on my heart. The question paper was sealed from three sides. I gently touched the question paper with the index finger.

'*This is it.*' I thought.

Before I could think any further, the bell rang.

I opened the seal from the three sides and quickly scanned through the paper. The format was simple. There were ten questions in all, each carrying ten marks. I had to solve around four questions to have a realistic chance of clearing the cut-off. I nervously searched through the paper to identify any familiar questions. At a first glance I didn't find any obvious ones. I recalled how my professors always emphasized the importance of picking the right questions.

"You don't need to crack all questions, be smart about the ones you pick, you don't want to be wasting your time on the ones you don't need to," I recalled Professor Sanjay telling us time and again.

I started attempting a problem from coordinate geometry, which I always felt was my strength. After banging my head for about fifteen minutes, I realized that I had probably overestimated my abilities. It wasn't strong enough for what I needed on D-day. I nervously looked at the watch to see how much time I had killed for zero return. It was slightly over 8:15 a.m. I decided to not waste any more time and tried picking something else. I was conscious that I couldn't afford to make another wrong choice. After a bit of deliberation, I decided to attempt a calculus problem next. Unfortunately, after spending a little over ten minutes, I met a similar fate.

I dreaded looking at the watch.

It was already 8:32 a.m. and I was yet to open my marks account. I tried to concentrate harder in the hope to get things moving. But the heat of the moment was getting to me. I nervously glanced around the room to see other students. They all seemed to be ferociously filling their answer sheets. I wondered how they could have so much to write. It was just ten questions after all, none of which made much sense anyway.

The next moment, I found myself thinking about a memory from years ago. Back then, my grandfather had a bicycle which he used to commute around. I used to accompany him for grocery purchases, sitting on the horizontal steel rod. I had often complained to him that I felt uncomfortable sitting on the steel rod. One fine day, he approached me with a gleam in his eyes as he excitedly showed me a baby cushion seat that he had gotten installed on the horizontal rod. 'Now you will never feel uncomfortable,' he had said with a gratified smile.

I again looked at my watch. 8:40 a.m.

I nervously adjusted my posture and concluded that it was oversight on my grandfather's part to have made that statement back then, for I was feeling really uncomfortable in that moment, more uncomfortable than ever before. By then, I had started sweating.

I always knew that it would be tough in there, but what I experienced that morning was colossal. It was like a calamity had struck me with all its might, rendering me numb and immobile, leaving me shattered and devastated.

'*So much for all the late nights and early mornings*,' I helplessly thought.

I desperately wished I could have spoken to Papa for fifteen seconds and asked, 'I am clueless. These questions are way beyond me. What do I do now?'

The very next moment I visualized what Papa would have answered. 'Don't worry. We will come back next year, even better prepared. For now, just think of it as one of the many mock tests that you have given at FIITJEE. This experience of a real mock will help when we come back next year.' He would have been unperturbed.

Those few seconds of imaginary conversation with Papa helped me immensely. I instantly felt relaxed. The comfort was very similar to what I had felt two years ago when I was terribly upset about my score of 2 on 25. On that occasion, Mama had calmly comforted me by sharing that even a score of zero was okay. I wondered why humans always needed a relative cushion to feel comfortable and how just by playing a few mind games, we could fool ourselves into feeling comfortable. Just a few minutes back, I was so nervous that I was almost trembling. But now I was feeling relaxed and completely detached from that monstrous pink question paper I was holding in my hand.

I again looked at my watch, not out of any pressure, but just to see how much time I had to sit through that practice mock test. I disinterestedly started attempting the questions again. To my pleasant surprise, I did manage to crack one problem in the next fifteen minutes. I felt ecstatic at having solved the first problem. It was not that I had any hopes of doing well in that examination anymore, but just the validation that I wasn't a complete dud felt good.

I glanced at the watch. Ten minutes past nine.

I still had about fifty minutes to continue practicing in that real examination environment. A part of me wanted to believe that it was no longer a practice match. The other part countered the thought by reminding me of the misery that had unfolded in the first hour of the examination. I consciously tried to ignore both thoughts and attempted the next question. Few minutes later I had cracked another one, much to my delight and surprise.

With just over fifteen minutes to go, I was confused whether I should have still been thinking of it as a practice match as I had indeed managed to crack a few problems. I realized that if I could somehow crack one more problem in the remaining time, I would have at least crossed the individual cut-off mark for that paper. I was cognizant that physics was the last exam for the day and that was my strength. If I could somehow get into that exam, clearing the individual cut-offs in mathematics and chemistry, then anything could have happened.

I glanced at the watch yet again. 9:47 a.m.

'Strange things do happen. Keep pushing.' I told myself.

I felt that my best chance to solve one more problem in the limited remaining time was with one of those problems that I had already spent some time thinking about. I went back to the question that I had started the paper with. The last ten minutes of the exam was the only brief period in that exam when I concentrated intensely hard. I did not allow any random thought to cross my mind in those final few minutes – no cricket fantasies, no blank staring around, no childhood flashbacks, nothing; just razor-sharp focus on that one question, as if my life depended on it.

I didn't realize, but in my quest to concentrate hard, I had become quite animated. I was frequently murmuring things to myself to keep the concentration going. Every few moments, I would partially raise my hand, as if deliberating a critical point. The next moment, I would nod my head in disagreement, and then the very next, I would nod in agreement as if I had managed to convince myself on the right approach. In between those animated gestures, I was writing as fast as I possibly could.

Apparently, the invigilator was noticing it and was getting increasingly annoyed.

"You may be distracting other students," he said to me in an irritated tone.

No response.

I had heard him, but had no time to respond to his worthless observation.

"Did you hear what I said? Be careful to not distract others," he shouted again.

I looked up with a cold face and nodded, while continuing to write on the sheet simultaneously. The nod was intended to acknowledge his command, though it came across as - 'Shut-up, you moron.'

"Last two minutes, please. I want all of you to instantly stop writing when I tell you to stop," he shouted.

I kept writing, a little faster.

"Stop, everyone. Stop!" the sadist shouted a few seconds later.

I banged the pen on the table and stopped writing with a jerk. The ordeal was over. I felt drained. But somewhere deep within, there was also a sense of satisfaction. Not from having done great, but from having put in every ounce of effort that I could have. The invigilator tied the answer sheets in a bundle as students slowly vacated the room.

I continued sitting there with my chin resting on my palms and my elbows supported against the desk. I was not sure of what to feel about the paper. Despite the seemingly fluctuating fortunes across the two-hour timeframe, I felt I had managed to do something. I could not be sure if that something was good enough, though.

With a lot of effort, I got up from my seat and left the examination hall.

Chemistry exam – Time to hang in there

As I walked through the corridors, I noticed the fellow students merrily chit-chatting. Some of them seemed to be talking about the mathematics paper, while there were others who seemed to be casually gossiping about anything and everything under the sun. They all looked happy and relaxed. I wondered why I couldn't be like them. I had no energy for a fake gossip session, so I tried to look for a quiet corner. After randomly walking around the school premises for a while, I found a corner at the far end of the school boundary. It was a soothing tree shade that offered the solitude I needed to regather myself ahead of the next paper which was due to start at noon.

I occupied a spot beneath a lush green tree, comfortably resting my back against the tree trunk. For a long time, I had wondered what it would feel like after walking out from the examination hall. I had often relied on my imagination and wishful thinking to create scenarios. Nowhere in my imagination had I created a scenario similar to the one that actually unfolded that morning. It almost felt like an anti-climax. I was in a state of trance.

When I looked at my watch a short while later, I was surprised to see that it had been over an hour since I had been sitting there. I hurriedly unpacked my tiffin box to have a quick bite. As I grabbed my food, I caught sight of that pink-coloured mathematics paper lying beside me. It jostled me from my state of trance, bringing me back into the real world. I immediately became conscious of the two more exams that I had to take the same day.

I remembered the wise words Professor Sanjay had shared on the day of the screening test – *'If at any stage you feel like it's all lost, just hang in there! That's your strength.'*

The thought helped me get my focus back. I gulped a few sips of water, shifting my thought to the next paper that was due to start in a little over thirty minutes.

The chemistry exam had always been my weak area. I just couldn't relate to the subject. Physics was still different. In physics, I could often link the concepts to something interesting that would make the pain of studying the subject bearable. The laws of motion made me think of Tendulkar smashing the cricket ball, the Archimedes' principle of buoyancy made me think of the Titanic movie, the aerodynamics concepts made me think of the joy of flying kites. On the other hand, chemistry concepts always reminded me of Kavita ma'am mercilessly butchering me inside the school laboratory.

By around quarter to noon, I had settled in the examination hall. I wasn't feeling the same level of nervousness as I had experienced before the mathematics exam. It was probably because the nerves had settled a bit after the first exam.

The invigilator distributed the answer sheets and a sealed question paper, a yellow one this time. I had developed such a strong association with the chemistry laboratory that every time I held a chemistry paper in my hand, I could feel the foul pungent smell of fumes. That moment was no exception. I almost felt the burning sensation of fumes in my nose.

At sharp 12:00 noon, I opened the seal and browsed through the paper. I was pleased to notice that unlike the mathematics exam, the chemistry paper did not have ten subjective questions of ten marks each. Instead, there were several short answer type questions, carrying three to five marks each. This format suited me better. For someone relatively weak in a subject, it is always better to have more short answer type options to keep moving forward rather than getting stuck with a ten-mark mega problem. I wondered if the change in format was a sign that the cosmic powers were conspiring to help me clear the exam, despite my limitations.

"Just hang in there!" I softly murmured to myself.

I navigated the next two hours stress-testing my fragile command over the chemistry concepts. Unlike mathematics, I did not have a preference for any particular topic to start with. However, I did have a repugnance for inorganic chemistry. That was a topic I was particularly weak in. Other than that, I could have picked questions through a simple pitch and toss of a coin – stoichiometry, chemical equilibrium, ionic equilibrium, organic chemistry – they were all the same for me. By the time the concluding bell rang at 2:00 p.m., I had attempted almost 70 percent of the paper, way beyond my self-expectations of the subject.

After completing the exam, I walked back to my resting spot under the tree. I was pleased to see that the spot had still not been invaded by the fellow students. I lay there under the tree with my eyes closed and my forearm gently resting over my forehead. I reflected upon the way the day had progressed till that point. It almost felt like an in-progress innings of a one-day cricket match. The mathematics paper was like the first fifteen overs played on a seaming pitch under over-cast conditions. I was clueless as to what was happening around me. During the second paper, it seemed like the conditions had eased up a tad bit, which allowed me to somehow hang in there. I concluded that if the one-day innings was the right metaphor, then the all-important slog overs awaited me in just over an hour. I decided to put in all I had in the final paper. I felt a sudden rush of adrenalin.

"Game on!" I shouted, thumping my chest.

Physics exam – It's not over till it's over

By around 3:45 p.m., I occupied my seat in the examination hall. Having been through two papers already, I felt reasonably relaxed ahead of the third and final exam for the day – the physics exam. The subject had always been quite close to my heart. In fact, in the years prior to commencing JEE preparation, I used to thoroughly enjoy the subject. Papa too enjoyed explaining me the concepts, conducting real experiments.

However, somewhere along the way, the childlike joy and inquisitiveness made way for mathematical equations. The simple projectile motion of grapes I had once enjoyed alongside my cousins had transformed into 'Y is equal to x tan theta minus g x square upon 2 u square cos square theta'. The joy had faded away. But deep within, I still loved the subject.

I was still thinking about when and how the transition had happened when the invigilator placed the question paper on my desk, a blue-coloured one this time. I recalled the wise words Papa and Professor Menon had shared with me during the preparation months.

'Your gut and instinct can let you down, but mathematical equations will never let you down. If your gut-based answer is different from what equations tell you then always listen to the equations. Equations never lie. Trust them blindly.' I recalled Professor Menon's words.

The very next moment, I recalled a slightly different version that Papa had shared – 'Never apply equations blindly. Always think and visualize the problem before you start applying mathematical equations.'

With just about five minutes to go, I found myself wondering who was right.

'Doesn't really matter. Not anymore,' I thought. *'No one cares how runs come in the slog overs, as long as they keep coming.'* That was the final thought that crossed my mind. Thinking in cricketing terms always helped me put things into perspective.

I opened the question paper seal.

The format of the physics paper was similar to that of the mathematics exam. There were ten questions carrying ten marks each. I scanned through the paper to get a feel for the type of questions. On a quick glance, I noticed three visuals in the paper – a pulley system with some masses connected around it, an object launched in a projectile motion along a cartesian plane, and an object placed in front of a convex lens.

I was conscious not to make the mistake I had made in the mathematics paper, of choosing a wrong question to begin with. I thought for a moment. For no apparent reason, I had a flashback from my first physics lecture at FIITJEE. Professor Menon had been kind enough to not overly embarrass me cutting short a conversation by saying – 'It's nothing important, just a dirty imagination of an example of a projectile motion....'

Back then, I didn't have the foresight or seriousness to understand how important it could have been for me to intently follow what Professor Menon was explaining. Almost two years down the line, here I was, holding a nice crisp blue paper in my hand with ten percent of my exam fortune depending on that same little projectile motion concept, the concept that had elicited the mental image of a boy peeing from top of a terrace once.

But why was I thinking about that sitting inside the examination hall where every minute could count? Maybe it was a hint from the higher power to guide me towards picking the right question. Or maybe, as always, I was just distracted.

I started the paper with the question on projectile motion. After carefully playing around with a few thetas and velocity vectors, I cracked the problem.

Phew.

'That was neat. Good start!' I thought to myself.

I spent the next hour and a half conserving momentum, maintaining thermal equilibrium, reflecting light beams, and playing around with free body diagrams. It all felt neat and elegant. No heart breaks, no stress, nothing. Just simple elegant application of physics concepts, something that Papa and I had practiced a lot.

With just about ten minutes to go for the exam to end, I scanned the paper to see how I had fared. I felt proud of the effort I had put in. I had solved almost 80 percent of the questions. I wondered how Professor Malik would react if he were to ever see my answer sheet. I could visualize him nodding his head with a sarcastic smile saying, *'Mr Singh, I always told you, you are good for nothing.'* The thought brought a frown on my face. I instantly cursed myself for again succumbing to that same age-old problem of getting distracted at critical moments.

'Idiot, it's not over till it's over. Keep the concentration going.' – I found a part of me shouting at myself.

I hurriedly scampered through the paper to identify any final unanswered questions. The only unsolved question that caught my attention was from the topic of modern physics, a topic that I wasn't very well versed with. I nervously glanced through the watch. We still had about six minutes to go. Despite my fragile understanding of the topic, I thought about the question for a couple of minutes.

"This one is only for you Mr Malik, with love from the one and only, Mr Singh." I murmured softly, while simultaneously writing in the answer sheet frantically.

"Stop. No more writing. Stop immediately!" shouted the invigilator.

I banged the pen on the desk one final time for the day, a simple gesture that somehow seemed to converge a sense of tension, relief, pride, anger, and tribute – all at once. It was a strange feeling, something that I had never experienced before.

I had somehow managed to crack that one final question too.

✩✩

By the end of the day, a huge crowd had gathered outside the school. Walking through the noisy corridors, one could hear all kinds of sentiments – misery, optimism, fear, excitement.

Since I had not spent any time with other students during the breaks, it was the first time I was gathering real feedback on how others had perceived the exam. I intently tried to overhear the remarks. My fortune depended as much on my performance as on how others had fared. Every time I heard someone crib, I felt good, and on occasions when I overheard cuss words, I felt elated.

'*I was not the only one who got screwed.*' I thought with a huge sense of relief.

On coming out, I saw Papa from a distance. He was standing beside our grey-coloured scooter. There was a hint of a smile on his face, as if to acknowledge the significance of the big day. As I made my way through the crowd, I wondered what to tell Papa.

The day had started off on a disastrous note with the mathematics examination, but I had somewhat recovered after that. Given the nature of the exam, it was impossible to know if the recovery was good enough. I felt I had a slim hope, but was not sure if that was significant enough to be shared. The last thing I wanted to do was to set unrealistic expectations.

On reaching closer to the scooter, I noticed a characteristic glow in Papa's eyes which seemed to be asking a question and revealing the answer he wished to hear in the same moment. With a subtle wink of the eye and a slight palm movement, he seemed to be asking the big question. I think he deliberately refrained from asking explicitly as it could have entailed a broad range of responses, including some potentially disturbing ones for me. I too tried to evade making an eye contact on the pretense of tiredness and exhaustion. It was fascinating that after months of hard work and singular focus on the D-Day, here we were, facing each other, but none of us having the courage to speak about it.

"It was tough!" I finally said.

"I am sure," Papa replied with a smile.

Underneath that smile was a faint hint of disappointment, which could never have been visible to a naked eye. It could only have been felt by someone who had been privy to the effort that we had both put in, as companions.

I quietly took the back seat as Papa drove the scooter. A few moments later, we stopped at a red light. I thought Papa would finally ask the big question, but he just looked at me in the rear mirror and smiled. Despite the eerie silence, there was a loud message – there was nothing more important to Papa than my comfort. I warmly reciprocated with a smile.

To my pleasant surprise, he never asked me about the exam. Never!

✩✩

Those pangs of cynicism

Mama and Didi were visibly curious to know how the day and had gone by, and unlike Papa, they didn't hold back their questions. I sat at the dining table with a glass of milk, with Mama and Didi sitting right across the table. There was a small little lull before Didi launched a volley of questions.

"How was it?"

"It was okay."

"Please don't play your usual games today. Tell me genuinely."

"I am not sure. I think I messed up the mathematics examination badly."

"How badly?"

"Quite badly."

"That doesn't say much."

I took another deep sip of the chocolate shake before giving a considered response. "For the first forty minutes in the two-hour exam, I had not been able to solve a single question," I replied.

"And then?"

"I panicked and my fingers started trembling," I said rather dramatically.

"No, I mean how many did you solve eventually?"

"I attempted a lot of questions and solved a few completely. In the last fifteen minutes, I even managed to crack the problem on which I had wasted the first fifteen minutes of the exam."

"Not bad! How was chemistry?"

"Chemistry paper was easy by JEE standards, and it would not be the subject that determines the final outcome. Despite my limitations with the subject, I did a decent job."

"Good. How was physics?"

"I cracked it!" I replied with a sense of pride underpinning my otherwise tense expression.

"Excellent. Then why do you look so tense?"

"I am not sure if I would clear the individual cut-off in mathematics," I replied with moist eyes.

There was an awkward silence for a few moments. Shortly thereafter, I excused myself, leaving for an early sleep.

I lay in the bed, blankly staring at the walls. Of course, I was not sleepy. I was just reflecting upon the day. It was interspersed with some silent weeping and a flashback of various incidents from the previous two years. I was not focusing on anything in particular. The incidents just came rolling by, one after another – the two marks in the computer test, the chemistry lab jibes, the naps in classes, the blank stares, the broken tooth, the misery at the sports day event, the bunked FIITJEE classes, the fun time with cousins, the late-night studies with Papa, the evening walks with Mama, the nasty confrontations with teachers, the silent fireworks, the derisive remarks from fellow students, the unexpected words of encouragement from MS Dos!

A lot seemed to have happened in just two years. It seemed like a bumpy ride. I had only hoped that it would all feel worth the toil after the big day. Somehow, that didn't seem to be the case.

At around quarter to midnight, Didi came over to the room with two plates of Maggi and a coke. I too was tired of sleep pretense.

"See what I have got! Get up, let's have some food and then you can sleep again," she said.

I instantly got up and carefully took my plate.

"You are a celebrity today!" she said, trying to start a conversation.

"Why?"

"Everyone is calling up to check how you fared in the JEE Examination today."

"Who all called?" I asked, somewhat irritated.

"Some friends from school and FIITJEE and some well-wishers."

"Bunch of hypocrites, if you ask me," I replied, slowly savouring the bite.

"What do you mean?"

"See, usually what people say is not what they actually mean. It is difficult to understand what's truly going inside a person's mind."

"What does that have to do with people calling in to check on your performance in JEE?"

I took a sip from the Coke bottle. "The only three people who truly care for how I fared today live under this roof. Other than that, it's all formalities. In fact, in some instances, I suspect it's a bit more than that. Some of the people who called today may have actually been hoping to hear that I messed it up badly. They won't say it on the face, but that's true. We all try to say things which adhere to the so-called decorum of civilized human beings."

I continued after a few moments. "I am not suggesting that people around us are bad. This is just normal human behaviour. I am no different either. I don't mind seeing people happy, but only as long as their magnitude of happiness is lesser than mine. I am fine for others to have similar outlook towards me, but I don't understand the need for pretense. More so, since it is so easy to see through that, it almost makes me feel that the other person is thinking I am a fool."

Didi said without blinking, "You were not sleeping for the last four hours, were you? I can see a lot of turbulence in your thoughts."

"Yes, I was not sleeping. I was just reflecting upon the last two years."

"I am glad that you have been so passionately thinking about it. However, at the end of the day, don't forget that it was just another exam. Don't take it so seriously that it leads you to say all the stupid things that you just said."

That little moment of redemption

In the days following the JEE exam, I had a tough time keeping my mind focused. There was a constant feeling of emptiness, as if something vital had been snatched from me. My tryst with JEE preparation may have followed an unusual path, but it had become an integral part of me. I did not consciously realize, but all I had been doing over the past several months was only centered around exam preparation. Now that it was over, I was struggling to keep myself engaged.

It was a bright sunny Sunday morning. The usual daily chores had already started for others in the house, while I was still struggling to get out of bed. It wasn't my sleep that was holding me back, but the complete absence of any plan for the day which I dreaded. I couldn't find the motivation to get out of bed only to stare at the walls the whole day, something I had been doing quite well of late.

At around 9:30 a.m., Mama came to the room to wake me up.

"I am preparing breakfast. Do you want to have something special today?"

"No. Anything will be good."

"Okay, so your bread-omelette and banana shake will be ready in ten minutes. Make sure to brush your teeth before that. Omelettes taste best when fresh. Come!"

I wondered how one could not get tired of saying the same thing day after day. Moreover, every day she would say it as if she was saying it for the first time.

Once at the breakfast table, I casually glanced through the sports page.

"Where is Papa?" I asked.

"I am not sure. I haven't seen him around. Maybe he has gone out to purchase grocery or something."

A few moments later, the doorbell rang.

"I think he is here. Let me check," said Mama.

As Mama opened the door, I faintly heard some soft whispers. I was not sure what was going on. Was it Papa at the door? If yes, why would he be whispering? Had he said something to Mama that I was not supposed to know? I could feel my heart sink. Before I could think any further, I saw Papa excitedly approaching me with rapid long strides. He had an unusually big smile on his face, a smile that seemed too generous for his usual demeanour. He was struggling to hold his excitement, but wouldn't say anything.

The very next instant, Mama followed suit. She barged in laughing with her hands thrown wide open in the air. They both hugged me tight. I was still not sure what was happening around me.

"What is it?" I asked innocently.

"560!" Papa replied.

I wondered if he was now taking his reticence to a new level, where he planned to communicate using numeric codes. I thought for a moment what that code could have meant.

"What 560?" I asked.

"Your All-India Rank in JEE Examination!" exclaimed Mama.

I was speechless. I didn't know how to react. Mama and Papa kept patting me on the back as I took a few moments to let the news sink in. I could still not believe what I had heard.

"How do you know?" I asked.

"I am coming straight from the IIT Delhi campus where they have put up the results on the notice board," Papa replied.

"I think there is some confusion. They must have put up the Delhi zone ranks. It can't be the All-India Rank," I said.

"There is no such thing as Delhi zone ranks," he said with a shrug. But I could observe the broad beaming smile making way for a cloud of doubt.

"But if you're doubtful, let's go back and double check?" he offered.

"Yes, let's please do that!" I replied.

"This is just not possible. This can't be true," I kept faintly murmuring as we headed out.

Without uttering another word, we stepped out. I settled comfortably on the back seat of the scooter as Papa drove us to the IIT Delhi campus. It was a 15-minute drive from our place, but it felt like eternity. After parking the scooter, we hurriedly walked towards the notice board. I found myself murmuring a few silent prayers in anticipation.

Papa carefully caressed the top row on the notice board. It read – 'IIT JEE 2000 Results – All-India Ranks of Selected Candidates'.

"You see that?" he asked.

I took a minute to read it, and then read it again, and then read it one more time, distinctly speaking out each word slowly so that I could hear it too.

"IIT…JEE… 2000… Results… All-India…Ranks of…Selected… Candidates" – I read from the board.

And then Papa quickly navigated down through a long list of roll numbers to point to my roll number.

"And here is our roll number. See it for yourself," he said as the faint cloud of doubt disappeared making way for the beaming smile.

"You are right!" I said sheepishly, uncertain about how to react. I kept staring at the roll number, feeling overwhelmed to say anything for a while.

"YESSSSSSSSSSSSSSS!!!!!!!" I shouted as hard as I could, punching the air with my fist. It took me a few seconds to regather myself.

Papa hugged me tight from the side, continuing to look at the board.

"You did it!" he said.

"We did it!" I replied, finally letting a happy tear trickle down my cheek.

☆☆

I had often wondered what is that one thing that I would do if I ever cleared the JEE exam. On most occasions I had thought of a rather unusual action. I had always imagined myself going back to MS Dos with the torn answer sheet of my computer science examination. The incident had shattered me when it had happened, and I had silently hoped that there would come a day when I would see MS Dos in the eye and continue the conversation that had been cut short back in the day. It may have been just half-a-mark, but that was *my* half-a-mark. I was not asking for any grace marks.

Next morning, I got up rather early. I lifted a few heavy books on my study table to pull out the book resting right at the bottom of the stack. I carefully opened the book to take out the torn answer sheet, something that I had preserved as a prized possession for almost two years. I had not seen it since that fateful day, partly because I didn't have the time, and partly because I wanted to wait for the right moment. That morning, it felt like the right moment had arrived. Soon thereafter, I went to the school.

"May I come in ma'am?" I said, carefully opening the computer science lab door.

"Yes please," MS Dos replied without looking up from the screen.

I stood there at the door for a few seconds, waiting to grab ma'am's attention. She did look up a few seconds later.

"Aman! What a pleasant surprise. I wasn't expecting you. Come right in," she said.

"Good morning, ma'am."

"Good morning, good morning. How have you been and what brings you here?" she asked.

"Ma'am, I wanted to share something with you."

"What is it?"

I couldn't say anything. "All well, Aman?" she asked, this time with a bit of inquisitiveness.

"Ma'am, the final result for the sport that I was practicing has come," I said.

"... And?" she asked, almost as if holding her breath.

"I scored an All-India Rank of 560. That should comfortably land me a seat in IIT Delhi," I replied struggling to hold back tears.

MS Dos immediately got up and whole heartedly patted me on the shoulder. "Well done! I am so happy for you!"

I just smiled.

"I know it was not easy," she continued.

I was speechless. I had been waiting for this moment for two years. But now that it was there, I just didn't know what to say.

"I know you want to say something," ma'am said with a warm smile.

I gathered the courage to take out my prized possession from the bag, as she watched me intently.

"Ma'am, I was really hurt when this happened two years back," I said, solemnly keeping the torn answer sheet on the desk.

"I am sorry for what happened," she replied.

"You don't have to be ma'am. A lot of people hurt me in many different ways over the last two years. I am not going to go back to any of them, and honestly, I couldn't care less about what they think about me. But for some reason, I wanted to come back to you."

"Why?"

"Because I think after that first incident, you have been very kind to me. Your words of encouragement during the sports week meant a lot to me and I wanted to thank you for that."

MS Dos thought for a moment before responding. "First impressions can be misleading, Aman. During our first interaction, I found you extremely lackadaisical and someone who lacked self-respect."

"I hope that has somewhat changed now?" I asked.

"Totally, I stand corrected on both. Someone who is lackadaisical wouldn't secure an All-India Rank of 560 in IIT JEE."

"...and what about self-respect?"

She again thought for a moment, as if to carefully evaluate her words. "Someone who lacks self-respect wouldn't preserve this piece of torn answer sheet for two years," she replied.

She kept staring at my total on the torn answer sheet for a few seconds, as if to evaluate the right next action. Then, she struck out my total of 2 marks on the torn sheet with a small note besides it – '2.5. I stand corrected. Well done!'

I gracefully bowed my head and warmly smiled back at her. "Thank you, ma'am. This means the world to me."

"Do well in life! Be assured that wherever you go in future, you will have a well-wisher cheering for you right here."

I waved her good-bye and left the computer science lab, feeling redeemed.

That's when I heard a familiar voice from behind.

"Mr Singh!" It was Professor Malik. No one else in the school addressed me so respectfully.

"Good morning, sir."

"Good morning, Aman. What are you up to these days? I guess you must be busy catching up on sleep, something you have been truly deprived of for the past two years," he said mockingly. Clearly, he had not been able to get the silent fireworks out of his mind.

"Yes sir. You are right. I am doing exactly that, partly to catch-up on the lost sleep and partly to get fully refreshed for what lays ahead," I said.

"So, what lays ahead for you?"

"I will be pursuing Mechanical Engineering from IIT Delhi," I replied. "Ah by the way, I don't think I shared with you. I secured an All-India Rank of 560 in the JEE Examination," I continued.

"What!!" he reacted in shock and dismay.

'You may be an expert, I may be a fledgling novice; you may be wise, I may be a moron; you may be right, I may be wrong. That still doesn't make you any greater or me any lesser, sir. The fact remains that you are you, and I am me. I respect you for what you are, and I am proud of what I am.' Even as these words came up in my mind, I preferred maintaining a dignified silence in that beautiful moment.

I stayed quiet, not because I wanted to be sober, but because I wanted to be louder. I continued looking at him silently for a few seconds, not with abhorrence or anger, but with complete indifference.

"Goodbye, sir," I said.

I walked out of my school corridors for one final time, ironically for the first time with pride and confidence. That was the end of my schooling.

Things could have unfolded in many different ways, but thanks to my parents, I walked off with my head held high and with memories to cherish forever.

IN HINDSIGHT

As I look back at the last leg of my schooling journey, one thing that really stands out for me is the power of perseverance, essentially the ability to hang in there when all seems lost.

No matter how hard you try, you will invariably end up encountering challenges along the way, some of them seemingly insurmountable. This is where it is important to just hang in there.

I also passionately recall my final interaction with Professor Malik. Somehow, that was the moment in which I learned the art of being proud of myself, yet respectful of others. I may have had my differences with him back in the day, but he played a critical role in shaping my personality and I am thankful to him for that.

KEY MESSAGES

- ✓ Actions speak louder than words. The best way to answer your critics is not through words, but through results. You may not have much to say today because of the mess you are in, but then you don't need to. You are better off silently working your way through the hurdles and wait for the right moment.
- ✓ Overcoming hurdles doesn't require exceptional talent or abilities – it just requires unwavering commitment and patience. Regardless of how hopeless a situation feels, just hang in there; never quit, never!
- ✓ A lot was done before you were born, a lot will be done after you are gone; and this fact holds for you as much as for others. Be respectful of others, yet proud of what you are.

July 2021
Current day

> Hindsight is a mysterious ability. It makes me experience joy and sorrow in the same moment; makes me feel significantly evolved yet diminished in the same moment; makes me wonder if all our worldly pursuits are for real or just an illusion. For despite having achieved all that I once wanted, I still feel the same old void.

The nostalgia

1:50 a.m.

My chain of thoughts was broken by a gentle knock on the table. I lazily lifted my forearm and opened my eyes. It was Mehr standing right next to me.

"You didn't sleep?" I asked.

"I had slept, but I noticed that you were still not in the room, so thought of checking in. Is there a lot of work left?"

"No, not much. Just the part that was left when we had dinner. I got distracted by something and have been thinking about it for a while," I replied with a tired smile.

"Is there something that I can help with?"

"Don't worry. I have it covered. It's not much. I will get to it now and make sure to complete it in a few hours. And yes, when I say few hours, I mean one or two hours, nothing more than that," I replied.

Mehr smiled warmly.

"You go to sleep. I will come over in some time."

"Okay. If you need anything, wake me up."

Just before she left the room, I asked another question. "By the way, what time do we want to sit for Ekkam's playschool homework tomorrow?"

She turned back and gently smiled. "Any time tomorrow evening," she replied and continued to stare at me somewhat quizzically.

"What?" I asked, becoming increasingly conscious about the way she was looking at me.

"What have you been thinking about?" she asked.

"Will share some other day. For now, let me just get this review completed quickly," I replied with a chuckle.

"Okay. Good night!" she said with a smile and left the room.

✩✩

Next morning, I got up with the usual sense of urgency. I rushed to the study room and switched on the laptop. A part of me was still thinking about the nostalgia that I had allowed myself to immerse in the previous night. It was a beautiful feeling, something I wanted to feel all over again. I decided to drive down to the same place where it had all started – the Pragati Vihar Hostel at Lodhi Road.

It took me about an hour to reach the hostel from my current residence in Gurugram. It was surprising that the place was so close to me, but I was visiting it after almost two decades.

As I came out of the car, I was engulfed with distinctive feeling of both joy and sorrow in the same moment. I stood there, overwhelmed. I took a stroll around the society, keenly observing small things that I had probably missed as a kid.

I noticed the narrow trunk of the tree that stood in the middle of the lane, at just about the right place to serve as wicket for our evening cricket games. It was a precious little tree, especially because of its position on the ground and the diameter of its trunk that almost resembled the width of a wicket. The tree still stood there, at exactly the same spot. It hadn't moved an inch. I engraved a sharp line on the trunk at about three quarters of a metre from the ground to mark the wicket, just as I used to do as a kid. I recalled how we used to waste precious ten minutes every evening to determine the precise height of the wicket. I continued staring at the line, silently wondering how such an insignificant looking engraved line on a tree could have been so important to me, and why after so many years I was still staring at it with a hollow feeling.

I moved closer to the other end of the ground, where I saw the society's central garbage bin. It was in exactly the same state the way it was over two decades ago. There was overflowing garbage leading to foul smell. Mama had once cajoled me into writing a practice letter to the editor of a national daily to highlight the unhygienic state of the bin. She was keen for me to use it as an opportunity to practice writing formal letters. After I was done writing the letter, she had checked the content for basic grammar and had shared with me the corrected version.

'Good effort! Look at the points I have marked and make sure you don't make these mistakes in the exam tomorrow,' she had said, handing over the reviewed letter to me.

A few weeks later, Didi spotted the letter in the editor section of *Indian Express*. Papa had furtively gone ahead and posted the corrected version to the editor of the national daily. The entire family had read the letter in jubilation and celebrated the moment. It was a special moment back then, as it was the first time my name had featured in a national newspaper. Mama had taken a cut-out of the letter and proudly shown it to all her friends. I took a deep breath cherishing the beautiful memory associated with that garbage bin.

As I moved closer to the building, I noticed a plastic ball falling from the lobby of one of the floors. A group of kids excitedly stared down from the fifth-floor lobby and frantically shouted.

"Uncle, ball please".

It took me a moment to realize that it was no longer me in the group of kids, requesting some stranger for the ball. It was me, the stranger, who was being requested for the ball. I could hear my voice reverberating from a time span of two decades - 'Ball please, ball please, uncle ball please.'

I didn't realize, but it was already well past lunch time. I instantly thought of the Chowmein stall in Meharchand market. Back in the day, I had found it embarrassing to mention the place in a discussion on fine-dining places, but today, I desperately wanted to be there. I recollected how all four of us used to cramp onto our Bajaj scooter and Papa would drive us down to the market. It was a shiny silver-grey scooter, DL 2S F 8026. It wasn't very comfortable when all four of us sat together on it, but it still did the job. I stared at my bright shining SUV and solemnly wondered why my luxurious car could not provide the same happiness that DL 2S F 8026 once did.

Shortly after lunch, I drove around the familiar roads of Lodhi Road. As I passed by the Lodhi Garden, I had a distinct desire to visit our once favourite spot, where Papa and I used to study. The spot looked exactly the same, yet so different. I vividly remembered how Papa had once bought two cups of ice cream to celebrate our mini victory. It was an important milestone back then, my first fledgling steps along the path to all the professional success I was destined to achieve.

I sat there, below the tree shade, slowly savouring an ice cream, though it did not trigger the same joy it once did. I reluctantly got up after a few minutes and drove back to the Pragati Vihar complex.

As I walked around the residential complex boundary, I passed by a comics shop. I recalled how crazy I used to be for comics. Didi often pleaded with me to read something more intellectual. Sometimes she would request me to at least switch over to the English version, though I never succumbed to her requests.

I was surprised to see that the same little shop still existed. I casually walked in and browsed through the collection. Looking at the familiar comic characters on those colourful pages, I wondered why they had not grown over the years. Or maybe it was a case of me having moved on too quickly, leaving them behind.

I casually glanced at my watch to see the time. It was close to 5:00 p.m. That used to be the time when all kids somehow found their way out to the park – some kids had to fight their moms, while there were a few lucky ones like me, whose moms actually forced them out to play. I recollected how on one rare day, I was flooded with homework. After a lot of deliberation, we had decided that I would have to skip the evening play that day to complete the homework. It was a tough decision for me; it was even tougher for Mama. Few moments later, Mama told me that she would complete my homework and I could go out to play. I was thrilled but was concerned that Mama's beautiful handwriting would stand out and the teacher would immediately know. 'Don't worry, I will write with my left hand to make it as illegible as yours!' Mama had replied, making me break into a broad smile.

I went to the park and silently stood in one of the corners, keenly watching the euphoric ambience. I noticed a group of young boys merrily playing cricket. I recollected how Mama used to stand in the corridor outside our house to watch me play from a distance. I had always requested her to not stand there, especially when it was my turn to bat. Every few minutes I would obliquely stare to see if she was still standing. On each occasion I used to hope that she would have gone inside, but she never did. I turned around to see the same corridor where she once used to stand. The irony was that this time, I knew she would not be there, but I wanted to see her standing there. A tear trickled down my cheek as reality sunk in that those beautiful moments were a thing of the past now.

I took a deep sigh and continued staring at the kids blankly. Despite the cheerful shrieks of young kids all around, I felt a distinct air of void and emptiness.

As I continued to reflect, I realized that as a kid, my horizon was somewhat limited, and I could never see things beyond the immediate vicinity – both in space and time. I was always consumed with the immediate goals, and everything revolved around that. I never realized that I would grow up one day and all those beautiful moments would be gone. It was this illusion of permanency that led me to believe that my existence and relationship to those beautiful moments was sacrosanct. Today, for the first time, I was watching those familiar moments from a time gap of two decades. I felt deeply aggrieved to observe that I was not a part of those moments anymore.

I went to the terrace and laid there beneath the open sky. There were beautiful memories, many of which looked painful when they actually happened, but I found myself longing for those same old moments. There were material possessions, all of which had once been my dreams and a reality today, but strangely I didn't seem to value them the same way anymore. A lot seemed to have changed, but there was much more that I wanted to change still.

I wondered if the pursuit of filling a void is real or just a mirage. Professor Malik always dismissed my efforts as a pursuit of void. I hated him for that, but inadvertently, he may have actually been right.

It may indeed have been a pursuit of void, for despite having achieved all that I once wanted, the void remained. The nature of void may have changed over the years, but the feeling of longing, the quest for contentment continues.

I gently closed my eyes and allowed a myriad of conflicting feelings to gradually sink in.